Morals and the Media

Morals and

Ethics

Nick Russell

the Media:
in Canadian Journalism

UBCPress / Vancouver

©UBC Press 1994
Reprinted 2001

Printed in Canada on acid-free paper ∞

ISBN 0-7748-0457-2

Canadian Cataloguing in Publication Data

Russell, Nicholas
    Morals and the media

Includes bibliographical references and index.
ISBN 0-7748-0457-2

1. Mass media – Canada – Moral and ethical aspects. 2. Journalistic
ethics – Canada. I. Title.

P92.C2R87 1994   302.23´0971   C94-910200-8

UBC Press gratefully acknowledges the ongoing support to its pub-
lishing program from the Canada Council, the Province of British
Columbia Cultural Services Branch, and the Department of
Communications of the Government of Canada.

UBC Press
University of British Columbia
2029 West Mall
Vancouver, BC V6T 1Z2
(604) 822-5959
Fax: (604) 822-6083
E-mail: info@ubcpress.ca
www.ubcpress.ca

To Sharon, Ian, and Geoffrey, for their patience and support

Contents

Preface

How and why do the media decide to publish what they publish and are they right? Why do the media do what they do? Are they ethical? Based on what criteria? Do they reflect communal mores or march to a different drummer? Are ethical decisions spontaneous, casual, uncoordinated, or really not decisions at all, the product of the headlong rush to meet deadlines and beat competitors? And if the consumers of news don't like what they get, what can they do about it?

These are some of the questions that have puzzled me for years, both as a journalist and as a journalism teacher. And these are some of the questions I explore in this book. I have no intention of dictating behaviour. Instead, I hope to identify how the mores of the media are developed and how they reflect society, and to offer some ideas on how journalists can approach ethical decision-making.

As US journalism teacher John C. Merrill suggests, journalism ethics are 'a swampland of philosophical speculation where eerie mists of judgment hang low over a boggy terrain.'[1] Anyone stepping here does so with considerable trepidation, knowing that there is rarely a 'right' answer. And what is 'right' will vary from community to community, from newsroom to newsroom, and even from person to person. So, at best, I can only offer ways to arrive at answers.

There are at least two things this book does not attempt to do. It does not examine the francophone media in Canada, partly because this book already represents a huge undertaking.[2] This is the *first* book on

Canadian journalism ethics. In the United States, literally dozens of books have been produced on journalism ethics in the past couple of decades, with the focus becoming narrower and narrower; there is, for instance, a book specifically on photojournalism and ethics.[3] But because this is the first, it must be an introduction to virtually all aspects of journalism ethics, covering all media and the vast range of ethical dilemmas contemporary journalists face. Other books will follow, and those can begin to zero in on, for instance, the ethics of sports journalism or of the entertainment pages.

The second thing this book does not do is provide an introduction to the philosophical underpinnings of journalism ethics. The reasons are somewhat similar and have to do with insufficient space and the fact that philosophy is not my field.[4] Moreover, it was not my intention to write a book that would only be read by academics. This book is also for students of journalism, working journalists, and news consumers – the mass of readers, watchers, and listeners who are increasingly interested in media. I very much hope that laypeople will read it, and a heavy chapter or two outlining Aristotle's Golden Mean, Judeo-Christian norms, Mill's Principle of Utility, and mixed-rule deontology might deter some. But, above all, philosophy knows few boundaries: there are already several American books outlining the philosophical framework applicable to all Western journalism ethics; these can be read in conjunction with this book.[5]

As a teacher of journalism ethics, I have always felt that I should not impose my own values on students. I preserve that stance here, but inevitably my own values will emerge, so perhaps they should be described from the start. I believe journalists must take responsibility for their actions, that journalists remain citizens with rights and responsibilities, that journalists should be sensitive, caring people, and that they have an implicit 'contract' with their audience to present a reliable, balanced, and constructive picture of the world.[6]

The perspective of this book is unabashedly Canadian. So what's peculiarly Canadian about morals or the media? Canada is not a melting pot of people in the American tradition, but rather a cultural and ethnic mosaic, a loosely knit confederation, linked together by CN and Air Canada, by *Maclean's*, the CBC, and the *Globe and Mail*, and by fibre optics, cable, wire, microwave, satellite, mail, and fax. And while we use the media a lot, we also like to talk to each other – privately – a lot, and are among the world's heaviest users of the telephone.

Within this cultural diversity there is room for the *Chinese Voice, Ukrainsky Holos, Western Producer,* and *Canadian Zionist.* Does all this variety allow for any common concerns or values among Canadians? Certainly the universals of food and shelter are of great concern to most Canadians, but again, their approach to these is significantly different from that south of the border: Canadians tend to care less about the right to bear arms than about the right to privacy; less about flag and country than about the protective umbrellas of government, pensions, insurance, and large savings accounts; and less about nukes and NATO than about Cruise missiles in our air space or American subs in our Arctic. These are, after all, the people who have great difficulty in remembering the words to the national anthem (and when there's any risk of everybody getting it right, they change the words). These are also people who care about hockey, acid rain, the War Measures Act, and Greenpeace, with much of this information conveyed – on TV at least – by grave, fatherly anchors rather than the bubbly blond airheads recommended by some media consultants south of the border.

What else moves Canadians? Abortion, the death penalty, keeping the streets safe, keeping hookers and skinheads out of sight, city taxes, the summer cottage, French, single-family homes. And if there's a theme here, it may be one of continuity, of security and privacy. Canadians seem to think of themselves as solid and reliable, and they want to be as solid and reliable as they wish, without public scrutiny.

Abroad, Canada is not known for its nationalism, its imperialism, or its interference in other nations' business. (We have little to equate with the CIA's influence in Nicaragua or military intervention in Vietnam, Somalia, or Iraq.) Instead, we are known for peacekeeping. We're still largely seen as a friendly, nonjudgmental, Western nation. So while we probably value the Mounties more highly than the military, we nonetheless send forces, when requested, to Cyprus, Bosnia, Haiti, or Kuwait – with no hidden agendas.

These shadowy values, in large part, have their roots in the Protestant work ethic, though the churchy part has dwindled significantly (with many jurisdictions having no prayers in school and no religion classes). The modern communicator has to beware of references to the Sermon on the Mount or the Four Horsemen of the Apocalypse, as they may be greeted with puzzlement.

These generalizations are, of course, just that. Analyzing a national psyche is difficult, and there are all sorts of exceptions. There are aggressive Canadians, there are pockets of macho white supremacists, there are RCMP 'dirty tricks,' and doubtless there are blond TV anchors thoroughly conversant with both the Sermon on the Mount and the national anthem.

But, in general, Canadians may be more protective of individual privacy than their southern neighbours. And logically this may lead to the belief that the individual's right to a fair trial outweighs the public's right to know the lurid details of that trial. Similarly, Canadians in general believe that society's right to be protected from armed thugs is greater than the individual's right to be an armed thug. And perhaps this is mirrored in an antipathy to sensationalism in the news media. The entrepreneurial spirit is accepted (despite some discomfort at the power of Bay Street), but the individual's right to publish violent comics, hate literature, or pornography is curtailed.

Having described the Canadian perspective of this

book, it would be useful to define the other two key elements in the title: media and morals. Oddly enough, some dictionaries don't even contain the word 'morals.' In this context, the sense is one of principles: how people (reporters, editors, and, by extension, 'media') behave, how they conduct themselves, particularly how they distinguish between right and wrong, good and evil. These are not terms everyone will agree upon. Even two friends may not agree on what is good and evil, let alone two enemies. What is good and what is bad is not the same for all people, for all times, or for all places.

What about 'media?' The dictionary may send you to 'medium,' the singular, in the sense of a substance through which impressions are conveyed, a means by which something is communicated. This book deals exclusively with news media: radio, television, magazines, the Canadian Press news agency, daily papers, weekly papers, and newsletters – the means by which news is communicated. Yet clearly the newsletter produced by the local scout troop is very different from the CBC's *Prime Time News*, which in turn is dramatically different from the *Ottawa Sun*, and the differences in their mores are worth exploring.

The word 'ethics' in this book refers to ideas or guidelines that help in the solution of moral problems. As one US lawyer defined it, ethics are 'where conflicts arise in the practical application of ideological principles to the realities of life.'[7]

This book, then, is designed to encourage debate on the issues of media behaviour in Canada. It aims to take the first steps into largely uncharted territory rather than be the last, definitive word on the subject.

Acknowledgments

I would like to express my appreciation to the many Canadian editors and news directors who completed my two surveys on codes of ethics. I am also grateful to Professor Ed Lambeth for including me in the 1986 journalism ethics conference at the University of Kentucky and to Professor Deni Elliott (then of Utah State University) for introducing me to the ideas of Lawrence Kohlberg.

Warm thanks are also due to Bryan Cantley, editorial director of the Canadian Daily Newspapers Association, for continuous support and encouragement; to Betty St. Onge, then at the University of Regina School of Journalism, for transcribing a lecture series and for locating various citations not easily available; to the University of Regina and colleagues there for granting me a sabbatical to begin this research; to my family for support during the year's relocation to Wales; to my dissertation supervisor, Geoffrey Mungham, for insight and direction; to Sharon Russell for her work on the index; and to UBC Press editors Holly Keller-Brohman and Carolyn Bateman for the wonderful job on the manuscript.

PART 1

The Framework

1 Values and Evaluation

A photographer is rushing on deadline from the premier's news conference back to her newsroom when she sees a car crash into a tree and catch fire. What does she do: Take pictures? Help the injured? Or keep going as she calls for aid on her cellular phone?

People are born moral. This is not to say that people necessarily behave well, but simply that they – we – have the ability to judge. We are not *a*moral, though we can choose to be *im*moral. We can judge our behaviour. We can judge our own judgment.

Journalists have to use that judgment constantly. Their working lives are filled with decisions. Their behaviour constantly involves decision-making – which stories to cover, whom to interview, which questions to ask, what to lead with, whether the story is fair, where a story is placed in the paper, how big to make the headlines, what TV footage to use. And those decisions constantly have impact on the lives of others.

Television journalist John Harvard once remarked, 'Every day, journalists sit in judgment over somebody, from prime ministers to policemen, from handymen to hookers ... Every day, we make moral judgments, from the picky to the profound.'[1] While this may contain a certain amount of hyperbole, it is true that no journalist can avoid such decisions for very long, and many of them are extremely difficult.

How do they decide? What criteria can they use? Are the decisions fickle, based on whims of the moment or the state of the stomach? Are they self-serving, based on greed for rewards, promotions, increased circula-

SHOE

tion, better ratings? Or are they carefully thought out, balanced, collegial decisions based on formal, articulated sets of criteria – rules – unanimously accepted and engraved on every newsroom wall?

In fact, of course, none of the above. Few Canadian newsrooms possess written codes of conduct, most decisions have to be made hurriedly, newspeople have a wide range of backgrounds and values, and every situation appears to be unique, needing to be weighed on its own merits rather than fitting into some neat pigeonhole. It might be a relief to say: 'This case falls under the rules on Invasion of Privacy, and I must therefore handle it in the following way.' But it rarely happens. And, in fact, if journalism were that simple, the job might have considerably less appeal.

Common Values in the Canadian Mosaic

The mosaic that makes up Canada's population represents dozens of different racial origins and religions. However, this does not prevent some modest generalizations, as some values appear to be universal.

Fundamental, for instance, to most societies are the basic moral principles of good and evil, truth-telling, promise-keeping, justice, gratitude, generosity, reparation, self-improvement, and not injuring others.[2]

Incorporated in these is the peculiarly human capacity for self-denial. We can, for instance, will ourselves to tolerate hunger (wait till lunchtime before eating), to respect other people's territory (stay out of their yard), and to control sexual urges (hands off the hunk in the elevator).

For such values to work, they must be mutual: a social contract. At its crudest, we agree, 'I won't try to kill you if you don't try to kill me.' In most societies – certainly in North America – we have extended this to include, 'I won't steal your ox/Chevy/husband if you won't steal mine. And I won't offend your values (e.g., I won't urinate in a crowded subway) if you won't offend mine.'

Much of this has been codified over the last three millennia into religion-based commandments and community laws. Over time, these are modified, but the basic premises remain. Complicating them is the increasing rejection by many Western people of the church as an authoritarian force. John Macquarrie

suggests that the human race is 'coming of age.'[3] 'There was a time when the church tried to legislate for most of the situations in which its members might be expected to find themselves ... In the enormously complex world of today, more and more must be left to conscience and responsible judgment ... It means ... that each one has to become his own moral philosopher.'[4]

This development puts a heavy responsibility on individuals, but society tends to compensate. 'Life is too short for innumerable agonizing appraisals undertaken *de novo*. Rules, customs and habits ... save time and effort by capitalizing on experience.'[5]

Those rules, customs, and habits don't by any means cover every situation, especially within specialized disciplines such as journalism. However, some have special application, such as truth-telling and not injuring others.

For such principles to work well, a good deal of freedom is required: freedom to speak out and to keep silent; freedom to respect others and to be respected; freedom to enjoy sex with willing partners or to abstain; freedom to behave in public ways or private ways; freedom to possess material goods, to share them, or to disavow them.

These freedoms imply trust: the belief that the other parties involved will deal as fairly as oneself. Whatever the role of the journalist is, it will not work without the trust of the audience – credibility – and a good part of that trust is based on the truthfulness, or perceived truthfulness, of the media in general, of the specific newsroom, and, indeed, of each journalist.

And whatever the consumers of news see as the role of the media, a primary requirement is information on which they can base life decisions. There is an expectation that the media will be honest and fair in providing the truth.

Free Enterprise vs. Journalism

A dilemma is posed by the nature of the paymaster. Gathering and distributing news is an expensive proposition. (Advertising contributes 80 per cent of the cost of producing a typical Canadian daily, so if a reader of the Toronto *Globe and Mail* were to pay the entire cost, instead of paying 50 cents she would pay $2.50 per copy.)[6] So most media have evolved with audiences only paying part of the cost, the rest being raised through advertising. Backers are usually needed to provide capital to build the radio station or buy the printing press, and these shareholders generally expect a return on their investment. Thus the individual journalist may be motivated by the most admirable personal principles, while working for a vast, multinational corporation driven by profit.

These are not ideal bed partners. Are media owners the greedy profiteers they are sometimes made out to be? It is risky to generalize, but human nature suggests some may be, while others are more benevolent and a few positively altruistic. History indicates that the Southam newspaper chain has in the past largely been run by benevolent, hands-off proprietors. Conrad Black, on the other hand, is proud to be a capitalist, and his company has not hesitated to close down unprofitable newspapers even if it meant grief for some employees, not to mention readers.[7]

Unquestionably, some proprietors do interfere with their newsrooms. Anthony Bevins cites Black for strongly criticizing the London *Daily Telegraph*,[8] but Black applauds interference by the owners: 'Non-Interventionist Proprietors Encourage Irresponsible Journalism by Their Abdication.'[9]

This is a convoluted argument, but at least readers and editors know where they stand with him. Long-time publisher Stu Keate maintained that owners almost never meddled in Canadian newsrooms.[10] Paul Rutherford maintains that the media have been treated as 'ordinary commercial property' for at least a century,[11] but that Canadian management has largely been benign: 'The masters of press, radio and television do constitute a media elite. They are not a conspiracy against the public good, however. Indeed, their reign has contributed to a marked improvement in the performance of the media ... Bigness and growth were necessary to survive.'[12]

Rutherford's description of Canada's papers in the 1930s is probably still appropriate. 'The newspaper industry was a business like any other, wherein reigned the twin gods of Profit and Stability.'[13]

Readers, too, have a form of investment in the media, both in trust and in time. If their relationship with the TV station, newspaper, or radio newsroom is

to work, they must be able to trust it, to know that if there is an advertisement for a special on turkeys at Safeway, they can expect to find the cheap turkeys if they go to the store. To know, too, that having absorbed the news about all electoral candidates, they can vote intelligently. Thus they know it is worth investing considerable time to read their daily paper – according to Canadian statistics, an astonishing average of 44 minutes a day.[14]

Many news consumers feel that this 'investment' gives them some sort of proprietary rights. (When the St. Catharines, Ontario, *Standard* had a promotion campaign in the late 1980s with the slogan 'It's Your Paper,' customers phoning with complaints frequently justified them with 'It's MY paper.')

Consumers naturally choose the station or the paper that best suits their tastes, in terms of when it is available, the style of the product, and the cost. Vancouver viewers may choose to watch BCTV supper-hour news because the time of the show suits them, they prefer the format, or they like the anchorperson. As such, they like it the way it is. Readers of the *Owen Sound Sun-Times* do not want it suddenly to resemble the *Winnipeg Sun*. And they expect the crossword and the sports section to be in the same place each day. (So it must have been very traumatic for regular readers of the Vancouver *Province* in 1983 to have a large, sober business paper one day and a brassy tabloid with the same name on the top the next.)

Pleasing the audience is important to the media because they must occasionally pay a dividend to those shareholders. But this raises a crucial ethical issue. Just how far should they go to please the viewers and listeners? Issues of prurience, violence, and vulgarity will be discussed later, but in broad terms, media managers have to decide whether 'anything goes,' or whether there are limits. Is 'publish and be damned' an acceptable ethos? Are the 'tits-and-bums' papers of Fleet Street any less ethical than the grey ladies of Front Street or Wall Street?

Limits are, of course, imposed by law, and to a certain extent these nibble away at press freedom increasingly each year. (Police demands for documents and sources are increasing in Canada, the United States, and Britain.) But toughening of the law is often a result of media excesses, provoking legislative 'revenge.' For instance, calls for tougher privacy laws usually follow some new outrage by the paparazzi.

Journalists do not often publicly admit this connection, but it was clearly stated by David Montgomery, editor of the British daily *Today*, when he was explaining why there are so many libel suits. 'We got above ourselves, took too many risks, and practised sloppy procedures,' he told a conference of the British Bar. 'And we did it in the face of increasing public disquiet about our antics. In short, we asked for it.' Montgomery described readers' response as 'a huge revenge for our misdemeanours.'[15] He is, of course, speaking for the desperately competitive British tabloids, but it is at least partially true of the Canadian tabloids.

However, the laws relating to journalism need neither threaten journalists nor allow them to feel free from making moral judgments. It's true that few laws affecting media are there to protect the media: most are there to protect Joe Lunchbucket *from* the journalists; but they are there only to protect Joe from the *excesses* of the *worst* reporters. The truly responsible journalist will rarely feel constrained by laws of libel or privacy, for instance, because his own value system brings him up short before the law takes hold.

As for the law freeing journalists from making ethical judgments, Stephen Klaidman and Tom Beauchamp summarize the relationship well in their book *The Virtuous Journalist*: 'Legal protections that permit irresponsible journalism do not imply that journalists have no moral responsibility. Quite the reverse is true: freedom from legal constraints is a special privilege that demands increased awareness of moral obligation.'[16]

The press can, for instance, legally get away with a great deal in terms of impugning people's characters, invading their privacy, using vulgar words, and printing suggestive pictures. This is not to say that it is good or desirable, but society does permit it. Page 3 of the *Toronto Sun* each day is living proof of the press's freedom (though some European tabloids, such as the London *Sun*, reveal much more; see Chapter 13, 'The Media and Sex').

But how far should they go in catering to the tastes of the audience? Pornography laws in Canada permit considerable latitude. Magazines such as *Penthouse* and *Hustler* are routinely admitted into the country without demur. If they are permitted, why shouldn't every newspaper publish the same lurid, erotic, and sexist pap?

Obviously there is a vast chasm between *Penthouse* and the *Globe and Mail*. A number of distinguishing features are relevant, the most important being the nature of a typical daily – the 'family newspaper.' Every major town across the country has its own daily, from the *Alberni Valley Times* to the *Corner Brook Star*. Half of every day's issues are picked up on the newsstand, but half are subscribed to, a familiar face, delivered each day, with predictable quality.[17] The papers appeal equally to the male and female adults in the household (with desperate efforts by publishers to attract younger readers as well). And despite proprietors' gloom, the papers are mostly prosperous and growing: both total circulation and total revenue increased steadily during the 1980s. Despite the competition from television, says Peter Desbarats, 'most daily newspapers continued to be highly profitable.'[18]

The Family Newspaper

Finding a definition for the term 'family newspaper' is difficult, but perhaps it can best be achieved by looking at some of its components. The family newspaper is seen as including ingredients of interest to all members of the family. (Newspaper managers are desperately trying to attract young readers, as audience demographics show the average age of readers is getting older and older.) So, if it must appeal to both grandparents and teenagers, it must not offend. This means that *most* newspaper language is acceptable, but it should avoid sexism and violence. The family newspaper obeys the house rules, and so does not discuss subjects that cannot normally be discussed at the dinner table in front of the children.

If this begins to sound numbingly dull, it should be noted that this is far from the whole story. The nature of what is acceptable varies with time and space, and with the medium. Styles change over the years. Abortion can now be discussed, where it used to be anathema; the transmission of the AIDS virus can be described, where it would have been impossible even a decade ago; incest can now be reported, where it used to be taboo. Similarly, it is clear that what is acceptable in a metro Toronto daily is not necessarily acceptable in the tiny *Times* of Tillsonburg, Ontario, or in a small Hutterite community.

The media themselves also provide variables. A broadcast obscenity is quickly gone, and offending images or language may soon be forgotten, where print has a permanence that means editors must take greater care, especially with weeklies, which often sit on the coffee table for seven days. Even within media, differences are evident. Late-night audiences are presumed to have tougher skins than supper-hour audiences, and a CBC FM program such as *Ideas* can use language that would cause howls of protest on prime-time TV (see Chapter 14, 'Hide the Paper: Here Come the Kids').

Though there are similarities between many newspapers, there are also dramatic differences. And though issues of ethics have not been addressed head-on as yet, clearly some of the questions suggested above are ethical questions. The very act of defining the nature of a paper, and therefore the type of journalism, is in part an ethical decision. Proprietors, seeing a market niche for their product, decide to aim for that demographic group with specific design and content concepts. They are therefore endeavouring to give those readers what they want.

Giving Audiences What They Want?

The editor who decides to give readers what they ought to have is going to produce a very different paper from the editor who chooses to give them what they really want. Sheer economics ensures that few in the daily newspaper industry are that rash. (Obviously, the editor of the Jehovah's Witness magazine *Watchtower* can ignore economics.) But it is interesting to compare our attitudes to 'up-market' and 'down-market' papers – such as Toronto's *Financial Times* and the *Sun*. Is one more ethical, less opportunistic, than the other? Editors of 'down-market' tabloids clearly believe they must serve the interests of their audience. (Awful evidence of this is seen in the pornographic British daily, *The Sport.*) The editor of another London tabloid succinctly described his audi-

ence: 'The basic interests of the human race are not in music, politics and philosophy, but in things like food and football, money and sex, and crime. – especially crime.'[19] Yet are not both the *Financial Times* and the *Toronto Sun* serving a specific audience? Why should one paper be respected for being dull and largely inaccessible to many people, while another is faulted for 'pandering' to baser instincts, when both do well in their markets?

It is a natural instinct for people to want to be entertained, even if that is not necessarily what they 'ought' to have. 'Ought' implies a degree of resistance: taking our horrid medicine unwillingly, even though we know it is good for us.

In a media context, people ought to have a broad base of information for making their own judgments, judgments on how to vote, what to eat, who needs foreign aid. (This is quite different from being told *what* to think.)

Some of this information we do not *want*, such as images of a famine in Africa, fascinating and horrifying information that readers and viewers may resist because it may make demands on them, but information they ought to have. Such material helps the audience make decisions about whether to give money to Oxfam or even whether to buy a bigger car.

The line between news-we-ought-to-have and news-we-want is narrow. Audiences may not recognize the relevance to themselves of a story about war in the Middle East, until prices go up at the local gas pump. Such connections can often be found, so that many stories that might be described as 'ought to' stories in fact are 'need to' stories. The leakage of PCBs from a truck on a remote stretch of the Trans-Canada Highway may in fact have far-reaching ramifications in terms of changes in regulations on transportation of dangerous materials, cleanup costs, and costs of equipment needed to replace transformers using PCBs. Similarly, an outbreak of AIDS thousands of miles away can have long-term local effects.

Many such stories can be said to help consumers face a complex world. As the Saskatoon *Star-Phoenix* put it in a 1990 promotion campaign, this is 'News You Can Use.'

It is often important to have such information in order to know how to act and how to react, to be informed before the disaster happens. The farmer who wakes up one morning to find the bailiffs at his door to evict him may be better able to cope with the disaster, or even prevent it, if he knows, *before* he buys a new combine, about the fixing of grain prices in Europe.

In addition to information on such things as politics and self-protection, newspapers are increasingly leaning towards information that helps the reader live a fuller, happier, richer life. This may come in the form of information about a breakthrough in arthritis research, or an ad about birth control, or a teen column on getting rid of zits: it's all useful information. The issue, for the news media, is how much the reader requires.

But there may be other forces at work:

- *Technical requirements.* The newspaper press often cannot print single pages and editors may not produce blank pages, so the size of the newspaper has to increase or decrease in increments of four pages, or at least two, at a time.
- *Economic considerations.* Shareholders like dividends, which means making a profit, so however much editors may want to open new bureaus or send correspondents to foreign news spots, the paper must still take in more revenue than it spends.
- *Visual and consumer concerns.* A paper typically needs at least 65 per cent advertising to 35 per cent news to balance the budget without increasing the purchase price; yet because editors hate having ads on page 1 and the editorial pages, some other pages will have to be stuffed with ads to compensate.

At the same time, the supply of news is fickle and unpredictable. It may be affected by some of the following:

- Is it a 'slow' news day, as often occurs in February and July, providing little news to fill the paper?
- Is the travel editor desperate for copy because there's a glut of travel advertisements early in the New Year?
- Does the food editor need more copy because the food stores demand a special section on Thursday to catch the weekend shoppers?

These are clearly not occasional decisions but decisions that are being made every moment in every newsroom across the country. And many editors will agree that their decisions are not based on any book of rules but on instinct, on a sense of what the audience wants and needs and can tolerate.

Codes of Ethics

Instinct is, in fact, probably not as capricious as it may seem, for it is based on experience and newsroom lore. Editors teach neophytes newsroom values mostly by example and oral advice in the office or the press club. In a 1990 survey of major Canadian newsrooms, only eight newspapers were identified as having formalized codes of ethics. (For a fuller discussion, see Chapter 17, 'Codes of Conduct.')

A previous survey, conducted five years earlier, turned up only three codes in effect in Canadian dailies but provided some fascinating insights into current thinking. Editors were asked to send a code if they had one. Neil Reynolds, editor of the Kingston *Whig-Standard*, replied simply: 'Our code of ethics is by convention, not constitution. We have no written version that I can send, although I believe that, like the good book says, it is "written on our hearts."[20] Wrote Geoff Stevenson, managing editor of the *Hamilton Spectator*: 'Personally I'm not a believer in written codes of ethics. I believe a better system is to discuss specific items when they come up and make a decision at that time.' Bill Peterson, then city editor of the Saskatoon *Star-Phoenix*, noted: 'My personal belief is that the most important – and powerful – newsroom code of ethics is the continuing discussion among news staff of the dilemmas we face.' (However, Peterson pointed out that his newsroom, even then, conducted seminars on such issues as naming names, and all reporters were given a copy of John Hulteng's booklet *Playing It Straight*, which evaluates one American code.)

Steve Hume, then editor of the *Edmonton Journal*, wrote in 1985 that his newsroom had no formal code and that codes tended to be restrictive: 'A written code of ethics would have done nothing to prevent the Janet Cooke fiasco at the *Washington Post*,' he wrote. 'Ethics, like morality, dwell in the hearts of individuals, never in documents.' (Southam Inc. [1979] had earlier distributed a two-page 'Credo' to all member newspapers, including the *Journal*, but this did state that 'there is no "Southam" editorial policy.' Within five years of

Hume's disavowal, the *Journal* had developed its own four-page code.)

And Sean Finlay, editor of the *Evening Telegram* in St. John's, Newfoundland, said journalists had no special rights and therefore needed no special code of behaviour: 'The Code of Ethics I adhere to and the one I demand of my reporters, editors and photographers is the same Code of Ethics – which is not written out – followed by any and all reasonable persons in society.'

Such firm repudiations of codes were noticeably absent in responses to the follow-up survey in 1990.

However, although there are still few written codes in Canadian newsrooms, it might be useful to develop a list of key questions to ask when making ethical decisions. The following is inspired by the traditional journalists' 'five Ws.' (The five Ws and *H* of Who, What, When, Where, Why, and How are frequently suggested as the basic questions a reporter must start with when following a typical story.)

The Five Ws of Ethics
- *Who* gains or loses by this story? *Who* cares? *Who* gets hurt?
- *What* does it do for our/my credibility? (Will the audience think less of this newsroom for running these details? Can I look myself in the mirror tomorrow?) *What* has been newsroom practice in the past? *What* are the alternatives?
- *When* should we publish this? (Is there a genuine rush to publish this story now, or are we giving only one side to beat the competition?)
- *Where* should this story be published? (the *Christian Science Monitor, Calgary Sun, National Enquirer*?) And *where* within the news package? (Top story on the supper-hour news? Hidden in among the truss ads on page 99?)
- *Why* withhold or run this? (To be first? To inform? To titillate? To have something to enter in the National Newspaper Awards?) *Why* is this source doing this? (Why does he want to buy me lunch?)
- *How* was this material gathered? (By fair questions to an informed source, from a properly identified reporter? Was it undercover?) *How* might the process affect the story? *How* was it corroborated for fairness and accuracy? *How* would the decision alter if the situation were reversed and I was on the receiving end?[21]

These questions do not resolve the debates or make the answers obvious. (And, of course, the five Ws are merely a mnemonic device. In reality, this represents about fourteen questions.) But they do begin to pinpoint the real issues and get away from emotional responses and loaded language. They help focus debates otherwise based on such emotive words and phrases as 'freedom of the press,' 'censorship' and 'the public's need to know,' or such grandiose abstractions as 'We're in the reporting business, not the secrets business.'

Here are a few, true scenarios where these five Ws may help to focus the debate:
- Sony is celebrating the sale of its millionth Walkman, and journalists are promised a free Walkman if they attend the news conference.
- A young woman is raped in a village vicarage. Should she be identified? Should the church or the village be identified?
- A reporter finds an advance copy of a provincial budget in a print shop's garbage.
- A cabinet minister is suspected of interfering with the justice system. A bright young reporter says he has the goods on him, with the documents 'right here' on microfiche.

It bears repeating that these five Ws do not resolve any ethical dilemmas. They may simply help focus the debate on the real issues, rather than on abstractions.

Kohlberg's Moral Ladder
How do people make value judgments, especially when those values are simply 'written in our hearts,' as two of the editors described above?

In the Canadian mosaic, a multitude of values are at work. Dominant, however, is the Judeo-Christian ethos, brought to this country by a mix of settlers over the last 300 years, and passed on by priests, teachers, parents, and laws to subsequent generations.

Such a setting dovetails with the theories of a professor at the Harvard Centre for Moral Development and Moral Education, Lawrence Kohlberg.[22] Kohlberg examines the values people acquire from birth onwards and concludes that North Americans in general demonstrate a range of decision-making strategies, starting from the crudest survival instincts and perhaps ultimately rising to the level of an 'ideal' person.

Such a vertical ladder of moral reasoning is easily accepted, for instance, by active Christians, who see themselves caught in a tug-of-war between hedonistic egotism and heavenly selflessness. But it is not necessary to share this philosophy to see the value of analyzing decisions through the Kohlberg filter.

Put very simply, Kohlberg sees Western society as rising through three general moral stages: pre-conventional or pre-rational morality (childlike), conventional morality, and post-conventional morality. Each of these is subdivided:

Pre-Conventional Morality
Stage 1: Fear of punishment. Authority defines wrongness, which is not debatable. Wrongdoing is always punished.
Stage 2: Hope for reward. While recognizing other views, this stage is primarily motivated by satisfying self. Important to keep promises so others will keep theirs.

Conventional Morality
Stage 3: Peer or community approval. Recognition of need to cooperate. Concern with maintaining trust and social approval. Do unto others, etc. Justice flexible.
Stage 4: Law obedience. The good of the majority is paramount. Rules are pervasive (societal, religious, internal). Respect for law is essential.

Post-Conventional Morality
Stage 5: Social good. Some rights are inviolable. Social welfare is vital. All deserve respect and dignity. Punishment is less important.
Stage 6: Universal principles. All are free, equal, and autonomous. Justice, dignity, and benevolence are important. Each must maximize quality of life and liberty for all. The disadvantaged deserve special care. No punishment or rewards.[23]

Kohlberg believes people should stretch themselves, striving always for a 'better' (i.e., higher) level of decision-making. However, perhaps for the average journalist it is enough to use Kohlberg's Stages of Moral Reasoning as a means of analyzing decision-making. Jew, agnostic, or Muslim alike can use Kohlberg to look at an ethical dilemma, determine what form of evaluation is at play, and therefore make an intelligent judgment.

The Kohlberg ladder is based on the assumption that it is better to be concerned with society than with oneself, and this is probably acceptable, in principle, to most Canadian journalists. Many reporters, editors, and news directors may not aspire to be a Kohlberg 'ideal person' but may well agree that they are in the news business not (just) for their own pleasure but to inform people and to help them live better, richer, more effective lives.

The writer may get fulfilment from a page 1 byline or from seeing herself on the nightly news, but there is also something *useful* going on, a process of informing, while building a reputation for veracity and good writing.

It may now be helpful to redraw the Kohlberg ladder as a circle. With this schema, we abandon the numbers in order to minimize the judgmental nature of the debate: It's clearly dangerous for newsroom colleagues to say, 'Well, she's only operating at Level 3, but obviously I'm a 5.'

At the core is Self versus Community, perhaps comparable to the strong/weak, active/passive dichotomies of Chinese philosophy. The second circle depicts the

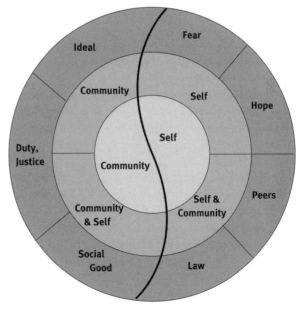

Diagram of Kohlberg's ladder

overlapping quality of value judgments, as one becomes more altruistic and less egocentric. And the outer ring further subdivides these into the overlapping motivations that Kohlberg offers.

In a journalistic context, Fear here represents fear of punishment from employer (for missing a deadline, being scooped, etc.), offset by the Hope for reward (a bonus, better ratings, promotion to a copy-desk job, a prize in the annual Radio Television News Directors Association competition). Peer approval is important in terms of the newsroom or the press gallery and, to a dwindling extent, the media clubs. Few people are immune to 'Nice story, Chuck!' bellowed across the newsroom by the city editor, or the raised eyebrow of the old-timer in the bar: 'Didn't you know we did that story last year?'

The Law plays far from a static role on this list. The law is, indeed, written and largely clear and well-known, in the specific sense of the statutes of Canada and its provinces. But there are also in-house policy manuals, codes, and intermittent memos. And even the statutes are treated differently by some than by others. Fearless Freda may say, 'Never mind what the lawyer says, let's go with it. The public needs to know,' where Timid Terry says, 'We can't do that. We might get sued.' *Is* the law sometimes an ass? Is it the responsibility of the media to test the law, to stretch the law, or simply to obey?

'The law says we mustn't identify minors who are victims of a crime, therefore we mustn't name this teacher/child molester, even after he has committed suicide.' Right or wrong?

It is with that 'greater good,' of course, that we begin to move increasingly into the realm of Kohlberg's Social Good, deciding issues based on what's best for the greatest number (a risky game). Only now does the issue become *effect*: What effect will the story have on individuals, or the audience, beyond the newsroom?

Finally, there comes the Justice/Duty stage. The journalist concerned with Justice or Duty has no concern for himself but is driven by abstractions such as dignity and integrity. At this level, the journalist may on occasion find it is necessary, for the greater good, to break the law. (A classic example of this might be pio-neer publisher Joseph Howe, who decided to run a letter that was clearly libellous by contemporary standards in the *Nova Scotian* in 1835, in order to clean up a decadent and evil government.)[24] The newsperson may also occasionally feel driven to put his or her job on the line, willing to quit rather than to behave in an 'unethical' manner.

At this level, the journalist is capable of weighing different ethical principles against each other, consulting colleagues (and superiors), and only acting after carefully considering the consequences of her actions.

Kohlberg No Panacea

Kohlberg's Steps were not designed with journalism in mind, but they may be a useful catalyst in debates about newsroom ethics. The reporter/editor/news director who spends a few minutes examining a dilemma from a Kohlbergian perspective may well find angles to the issue that he or she had not expected, and may draw conclusions quite opposite to first impressions.

It might be instructive, here, to try applying the five Ws and Kohlberg to the scenario outlined at the beginning of this chapter, in which a photographer encounters a serious accident as she returns from covering an urgent assignment.

Who: The accident victim may benefit from the photographer's intervention, or may suffer if she does not stop to help. But perhaps the photographer will miss her deadline, and so the public will be denied the picture from the news conference. Is it either/or? Is one more important than the other?

What: The photographer's credibility may suffer if she fails to help the victim. If the hurt driver dies, will the photographer be to blame? What other alternatives are there?

When: Is a press conference picture really that urgent? If the local TV station runs coverage tonight, does that mean the paper must have pictures, too?

Where: Not really applicable here.

Why and **How:** Why drive on by? Perhaps the photographer is using the excuse of the deadline to avoid getting involved in the accident. Why help the victim? Because media people are citizens, too. Journalistic detachment does not extend to ignoring suffering that the newsperson can help to alleviate. And the reversibility rule suggests that if *we* were trapped in a car wreck, we would like to think somebody would stop to help *us*.

Kohlberg's Reward and Punishment

Clearly the photographer risks getting in trouble if she fails to deliver the picture on time. It is likely that space is being held for the picture, and editors will be less than pleased if she fails to deliver since they may have to tear apart a page to accommodate different material. This may take precious minutes, conceivably resulting in hundreds of dollars in overtime for press-workers, drivers, and carriers. On that basis, this is scarcely a decision the photographer should take alone. She must get on the cellular phone to the news-desk and ask for fast guidance.

Peers

Even the most cynical newsperson would probably acknowledge that helping the injured is acceptable. (Though she may tell the old story of the reporter at a fire who got so engrossed that he told his editors he couldn't file a story 'until we've put out the fire.') There's little doubt the *community* would expect the photographer to drop her camera and start aiding the victim, so why should the editor's values be different?

Social Good

The welfare of the individual victim here overwhelms the need of the community to see the premier's picture.

The result of this analysis is scarcely surprising. The photographer should (1) phone for emergency help, (2) phone the newsdesk to advise what's happening, (3) help the victim, and (4) rush the picture to the office as soon as possible. This analysis reinforces instincts and demonstrates which values are at work. Weighing these issues, we can conclude that the photographer should be able to help the victim while not jeopardizing her own job, although risking some considerable criticism from the news desk.

However, it must be added that few ethical judgments need to be made in quite such haste. Under such circumstances, nobody is going to stop to mea-

sure the situation by the five *W*s or by Kohlberg but hopefully will react as a feeling human being. And every situation is different. If the photographer was rushing back to the Victoria *Times-Colonist* with pictures of a major earthquake in downtown Victoria, she might be justified in telephoning for help, but not stopping at the car accident.

TOUGH CALLS

Here are some scenarios taken from real news stories. It is useful to draw up a list of the five *W*s suggested above. Do these help in deciding how to handle each situation? Does Kohlberg help?

1 One of your copy editors is handling a brief wire story about a 71-year-old hooker spending her birthday in jail in Knoxville, Tennessee. His ingenious headline is: 'Very Old Dame Plays Very Old Game.' Is that suitable? Is the item newsworthy?

2 Your TV newsroom has shots of a local hotel fire, including two people dead. Do you run them? On the supper-hour news?

3 Your best reporter wants to research a story on the white supremacist Aryan Nations movement by infiltrating the group incognito. Neat idea?

4 You have the names of several men charged with buggery following police surveillance of a public washroom. Do you run the names on your newscast?

5 Your reporter finds himself in the motel room next to the premier, out on the campaign trail, and overhears a most revealing phone call. Can he write a story about it?

2 The Nature of News

What is this abstraction, news? How do journalists decide that Dog Bites Man is not news, but Rottweiler Bites Baby is? Why are the amours of a cabinet minister given equal play to the atrocities of a Middle Eastern massacre?

Every journalism textbook author has tried his or her hand at defining news. The consensus, after the smoke has cleared, seems to be something as simple as 'News is what interests people,' 'News is what makes people talk,' and 'News is information that helps people to live a full life.'[1]

A simple checklist of criteria is often attached to such statements. A good news story, it is said, includes some of the following: proximity, immediacy, impact, conflict, important people, disaster, human interest, the bizarre, etc.[2]

Some of these are worth describing further, with the caveat that they are merely *flags* to indicate newsworthiness. A story may be news and still not fit any of the categories, and a story may be news and yet contradict some of these.

Proximity. This yardstick of newsiness implies that the closer an event is to the reader, the newsier it is. A two-car fender-bender in Kuala Lumpur may be of little interest in Stony Plain, Alberta. But a similar accident on a side street in Stony Plain may be the talk of the town.

However, if that accident in Malaysia involved, say, the pope, then it might well get into the daily *Stony Plain Thunderer* and most other news media round the world. So the criterion of proximity would be overwhelmed by the criterion of important people.

Immediacy. This refers to the essential meaning of news: that which is new. Old news is not only a contradiction, it is boring. (Yet when Prime Minister Mackenzie King's diaries were released, after decades of secrecy, they revealed such intriguing insights into the leader's psyche that they were unquestionably news: the bizarre quality and the importance of the central character over-rode any reservations about the antiquity of the events. The information was still 'new' to the audience.)

Impact. This refers to the consequences of the event. A Middle Eastern war may be remote but may have direct impact on the reader at the gas pump.

Important people. Famous people are a never-ending source of fascination for the un-famous. Whether they be movie stars, cabinet ministers, pop singers, popes, or NHL hockey players, there seems to be no end to the appetite for details of their lives. Even the most public of people deserve a modicum of privacy, but once they have thrust themselves into the public spotlight they can expect, as US presidential aspirant Gary Hart discovered, that they are almost never off-duty. Editors recognize this fascination and have to struggle with the question: How far can we reasonably go? Is it useful to picture the brassiere discarded by the wife of former president Ronald Reagan?[3] The debate is explored fully in Chapter 11, 'Privacy.'

Conflict. War – obviously – is news. World war is clearly all-consuming. Civil war in the Hindu Kush is less widely interesting. But when two neighbours in Our Town battle each other with bulldozers over a disputed fence ... that, too, is news. So conflict may range from the enormity of the nuclear threat to a simple dispute between two individuals.

Disaster. Like conflict, disasters can vary in size, and their interest will be in inverse proportion to their distance from the audience. The journalist may have to work extra hard to arouse reader interest in, say, an Eritrean famine. But that interest CAN be provoked, especially when pictures (or TV footage) bring the starving children into the living room, and when the human interest elements outweigh the distance.

Human interest. One of the most controversial of these news criteria is human interest. Unquestionably, people do like to be entertained. And they (we) do like to know the pains and peccadilloes of fellow human beings. Most people don't want an unrelieved diet of budget news, but at least occasionally would enjoy a yarn about Martians landing in Phoenix or about an 80-year-old man getting eleven women pregnant. Some sceptics will label this gossip, for many human interest stories are not really 'important.' For example, a story from Winnipeg described how a small boy fell in the river and how another child managed to hook him out by his mitts, which were tied together with a string. Yet that is hardly news, in terms of the cataclysms around us, the volcanoes, the earthquakes, the bomb threats, and, indeed, the number of children dying around the world every day.

The old saw says, 'Dog bites man is not news, but man bites dog *is*.' Even better is, 'Local man bites dog.' Clearly this is a light-hearted analysis. Yet when a *pattern* emerges, a repetition (an outbreak of attacks on people by pitbull terriers), then the exception proves the rule, and 'Dog bites a*nother* man' makes headlines.

But do the newspapers have a responsibility to publish a story like that? Surely they shouldn't be bothering because it is not data that we need to survive, or even to live a much richer life (except for avoiding pitbull terriers). Yet such tales arouse interest, sympathy, and perhaps even restore faith in human nature.

Such stories are often remembered long after the event. When a British ferry capsized in the English Channel and more than 100 people died, one image

was permanently etched on many people's minds: a passenger who made a human bridge of himself, so others could crawl over him to escape.

The 'news,' in terms of what the audience ought to have, is how many people drowned, how many people were saved, what this accident is going to do to the ferry business, and what is being done to prevent this happening again. But for many, it is the 'human bridge' that will be remembered.

Similarly, many people will remember (from the early days of television) Soviet premier Nikita Khrushchev at the United Nations, not for what he said but for the dramatic way he said it, banging his shoe on the desk in a most unstatesmanlike way. That isn't *important*, but it is a colourful gesture, and it made news right around the world because it summarized his anger, and it was such a human thing to do.

The human interest story may also *move* the reader. For instance, in 1971 there were news reports of a small California earthquake. There weren't a lot of people killed, but on the second or third day, one story described one casualty:

LOS ANGELES (AP) – At 10, Angel Ferrer stood only four feet tall and weighed 59 pounds, but he dreamed a dream with more intensity than many bigger boys could muster: He wanted to be a Cub Scout.

But the $3.50 registration fee couldn't be squeezed from his family's welfare budget.

Angel clung to his dream. He collected old pop bottles and aluminum cans and saved up 53 cents.

He used the money to buy a used Cub Scout uniform at a Salvation Army store. It was baggy and tattered and had unfaded spots where someone else's badges were once sewn, but it was 'regulation.'

The cap and scarf could come later.

Still without the registration fee, Angel and his father, Julio, went to a Cub Scout pack meeting on Jan. 28.

'The little kid sat there in his uniform and watched everything like a thirsty man looks at water,' the pack leader, policeman Richard Jesson, recalls.

'Afterwards, his father told me he'd find the money somewhere, and we made plans to take Angel on our next camping trip.'

They went, Cub Scout Pack 44 and Angel.

'You should have seen that kid on our trip,' recalls Jesson.

'He was the first in line for everything, and did everything three times harder than anyone else.

'The poor little guy didn't have a sleeping bag or regulation mess kit like everyone else. He'd brought all he had – a regular dinner plate, a plastic fork and a plastic cup.

'He guarded them with his life. I guess his mom had told him not to break the plate because when he went through the chow line, he held it with both hands.'

The pack returned home Sunday, Feb. 7, and for two days, all Angel talked about was the outing.

Then, the Southern California earthquake came on Tuesday, and San Fernando, where Angel lived, was one of the communities hardest hit.

He died.

Angel's father, an unemployed laborer, suffered leg and internal injuries when their house collapsed.

Angel was to have received merit badges in front of the other boys of Pack 44 in two weeks. Instead, a funeral director pinned them on the coffin.

The funeral director recalled that Angel's Cub Scout uniform looked new.

It was. Angel's parents had bought it only four hours before the funeral.[4]

This story, too, is not 'important,' but it is moving. It reaches out and grabs the reader by the lapels, saying, 'This was not a remote event involving a bunch of statistics: it's Everyman, and the kid next door.'

It should be repeated that these criteria for judging news value are imperfect and highly fallible. As Ericson et al. point out, the news industry 'is not tightly rule-bound,' but works under conditions of 'equivocality, change, fluidity, and discovery.'[5] Such decisions are based more on 'a vocabulary of precedents' and a 'nose for news' than on any hard rules or formal definitions.[6]

For journalists, the ethical questions are constant, as they struggle to give audiences a healthy mix of what they need leavened with style and humour.

Good vs. Bad News

It is often argued that these criteria are artificial (they are), and that they emphasize the bad news at the expense of the good. And there is a lot of merit in that argument.[7] When push comes to shove, although

readers may well tell pollsters there is too much 'bad' news in the media, they would almost certainly be more interested in a story about a plane crash than a story about all the other planes that didn't crash. However, the fierce arguments that have ensued in recent years on this topic may well have helped to focus journalists' attention on the need to actively seek and promote positive stories. Certainly, good news does come along and can usefully be played large. In 1987, for instance, a Moose Jaw child was kidnapped by a pedophile with a long criminal record. Bad news. But the pair were tracked across the country, the man was arrested, and the child released without physical harm. Good news! And the stories were played prominently not only in the child's native province but across the country.

All the News that Fits

The result of mixing such stories – what we need and what we want – is that peculiar amalgam that the media carry each day, under that vast umbrella label of 'news.' It is not fixed in time or place. It is not fixed even in any one newsroom or any one editor's head, but rather it is an instinctive judgment, often made under real or imagined deadline pressure, based on gut feelings, experience, education, and peer pressure.

For editors, these decisions are further complicated by the actual supply of news vs. the space available. The amount of news that comes into a newsroom is not equal to the amount of news that gets into the paper every day. It may in fact be twenty times as much as the editor has room for: for every one story that gets in, perhaps nineteen stories will be thrown out.

These are the sorts of questions that the editors are subconsciously asking:

- What is it that makes news?
- What is it that is going to interest my readers?
- What have they *got* to have?
- What *ought* they to have?
- What would they *like* to have?
- How can we mix this all up and give them a news package they will like and enjoy?
- How can we give them a mix that will make them read *this* paper, and make them want to read it *every* day, so that we get the same readers, loyally looking for us regularly?

Like the audience, the editor needs continuity: she does not want only the Joneses reading it on Monday and only the Smiths on Tuesday, even if the numbers are the same, as this would completely confuse the advertisers.

Only when the same readers are regularly loyal can the management tell the advertisers, for example, 'We know a fair bit about our readers: they are 80 per cent Joneses – business-oriented, thoughtful people with an average income of so much, who like entertainment but don't care much about sports, and who have two cars.' Then specific advertisers can say, 'Those are the people we want to reach, so we will advertise our products in your paper.'

The Personality of Papers

The *Moose Jaw Times-Herald*, the *Mississauga News*, and the *Wall Street Journal* all have at least one element in common: their 'newspaperiness.' But their differences are perhaps more obvious. Each paper is distinctive in how it responds to the needs of its audience, and the audience that its advertisers want. The differences are far more than geographical (though the audiences certainly do differ from Moose Jaw to Toronto to New York) and are modified by other elements, such as the presence of *other* media. The Moose Jaw paper is the only local daily in this small agriculture-based community, and so to serve its readers well and respond to the whole spectrum of their interests it must reflect all sides of local debates. As well, its editorials must recognize that there is no other platform for opposing views. (To a small extent the paper competes with the Regina *Leader-Post* and the Toronto *Globe and Mail*, but only the *Times-Herald* covers the fine detail of Moose Javian life.) In Toronto – a vastly bigger, more cosmopolitan, polyglot city – the *Globe and Mail* competes head-to-head with several other dailies, plus still others in other Ontario communities, and also defines itself as a 'national' paper with special strength in business journalism. The Wall Street paper, too, faces other dailies, such as the *New York Times*, *Newsday*, and *USA Today*, but competes by appealing to a very narrow slice of audience. (No comics, no front-page pictures, a grey, repetitive layout. The paper deliberately excludes many readers.)

The editors and news directors in each newsroom must, therefore, be conscious of the specific audiences they serve, so that the implicit contract between newsroom and consumers can be maintained.

Credibility: Hard Won, Easily Lost

What tends to happen, when something goes wrong, is that the consumers, consciously or unconsciously, dismiss the media en masse. When readers laugh at a supermarket tabloid headline ('Swiss Cow Gives Birth to Human Twins'), they are laughing at all media, and all media lose another tiny fragment of credibility. This tarred-with-one-brush syndrome makes the metro TV station responsible not only for its own credibility but that of all its peers, even that of the little weekly in Squamish, BC.[8] Does that really matter? 'Our credibility is the central pillar of the media's strength,' said Knowlton Nash, respected anchor of CBC-TV News in 1981.[9] He defined credibility as, 'our fairness, our honesty, our accuracy, our ability to combat effectively the accusation of being harlots with power without responsibility.'[10] Nash reiterated its importance when he added that the media must sometimes risk public irritation by rocking the boat: 'But in doing our job, in getting some people riled up, our effectiveness boils down to one word: credibility. As I said at the very beginning, without credibility, we've got nothing ... The heart and soul of our business is credibility. We get that credibility, and the respect and the power that go with it, only by being a socially and professionally responsible agent for the public.'[11]

In the last couple of decades, the media have begun to recognize the vital importance of credibility, as well as its fragility. As US journalism teachers Jay Black and Ralph Barney have remarked, 'Almost without notice in the popular or trade press, credibility has ascended to the top of journalism's list of virtue words.'[12] Many factors constitute credibility. Donald Jones, ombudsperson of the *Kansas City Star and Times*, for instance, summarized the main things that readers complained about, and he concluded that inaccuracy topped the list. Other factors that his readers complained about included unfairness, arrogance, invasion of privacy, and lack of independence by the media.[13] Bob Clark, vice-president for news of Harte-Hanks newspapers, brought a list back from an American Press Institute seminar: inaccuracy, invasion of privacy, rudeness and lack of accessibility, ignorance of community issues and people, bias/lack of balance/unfairness, inadequate coverage, the image of reporters seen on TV and portrayed in books and movies, too much bad news, mixing opinion and news, and so on.[14]

The word credibility means, literally, believability, but it translates as trust, the audience's confidence in the media that they read, watch, and listen to. And the more 'in-credible' the media are, the less people will rely on them. Credibility is devilishly difficult to measure and is a constantly shifting issue. To ask people if they 'believe' the media is to suggest that they may be gullible and uncritical, and who wants to admit that? But to ask which medium is most credible – radio/TV/dailies, etc. – is to ask people if they believe what they have 'seen' happen (newsclips on TV) compared with what they have merely heard or read. And a shift of a few percentage points may simply reflect different respondents. A Gallup poll concluded 64 per cent of Canadians think newspapers are doing a good job of presenting the news. But while 68 per cent of people in the East were satisfied, only 57 per cent in BC were.[15] Does that mean eastern papers are 11 per cent better than BC papers? Or could it be that the critical faculties of Maritimers are less aroused? So the specific numbers may not mean much.[16] What counts is the overall trust and the direction of those numbers, and how they translate into circulation figures and the democratic process.

Accuracy

Unfortunately, a small detail is all that it takes. Some years ago, the Toronto *Globe and Mail* reported that police dogs were being used to harass Indians in Regina, and that in one year 'there were 81 people bitten by the city's police dogs.' But city officials showed that the figure the reporter had used was actually the number of people who had been injured while trying to escape arrest, such as climbing over fences, etc. The reporter lamely described his number as a 'typo,' and the result was that the mayor called the whole *Globe* story 'garbage' and 'misleading.'[17] Inevitably, other people may have shared this view, and thus attention was dis-

tracted from the real issue. (Accuracy is explored much more fully in Chapter 3, 'The Role of the Media.')

Fairness

Fairness can refer to, say, a paper's broad overall coverage of major controversial topics like elections or abortion, or it can refer to the tiniest decisions of word choice: selecting a loaded word versus a neutral one.

In general, the staff of any given newsroom will strive to give a balanced record of the world, driven by their own sense of fairness and the consumer's response to that (see discussion of objectivity in Chapter 3, 'The Role of the Media'). This will include trying to achieve balance on controversial issues, trying to give both sides of an argument, and generally trying to provide the news consumers with the raw material upon which to make decisions. Such balance is, by definition, intended for the 'news' columns, and does not encompass the intrinsic bias reflected in editorials and signed columns. But, increasingly, even these are seen as needing to be fair and to allow for other points of view, particularly in communities with limited media, such as one-paper towns.

Loaded Language

But fairness can be subtly and seriously distorted by the actual language used. A writer can easily prejudice his audience with his choice of words, even though the story may report 'both sides.'

The key is the use of neutral vocabulary rather than loaded words. Neutral language refers to colourless words such as 'accident,' 'house,' or 'meet.' Loaded words not only convey a simple meaning but also carry a burden of emotion. The US linguist S.I. Hayakawa has divided such words into two categories: 'snarl' and 'purr' words.[18] These include such highly emotive terms as 'admit,' 'scabs,' and 'tragedy.'

Compare, for instance, the effect of these two statements:

'Prime Minister Ethel Kugelschreiber revealed today sweeping reforms to Canada's abortion laws.'

'Prime Minister Ethel Kugelschreiber announced today major changes to Canada's abortion laws.'

Compare 'seal harvest' with 'slaughter of seal pups'; 'fetus' with 'unborn child'; 'management offers' versus 'union demands'; 'terrorist' versus 'freedom fighter.'

No list could contain all the 'snarl' and 'purr' words in the language, but others that journalists encounter include: deny, claim, democracy, breakthrough, realistic, exploited, bureaucrat, censor, commercialism, and regime.

The English language is so rich (the single-volume *Concise Oxford Dictionary of Current English* has 120,000 entries, according to the 1990 dust jacket), that most loaded words are easy to avoid, simply by using a more neutral synonym. Sensitive journalists have long ago learned to eschew terms such as housewife and anchorman, or labels such as cute and brunette. But it is easy to fall into the trap by using catchphrases such as 'the Italian vote,' 'student rioters,' and 'teenage drug-addicts.' It takes an extra effort for the writer to ask herself: How do I know all the rioters were students? Or, Do all Italians vote the same way?

Increasingly, lobby groups use such loaded language to try to influence the media (and through them, the public). The abortion debate is a constant reminder of this. But there are also pressures on the press to substitute absurd circumlocutions for simple, recognizable words. I will probably get into trouble for citing 'physically limited' and 'physically challenged' as examples of these, but are 'disabled' and 'handicapped' such patronizing or pejorative terms that they should be excised from our vocabulary? There's a thin line between sensitivity and political correctness.

Journalists must also take special care with political stories, which, by their nature, involve philosophical polarities. A small example will suffice: Saskatchewan Liberals elected a new leader in 1989, and after a few weeks she held an important news conference. A reporter described her speech as 'vitriol,' said she 'deflected reporters' questions about her failure to garner much media attention,' and said that, as leader of 'the moribund Grits' she had 'kept a low profile' during important debates in the House.[19] The net result, for the reader, is a picture of wimpish incompetence that must have delighted the government.

Journalists must also exercise some caution in adopting new words before they are current or in overusing fad words. The audience becomes numbed with the repetition of abstractions such as 'interface,' 'scenario,' 'cutbacks,' 'guidelines,' 'bottom line,' 'time frame,' and 'task force.' And neologisms, often invented by special interest groups, may be designed to disguise a nasty truth, and can change the nature of an event or a report: words and phrases such as 'revise downward,' 'downsize,' and 'privatize' may camouflage unpleasant realities. Even simple words – 'crisis' and 'disaster' – become devalued with overuse.

Irony: Easily Abused

Another verbal tool that has to be watched warily is irony. The word comes from the Greek for 'dissembler' and is defined by the *Concise Oxford Dictionary* as the 'ill-timed or perverse arrival of an event or circumstance that is in itself desirable.'[20] It is a literary device that can strongly influence the audience response to a story and, hence, may distort the event.

Should reporters have been more sceptical, for instance, in 1980, when Joy Adamson died? One wire story began,

NAIROBI (UPI) – Joy Adamson, who captured the hearts of millions with her book Born Free about how she raised a motherless lion cub, was attacked and killed by a lion, police said today.[21]

It was a natural story, apparently based on a police statement. But there was a catch. It emerged later that there were no claw marks on the body, and Adamson's car had been stolen. Smart lion.

Listen to the tone of these leads from wire stories back in the 1970s:

LONDON (Broadcast News) – Lord Wrottesley, 88-year-old naturalist peer, died yesterday with his lifetime ambition unfulfilled. He never succeeded in breeding the ideal spotted mouse.

LONDON (Reuters) – A court granted a British businessman a divorce Wednesday because of his wife's 'massive adultery' and cruelty, including jumping on his bowler hat.

Presumably every word of both these items is true. But is that enough? Perhaps Lord W. left other marks on the world, beyond his failure to breed spotted mice? Perhaps the businessman's wife did other, crueller, things than jumping on his hat? One way to judge these and similar items is to ask some of the five *W*s:

What is normally done with such stories? Do Canada's broadcast newsrooms normally carry obits of minor British nobles? Do Canada's dailies normally carry reports of British divorce cases? And, of course, the answer in both instances is no. It is only the perceived irony of these stories that gets them a spot on the wire.

Similarly, *why* are we going to run this story? And the answer must be, 'for a laugh.' This is today's 'Bizarre British Brief.' But are we laughing *with* the protagonists here or *at* them? Would they and their friends be laughing too?

And *whom* do these stories hurt? Nobody, directly. These citizens are a long way from Canada (remembering, however, that many Canadians have close relatives in Europe). But whom does it benefit? Is the audience any the richer for this information?

Now compare this:

TERRACINA, Italy – Twenty-eight-year-old Maurizio Sarra, a noted Italian underwater swimmer who wrote a book called 'My Friend The Shark' died in hospital during the night after being attacked by a shark.

Is there, perhaps, a difference here? Did the central character thrust himself onto the public stage by writing a book (hence making the story of North American interest, not merely local)? Don't those readers have a right to know what happened to this man who, in effect, tempted providence? (This is identical to the Joy Adamson story ... except that it is true.)

The issue of laughing at other people's misfortunes is important and will be further explored under the rubric of Privacy. But it must also be eschewed in headlines. Several years ago, one tabloid sports page headlined: **Brewers Open Camp with a Bang**. The story described a gas explosion at the Milwaukee Brewers' training camp in which the manager and general manager were both hurt.[22] A funny story? Hardly. But certainly a light-hearted headline.

Much further afield, the *Singapore Straits Times* once ran a story about a woman who committed suicide after her dog was killed in a car accident. The headline: **Woman, Dogged by Grief, Found Dead**.

And perhaps it is apocryphal, but a story about fatalities caused by a cold spell in Britain was said to have been headlined by one US daily as **Stiff Upper Lips**.

None of these reservations about the use of irony should be construed as implying that it is not a valid journalistic tool. The definition of irony as 'the ill-timed or perverse arrival of an event or circumstance that is in itself desirable' is usually extended to refer to any ill-timed or perverse event, and the world is certainly full of such things. The press would be distorting reality if they ignored the fickle finger of fate.

For instance, it is scarcely news if somebody faints at a blood donor clinic; but when the fainting donor is trying to promote a charity and goes to the blood bank dressed as Count Dracula – that's news! Similarly, when a man charged with heroin possession ducks out of the courtroom while the jury is out, only to be found Not Guilty and to be arrested for jumping bail ... that, too, is news.[23] Nobody is hurt by such tales, and readers are hungry for a little humour in a gloomy world.

Privacy

Reporting the intimate details of divorce or death may cause further grief for the participants, and such incursions need clear justification. Audiences seem to be highly protective of individual privacy and resent invasions, even when they are justified and unavoidable (for a fuller discussion, see Chapter 11, 'Privacy').

Sensationalism

One of the perennial accusations thrown at the media – the newspapers in particular – is that they are sensational.

The *Concise Oxford Dictionary* definition of sensational is simple: 'Causing or intending to cause great public excitement,'[24] which sounds harmless enough. But when the word is aimed at the media, it is usually meant to imply that the *motives* are wrong, that the story is, indeed, intended to cause great public excitement, not because of its own intrinsic merits but to sell newspapers. Hence it is seen as symptomatic of the media's capitalist greed.

Mostly, in fact, the mainstream Canadian media are

BLOOM COUNTY   by Berke Breathed

fairly calm these days.[25] When something sensational does slip through, it is usually an aberration rather than a habit or a trend. Take, for instance, this headline: **Beautiful B.C.: A Good Place to Sit Out Nuclear War.** This was yelled from the top of page 1 of the Vancouver *Province* (well before it converted to a tabloid).[26] The story began, 'B.C. may be the safest spot in North America if the bombs begin falling in nuclear war, experts say.' Quite apart from the doomsday quality of this message – which seems absurdly apocalyptic today – the 'experts' in this story turned out to be one local emergency planning official, and a retired American 'who spent much of his professional life working at a major U.S. nuclear test centre in Nevada.' This 'expert' (scientist? janitor?) was given the pseudonym Adam Light. And that was it for sources. That must have been a slow Thursday.

Here is another, minor, story, which seems to be distorted by preconceptions. **Clark Surprised by Poll Results** said the *Calgary Herald*. A picture showed a bemused Joe Clark, and the story began, 'The latest Gallup poll came as such a surprise to Joe Clark that the former prime minister almost left his newly received honorary degree sitting on a Jubilee Auditorium chair Friday.'[27]

The actual assignment for the reporter was to cover the university graduation ceremonies at which Clark was to get an honorary degree and make the convocation address. But when one reporter buttonholed him to show him some poll results, as he was unwinding from his starring role, he was taken by surprise and ad-libbed a response. This spontaneous – and largely

meaningless – answer got two paragraphs in the story. His convocation speech got one paragraph. And would it be any wonder if he had walked away from the unexpected scrum, leaving his newly acquired degree behind? Or at least, does it rate the lead on the story?

Perhaps the best way to handle this would have been to write two separate stories, one actually reporting the convocation, and the other a sidebar on Clark's poll reaction. (This knee-jerk packaging, probably a result of too little thought by a desk editor, is particularly associated with Joe Clark, who has been consistently pictured as inept since his accident-prone travels as external affairs minister.)

Canadian author and journalist Maggie Siggins, talking to journalism students about sensationalism, made this telling remark: 'It is much easier to do sensationalism than it is to do journalism.'[28] Siggins used as an example a 1981 documentary piece on arson produced by CITY-TV in Toronto. The 'City Pulse' item included marvellous fire footage – but they were not all arson fires, she maintained. The images included a disfigured burn victim groaning loudly in a hospital bed and a fire being set in an alley waste bin by some lads Siggins felt closely resembled newsroom copyboys. The story, by a trench-coated writer who is now a senior reporter for CBC-TV, described arson as 'the crime of the '80s,' called it 'the fastest growing crime in Ontario,' and quoted a fire chief who said, 'It's going to be out of control within the next two or three years.' But in retrospect, it is evident that arson is not nearly as pervasive as implied. The story was a good example of a television item in which the need for visuals and drama overcame any sense of calm reportage. The story 'yelled' at viewers.

Nor is radio immune to this sort of theatricality. The following was the start, years ago, of a one-paragraph item from Broadcast News, the Canadian broadcast news wire, no doubt picked up from Associated Press:

TRAGEDY INVADED THE SPORTS WORLD TODAY. IN OKLAHOMA CITY, OKLAHOMA, FRIENDS FOUND MRS. ESTELLE MURCER IN HER CAR IN A GARAGE, APPARENTLY AFTER TAKING HER OWN LIFE. SHE WAS THE STEPMOTHER OF BOBBY MURCER, AN OUTFIELDER WITH THE NATIONAL BASEBALL LEAGUE SAN FRANCISCO GIANTS ...

The average listener in Dauphin, Manitoba, may be forgiven for feeling less than moved by this remote domestic incident. If that can be described as 'tragedy invaded the sports world,' what superlatives are left when an entire soccer team dies in a plane crash, or gunmen kill a dozen at the Munich Olympics?

Sometimes all that stands between calm reporting and sensational reporting is sensitivity – awareness of the nuances of a story, such as tone of voice. Take, for instance, an incident years ago when Ross Thatcher, then premier of Saskatchewan, was chatting with reporters informally. Tax talks between Ottawa and the provinces were in progress, and one reporter asked Thatcher what he would do if the talks broke down: 'Oh shit, we'll secede and join the U.S.,' joked the provincial leader. Next day, one Ontario daily trumpeted: **Sask. Threatens to Secede.**[29] Did that headline reflect the event? Was it fair? And yet the report was – in a literal sense – accurate. Those were Thatcher's words, though clearly not his intent. It could well be argued that a provincial premier should know better. As a wily and experienced politician, he should have known that every word he said to the media was fair game. But was the public well served?

One of the intriguing aspects of sensationalism, which gets overlooked, is that it may not be as big a seller as it is sometimes made out to be. Clair Balfour, ombudsperson for the *Montreal Gazette*, analyzed which issues had the biggest street sales during one year and found that old-fashioned hard news was the easy winner. The day after Montreal suffered a huge downpour leading to widespread flooding, the *Gazette* sold 8,000 more copies than expected;[30] when former

Designing this *Ottawa Sun* double-page spread reviewing the life of Andrei Chikatilo must have been fun. The Red Ripper headline, three inches high, was in scarlet, and the pictures were full colour. Writer Peter Conradi produced a 'quickie' book by the same title a couple of months later. The Russian had been sentenced to death for killing and mutilating fifty-two women and children. Most Canadian dailies recorded the trial with a few inches of copy.

premier René Lévesque died, nearly 7,800 extra copies were sold; the 20 October stock market dive sold 6,000 more copies than expected. Issues that included special business or fashion magazines were also heavy sellers. These, then, were the issues that sold unexpectedly well. Yet as Balfour pointed out in a newspaper column, the list contains 'no sex, no violence.'[31] Balfour's point was that editors perhaps misread the audience's appetite for excitement. It is easy to get carried away with the potential excitement of an event, especially in the midst of a major, developing story. Take, for instance, the huge headline on the top of the daily *Nanaimo Free Press*, back in 31 March 1964: Alaska 'Quake Toll 178; Town Is Wiped Out. The only problem with that Associated Press story was that the final death toll was just seven. But the initial story, based on rumour and hearsay, actually said that 178 were 'dead or presumed dead.' Today, responsible news agencies have precise guidelines on handling – and corroborating – such estimates.[32] Mostly, newspeople are much more sceptical today. But the *New York Post* certainly won itself a place in history for its coverage of the Chernobyl accident.[33]

THE WORLD TREMBLES screamed the main headline in two-inch high capitals, followed by: 2000 Dead 25,000 Flee as Soviet Nuke-Plant Fire Rages. (Probably only about a dozen people died in the initial explosion, though of course hundreds more have since succumbed to radioactive fallout.)

Disasters are difficult to report because of the urgency, the drama, and the probable lack of good communication facilities. War reporting imposes similar difficulties, and Canada was under the rule of the War Measures Act when the following eight-column streamer topped the *Vancouver Sun*: NEW FLQ WARNING: 'Women and Children Next' Hull Torture 'Message to PM.' This inflammatory story, which topped page 1 of the Saturday, 17 October 1970 edition, described a woman who had been tortured by the Front de Liberation du Québec (the French terrorist cell that attempted an armed revolt in Canada). The War Measures Act had been invoked across the country, censorship had been imposed, the army was patrolling the streets of Quebec, and the nation was extremely jittery. Only several days later did the *Sun* run a brief story inside the paper, reporting that the entire incident was a hoax. All evidence suggests that such a story would be handled far more circumspectly in the 1990s.

By contrast to such inflammatory displays, modern Canadian dailies are largely pretty quiet. 'Perhaps the most serious knock on the press of Canada is that it is dull,' asserts Stu Keate.[34] Certainly by comparison with their British counterparts they may be so. A survey of public opinion about the UK press asked readers of the 'popular' dailies (*Mirror, Sun*, etc.) if they thought their favourite paper tended to exaggerate the sensational aspects of news: 80 per cent said this was 'very true' or 'fairly true.'[35]

It would be fascinating to see similar figures for Canadian dailies, but even readers of the *Toronto Sun* probably have more faith in their paper than their British counterparts.[36] Even so, the readers still feel free to criticize. *Maclean's* magazine was fiercely attacked by readers after doing a Christmas cover story on violent toys showing Santa Claus on the cover dressed in a camouflage suit and carrying a machine gun. (For further discussion, see Chapter 10, 'The Media and Violence.')

Arrogance and Independence

These two causes of public distrust of the media may well be related. They emanate from a sense that the media are isolated from their audience. On the one hand, journalists are seen as egotistical, power-hungry, driven by their own agendas; and on the other hand, the media themselves are seen as remote, and driven by absentee landlords with a greed for profit. Hence audiences will often imply that a Toronto-based company has little interest in serving the interests of, say, Port Alberni or Cape Breton (hence, there's a demand for more local news). But they will generally fault the media for not having enough world news. Charles Bailey, former editor of the *Minneapolis Star and Tribune*, commented: 'Journalists, particularly in Washington, are perceived as richer, more elitist, more arrogant, more sensation-seeking. They are less liked, less respected.'[37]

It is a no-win situation, and it is unfortunate that so many journalists are uncomfortable being on the receiving end of criticism because it is part of the job description. The retiring president of the American Society of Newspaper Editors, Creed Black, described it as an 'occupational hazard': 'The irony here is that because newspapers are better than ever, we may be gaining in unpopularity in some circles as we improve the watchdog role.'[38] J. Patrick O'Callaghan, then publisher of the *Calgary Herald*, put it neatly: 'Let's face it, by their very nature, newspapers are not beloved, even by their most avid readers. Even our best friends have trouble with us. We are often not nice to know. We don't know our manners or accept our place in the scheme of things. We tend to express opinions in outrageous terms, often shocking our owners as much as we irritate and annoy our readers ... We are not a nice cuddly institution.'[39]

This alienation was echoed by Fred Bruning of *Newsday* in a thinkpiece in *Maclean's*, in which he argued that people were delighted that journalists had been kept out of Grenada by the US military. The press has a role to protect the audience, he said, but, 'The screwy thing is that the public doesn't want to be protected, at least not by the press.'[40]

Another factor contributing to this sense of arrogance may well be the remoteness, or perceived remoteness, of the media. With increasing chain ownership, there are very few independent news media any more, apart from the weeklies (and only some of them). With only a handful of independent dailies,[41] with most TV stations being seen as creatures of CBC or CTV, with most radio stations being part of vast networks, the audience may *feel* 'their' media aren't theirs at all.

Complaints were made to both the Davey Senate Commission on Media and the Kent Commission on Daily Newspapers suggesting unhealthy centralization of ownership and lack of local independence. Interestingly enough, neither commission found much specific hard evidence of interference by managements in the daily news operation. (Though both, nonetheless, sounded the alarm against increasing chain growth.) And this seems to be consistently backed up by senior news managers. Stu Keate, recalling the tyrannical Max Bell's control of FP newspapers, concludes, 'Each [paper] was left to determine its own editorial policy.'[42] But he implies that Brig. R.S. Malone, who took over from Bell, constantly interfered,[43] and

that John Bassett, too, was not averse to interfering as Toronto *Telegram* publisher.[44] Keate's statement about the Thomson chain is perceptive: 'The Thomsons, for instance, liked to say that their papers enjoyed local autonomy and in the editorial sense this was probably true – but what did it matter if a rigid budget structure, imposed on every paper, prevented the publisher from making necessary improvements?'[45]

Frequent interference in newsroom activity is virtually impractical, as the chains are simply too big for a proprietor to be involved in daily newsroom decisions. However, cases do undoubtedly occur. Nick Fillmore, a CBC producer and activist with the Centre for Investigative Journalism, cited several in 1986.[46] Interestingly enough, the CBC seems to have managed to stay at arm's length from its 'owners,' the federal government.[47] At the same time that newspapers have relinquished their turn-of-the-century ties with political parties and moved to the moral high ground, so owners, making a substantial profit, may have simply concluded, 'If it ain't broke, don't fix it!'

But their attitude is often depressing. Desbarats cites a chilling remark attributed to Roy Megarry, then publisher of the Toronto *Globe and Mail*: 'By 1990, publishers of mass circulation daily newspapers will finally stop kidding themselves that they are in the newspaper business and admit that they are primarily in the business of carrying advertising messages.'[48] The Kent Commission bitterly concluded that 'the power exercised by a chain, shaping the editorial content of its newspapers, is pervasive.'[49]

The lack of daily newspaper competition is also a worry, though it solves nothing to blame it all on newspaper publishers who are unwilling to maintain unprofitable papers. (In fact, between 1981 and 1990, Canadian daily chains folded four titles, but founded four, for a zero loss, according to the CDNPA statistics cited above.) But ownership of a monopoly operation – TV, print, or radio – brings with it a considerably increased responsibility to provide rounded coverage and broad public access.

To respond to the accusations of arrogance, the media have to work overtime to reassure audiences that they are not concerned exclusively with the bottom line, that the corporate giant, with headquarters

1,000 kilometres away, cares about the small communities and the individuals they comprise (for further discussion of accessibility, see Chapter 16, 'Righting Writing Wrongs').

That, too, is an ethical decision.

TOUGH CALLS

1 'Jim Fixx, who started the running-for-fitness fad, died of a heart attack today, while running.' Is this a good lead?

2 At one time, the Prairie weekly *Farm, Light and Power* required its writers to submit stories to sources for approval before they were published. Does such interaction build reader confidence? Is there a downside?

3 The satirical magazine *Frank* runs a story implying that Prime Minister Mulroney has had a drinking problem. The yarn is picked up by other media. *Maclean's* magazine, for instance, goes to some trouble to deny the 'widely circulated' rumours. Does the first story legitimately put the matter on the public agenda? Can editors ignore it, once another medium has published it?

4 The pope made a tour of Latin America. One reporter wrote about what he saw as the irony of the lavishly expensive tour amidst poverty and hunger. Was he right to do so?

The Role of the Media

Objectivity and *truth* have long been the two cardinal catchwords of journalism. This implied that the reporter's role, as Peter Desbarats rather disparagingly put it, was 'simply to report' what he or she observed,[1] recording the facts without any personal intrusion (the use of 'I' was absolutely banned). What the reporter observed was, as far as possible, true, and therefore *truth*. What he or she wrote was, as far as possible, impersonal, and therefore *objective*, concentrating on the objects observed and minimizing the writer's own views.

While this may be something of an unfair simplification, it probably represents the way many young reporters were trained, including this writer. Age has a way of giving one, if not wisdom, at least awareness of one's ignorance. With experience, thoughtful reporters and editors came to recognize that truth and objectivity were complex, indefinable, and difficult to achieve, though perhaps still worth seeking, especially as nobody had come up with a better idea.

Certainly journalists are not inanimate or unfeeling. As newspeople examined their souls, they recognized that what had been billed as one of the eternal verities of the craft was in reality unachievable. The Canadian newscaster and TV host Peter Trueman put it this way: 'Good journalists seethe with opinions, and those who do not have opinions on the issues that beset us are airheads.'[2] Nonetheless, Trueman, in discussing the case of Dale Goldhawk (a CBC host who was taken off the air during an election campaign because he was president of the outspoken actors union, ACTRA), rejects any suggestion 'that reporters should have the right to express personal opinions in hard news stories.'[3]

So, how can we define objectivity? Here is a light-hearted multiple-choice test. Objectivity is:

1 Impossible and obsolete.
2 All that is necessary to be ethical.
3 Impossible but still worth striving for.
4 A management tool to suppress bright writers.
5 All of the above.

Perhaps no. 5 is the closest we'll get. Objectivity varies depending on whom you ask. *Objectivity is an attitude. It is the attempt by journalists to keep personal views out of news reports and to give as fair and full a report as possible and suitable.*

Objectivity is not a new idea, nor is it necessarily universal. Rutherford notes that 'by the 1920s the ideal of objectivity had fixed itself in the minds of journalists and readers as the guiding principle of proper reporting. News columns are more impartial than in times past. Reporters were trained to witness rather than interpret events, to provide copy free from any personal views ... Myth though it was, the ideal of objectivity enhanced the credibility of news.'[4]

Objectivity and Truth

Objectivity is closely associated with truth. John Merrill remarks, 'It has to do with truth, but objectivity implies something more than truthful information, it implies *thoroughness* as well; it implies realistic organization and balance; it implies proper focus; it implies unbiased selection of facts and true-to-nature emphasis and deemphasis of these facts.'[5]

Several of these points are valuable. Merrill seems to put truth as the first criterion, but it would be a mistake to become obsessed with truth to the exclusion of other issues. At best, truth is only holding a mirror up to society, and generally society needs more than that. (And it is impossible to tell 'the whole truth and nothing but the truth.' Even the reporter at the scene of a minor accident does not see it all, hear it all, and smell it all, let alone capture every detail on paper or film: the steering wheel was not bent, the driver was wearing blue underwear, the transmission leaked 16 cc. of 10/30 oil, the seventeen Holsteins in the neighbouring field were calling to be milked. All this is part of the 'truth' of the moment. And even if every fragment were captured, no editor would give it space and no reader would read it. The average sixteen- or eighteen-minute TV newscast could not tell *all* of one tiny accident, let alone all *The World Tonight*.)

Is everything that appears in the news media true? Certainly not, if one includes advertising, horoscopes, quotes from the occasional politician, and even accidental errors in news stories. Newsrooms generally take no responsibility for the extravagances of advertisers or stargazers. (At least one US paper has begun putting a disclaimer with its horoscope, but we should not hold our breath waiting for media managers to do the same for advertising.) Does some of the exaggeration of advertisers chip away at the newsroom's credibility? When newspapers carry an ad that looks like news and is headlined, 'Device may increase gas mileage by 22%' do readers believe the ad, or tend to disbelieve *all* headlines?[6] At best – once again – all the press can hope to achieve is a close proximity to truth.

Merrill adds thoroughness, balance, focus, and lack of bias as essential elements. These ingredients, all well stirred, produce – with a sprinkling of luck – something approaching a fair report.

Is Truth Accuracy and Accuracy Truth?
Truth is a slippery creature, never attainable. But accuracy suggests, instead, that what the reporter reports is of itself true, though not, perhaps, the whole truth. (It is 'true' that there was a burglary on the High Street last night; it is irrelevant, though also true, that it was a warm, windy night and there were Halloween decorations in the windows.)

In *The News Media: A Journalist Looks at His Profession*, John Hohenberg cites a classic example of what can happen when journalists become myopic in the pursuit of accuracy. McCarthyism, he says, could never have grown into the horrific national witch-hunt that it did if journalists had been doing their full job, manning the watchtowers. By accurately reporting McCarthy's outrageous claims, journalists were abetting him, he maintains.[7]

As if that lesson were never learned, the same happened in Canada in the 1980s, with the emergence of anti-Semite Ernst Zundel. The press covered Zundel's trial, for distributing hate literature, faithfully and fully. But in so doing they gave publicity and even credence to the views of kooks and hate-mongers. A York University historian, Ramsay Cook, was quoted by the *Globe and Mail* as blasting the media: 'Those people who denied the Holocaust were given the same objective treatment as the others so it sometimes appeared in the newspapers that this was really a matter that was open to question.'[8] Very true. The Holocaust is *not* negotiable. Of course it happened. But how is the reporter – perhaps a court reporter trained specifically in this craft – how is she to know that some evidence in court is indisputable while some is debatable or even wrong? Or, to put it another way, which 'facts' can reporters take as incontrovertible, and which ones need parentheses or disclaimers? Does the reporter take it as indisputable that Christ was born of a virgin? Or that zero population growth is desirable? Or that clearing Brazilian rain forest is bad? And what about wartime? As an early US senator intoned, 'The first casualty when war comes is truth.'[9] This is effectively documented in *Gotcha! The Media, the Government and the Falklands Crisis*, the story of media manipulation during the Falklands War, which quotes Winston Churchill from 1943. 'In wartime, truth is so precious that she should always be attended by a bodyguard of lies.'[10] Even if the politicians' motives are entirely high-minded, using truth as a weapon of war leaves the media in a very precarious position. As Philip Knightley's excellent study, *The First Casualty*, shows, the media have often been quick to massage the truth 'in the national interest.'[11]

Another increasingly difficult area is photography. It used to be felt that 'the camera cannot lie,' but, especially with the emergence of digital technology, the camera can lie prodigiously (see Chapter 15, 'Different Media, Different Problems'). So extra effort is needed to protect the integrity of pictures.

Finally, of course, truth can be distorted by omission as much as by commission. Bob Edwards, celebrated editor of the Calgary *Eye-Opener* newspaper, observed back in 1920, 'Occasionally a man tells lies by keeping his mouth shut.'[12] This, too, is explored further in Chapter 7, 'Manipulating the Media.' But journalism must sometimes be pro-active, not simply re-active. During coverage of the Westray mine disaster in Nova Scotia, for instance, it became embarrassingly clear that the media had simply failed to see the warning signs before the mine explosion. Commented Bruce Wark, a CBC reporter and now journalism teacher at King's College, Halifax: 'It was a huge media failure, me included ... The media went with company propaganda, and ignored the problems.'[13] Wark said journalists had heard rumours of safety problems at the mine but, for a variety of reasons, ignored them. 'I believe that those miners would have been alive today if the media had done their job. We're all implicated,' he said.[14] The recurring sexual assaults on boys at the Mt. Cashel Orphanage might come under the same heading: a story that wasn't told until it was too late.

Objectivity and Motivation

But there is one other ingredient that John Merrill does not fully explore, which has less to do with technique and more to do with motive: WHY be objective?

It has already been argued that various media, over the years, have been highly selective and even subjective in their handling of the news, despite their avowed position of objectivity.

Partly because of the sheer difficulty of achieving objectivity, a lobby has emerged in recent years to abandon the whole idea. Peter Desbarats argues persuasively that objectivity reflects 'the old rules,'[15] concluding that it is impossible and therefore should be abandoned. His bottom line is that reporters 'should not pretend to make comprehensive, objective reports,' but instead should produce 'intelligent assessments of news events for the guidance of viewers.'[16] (However, he feels that this is impossible without more newsroom researchers.)

Desbarats is joined by the outspoken CBC public affairs radio producer Max Allen, who has argued that 'objectivity is an artificial convention: It protects us politically, and it's easy to do.'[17] Therefore, he told a conference of the Centre for Investigative Journalism in 1985, objectivity should be wholly rejected.

However, I am not entirely persuaded. Certainly humans cannot be objective. Living is a continuum of choices, and choices are necessarily subjective: What shall I wear? What shall I eat? What shall I buy? What shall I tell the boss? Journalism just exaggerates this process. The assignment editor chooses which stories to cover. The reporter chooses which quotes to use. The item producer chooses which footage to show. The anchor chooses which words to emphasize. And, as Desbarats asserts, it is a charade to 'pretend' otherwise.

But why pretend? Perhaps, like the provocative movie that begins with a warning 'the scenes you are about to witness may contain violence and coarse language,' news should be preceded by a warning: 'This newspaper/newscast represents the best efforts of our staff to capture fairly the material that they believe is important today. They try hard, but they are not infallible ...'[18]

Such a show of humility might go some way to assuage the accusation of media arrogance. ('All the news that's fit to print'? Who knows it all? Who has space for it all?)

It is, of course, frustrating to be imperfect, frustrating for a journalist to know that as long as she espouses objectivity she strives for the impossible. But is that sufficient reason to stop trying? (At the risk of everyone abandoning the debate, and all journalists deciding to do something simple instead, such as micro-surgery or astrophysics, one could argue that *all* journalism is impossible. If journalism is capturing twenty-four hours of the world in a single newspaper or – worse – in a single newscast, it is, of course, impossible. If journalism is the reporting and interpreting of everything that the audience needs regarding wheat futures, Palestine, the Rough Riders, chess, child abuse, space travel, love, and city taxes, what hope is there? But it is. And the only hope is that journalists will do their level best.)

Certainly, Bill Morgan, a senior CBC newsman who now directs the marvellously named 'Office of Journalism Policy and Practices' for the CBC, maintains journalists should reach for the unattainable. He told a seminar of the Canadian Communications Association: 'Journalism is the task of endlessly doing the best you can, yet being disappointed ... Impartiality is something worth striving for.'[19]

The Corporation is, of course, something completely different. Through its network of networks (radio, TV, French and English and All-News), it serves every Canadian, from Sooke to Twillingate, from yuppies in Vancouver to radar operators in remote settlements of the Arctic. And every Canadian is its critic. Therefore, its need to be fair and balanced is even greater than, say, 'Canada's National Newspaper,' the *Globe and Mail*. So Morgan's – the CBC's – mandate will be different from commercial media: 'The airwaves belong to the people and they are entitled to hear the principal points of view on the issues of the day ... The hotter the controversy, the more important it is to condense the time between the expression of points of view.'[20]

Morgan's credo applies primarily to news programming, but it is not without challengers, certainly in the public affairs area. Like Desbarats, the CBC agent provocateur Max Allen says people should quit pretending to be objective: 'People should write what they believe to be true ... and sign it, and say, "These are my views."'[21]

Allen implies that objectivity is, in fact, unethical, as it is a cop-out. It means, in his view, that the ideal journalist is 'dumb' – he or she would have no opinions and could draw no conclusions.

Interestingly, one of America's most eminent journalism teachers, John C. Merrill, argues that worrying about ethics is virtually unnecessary, if only journalists *are* objective.[22] Clearly, he, like many people, has not heard that objectivity is obsolete: 'Conventional wisdom among journalists is that objectivity in reporting is paramount,' he begins an article on the subject, 'and that the newsperson who is objective has fulfilled the highest and most responsible expectation possible.'[23]

Merrill, who admittedly is not known for his liberal views, seems to feel that the jury is still out on whether objectivity is possible, but that striving for it remains a laudable goal, and striving for it is, per se, ethical behaviour.[24]

In *Philosophy and Journalism*, Merrill introduces a nice paradox:

It is impossible for journalists to detach themselves from their stories if they are to give an honest and full account. And in this reluctance to detach themselves, journalists dedicate themselves to subjectivity. But it could be said that this dedication to subjectivity is the pathway to greater objectivity ... We are simply saying that subjectivity is essential to what might be called objective reporting.[25]

This is a fairly metaphysical way of saying that the finest journalism involves the journalist doing his best to be fair and thorough, while recognizing and admitting his limitations.

But there is a danger that objectivity may be seen as an end in itself rather than as a means. It should not be confused with the role of journalism, which is what both Merrill and Desbarats seem to do. Merrill clearly equates objective reporting with ethical reporting.[26] Somehow, he convinces himself that the reporter who makes NO judgments is more ethical than she who worries her story to death: 'Why not just report and let the chips fall where they may?' he asks rhetorically.[27] He defines objective reporting as 'full-disclosure' reporting, and pours scorn on those who debate a story's consequences or who worry about the feelings of the people caught up in the story.[28]

So Merrill pits objective reporting against what he calls 'morally inspired reporting.' (He labels a story in which the reporter declines to give a rape victim's name as 'flawed' and 'incomplete.')

But *is* objectivity simply full disclosure? It is impossible to tell the 'whole truth,' but isn't that exactly what 'full disclosure' implies? Merrill indicates that full disclosure involves not leaving out details from a story to satisfy some private agenda, and he longs for some mythical good old days when men were men and editors judged a story to be good simply because it was 'truthful, balanced and complete.'

Arm's-length objective journalists, presumably, must not be moved by compassion for the people caught up in the news or by concern for the results of a story.

On the surface, this sounds very much like the argument advanced by Ann Medina, a respected CBC television reporter, who joined the debate in 1988. Giving a Minifie Memorial Lecture at the University of Regina, Medina argued that too many reporters today apparently feel a need to report 'in order to' – for instance, in order to save lives, to stop corruption, or to bring about peace in a region. She went on to say, 'These goals sound very lofty. Surely, one might say, no one could question a reporter with those kind of concerns ... Well, I do. Too often, those who report "in order to" end up playing God.' Medina's conclusion was that 'we should not play God. We should not look into a crystal ball. We should publish the story even if we think it might end up costing lives ... It's our job to be fuddy-duddy journalists and ... once again, report what we see, what we hear, what we can touch and what we know.'[29]

She, too, appears to espouse the journalist-as-pipeline view, as if she can be neutral, and as if her choice of whom to interview, whom to film, and which clips to use are in fact not subjective choices. Yet surely part of her own excellence as a reporter is precisely her ability to go beyond being a mere conduit, a fly on the wall, and to report selectively what the audience wants and needs to see and hear?

The implicit contradictions in such a position were emphasized when Medina talked about her craft to journalism students before giving the Minifie lecture. Among the qualities of the good reporter, she said, were curiosity, drive, patience, tolerance, a cast-iron stomach, and 'emotional stamina: You want to get close to it [the story], touch it, and let it touch you.'

So the reporter is encouraged to become emotionally involved with the story. However, it mustn't show. Medina urged young reporters to remove themselves from their stories: 'Dwindle, shrink, remove the reporter as much as you can.' Why? 'I don't want the audience to be aware that I am the filter through which they are seeing the story.' The filter? Can one filter, and still claim to be 'objective'?

Another TV journalist used a similar metaphor when giving another Minifie lecture. Helen Hutchinson chose the term 'sieve':

The fact is that each of us carries around his own intellectual and emotional sieve through which all information is strained. Each of us edits his or her own life.

As broadcasters, one of our jobs is to edit other people's lives. As viewers, we need to remember, even when we're watching 30-second news clips, that someone has edited them according to his or her own lights.[30]

This is a clear recognition of the subjective nature of the job, without wanting to embrace subjectivity exclusively.

John Miller, head of the Ryerson School of Journalism and former deputy managing editor of the *Toronto Star*, raises another problem. He defines objective reporting as having come to mean 'reporting that legitimates ideas only if they are spoken in public by suitable officials.'[31]

That's a fascinating snapshot: the knee-jerk reporter who thinks he's being objective by simply using the familiar old 'official' sources – the minister, the police chief, the coach, etc. This reporter clearly leaves himself dangerously vulnerable to manipulation. (An example of this would be the mayor who calls a news conference to announce that the heritage buildings downtown are to be bulldozed for a shopping mall. So reporter Freddie Farkleberry solemnly reports the announcement, with no attempt at ascertaining if this is the best thing for the community.)

On the other hand, Peter Desbarats refers disparagingly to 'any lingering pretensions to objectivity that journalism might still hold'[32] and peremptorily dismisses objectivity in the past tense, tying it together with the role of the journalist: 'When objectivity was still regarded as the touchstone of good journalism, the role of the news media seemed relatively easy to define: it was simply to report.'[33] As the job was easy back then, he argues, so the reporter needed little skill: 'When objectivity was the rule, journalists, at least in theory, needed little more than a pencil and notebook, good eyesight and hearing, and an open mind.'[34] Such dismissal of journalism 'greats' of the past – Ross Munro, James M. Minifie, Norman DePoe, John Dafoe, and Joseph Howe – seems a trifle high-handed. Was that all they brought to the craft – tools and an open mind? Or were they actually the advance guard of a new kind of journalist? Certainly subjective journalism is not new. It began with the birth of newspapers in the mid-seventeenth century, and has a fine tradition, which has carried on through Dafoe and Bruce Hutchison to some classic contemporary journalists. Helen Hutchinson, an admirable television host and reporter, recalls covering a devastating earthquake near Naples in 1981 and being deeply moved by the grief and suffering. Her training told her to suppress her tears on camera, but subsequently she regretted not showing her feelings: 'I should have simply been me.'[35] Brian Stewart allowed his passion to show, and his emotional plea on CBC-TV for help for the starving in Eritrea touched off a worldwide campaign to aid them.

But objectivity – bringing truth, accuracy, fairness, and balance to a story – needs considerably more skill than critics seem willing to admit. Certainly, if objectivity is rejected, the reporter thereby acquires a monstrous burden: 'If all reporting is to some extent subjective, then every report except the simplest transmission of data (weather, stock-market reports, sports results) contains an element of commentary and influences public opinion.'[36] Adding a few newsroom researchers won't relieve that burden. Every two-car crash will have the potential to 'contain an element of commentary,' and every Women's Institute tea could 'influence opinion.' The vast knowledge and wisdom required of each journalist to achieve this would be overwhelming. 'Subjective journalism, in an age of shifting truth, requires experience, knowledge, judgment, and unusual skill in the use of verbal or visual language. It demands a new kind of journalist.'[37] Newsroom salaries may have to increase a bit before this nirvana is reached.

But what does this all say about the consumers of news? It might be instructive to ask the advocates of subjectivity their opinion of news audiences. Are readers, watchers, and listeners basically stupid? Too stupid to distinguish between fact and opinion? Too stupid to make their own minds up on issues, always needing to be told how to think and what things mean?[38]

Objectivity and the Five *W*s

The question brings us, once more, to the five *W*s of journalism ethics offered in Chapter 1:

Who benefits/gets hurt by objectivity versus subjectivity? The audience, surely, is best served by a true, fair, and balanced report of the facts. Is the audience better served by being denied this raw data? (Ottawa columnist Charles Lynch notes that readers have on occasion complained about a lack of basic information. When his commentary gets in the paper but the news story reporting the event he is commenting on gets left out, people don't like it, he says.[39] So the first priority is giving the audience the facts on which it can base its own decisions. Where necessary, a constructive analysis of a situation may be of further help.

What does objectivity/subjectivity do for the credibility of the journalist and the newsroom? If credibility represents trust, will the audience trust the writers and editors more if they come out of the closet, analyzing and commenting on the events that they cover as news, as Peter Desbarats suggests?[40] Or will they prefer to get the 'facts' without the polemic?

When and **where** don't have great significance here. But, if objectivity is formally declared dead and pointless, does the reporter then have the freedom to rush into print as soon as she wishes, without having to fret about getting 'both sides' or balance? Conversely, does she have the freedom *not* to rush into print, but to publish only when satisfied that the analysis is absolutely complete, days or even weeks later?

Why air or suppress this? Why write it? Why, indeed, *be* a journalist and pursue this arcane craft? Does the subjective reporter have a new role to play in society, beyond gathering and presenting information? Does every event need analysis? Is every story interpretive, or is this role reserved – as now – for the major stories?

How is news normally handled? If readers are raised in the belief that journalism does strive for objectivity, will it confuse them to find that all stories contain the writer's interpretation, in addition to raw facts? And how does the reversibility rule work here? Would the journalist who believes interpretation is necessary to every story accept subjective journalism in all the news that *she* reads, hears, and watches?

Clearly, it is the view of this writer that objectivity *is* impossible, but that every reporter should make every effort to be objective – to be fair, full, and accurate – nonetheless.

Reporters Report?

The very term 'reporter' implies an element of neutral recording for posterity. News has itself been dubbed 'tomorrow's history' and 'history on the run.' This suggests that the media are primarily event-oriented and that their role mainly involves recording today's events, providing the raw data for tomorrow's historians.

The Davey Report, however, was more rigorous, insisting that it was easy to chase fire engines, but a good journalist must delve deeper: 'How successful is that newspaper, or broadcasting station, in preparing its audience for social change?' it asked.[41] For instance, it may seem adequate, in terms of history, for a radio station to report that there has been an influx of oriental immigration in Vancouver, or for a newspaper to report that there has been considerable oriental investment in Vancouver. But what effect will this have on real estate, on social services, and on second-language schooling? That is information that the audience can act on: News they can use.

The best media, by that definition, are those that take the surprise out of tomorrow. They don't merely tell what *has* happened but what *could* happen and what *may* happen. A newscast might tell listeners that the sales tax will go up 2 per cent next January, thus helping the audience decide whether to buy a new car before New Year's Day.

This does not involve the media in reading crystal balls or chicken entrails. The journalists must make connections and locate experts who can help predict whatever the roller coaster of the future may offer, be it racial tensions, government pensions, banking reliability, or the future of wheat amidst American price subsidies and global warming.

Despite this, ordinary, old-fashioned reporting is still essential. Chasing fire engines is still essential. While it is important to explain WHY the fire engines are out and what an increase in arson means to society, it remains vitally necessary to simply report the events as fairly and accurately as is practical. But the media

must sometimes go beyond this, putting ideas together, seeing connections and consequences, analyzing data, for instance, to indicate *in advance* that the government will be forced to increase taxes, rather than waiting for the announcement. Informed analysis and intelligent guidance can provide important leadership. This is what Helen Hutchinson calls 'putting the beads on the string.' The journalists' role, she says, is

to put events into context, to try to make some sense out of all the information with which we're bombarded, before we scatter it ...

The string is the continuum of time. Everything goes on the string ...

Some beads are larger than others, but they're all there on the string. Nothing exists in isolation. When you look at an event or achievement in this way, when you sit back and contemplate that big string, it's much easier to get the perspective in place and to decide how each bead fits in with the others.[42]

Part of this simply involves good news judgment. Editors, choosing assignments, must consider the long-term potential of events. To send a reporter to a large, distant medical conference may sound boring, specialized, and expensive. But the reporter may extract important data on AIDS, for instance, which may enable readers to make crucial decisions about their future sexual activity, and which may help governments to make crucial decisions about AIDS prevention and treatment. So the editor, especially the assignment editor, who decides which stories should be covered by whom, must make value judgments, based in part on which stories may turn out to be important in the future.[43]

But people don't necessarily want to be protected by the media. The press has to watch on behalf of the public, protecting them and telling them what is going to happen. If there is a strong central government – with a landslide majority, such as New Brunswick had in the late 1980s – then the Opposition has a very small voice. Under those circumstances, the press must challenge and question the government, to keep it honest.[44] Such a role puts the press in an invidious position; it seems always to be carping, criticizing the government. Southam News columnist Charles Lynch has suggested that some journalists profit by negativism, arguing that 'every knock is a buck.'[45] Lynch says that negative commentary on the government is a peculiarly Canadian syndrome. However, wherever there are good reporters, there will be critics of government who are willing to slip them brown envelopes with ammunition for further attacks. By their very nature, these tips are going to be negative. There's little impetus for a civil servant or an Opposition MLA to slip a brown envelope to a reporter containing information that *praises* government activities. So the media have always to be on guard against manipulation. The existence of the leaked document doesn't automatically mean there's a story. The fact that a Global news reporter was slipped a leaflet summarizing the federal budget, due for release the next day, did not mean he *had* to publish it. Certainly the fact that the data was *available* was news. But to publish the contents of the data was to interfere with the event itself, conceivably influencing world markets. (For further discussion, see Chapter 8, 'To Press or to Suppress?')

In a way, this is a no-win situation for the journalists: The Global reporter was charged with possession of a stolen document, though he thought he was performing a public service. The majority of such leaks involve criticism of government – accusations of kickbacks, patronage, conflict of interest, poor security – but the government was elected by a majority of the community. Criticism of government may be seen subconsciously as criticism of the electors for their poor judgment.

The Media and the Status Quo

At the same time, while the media watch and warn, they surely cannot be preaching revolt. Most media are creatures of a capitalist environment, and they themselves can only function effectively in a stable environment. Hence, their first instinct is to protect the status quo. (Even the communist *Canadian Tribune* would have trouble selling subscriptions and distributing papers during a civil war.) Writers and editors may feel a duty to promote a better environment, but there's not much incentive to preach the total overthrow of the current economic system. The news media tend to

say, mostly subconsciously, that society is satisfactory the way it is. This attitude may be seen at first glance as 'objectivity' (reporting fairly, without taking sides), but it could also be dubbed 'conservatism': *Why rock the boat?* (the theme of William Weintraub's novel of the same name, about Canadian journalism). There is also, therefore, a clear likelihood that the media implicitly will defend the capitalist system under which they operate. Paul Rutherford notes this as happening from the early days of journalism: 'The Colonial press had served to reinforce the values and strengthen the institutions of an emerging Victorian Canada.'[46] Rutherford characterizes this as 'the defence of affluence'[47] and finds it entrenched today, 'for the multimedia have become, above all, the voices of affluence.'[48] Peter Desbarats describes very effectively how growing dependence on advertising brought journalists 'to identify their own interests with those of the economic and political systems that supported them.'[49]

By and large, the promoters of radical change have been greeted pretty coolly by Canadian media. The unemployed, making the On to Ottawa Trek in 1935 to seek a better deal than pennies a day in a work camp, got a very cold shoulder from the media along the way. Tommy Douglas and the CCF met considerable press hostility for suggesting state medicare in 1962. In the days of flower power, in the late 1960s, the radicals were dubbed 'hippies' and 'flower children' and were depicted as decadent druggies with long hair and beads, bent on destabilizing society – not as creative youngsters trying to make a better world.

Social Responsibility

Asking the fifth *W* – Why? – about objectivity, accuracy, and truth raises a large and crucial question: Does journalism have a purpose, beyond, as some cynic put it, keeping the ads apart? If we accept that it is purposive, then are we subscribing to what Medina condemns: reporting 'in order to'? But she, certainly, would not define journalism as mere ballast to fill the newshole, providing enough material so that the newspaper meets postal regulations for second class mail, or so the newscast can justify the commercial breaks.

Most journalists would probably say they were drawn to the craft for a range of reasons, among which 'informing people' ranks high. Media analysts go a lot further, identifying a range of roles for the press, differing with time and place.

Arthur Siegel summarizes these effectively in *Politics and the Media in Canada*, drawing heavily on *Four Theories of the Press*, by Fred Siebert et al.[50] Siegel concludes that the Authoritarian mode (in which the media are used to retain political power), the Developmental concept (which argues that Third World communities should develop their own news services to foster local interests and reduce Western influence), and the Soviet-Communist mode (where the press is seen as a tool of state and party) are inapplicable to the Canadian scene. Siegel sees Canada's media today as a blend of the old Libertarian Theory and the more recent Social Responsibility Theory. In the former, a free press is seen as paramount, crucial to democracy; in the latter, the media are seen as limited by a need to be fair to all segments of society, obligated to nurture the underprivileged.

This conjunction of competing philosophies (a press permitted complete freedom in order to preserve democracy, and a press constrained to respond to certain needs in society) is at the root of many debates about the press in contemporary Canada. Clearly, the Libertarian idea is weakened when few people can afford to own a press and few can get access to the news columns or airwaves. And clearly the social responsibility concept is weakened by the pivotal questions of who decides whom the media should be protecting and how this should be enforced. (As Paul Rutherford argues, the social responsibility theory makes the media very vulnerable, justifying 'an easy recourse to authoritarian measures.')[51] As somebody remarked, there's freedom of the press for everyone who owns one ... So it's freedom for the people who have got presses and not for the rest. Certainly not for the poor, the aboriginals, or the immigrants.

The social responsibility theory suggests the media must encourage the underprivileged to speak out, that it must actively seek to protect their interests, looking at poverty, at life on the reserves, at discrimination, and at jail conditions, even though this may not produce the event-oriented news of old.

Canadian editors, raised on a blend of the libertarian theory and the social responsibility theory, have to juggle these issues while making hundreds of news decisions each day – decisions on which stories to choose, where to run them, and with what pictures and headlines.

On the one hand, Canada has considerable freedom of the press, resulting in a feeling that anybody ought to be able to express their opinions in the papers, that the media can get away with a great deal, that a paper can be liberal or left-wing or right-wing, and that a newsroom should be independent even of its capitalist owners. On the other hand, readers expect media to demonstrate a responsibility to their society, to their audience, and to acknowledge an unwritten contract, especially in a single-media environment. In most mid-sized Canadian communities, there is only one local daily newspaper, and often only one local TV station. In the small towns and villages, there may be only one weekly, plus, perhaps, a radio station. In such communities, those newsrooms have an extra responsibility to try to carry 'all' the news and all the views, if they are to satisfy the whole spectrum of the audience. This puts a very heavy responsibility on the newsroom.

In addition to this witch's brew of competing demands, the public increasingly wants to be entertained. Television, of course, does this very well. Television entertains people and keeps their attention because of the constantly moving images, the sounds, and the colour. The print media, therefore, increasingly have to entertain to compete and do so by adding features, columns, horoscopes, comics, bright colours, and graphics to the news.

The ethical journalist has to balance and evaluate all these competing demands and competing techniques, which is much harder than simply saying, 'If it's true, we print it.'

How does this fit in with ethics? Understanding why journalists do what they do, their motivations, purposes, raisons d'etre, is necessary before we can resolve ethical questions. If we believe objectivity is paramount, the answers may well be different from those based on a belief that journalists have a crusading role. Objectivity in hard-news reporting is beyond reach but must nonetheless be reached for. Journalists must not report 'in order to,' but neither must they hide behind objectivity and balance to avoid responsibility for their actions.

Up to this point, the terms 'reporter' and 'journalist' have been used interchangeably, but perhaps we now come to the parting of the words. A *reporter* does, indeed, report, gathering and disseminating as full, fair, and accurate a report of the world as she is able, often without glory (though she can still be a network TV celebrity) and often even without a byline. The best reporters *write* extremely well. (By extension, an editor handles the reporter's work with the same high-minded dedication.) Contemporary names such as David Halton and Ann Medina come to mind.

The *journalist* is the gifted, informed reporter who can go beyond this to make connections, write analyses, explain, predict, and initiate, manning the watchtowers, protecting the underdog, and writing always with a byline and suitable descriptors ('Analysis by ...'). Perhaps the late Bruce Hutchison and Richard Gwyn fit into this category.

A limited number of people are capable of being good reporters, but it is an admirable and essential function in society, and the best reporters should be heralded and rewarded. A far smaller number rise from the same ranks to become the best journalists.

Neither reporters nor journalists are vegetables; they are not mere inanimate conduits of data. They can cause death or at least misery by their actions (for instance, by naming a mafia informer or a rape victim); they can cause death or misery by their inactions (for instance, by ignoring the homeless or the child-abuse victims). The news media are an important part of the social fabric, and as such reporters and journalists must take responsibility for providing a full and fair supply of information to the community so that its members can grow and the world can be a better place in which to live.

Any news worker (writer, picture editor, copy editor, or publisher) should be able to hold his head up when he meets his sources after the story is published. And any news worker should be able to respect the person he meets in the mirror each morning.

The Journalist as Advocate

It is extremely risky, though tempting, for the journalist to conclude that a particular public official is incompetent and say, 'I'm going to get him.' It is unwise even for the columnist, who may well be viewed by readers as just another journalist. It is risky not only because the journalist immediately sheds her cloak of objective credibility, but because there is a real danger that the public will not distinguish between that journalist and others. Even the most astute and critical news consumer will tend to feel that 'the media are after Joe Clark,' rather than the narrower, 'I see that columnist Alan Fotheringham is really going after Joe Clark.'

What may seem to the writer to be helpful insight may in reality be a crusade, vindictiveness, or an individual personality clash.

Certainly some politicians (*particularly* politicians) *are* ineffectual, and the media have a duty not to protect the inept and unfit from public scrutiny. But when a former British chancellor of the exchequer leaves

SHOE

home one morning with his trouser-fly undone, does that really deserve a substantial photograph and commentary, as the *Daily Mirror* did on 24 October 1990?[52] Certainly, too, a columnist must be allowed huge latitude in commenting, criticizing, and even ridiculing. (And, as Allan Fotheringham has pointed out, the same may be true of sports writers.)[53] But a crusade to 'get' someone may well influence events. Once the journalist begins to interfere with the course of history, she must step exceedingly carefully. Evidently, there are a few occasions when the writer feels the need to reach out even beyond the roles defined above, 'in order to' achieve some higher purpose, such as helping starving children in Eritrea. But this is very rare indeed, and the answers to WHY? must be overwhelmingly convincing to offset the loss of objectivity.

TOUGH CALLS

1 A newspaper photographer works for months to develop strong rapport with a single parent on the verge of child abuse. The resulting seventeen-picture photo feature includes a picture of the mother spanking her child. Should the photographer have intervened? Should she have helped the mother, rather than documenting the abuse?

2 Strong words were exchanged in the House of Commons on 11 June 1986. The *Toronto Sun*'s report of the incident began:

House a Zoo as MPs Go Ape

OTTAWA – Shocked tourists watched cabinet ministers mouth obscenities yesterday and saw Brian Mulroney purple with rage as the opposition called him a liar and sleazy.

MPs acted like wild animals in a rutting rage as House of Commons security officials worried that violence in the chamber was a hairbreadth away.

Associate Defence Minister Harvie Andre fled his seat ... Toronto Liberal Sergio Marchi was turfed out for saying he wasn't taking any more of the prime minister's 'bullshit' and Speaker John Bosley lost any control ... Hnatyshyn further stirred the fires of hate by neatly calling the Liberals 'f— bastards' in the House of Commons while Mulroney accused Marchi of something he called 'inverted racism.'

The rattled Bosley finally shut down question period two minutes early when it became clear the inmates were in danger of running the asylum.[54]

If objectivity is dead, does this fill the vacuum?

3 When a US university researcher asked for help in locating a woman with a very rare blood type for important research, Detroit medical reporter Sandra Tessler joined the hunt. She helped locate the woman, who had joined an isolated black sect in Israel, and assisted in byzantine negotiations to get her to donate blood.[55] Certainly she went far beyond simply reporting (which would have meant just reporting the researcher's quest), but she felt she was justified because she was serving the interests of science and humankind. Was she?

4 In the late 1980s, as the AIDS story built, a Minneapolis TV newsroom decided to do a documentary on how a victim coped. In the process, the crew discovered the infected man was still sexually active. The newsroom alerted the health authorities and the man's doctor. Should they have? (For further complications to this story, see Chapter 4, 'The Media and Money.')

5 Your newspaper's motto is, 'If the press doesn't make a lot of people mad, it isn't doing its job.' Is that suitable?

PART 2

The Pressures

The Media and Money

Money is not the root of all evil in journalism, but it is certainly the root of a lot of difficulty. With most news media being profit-driven, it is difficult for any newsroom to ignore the balance sheet. Some proprietors may be generous with newsrooms and may not count the pencil stubs or the holes in the carbon paper. But at the end of the year, the investors will want a return on their investment – and a better return than they would earn by simply investing in savings bonds.

In times of economic recession, the newsroom will suffer belt-tightening, even in such 'non-profit' environments as the CBC, in common with other media departments such as advertising, promotion, and circulation. Even if the newsroom is at arm's length from the commercial side of the business, it is not immune from the vicissitudes of the whole operation.[1]

Given that many of these media feel the pressure for profit, there is a widespread drive to growth: the biggest circulation gets the biggest slice of advertising. This meshes with the journalistic instinct to be 'first' and to be 'best' (measured in audience ratings). The adrenaline of competition may militate in favour of getting the story 'at any cost.'

Chequebook Journalism

One form in which this is manifested is chequebook journalism. While this phenomenon is not widespread in Canada – certainly not as pervasive as in the UK or the US[2] – it does appear, even if sometimes described obliquely as 'program expenses.'

Chequebook journalism can be defined simply as paying for news. It most commonly involves paying sources for exclusive interviews, but money may simply be offered to induce sources to speak.[3]

Examples of the latter in Canada include a CBC payment to a so-called 'Mafia enforcer,' and payment to a drunk driver to persuade him to describe an incident for television.

In the first of these, the Mafia thug was paid $3,700 by the CBC for an interview with *The Fifth Estate*, in which he described how organized crime works. This was later defined as a 'reasonable program expense' by Bill Morgan, who was then the director of television news. The man, who admitted one murder, was a police informer. 'There was important material, some of which, I think, would have cost a fair bit of money and time to uncover any other way, and some of which was not directly available,' said Morgan.[4]

The CBC manual, *Journalistic Policy*, in effect at that time, contained a section titled Payment of Fees: 'As a general rule, the CBC does not pay news sources; the journalist's task is to gather information freely given ... If exceptional payments of this type should be contemplated, approval of the Director of Information Programs is required. The fact of such payment must be reported in the broadcast.'[5]

In the other incident, later the same year, a private producer in Red Deer, Alberta, paid a man $1,500 to participate in a TV documentary on drinking drivers. The driver had killed a motorcyclist and served a two-

Newspapers competed to buy the wedding photographs of Paul Bernardo when he was charged with being the Scarborough Rapist in 1993. The *Toronto Sun* won, and ran ten pictures, mostly in full colour.

Chequebook journalism: The *Toronto Daily Star* 'bought' Gerda Munsinger, by paying her for an exclusive story. A small investment got them the scoop of the decade and left competitors grinding their teeth, at least for a few hours.

year jail term for criminal negligence.[6] The public can easily assume from such activities that in fact crime *does* pay.

In a more recent example, the *Toronto Sun* paid $10,000 for pictures of a defendant in a sordid rape-and-disappearance case – or, more accurately, for his wedding album. The *Sun* beat the rival *Toronto Star* in February 1993 in a bidding war for the pictures of Paul Bernardo (who later changed his name to Paul Teale) and his wife, Karla Homolka. At the time, Teale faced charges of rape involving two teenage girls who were murdered. The *Sun* ran several pages of colour pictures.

Chequebook journalism cannot be discussed in the Canadian context without reference to one of the sagas of Canadian journalism, the Gerda Munsinger story.

Munsinger was at the centre of a sex-and-security scandal. Between 1958 and 1961, the attractive German woman had been good friends with at least one cabinet minister. When questions were raised in Parliament in 1966 about the security risk, the justice minister said Munsinger had died. However, *Toronto Daily Star* reporter Robert Reguly found her in Munich.

Reguly was told by his editor to 'lock up' Munsinger for an exclusive story, and $1,000 was telegraphed to him. Scott Alexander describes the scene in Munsinger's fancy apartment: 'Reguly paid Gerda $980 ($20 had been lost on the exchange rate) and drew up a contract on a piece of scrap paper. Gerda had been bought. She was the *Star*'s, if not to have and hold, at least to talk with. And her story would belong to the paper.'[7]

The story was an enormous scoop for the *Star*, to the huge chagrin of the competition, especially the Toronto *Telegram*. Was it good journalism? It was certainly historic journalism, in the cloak-and-dagger tradition of classic investigative reporting. Was it ethical? There is no evidence Munsinger was a criminal, or anything more malevolent than a good-time girl, so it does not seem to be a case of a criminal benefitting. If the *Star* had not bought the exclusive story, then the other reporters who were on Reguly's heels would have had their stories a few hours earlier. But there's no indication that things would have transpired much differently without the *Star* coup.

However, there may be a danger in such cases that sources, once having learned that information is marketable, will withhold it until they can profit from it, and may indeed encourage a bidding war. This in turn could lead to the source exaggerating the value of whatever her or she may have 'for sale' and even exaggerating or inventing the 'information' itself.

It is inappropriate for people to capitalize on antisocial activities, and consequently it is inappropriate for the news media to do so.

In Britain, this has been spelled out by the Press Council in its *Declaration of Principles* on chequebook journalism, which says in part that the Council 'unhesitatingly condemns as immoral the practice of financially rewarding criminals for the disclosure of their nefarious practices.'[8] This was expanded in 1983 after the Yorkshire Ripper case: 'It is wrong that persons associated with the criminal should derive financial benefit from trading on that association. Associates include family, friends, neighbours and colleagues. Newspapers should not pay them directly or indirectly.'[9] Even peripheral activities, such as buying serial rights for books, may bring discredit to the newsroom.[10]

But this speaks primarily to the issue of paying criminals. What about paying law-abiding citizens for their information? Unlike the BBC, the CBC specifically forbids payments being made to elected officials such as members of Parliament.[11] This is in concert with the Senate and House of Commons Act, which prohibits MPs and senators from accepting remuneration from Crown agencies.

A Toronto incident in 1985 had the appearance of being much more benevolent. CFTO, Canada's largest commercial TV station, agreed to underwrite expensive surgery for a Guyanese child with neurofibromatosis – 'elephant man's disease.' CFTO donated at least $10,000 in return for the exclusive story; the Scarborough General Hospital agreed to cooperate to protect the thirteen-year-old's privacy. Clearly, however, there was a quid pro quo for this benevolent gesture – exclusive coverage of the story. CFTO then 'sold' print exclusivity to the *Toronto Star* (the country's largest daily) and radio rights to CFTR (the country's largest commercial radio station) in return for donations to a fund for the boy.

The competing media, notably Toronto's other two dailies, were livid, especially at the participation of a

publicly funded hospital. M.K. Guzda, writing in *Editor and Publisher*, quotes a most revealing complaint from John Paton, city editor of the *Toronto Sun*: 'Speaking for myself, we shouldn't pay for information. It is tainted. If we're in the business to disseminate information as accurately as possible, we shouldn't buy it. Having said that, I do work for a paper that does try to buy exclusive rights to some stories.'[12]

The issue of paying for news becomes clouded when the newsroom is actually benefitting the sick child in such a direct way. But the fact that the station 'locked up' the family and the hospital for an exclusive story indicates that this transaction signified considerably more than an act of charity.

An American incident posed some special problems for journalists. Minneapolis TV station WCCO was doing a documentary on AIDS which focused on one individual. The destitute homosexual who agreed to be featured caused them much soul-searching when he revealed he was continuing to have sex, despite the disease. At one stage the journalists bought the man meals and paid his hotel bills. WCCO's public affairs director, Mike Sullivan, found himself justifying this to critics: 'We made the choice on humanitarian grounds. We figured that if we didn't do that, he'd find somebody to stay with and maybe have sex with them.'[13]

But although the man died a few months later, providing him with accommodation for a few nights can have done little to protect the community. (The TV station actually reported his sexual activity to the medical authorities, hoping he could be prevented from infecting more people.) It may, however, have made him more amenable to being interviewed.[14]

Such practices present clear dangers: the danger of a price being put on stories, the danger of bidding wars, and the danger of sources demanding payment for interviews as a matter of right (as British MPs appear to do).[15] These situations are worsened when the sources are criminals.

Nonetheless, there may be occasions when paying a source seems the only way to get the story. The journalists have to balance the need for the story against the possible loss of public trust, and they must avoid any implication that they are taking over police responsibilities by paying informers.

Brass Cheques

With the typical 'brass cheque' transaction, an advertiser agrees to place an advertisement in a news medium in return for favourable mention in the news columns. The procedure has been popular with advertisers for a long time – and unpopular with journalists for just as long.[16]

The process may take several forms: A sensitive advertising manager may suggest to his newsroom that 'there's a good story in the renovations at Kugelschreiber's shop,' hoping they will take the hint and having assured Kugelschreiber he would urge a story on the newsroom ('but I can't promise').[17] He may put more pressure on – or work differently – by going to the publisher and suggesting that *she* urge the newsroom to write a story about his client, knowing the publisher's 'suggestion' is hard to ignore. Or, in the most unscrupulous environment, the salesperson (who in this case will likely also be the publisher) will sell the advertisement at the same time as guaranteeing a glowing 'news' story.

The critical media reader can often identify material in the 'editorial hole' (the section assigned to newsroom, as opposed to advertising, control) that is clearly designed to please advertisers. Angie Gardos asserts that 'Homes' sections concentrating on new housing developments have different standards from other news pages.[18] Noting that a full-page advertisement in the *Toronto Star*'s 'New In Homes' section costs about $14,000 (1989 figures), she suggests that advertisers carry considerable clout. She quotes a *Toronto Sun* salesperson who remarks simply that the more you advertise, the more 'editorial support' you get.[19] Furthermore, the 'New Homes' editor at the *Sun* is quoted as saying, 'These stories are supposed to be accurate but they're very positive,' and one frequent advertiser describes the copy as 'a form of free advertising.' And in most cases, there is no disclaimer saying this material is not regular news, no admission that most of the information is provided by the advertisers, and no attempt to signal the difference typographically.

Do ordinary readers instinctively understand the difference between regular news and the copy in these 'brass cheque' sections? Gardos is sure they do not. And she's equally sure the editorial copy boosts the developers: 'Despite what editors say, site stories do lend builders credibility and, for many readers, appear to be an endorsement of the product ... The builders couldn't be more pleased with the content if they wrote it themselves.'[20]

For the journalist, the issue is one of journalistic integrity (making judgments based on news values) versus realistic relations with the employer. Frequently, the enterprising reporter, when assigned to do so, *can* find a story in the opening of a new shop, the arrival of a new manager, or even an innovative display in the showroom in a small town. There may be something to be said for gritting one's teeth, writing the rather sycophantic piece, and gradually working from within to persuade the management not to permit such compromises. The alternative – resigning in high dudgeon – may be heroic, but such a grand gesture should best be reserved for the grand incident.

In some jurisdictions, organized employees have negotiated contractual language that provides for such material to be prepared outside the newsroom, without any journalistic involvement.

The following examples come from a variety of media:

- The weekly Stettler, Alberta, *Independent* ran a full broadsheet page with the headlines: **Grand Opening: New Company Philosophy, New Owner Means Big Changes at Macleods.** The 'newshook' for the story was the arrival of a new owner at the franchise hardware shop – four months earlier – and a remodelling sale. The fulsome text was accompanied by an astonishing ten photographs, mostly of loaded shelves.[21]
- The tiny weekly Ituna, Saskatchewan, *News* carried a much smaller promotional piece for a local building shop – on the front page.[22] In this village, the opening of a new store was certainly newsworthy, but writers still need to keep at arm's length from the topic (even if the retailer might buy lucrative advertisements). Ending the story, 'They are open six days a week for your shopping convenience' may make the reader suspect the store owner wrote his own story.
- In Prince George, BC, a new rodeo was started in 1985, and the daily *Citizen* agreed to provide prizes for winners. The reporter covering the event was instructed to 'Make sure you mention that.'[23]
- Radio statio CKCK in Regina, Saskatchewan, spon-

sored 'Lifestyles '89,' a homes show, and news staff were urged to feature the show and mention the sponsorship, resulting in several larger-than-usual news items. In the mid-1980s, the same station ran a large promotion for the Honda company, so a reporter was assigned to do a story on the company.[24]

- The daughter of a Calgary, Alberta, newspaper publisher played in a local band. A reporter was assigned to write a feature on the band. Would that have happened if she were not a player?[25]
- The Humboldt, Saskatchewan, *Journal* frequently writes about its advertisers. One broadsheet page featured the village of Muenster, with three stories plugging local companies. Sample writing:

Bunz Electric Ltd. of Muenster serves all electrical needs for its customers.

The Muenster Credit Union opened its doors in February 1943 and since then has moved upwards and onwards to give its customers the latest in business practices.

Varga's Lumber ... carries a good selection of lumber, hardware, Kem paint, plumbing, electrical, automotive, hand and power tools, fasteners, garden and welding supplies, radios, televisions, video rentals, sporting goods, housewares, carpet, linoleum, ceiling fans, wood stoves, windows, doors and a full line of heavy-duty power tools.[26]

Not uncoincidentally, the page was completed by three ads for Bunz Electric, Muenster Credit Union, and Varga's Lumber.

- In 1985, the newspaper *Farm, Light and Power* assigned a reporter to write about mice and rats on the farm, after receiving a rat poison advertisement.[27]
- The Lloydminster, Alberta, *Meridian Booster* ran a regular 'Business Profile' page, which focused on a local shopkeeper each week. These items – perhaps one-third of a broadsheet page with pictures – were boldly labelled 'An advertising feature for ...' and were accompanied by a substantial ad for the featured company. The reader will be forgiven for guessing that retailers who chose *not* to advertise would not be selected for a profile. But the package was clearly labelled and as such there was no attempt to mislead

readers into thinking this was a genuine news story, though the reporters assigned to such tasks may sometimes cringe at having to interview sources with no news story to tell.

The concept has been developed to a far more sophisticated level in the magazine field. An illuminating analysis by Michael Hoyt in the *Columbia Journalism Review* shows that what he calls 'value-added advertising' emerges in many forms.[28] Hoyt describes *Lear's* magazine running a front-cover picture featuring an advertiser, and a number of other gimmicks that are not editorial-related. 'But there is another kind of added value that magazines can offer for sale – their own editorial content.'[29] Hoyt describes one unnamed US magazine where three editors quit over ethics – editorial coverage promised in return for advertising. One editor is quoted as believing that in the long run the magazine is the loser: 'Once the editorial content is devalued, he figures, the magazine becomes less valuable to advertisers.'[30]

Hoyt's implication is that the practice is widespread, and readers should be suspicious of any 'editorial' matter featuring products or firms that advertise in the same publication.

Boilerplate

Promotional material that arrives in the newsroom ready to be incorporated in the newspaper layout, set in type and complete with headline, has traditionally been called 'boilerplate.' It gets its name from the days of hot metal newspapering, when lines of type were cast in a lead alloy and locked into a steel frame for printing. Promotional material would arrive by mail already cast in metal and ready to lock into a hole in any page. The modern version of this arrives printed on glossy white paper, complete with pictures and captions, ready to be waxed and placed on a photo-typeset page pasteup.[31] Sometimes called slicks because of their glossy appearance, these are insidious – and occasionally invaluable, as they will fill a hole on a page or provide pictures where no art is available.[32] They do not only represent free advertising for commercial products. Increasingly the technique is being employed by non-profit agencies such as Foster Parents Plan and Participaction.

What is the downside of such free material? The motivation of the distributor is usually to promote a product. Consider, for instance, the text of material distributed in 1988 by the Chevrolet company for newspaper automotive pages, which began:

The 1988 model Chevrolet Corsica was recently named 'Family Circle' magazine's first 'Family Car of the Year,' in the category for families with young children. Chevrolet's newest sedan was ...

'Corsica continues to represent a new generation of cars for Chevrolet ...' says Chevrolet general manager Robert Burger. 'The versatility of the Corsica ...'[33]

In this example, the first two (excessively long) paragraphs use the words Chevrolet or Corsica a total of eight times.[34] And precisely because the material is so accessible (already typeset to the newspaper's specifications) it is very awkward to eliminate such references. And to do so would likely result in the newspaper being cut off the mailing list for future slicks.

At any one time, dozens of Canadian firms are using this technique to distribute material to newspapers. Much is wasted, but evidently enough is used to justify the modest expense.

This concept has been carried a step further by at least one Canadian company that specializes in mass-producing slicks for clients. The twelve-page glossy tabloid *News Canada* is stuffed with 'news stories' that editors are invited to 'just cut and paste.'[35] Much of the copy is barely disguised promotional material. A typical issue, such as August 1988, contained a page of cooking recipes that mentioned Robin Hood flour nine times in four articles and a page of five articles on home heating and air-conditioning that mentioned the ICG brand eleven times. But some copy is more subtle. Features on cars discreetly mentioned General Motors 'in passing.' And some are even more soft sell. Articles on home insurance, car care, or gardening mentioned no brands, but promoted the concepts of increasing one's insurance coverage, getting frequent car check-ups, and using pesticides frequently. Some material is provided by government agencies, promoting various programs such as employing the disabled.

The monthly publication is also available to editors on Macintosh or IBM disks. As editor Dan Dilks clearly stated on the editorial masthead of the publication, the bottom line for his 'camera-ready news service' is 'that we want to make *News Canada* fit your publication.'[36]

In addition to this highly accessible package, the more enterprising promotion departments of some big firms are extending the concept to great effect. For instance, back in 1973, R.J. Reynolds, the US tobacco company, introduced a 'weekly news service' comprising pseudo news plugging its product, all obligingly set in nine-point Times Roman type.[37]

(Electronic delivery makes such distribution even easier, with material sent computer-to-computer from the promotion department to the newsroom, complete with suitable typographical specifications.)

Advertorial

Several of these concepts are combined in 'advertorial' – material that closely resembles news but is in fact a paid advertisement. Fortunately, most newspapers insist that such material be labelled advertising, but such a descriptor is often extremely small and easily missed on the edge of a large and busy page.

Why should advertisers not be allowed to disguise their message in this way? Their reason for doing it is the very reason to refuse it. Advertisers want the audience to be fooled into believing their material is not merely the extravagant claim of product promoters, but that it is *true*. If the reader thinks it is news, he or she is much more likely to believe it.

This material appears to be on the rise in Canada, judging from the spate of recent criticism.[38] Senator Keith Davey, who twenty years earlier had chaired the Special Senate Committee on Mass Media, identified advertorial as one of the problems facing Canadian journalism in the 1990s: 'What are we to think about the recent regrettable trend of allowing print advertising to pass for journalism? That is happening more and more, and it is a very distressing situation.'[39] (However, Deborah Melman-Clement, a journalism student writing in the *Ryerson Review of Journalism*, notes that advertorials, though not so named, were in wide use at least thirty years ago and remarks that they 'haven't changed much over the last three decades.'[40]

She quotes an apt description from Robert Fulford, a former magazine editor: 'Advertorial is to journalism what Muzak is to music. Muzak fills up the dead air in elevators. Advertorial just fills up the empty spaces between the ads – so you don't have a lot of ads running side by side.'[41]

Melman-Clement cites examples of advertorial in *Saturday Night*, *Goodlife*, *Canadian Business*, and, particularly, *Maclean's* magazines. Marina Strauss, writing on the same topic in *Content* magazine, found a four-page example in a twelve-page supplement in the *Financial Post*.[42] She also noted a 'sponsorship' concept, where, for instance, an insurance company sponsored a weekly column on health and lifestyle in the *Globe and Mail*.

However, Melman-Clement notes that some publications insist that advertorial copy have some visual differences from regular copy (typefaces and column widths) and that they not be written by staff writers. Do such subtleties clarify the difference between news and advertorial for readers? Concludes Melman-Clement: 'Such subtle distinctions as a different typeface and a different number of columns might just go unnoticed by the untrained reader.'[43] She quotes Marq de Villiers, editor of *Toronto Life* magazine, who labels advertorial as 'fraudulent,'[44] and Robert Murray, publisher of *Canadian Living*, who calls it 'dangerous ... a form of prostitution.'[45] Both de Villiers and Murray compensate with what de Villiers calls his 'preemptive approach,' running feature supplements with genuine editorial criteria, to attract advertisers.

A few newspaper examples:

- The opening of a new clothing store in Regina, Saskatchewan, is marked by what resembled a news story in the local daily *Leader-Post*, headlined 'New Off-Broadway' and beginning: 'It's totally new – awesome – and outrageous! It's Off-Broadway, the off-price store that just may change Regina women's shopping habits.'[46]

The typography, picture, headline, and caption all resembled a regular news story: Only the tiny disclaimer, 'advertising feature,' told the real story.

- An insidious ad appeared sporadically in North American newspapers throughout the late 1980s, promoting a highly suspect gasoline-saving gimmick.

Closely resembling a newspaper story, it not only had a news-type headline ('Device May Increase Gas Mileage by 22%'), but bore the label 'Reprint from *Albuquerque Tribune*,' which could only be intended to extend the fiction that this was a genuine news story.[47] Credibility of the newspaper may be further eroded by the absence of any company address, only a long-distance phone number. One grim example of this occurred some years ago when *Penthouse* magazine ran a contentious advertisement in many Canadian dailies allegedly in support of free speech. The ad gave no hint that *Penthouse* was behind it.

- A reporter for Saskatoon's *Star-Phoenix* wrote a bona fide news feature about a company that repaired chips in car windshields. The company then recycled the entire item, complete with his byline, as an advertisement.[48]

This concept has been taken a step further by some advertisers (or advertising salespersons) with 'sponsored' news and ad/news packages. Take, for instance, a double-page spread appearing in the tabloid daily *Winnipeg Sun*, 24 June 1988. The spread, in full colour, had advertisements for Sarasoda citrus drink across the bottom and down both sides. Information on coming events filled the central cavity, under the huge headline 'Guide to summertime FUN.' This listing of weekend activities in Winnipeg was written in a highly promotional style complete with a byline, 'By Karen Crossley, for the Sun.'[49] Only the most discriminating and curious readers might wonder who Crossley was and why she was not described as 'of *The Sun*' or '*Sun* staff.'

In 1981, R.J. Reynolds introduced the 'Camel Scoreboard,' a cigarette advertisement with a blank centre meant to be filled each Monday morning with the weekend sports results.[50] Miller Beer emulated this with a full-page box saying 'Welcome' at the top and 'to Miller Time' at the bottom. The rest of the page was regular sports news.

In such situations, the newsroom has not been directly compromised, but the reader may be confused or even believe that the news department cooperates with preparing ads that resemble news. Either way, there is a clear threat to credibility.[51] This may be further stretched when newsrooms run editorial features that focus on products largely or wholly beyond the means of most readers. For instance, the Regina *Leader-Post* ran a full-colour, full section-front headlined 'Luxury,' with a paean of praise (and four large photos) promoting a Toronto fur and leather coat maker.[52] The unctuous copy (with no byline) noted that the garments (which included grey fox, silver fox, and crocodile) cost between $1,000 and $4,000 – a lot of money in 1987. Was it advertising? Was it news? Or was it, perhaps, merely boilerplate?

In another example, *Western Living* magazine ran a nine-page cover story titled 'Green Acres.'[53] The cute first-person bylined piece described the joys of living on a Vancouver Island farm, and was profusely illustrated with some twenty-five full-colour pictures of the family enjoying themselves on their property. Credits for the package included 'fashions produced by Jane Mussett' and 'interiors styled by Brendan Power.' Cutlines helpfully offered such descriptions as, 'Branlin's navy blazer and burgundy print shirt are both by Alfred Sung Kids, jeans by Grant, desert boots by Roots.' The piece ended with a half-page 'shopping directory,' listing the sources for all the clothes. So presumably the clothes weren't theirs. And nor were the interiors? How about the llamas and the dog? Quickly

such a piece takes on an aura of complete fabrication: Readers may wonder if there really was a farm. Was the whole thing a lie, a fashion ad?

Advertisers' Clout

The situation is exacerbated by incidents where advertisers clearly do have – or try to have – some impact on newsrooms. In some cases, dissatisfied advertisers try to punish newspapers, and if the papers are small or vulnerable this may well have repercussions in the newsroom. Stuart Keate describes in his memoirs an incident in which journalist Moira Farrow reported that car salesrooms were being electronically 'bugged' by dealers; the story resulted in the loss of considerable advertising, though 'in due course the dealers drifted back.'[54]

Alec Ross, a freelance writer in Kingston, Ontario, describes another incident, where real estate agents were angered by a 'Homes' editor who refused to be sycophantic.[55] A staff reporter for the Kingston *Whig-Standard* profiled an author promoting the concept of owners selling their homes directly, without using real estate agents.[56] 'That decision has cost the newspaper more than $100,000,' said Ross.[57]

Such a sum is huge for a modest, independent daily, especially during a recession, and may have con-

Where does the advertisement end and the news begin? This colorful Sarasoda ad embraced a double-page spread in the *Winnipeg Sun*. Increasingly, advertisers are trying to wrap around or thrust themselves between news stories.

tributed to the decision to sell the newspaper to the Southam group four months later, after a century of independence.[58]

Two further examples in the weeklies:

• Several years ago the Zellers store in Weyburn, Saskatchewan, requested news space for a charity promotion in the *Weyburn Review*. The newspaper refused on the grounds that many other businesses supported local charities. Zellers subsequently cancelled its substantial advertising program with the paper.[59]

• A Yorkton, Saskatchewan, car dealer was taken to court for rolling back car odometers. The dealer asked *This Week* newspaper to withhold any news story, and when the paper refused, the dealer pulled his advertising.[60]

This attitude is partly a holdover from the old days when advertisers freely influenced news content. Peter Desbarats, describing the evolution of attitudes, notes that journalists always resented blatant interference – but it was not always necessary to be blatant: 'What happened over a period of many years was more subtle – the growing dependence of newspapers on advertising gradually brought them to identify their own interests with those of the economic and political systems that supported them.'[61]

The evident increase of advertorial matter implies that this symbiosis, while being a positive influence for the media's economics, may have a seriously negative impact on journalistic credibility.

Junket Journalism

The pressures exerted on newsrooms through brass cheques and advertorial are by-and-large subtle and indirect. However, given that there is evidence that some newsrooms *can* be influenced, it is no surprise to find that there are frequent attempts to exert overt economic influence in other ways.

Decades ago, it was not uncommon for Canadian journalists to accept 'presents,' particularly at Christmas. Charles Lynch describes the situation:

Businesses and politicians can't buy coverage the way they used to. Within my memory, the reporters in Ottawa were paid or were given gifts at the end of the year by the government of the day, and very much more recently, up until following the Second World War, this same practice was followed in the press gallery in Quebec. It was taken for granted that newspapermen could be bought and we had freebies of all kinds ...

News is not as easy to suppress as it used to be, and journalists are not for sale to advertisers or powerbrokers as they used to be. The bribes that I speak of existed in all parts of the country, and they were there to slant the news.[62]

Today, the most common incidence of this shrinking phenomenon is probably so-called 'junket journalism' – taking trips at newsmakers' expense.

At first glance, it seems obvious that the media should not accept patronage in any form, including free trips, but it has certainly been widespread practice in North American media for decades, and at least one argument has a modicum of validity: How else would the small newsroom have access to some important data?

The test case involves travel writing. There is a perpetual demand for travel copy, especially in the spring when travel operators advertise widely. As Canadian readers acquire more disposable income and leisure time, they want to travel further afield. To meet this demand, travel editors have to obtain material about increasingly remote and exotic places, and many simply do not have the budget to provide all-expense-paid trips for writers. Traditionally, the solution has been to let travel agents, airlines, hotels, and tourist bureaus carry the cost in return for the publicity.

What's the harm? The British columnist Katharine Whitehorn, discussing bribes, put it in a nutshell: 'This comes up all the time. There are so many public relations activities which aren't exactly bribes – not exactly – but if the BBC food programme gets taken to Spain by the sherry industry, it's unlikely to say the sherry tastes of tar.'[63]

One former travel writer, Daniel Grotta, described the pressures on such journalists:

The travel industry tries hard to insure that the travel writer produces only positive-sounding articles ...

This is done primarily through an unspoken system in which favorable articles are rewarded with regular invitations on future press trips, familiarization tours or inaugurals while unfavorable pieces are punished by placing the writer on a supposedly nonexistent blacklist that would bar him from receiving further invitations.[64]

Ian Gillespie, writing tartly about the whole travel writing genre, concludes that 'travel pages serve mainly the advertisers, whose dollars allow the travel pages to continue and who threaten to pull their ads if the stories – the annoying stuff between the ads – veer into unpleasant reality.'[65] He calls on travel writers to eschew places where human rights are abridged, and to write about the bad as well as the good. But he quotes one travel editor as saying, 'We wouldn't waste our space by telling people, "Don't go,"'[66] and he ends with a quote from Helga Loverseed, chair of the Canadian chapter of the Society of American Travel Writers: 'We are not qualified, as travel writers, to take a political or economic stand. The bottom line is that travel articles are selling tools. They should make people want to go to those places.'[67]

Such unabashed boosterism would not be tolerated in other areas of review writing (and travel writing really is a form of reviewing) such as drama or movies, although free tickets are often provided there too. It is that attitude that provokes Walter Stewart to liken travel writers to prostitutes: 'Journalists who allow themselves to take freebies are not real journalists. They're the hookers of the trade.'[68]

With such vitriolic condemnation, it might be expected that free travelling would be on the wane. Discomfort with the concept goes back a long way. (Gillespie recalls Gerry McAuliffe's single-handed attack on the genre more than fifteen years ago, when he took the unusual step of filing a complaint with the Ontario Press Council against a fellow journalist for not revealing his subsidized travel.)[69] A 1973 article by *Newsday* food editor Barbara Rader blasted food editors (150 from the United States and five from Canada) for attending a five-day freeload in Philadelphia sponsored by food manufacturers.[70] And in 1974, the CBS program *Sixty Minutes* criticized TV critics, forty-six of whom went from newspapers all over the United States for an annual press bash in Hollywood, all expenses paid.[71] Discussing this, *Vancouver Sun* TV critic Lisa Hobbs remarked that 'accepting freebies was a way of life at the *Sun* until a few years back,' and was 'one of the compensations the trade offered.' But, she said, attitudes had changed since those days. 'Any viewer watching this show [*Sixty Minutes*] could be excused for thinking the time and talents of any

reporter could be bought with a junket. Not so, and it's even less so today.'[72]

And Karin Winner echoes this in a report for the Associated Press Managing Editors. 'Until recently most newspaper editors swallowed hard perhaps, but accepted junkets and the accompanying freebies ... Times have changed. Newsrooms across the nation are shedding the last vestige of the appearance of "being on the take."'[73]

If they are, not everybody has been told yet. Writing in the *Guardian* in 1986, one journalist described the appalling behaviour of fellow London journalists on one such trip – the inaugural flight of Virgin Atlantic's London-to-Miami route. Richard M. Evans, CBC correspondent in London, said the travellers made a grotesque spectacle of themselves: 'I have never seen such drinking as goes on amongst the British Press. Drinking seems somehow tied up with their very identities ... I wouldn't take seriously anything published or broadcast about that trip.'[74]

Evidently, the Walt Disney Co., at least, does not believe junkets are over. A party for more than 5,000 journalists at Walt Disney World, Florida, in 1986 must surely rate as one of the biggest freebie events ever. The $8-million party was co-sponsored by the Disney Company, airlines, hotels, resorts, and tourism agencies. Many of the visiting journalists had their way paid by their companies – but the hosts paid the expenses of all those who accepted the offer.[75]

Even if taking free trips is dwindling, does it compromise the writers? Many of those discussing the issue share Walter Stewart's 'prostitution' analogy. But some believe otherwise.

Canadian freelancer Glen Warner: 'I don't think any writer worth his salt is going to be compromised by a few nights' worth of free hotels.'[76] Nobody, of course, is suggesting he can be bought for a bowl of potage. But do the *readers* know that? Concludes Ontario media commentator Barrie Zwicker, 'Writers who believe they can't be influenced are self-deluded or attempting to cover their ass.'[77] And Denver journalist Alan Prendergast quotes an effective *New York Times* editorial, inveighing against the Disney jaunt: 'Accepting junkets and boondoggles does not necessarily mean that a reporter is being bought – but it inescapably creates the appearance of being bought.'[78]

There may be one further way that freeloading writers are compromised. In the late 1970s, the *Toronto Sun* campaigned against airline employees having bonus passes, until Air Canada ticket agents pointed out that *Sun* management were not above using free passes themselves, noting the president's wife had just used a $1,500 free ticket to London.[79] When the pot calls the kettle black, the pot is not taken very seriously.

This inability to criticize may be felt particularly in media sports departments, where there has been a long tradition of travelling with the home team, often at the team's expense. In the past, this has often included free food, cigarettes, and alcohol. In 1979, a *Globe and Mail* writer, James Golla, was quoted as saying, 'If they are [accepting freebies] it's because the employers don't pay them enough.'[80] Reporter Stephen Overbury was describing a panel discussion by journalists in Toronto, at which many of those present apparently did not treat the issue seriously or scoffed at its implications.[81] A decade later, journalists appeared to be much more concerned about the dangers of sports writers becoming 'part of the team.' For instance, during the 1980s, the *Globe and Mail Style Book*, which says very little about ethics, curtly forbade junkets: 'Accept transportation, food and lodging only on the understanding that the grantor will be reimbursed the full commercial value.'[82] But this was expanded somewhat in the 1990 revision: 'Reporters and editors are not to accept lavish entertaining, free trips, free equipment to try out or anything more than token gifts. Gifts should be returned or, if that is impractical, donated to charity in the giver's name.'[83]

Much of this angst may have been stirred up by Gerry McAuliffe's consciousness-raising exercise (mentioned above), complaining to the Ontario Press Council about travel freebies. His complaint led not only to the Press Council's study of the issue, but to its conducting a national survey and a public forum on freebies and eventually publishing its conclusions in the booklet *Press Ethics and Freebies*, all of which served to put the issue on the journalistic agenda.[84]

There is yet one other area, of course, where a great deal of expensive travel is needed: the campaign trail. And once again, where 'the boys on the bus' used to travel at the expense of the candidates they pursued, most media now insist on paying their way, perhaps because of the perception that it is even more important to remain at arm's length on political matters than on sports matters. Summarizing the 1988 election campaign, Tim Naumetz notes matter-of-factly that newsrooms had paid $14,000 for board and travel per reporter following Prime Minister Brian Mulroney.[85] And he remarks on the changed atmosphere on the trail, with reporters staying sober, feasting on fruit and fresh broccoli instead of liquor.[86]

No Such Thing as a Free Lunch

These, then, are the larger issues. But what about the smaller items, the individual gifts?

Certainly these used to be in constant supply. 'I was enchanted to discover,' wrote Stu Keate of his initiation as a cub reporter, 'that newspapermen were granted front-row seats, at no cost, at baseball games, wrestling, movie houses and circuses. When reporters were offered books for review, they were permitted to keep the books and thus started building a library.'[87] Many of these free passes were obtained by the newspapers in exchange for advertising space, so hotels, meals, liquor, and train tickets might also be available.[88] Val Sears recalls the same pleasant bonuses in Toronto, and the reason:

The pay was low – new reporters started at $45 a week – but there were compensations that the morality of the seventies and eighties forbids – free rail passes from the kindly PRs on the railway, vacations in Bermuda in return for a travel page piece, liquor at Christmas and, up at the provincial legislature, a personal 'stationery allowance' from the government and a chance to serve as paid secretary to an obscure government commission. It was corruption, thin but wide.[89]

The guileless acceptance of such perks has now largely disappeared, though not without some regret. But many of the donors apparently still have not got the message. *Toronto Sun* business editor Garth Turner noted in 1986 that the offers still flowed in, and he even described it as 'a growing trend.' 'More than ever I am finding companies trying to give me things in return for covering their "news" events. This is a lousy way of

doing business. Unfortunately, it works – but elsewhere, not here.'[90] He described recently receiving the following inducements:

- A bottle of brandy from Bell and Howell, with an invitation to meet a visiting executive
- A full continental breakfast delivered to the office by the Toronto advertising agency Palmer, Bonner Inc., with an invitation to a subsequent breakfast seminar on the company
- A bottle of vodka from Hudson Bay Distillers Ltd., with a press release about a change of label design
- An offer of a Sony Walkman for journalists attending a luncheon and press conference celebrating the sale of the millionth Walkman.

Turner (later served briefly as federal finance minister) lays the blame for such transparent bribes firmly at the journalists' doors: 'If reporters sought out news and left the gifts on the table, corporations would stop giving them. And you'd know what you read in the paper, heard on the radio and saw on TV got there because it deserved to.'[91]

There is certainly little subtlety about such handouts, and an amazing range of items on offer.[92] Efforts to defend accepting such things are increasingly rare. One Miami newspaper reporter attempted, back in 1974, to justify acceptance, but his arguments seem very hollow in retrospect: 'I submit that taking away a newsman's freebies is (a) phony, (b) unjustified, (c) stupid and, (d) above all, pointless – although not necessarily in that order,' wrote Rick Garr. 'The only way a reporter can be harmed by a freebie in the absence of public knowledge is by his own weakness of mind and

judgment.' Garr seems to feel that most reporters cannot be bought 'for a bottle of Cutty and a filet mignon,' and that the recipients should just make sure that 'only a few people would know.'[93] But even if they cannot be bought, the perception is there, in the words of the poet, that 'Whose bread I eat, his song I sing.'

Ironically, senior media managers have been among the last holdouts in the consistent acceptance of free gifts. Although, for instance, in 1975 the National Press Club in Ottawa cut out freebies from its annual dinner and dance (an astonishing $25,000 worth of gifts, leaving a surplus of $9,000 for journalism student scholarships),[94] weekly newspaper publishers were still accepting substantial support for their conferences as late as 1993.[95]

Two further issues should be addressed. What should newsrooms do with the loot? And what about journalism competitions?

Disposing of the free items that continue to flow into newsrooms remains a dilemma. Carla Johnson described a constructive idea at the Spokane *Spokesman-Review/Chronicle* – a newsroom sale, with all the handouts (from a six-foot inflatable pickle to off-colour books) being sold to staff members and the proceeds going to charity.[96] Such a manoeuvre should not only provide useful funds for good causes, but should eventually send a signal to even the dullest public relations people that the gifts are not having the desired effect.

Media writing and photography contests have been in vogue for years, but in the 1980s they were being eyed with increasing suspicion. Some of these awards are clearly promotional by nature – prizes offered by a US tobacco manufacturer for the best picture of someone smoking a cigar could only be designed to encourage photographers to get cigars into their pictures. An annual competition by the Toronto Police Association offering cash prizes for writing and pictures about police work would not likely attract many entries critical of the police. Similarly, a contest sponsored by the Canadian Petroleum Association to promote 'a better understanding' of that industry would be unlikely to award writing about oil spills or pollution.

In a 1984 examination of this issue, the Ontario Press Council condemned as 'objectionable' participation in contests sponsored by self-interest groups where the entries must deal with the sponsor's special field and the sponsor is directly involved in the judging.[97]

Finally, in 1987, crusading Gerry McAuliffe struck again with a complaint to the Ontario Press Council about sponsored awards. The following year, the council suggested guidelines for such awards, including an arm's length relationship between contest and sponsors.[98]

In the same year, the National Magazine Awards went through a soul-searching exercise to distance itself from sponsors, and the National Business Writing Awards were folded by the Royal Bank, the main sponsor.[99]

In these, as in so many of the preceding examples, the fundamental issue remains the same. In the business environment, there is very rarely any such thing as the 'free' gift. The last of the five *W*s is crucial: WHY is this person doing this? And even in the rare instances where the answer is 'Simply because he likes me,' there must be one further question: WHAT does this do to my credibility?

It would be foolish to ban every gift of every nature and to let rule-obedience ruin friendships and the natural flow of relationships – insisting, for instance, on paying for a coffee offered casually in a source's office. But real friends generally return the favour. If the source buys lunch today, the reporter needs to ensure it is understood that *he* buys lunch tomorrow. Are some things too small to bother with? One simple yardstick is applied in some newsrooms: no journalist should accept more than can reasonably be consumed at one sitting. In other words, a modest lunch does not need to be the subject of guilt and acrimony, but the Caribbean cruise and even the bottle of Scotch whisky are to be refused or paid for.

Like Caesar's wife, journalists must be above suspicion. Exemplary behaviour will not instantly give journalists popularity and credibility – there are too many old films still in circulation, popularizing the stereotypes of the reporter with a press pass in his trilby and a mickey of Scotch in his raincoat pocket. But it is a beginning.

However, there are several other ways that journalists can find themselves in a conflict of interest, without bribes ever changing hands. Issues such as whether journalists can safely freelance, run for office, or marry a politician will be explored in the next chapter.

Tough Calls

1   Your newsroom is offered a press pass to a blue-plate fundraising banquet, with the prime minister as guest speaker. Tickets are $125 each for everyone else. Do you go? Do you pay? Do you brown bag? If a special press price of $25 is offered to cover the food, do you go and pay? What are the issues?

2   The editorial page editor proposes that your paper cease accepting ads for escort services, happy hours, and X-rated movies. This would cost an estimated $50,000 a year in lost revenue, the equivalent of two young reporters. The advertising manager says this is censorship and strikes at the foundations of freedom of the press. Who's right?

3   The police make a drug bust. Among those charged is the daughter of a major advertiser, who asks the news director to kill the story. The station manager is happy to rationalize it as a minor event ... but the news director knows names make news – and so do drug busts. What does he tell the manager?

Conflict of Interest

To the layperson or to the apprentice reporter, the journalist may cut a romantic figure, seen as hobnobbing with the powerful, and perhaps even having some power of his or her own. But there's a downside that is much less commonly known. Journalism imposes limitations on its practitioners. At some levels, the journalist may find his choice of friends is limited, his political activism is curtailed, and even his ability to 'do good,' supporting social agencies as a private citizen, is constrained, all in the name of conflict of interest.

Unlike issues of freeloading and junketing, conflict does not by any means exclusively involve private gain, though it clearly does when it concerns freelancing for outside agencies. But in matters of friendship (e.g., whom a journalist consorts with) or of volunteerism (e.g., the journalist who serves on the school board), the writer may be motivated by nothing but the best of intentions.[1]

It should be said at the outset that employers do not, in any way, 'own' their news staff. They do not today have the right to interfere in the reporter's private life.[2] But – just like the people she writes about— the journalist loses a degree of privacy and independence simply by joining this very public profession. It would be unrealistic for a high-profile, 'objective' television news anchor to think she could also be a member of Parliament. It would be outrageous for a news manager to tell his reporters how to vote in an election. But somewhere in between there is a demarcation line, defining what the news worker can reasonably do without compromising himself and his newsroom.

When is a Freelance Free?

Freelancing used to be a way of life for journalists, a means of eking out a few extra pennies in a grossly underpaid profession.

Today's journalist is generally far better paid than in the past (at least in North America, though frequently not so in developing countries), so the need to freelance to survive is not quite such a motivating factor. But journalists *are* writers, so why should they not write in their spare time, too?

The arguments against freelancing are largely management-driven: no writer should work simultaneously for two competing media; no writer should use the facilities of one newsroom to write for another.

Both rules are simple and not unreasonable. If one is employed 'full-time' (i.e., that is one's primary occupation, probably for about forty hours a week, for a semblance of a living wage), then it is not fair to the employer to work 'against' her by also working for a competing employer. So, the daily paper reporter should not moonlight in the newsroom of the local radio station, and so on. Generally, employers will not object if their staff work, say, for out-of-town media. So it is probably acceptable for a *Halifax News* reporter to 'string' for *Maclean's* or for a US supermarket tabloid magazine. But wise journalists will check with supervisors in advance, to clarify their reaction. And the full-time employer will expect the writer's first loyalty to be to her. If he has a 'scoop' it should first go to his main newsroom, and only later to the freelance outlet.

Similarly, if a reporter is hired and paid to work full-time, then even if he is freelancing on his own time (after work, lunch-hour, etc.), he should not be using company facilities. A lot of freelancing in a newsroom would quickly add wear-and-tear to equipment, clog up computer storage space, inflate already-huge telephone bills, and consume reams of printer and fax paper. Is this one of the perks of the business? Many employers turn a blind eye, anyway, but that is something to sort out with management before bad feelings are aroused. These problems can quickly be aggravated when the reporter is on deadline for his 'other' job, or when he has to make or receive phone calls for freelance assignments during his regular shift.

The issue quickly becomes one of divided loyalties. Can the servant have two masters?[3] This leads to the audience-driven argument against freelancing. What is the news consumer's perception of this writer if she writes for two media? Does the audience distrust the writer because of this, or at least subconsciously question the writer's loyalty, perhaps seeing the writer as a 'hack' willing to write for anyone who pays enough, rather than being strongly, exclusively loyal to one outlet?

Freelance work can also threaten the integrity of the reporter himself. When he is interviewing, for instance, the police chief, does he make it clear he is not wearing his normal hat of *Fort McMurray Today* police reporter, but is now interviewing as a writer for the *Police Gazette*? Does the source recognize the difference?

Some forms of outside work may not involve writing but, even so, can involve a conflict. In 1982, the sports editor of *La Presse* in Montreal ran into difficulties when the opposition *Le Devoir* revealed he had received more than $50,000 for helping bring a major boxing event to Montreal. When a newsperson himself makes news in this way, that may be sufficient indication of a problem. *Le Devoir* clearly felt the public ought to know that the rival sports editor profited from the sports event. Whether or not his desire to bring the match to Montreal had any effect on the columns of his newspaper, the public might perceive that possibility.[4]

Similar incidents recur regularly across Canada. For instance, some radio reporters also voice radio commercials. Especially in cases where the voice is highly distinctive, the listener may well recognize it as belonging to a 'reporter' or even that specific reporter. And in some cases, they go further. One respected BC news director regularly voiced radio commercials on his own station, identifying himself and endorsing a particular brand of roof guttering. Another veteran prairie reporter regularly did commercials beginning 'This is X with a message from Anik Travel.' Such a message may be harmless enough, but what if he was assigned to report on some negative news about Anik?[5]

In another case, a CBC television anchor on the Prairies reportedly balked at reading a story about the Amway company being sued because he sold Amway products on the side and believed in the Amway sales concept.

In an interesting variation on this, a British Columbia journalist ran into difficulties when he did some editing work for the provincial government. The writer was, in fact, a full-time freelance writer, sending columns to more than forty BC weeklies. But while writing about the government from the press gallery in Victoria, he also received substantial sums for editing the provincial ombudsperson's annual report for three consecutive years. On the face of it, such editing work seems to be entirely neutral and nonpolitical, but his colleagues in the press gallery were very uncomfortable when they discovered the arrangement. The implication was that someone receiving money from the provincial government might be seen as unable to write freely about that government. Aggravating the incident was the fact that his wife was also a government employee.[6]

Certainly, in such cases the journalist needs to clarify whether outside work is acceptable *before* he does it. And it is advisable to publicly declare any possible conflict. When the Saskatoon *Star-Phoenix* found itself writing about poor conditions in a local apartment building, the story wisely declared that the newspaper's parent company also owned the building.[7]

Private Wives, Private Lives?

One of the difficulties for the Victoria press gallery reporter was that his wife was a government employee. Yet surely no news proprietor also 'owns' his employees' spouses?

Clearly not. But can the press gallery reporter write with total freedom about a subject in which his bed partner is involved? If there are leaks to the media from the spouse's office, will she not be immediately blamed? If he must write critically about her department, will he not be compromised? If the reporter worked in, say, the sports department, or was a desk editor, instead of a press gallery reporter, there would be far less likelihood of conflict or the perception of conflict. So the only safe solution may be for the press gallery reporter to transfer to a less sensitive beat.

When challenged, that reporter pointed to a columnist on the Victoria *Times-Colonist* whose spouse was also a government employee. Other writers have cited other examples:

- Veteran Southam columnist Charles Lynch ended a long marriage to marry Claudy Mailly, press officer for both Joe Clark and Brian Mulroney and, later, a Conservative MP.
- CBC network anchor Peter Mansbridge and Nancy Jamieson, an economic policy advisor in Prime Minister Joe Clark's office, were a couple.
- Keith Morrison, anchor of CBC's *The Journal* married Suzanne Perry, who worked in Prime Minister Trudeau's press office.[8]
- Margot Sinclair, legislative reporter in Victoria, BC, for CKVU-TV, resigned after an affair with Attorney-General Bud Smith was revealed when somebody monitored and taped their cellular phone calls.[9]
- Between 1978 and 1982, Toronto television reporter Carole Jerome had an affair with Sadegh Ghotbzadeh, foreign minister of Iran, and resigned from the CBC in order to stay in Tehran. The affair ended only when the minister was executed by the Ayatollah Khomeini.[10]

Why do such relationships occur? Journalists and politicians are perpetually rubbing shoulders, needing each other, and feeding off each other, leading to what columnist Allan Fotheringham has described as a journalistic 'Stockholm syndrome.'[11] Such intimacy is bound, occasionally, to lead to close relationships.

A *Vancouver Sun* editor, Barbara Yaffe, likened the relationship to two swarms of bees buzzing round each other, some carrying honey, some out to sting: 'It's a tenuous, tortuous relationship between politico and press hound, and the hive is usually rather active ... It's pure symbiosis. Each side uses and feeds off the other, each a little fascinated by and in awe of the other.'[12] Yaffe, who has worked in four provincial press galleries plus the Ottawa gallery, was commenting on the Smith-Sinclair incident, which resulted in both the cabinet minister and the reporter resigning. She recalled having occasionally had dinner with male politicians, but even this had been questioned.[13] But the rules were simple: 'To have anything more than a friendly acquaintance with these or any other politicians clearly would have left me in an impossibly vulnerable position.' And 'both reporters and politicians know the rules, and the risks, before they indulge in so much as a handshake.'[14]

Interestingly, another newspaper commentator dismissed any intimacy between Smith and Sinclair. 'This aspect of their relationship is none of my business and, quite frankly, none of yours,' Brian Kieran told readers of the Vancouver *Province*. But then he continued, 'What is our business was her conscious decision to run by Smith drafts of her stories before they were aired, her efforts to coach Smith on how to better his political image ... The tapes reveal a too-cosy relationship in which Margot, in effect, became Smith's agent in the press gallery.'[15]

But how can the two – the intimacy and the political actions – possibly be divorced? The audio tapes of telephone conversations between the politician and the reporter show their mutual affection, which helps explain their asking each other for advice and support about their respective jobs. Without the affection, the reporter would have seemed coldly calculating and wholly politically committed. The intimacy helps to explain the relationship, though it in no way excuses it.[16]

There are two parts to this equation: First, Sinclair should not have let herself get into a serious relationship with a cabinet minister, because as soon as it became known, it raised doubts about her ability to report fairly. Second, the fact that she advised the minister on his politics, asked his advice about her stories, and described to him her activities on his behalf merely proves the dangers of such a relationship developing.

Former *Globe and Mail* managing editor Geoffrey Stevens (giving a lecture at UBC in 1990, aptly titled 'Uneasy Bedfellows: Politicians and the Press') has called the relationship between journalist and politician a 'conspiracy of self-interest ... sometimes incestuous, sometimes antagonistic.' But whatever other ramifications it may have, news consumers are bound to be suspicious of the journalist who shares a bed with a politician. Can he or she be objective? Can she be fair? Can she resist asking probing questions at breakfast or dangling hints over dinner? Above all, can she be tough on that friend if the necessity arises?

Several years ago there was a brief but rancorous debate in the Canadian media about journalists who merely socialize with politicians – count them among their friends, without getting into bed with them. The row developed after a silly incident in Washington in which Sondra Gotlieb, wife of the Canadian ambassador, slapped her social secretary at a dinner party. Several Canadian journalists (dinner guests) witnessed the event, but some declined to report it. Allan Fotheringham described it as a tough decision: 'Washington dinners, and especially Gotlieb diplomatic dinners, are conducted under the unwritten rule that there is no reporting.'[17] But for Canadian Press reporter Julie O'Neill it was no dilemma. She filed a story because she was at the event as a pool reporter. In other words, she was on duty, wearing her journalistic hat. Other journalists who were there as off-duty guests were there on the understanding that they would *not* report the occasion. If they were comfortable with that relationship, that was their decision. (But one wonders how far they would take that. If a serious incident had happened, for instance, would they have reported it?) Did they feel comfortable with themselves not reporting something others evidently felt was eminently newsworthy? How did they feel *not* running for the phone but instead withholding the story to protect their relationship with the politicians?

Without opening the 'off-the-record' debate yet (it is explored in Chapter 13), it may be pertinent to ask if the reporter is ever really off-duty? If he agrees to attend a social function but not report it, is he not tying his own hands, agreeing to a form of prior restraint? Certainly politicians, such as the ambassador and his spouse, have to be able to relax and lower their guards sometimes. But why, then, invite journalists to join in? Has the arm's length relationship gone a step too far? Should the journalist become so comfortable with her sources? If she picks up some juicy story idea at the event, must she ignore it? If she's woken in the middle of the night by an explosion, does she roll over and say, 'I'm off duty'?

When, for instance, reporters in the BC press gallery play volleyball regularly with the politicians, has the jolly familiarity – the banter and the back-slapping – gone a fraction too far, tempting reporters to 'go soft' on their sources/friends?

US journalist Walter Lippmann once remarked (in discussing the friendship between President John F. Kennedy and then *Newsweek* editor Ben Bradlee), 'Newspapermen can't be the cronies of great men. There always has to be a certain distance between high public officials and newspapermen. I wouldn't say a wall or a fence, but an air space, that's very necessary.'[18]

Defining and policing that air space is the difficulty. Some newsrooms do have no-conflict rules. For instance, the *Western Producer*, an agricultural weekly, devotes about one-third of its admirable code of ethics to conflict, carefully banning free gifts and freelancing 'that compromises journalistic performance,' and requiring that 'all actual or apparent conflicts of interest ... will be disclosed to readers.'[19] But it does not encompass the issue of fraternizing with sources.

The *Windsor Star* policy manual covers a number of aspects, including a useful perspective on conflict: 'It is not appropriate for journalists to be at once actor, chronicler and critic. If we are to discharge our editorial responsibility we must be free to write about or comment on the activities of any public body or special interest group without the slightest suggestion of a real or perceived conflict of interest or responsibilities.'[20]

That phrase 'free to write about ... any public body or special interest group without ... conflict' could well cover the Washington slapping incident if interpreted in principle rather than according to the letter of the law. The reporter who agrees to attend the 'off-the-record' event is asking for problems and is inviting the politicians to take advantage of the occasion.

Following some brief rules on running for office and revealing their politics, the section concludes usefully: 'It is understood that staffers have a right to determine what to do in their private lives and with their private time but such activities could have a detrimental effect on how impartially those staff members are able to carry out their journalistic functions. When such conflicts, real or perceived, occur, *The Star* has a responsibility to take appropriate action.'[21]

Again, there is nothing here about getting too close to sources, and very little about freelancing (it urges sports staffers to avoid acting as sports officials or scorers).

The American academic, Katherine McAdams, concludes that codes generally cover only monetary aspects of conflict, 'because money is a material, verifiable exchange and because news people – and their publics – are unified in the opinion that payola is clearly taboo.'[22]

Making codes stick is a continuing difficulty, which will be explored later. It is particularly difficult, however, when the code is administered by one's peers. When the BC press gallery was faced with the Sinclair-Smith incident, the logical thing was to follow the gallery constitution and strike an ethics committee to examine it. But the colleagues and friends who made up the gallery balked. President Keith Baldrey was quoted in his own paper, the *Vancouver Sun*: 'The press gallery is not in the business of investigating and policing individual members for anything. Journalists should not put themselves in a situation where they hold court and become judge and jury over their colleagues and contemplate taking any disciplinary action against them.'[23]

This position is arguable – but not, perhaps, by the president already elected to uphold an existing constitution. Baldrey rightly pointed out that the heat being generated by the controversy (which was much complicated by the phone monitoring, leaking of documents to politicians, and other issues) made logical debate difficult: 'The emotions are running so high and the tensions are still at such a high level that getting together in a large group to talk about the actions of individual members could be counterproductive and worsen the situation.'[24]

The Ottawa press gallery was having a similar debate at about the same time, though on a less inflammatory incident. A gallery member was found to be doing some writing for the government, and the gallery sus-pended him briefly, but then learned that several other members had also received modest cheques from government agencies, mostly for delivering speeches or writing speeches for politicians. A committee of past presidents and a journalism professor was struck – only to recommend that the gallery delete its ethics clause from the constitution. The issue was not as simple as presented here, but one clear message came through in the ensuing debate: Individual newsrooms should police their own staff (establishing and enforcing rules internally), rather than assuming peers will take that responsibility. But that leaves the freelancer as the wild card in the pack – apparently answering to no higher ethical authority, unless the buyers of her product develop appropriate criteria.[25]

In every community, there is a dearth of individuals willing to contribute their time, energy, and expertise to 'good causes.' Whether it is leading a Cub pack, knitting for the homeless, fixing the church roof, visiting the hospice, driving the disabled, delivering hot lunches to shut-ins, or fundraising for everyone, there are never enough volunteers. Journalists are exposed to more of these causes than most laypersons, and as caring people they may often be drawn in.

The process may be subtle. First, the reporter as a private citizen makes some harmless remark at a parent-teachers' meeting at his daughter's school, then he finds himself on the PTA executive, and he's soon urged to run for the ('entirely non-political') school board. He asks the publisher's permission and is duly elected, on the understanding that another reporter will cover school stories. After some time at the paper, he is named newspaper editor and finds himself writing editorials. When the teachers go on strike, as a school board member he is in an excellent position to write editorials about it. Or is he?

Though this scenario is invented, it fits quite well an Ontario incident, when the editor of the *Huntsville Forester* was taken to the Ontario Press Council for a perceived conflict – writing editorials about a teachers' strike while serving as a school trustee. To its credit, the paper immediately conceded it had erred, telling the Press Council, 'Our case stands as another example and warning to newspaper editors and publishers across the country. Those in our business, who are directly involved in the collection and presentation of news and opinions, should not run for public office.'[26] However, the Press Council roundly condemned the conflict: 'It is improper for a newspaper publisher, editor or reporter to hold office in any public or private body likely to be in the news,' they ruled.[27]

And what organization can be guaranteed never to be in the news? Especially if the helpful journalist has been dragooned into writing the group's press releases.

Public Service: Private Conflict

As journalists probably care more and know more about their community than almost any other career cluster, they may be better prepared to exercise their franchise than many other citizens. Certainly they should not be penalized for this caring and knowing by not being allowed to vote, in order to protect their independence. But how politically active can they be? 'The reader has a right to expect a news story to be told by an observer, not an advocate,' wrote Andrew Barnes, editor and president of the *St. Petersburg Times*, in his paper.[28] He was referring, of course, to mainstream, 'hard news' reporting, not to editorials, columnists, or fringe publications that do not pretend to objectivity. His column was prompted by the recent sacking of a reporter at a nearby small-town paper because she had become an abortion activist. As an education beat reporter, she had wisely asked her editor to avoid assigning her abortion stories *before* getting active, and she had done her lobbying from home, as a private individual. Nonetheless, an opposition paper had made an issue of her activity, and at that point her employer called foul. But Barnes, balancing the issues, sagely commented that had the woman worked at his paper she probably could have continued work: 'If it happened here, and a reporter said publicly her views are her own and not those of the paper, and further that she has nothing to do with the paper's coverage of that issue, well then, we would conclude it was beyond our control. It might be more convenient to hire people who are not caught up in the issues of our times, but it seldom works that way.'[29]

That's bravely said, if he can make it stick. Barnes addresses a number of elements here. The public disavowal is helpful, but it's particularly important that the reporter *not* be assigned to cover the issues she feels strongly about (just as this reporter asked). And he's quite right that employers cannot expect newspeople to be unmoved by the issues of the times. But that, of course, is the irony. Many journalists are in the business precisely because they *do* care about the community. In the process of doing their jobs – particularly reporters on beats such as legislature, city hall, and school board – they become better informed than most members of the public, and they may be less politically biased than many of the citizens whom they see being elected and performing – occasionally – like buffoons. They may, at that point, also be writing bylined columns, full of wisdom and balanced advice. Even if the idea of serving does not occur to them, sooner or later somebody may well say, 'Come on, Smith, if you're so smart, why don't you run?'

Evidently, a line needs to be drawn between activism and volunteerism. There's a vast gulf between the reporter who, for instance, becomes a card-carrying political party member, and the reporter who is drafted onto the Scout parent committee.

Furthermore, conditions may be different in the remote village than in the big city. The local reporter may be virtually the only member of the public to have regularly attended meetings. She has the background, and the interest. Politics in such an environment may well be much less partisan, less ideological; they may, in fact, be non-existent, in the sense that members of many smaller councils and boards are simply elected as individuals, with no party affiliations and no 'government/opposition' polarity.

As one Ontario weekly newspaper editor-publisher, Doug Brydges, argued:

I am a lifer in Geraldton. I grew up in the family business at the *Times Star* ...

I was continually solicited to run [for council] for a year or so, by many citizens, most of whom I know well, and after considerable thought I decided to do so. My decision was based on my willingness to make an extra special commitment to open-mindedness and objectivity ...

I have served on countless Committees and Boards, through Rotary and the Municipality from Planning to Youth work. I work for my community.[30]

For Brydges, the responsibility was clear: in small northern communities, people resources are limited and every volunteer is needed. But the same argument may not be translated to Victoria or Fredericton, Kitchener or Nelson. A reporter in Nelson, BC, found that his own high principles did not convince his readers. Resigning from the local executive of the New Democratic Party and from the party itself, Gerald Rotering also renounced his seat on council. He wrote:

The decision was forced by a growing conflict between my roles as a non-partisan journalist and as a local political figure.

In the past I have maintained, and so has this newspaper editorially, that a career as a journalist should not deprive a citizen of his democratic right to run for office, nor to take part in party politics.

While I stand behind that right, the reality is that the two roles are in opposition to one another and my credibility has suffered ... [It] unacceptably compromises the work of a news reporter.[31]

Rotering had strived to be honest with his readers, making sure they knew his political affiliations so they could evaluate his writings appropriately, but nonetheless he found that 'many people simply dismissed them out of hand.'

However, Rotering had been more 'political' than Doug Brydges, who had no party affiliation and was driven by no specific ideology, other than that implicit in newspaper proprietorship. It's that commitment to a particular philosophy that sinks the overzealous journalist. Consider again the *Windsor Star* statement: 'We must be free to write about or comment on the activities of any public body or special interest group without the slightest suggestion of a real or perceived conflict.'

The CBC's *Journalistic Standards and Practices* is equally clear on this issue. All journalists must be neutral: 'In order to maintain their own credibility and that of the CBC, on-air personnel, as well as those who edit, produce or manage CBC programs, must avoid publicly identifying themselves in any way with partisan statements or actions on controversial matters.'[32]

The manual specifies that reporters must never express personal opinions: 'Hosts and interviewers [must] ... refrain from personal advocacy ... The role of the CBC reporter is to convey news to the audience, with maximum fairness, accuracy and integrity. Therefore, a CBC reporter must not take a partisan position on a matter of public controversy.'[33]

In a section titled 'Credibility,' the manual urges management to consider people's background when hiring: 'In the engagement and assignment of persons working in information programs, the organization must be sensitive to their published views, their personal involvements and their associations and backgrounds in order to avoid any perception of bias or of susceptibility to undue influence in the execution of their professional responsibilities.'[34]

And under 'Political Activity' the *Journalistic Standards and Practices* manual warns of the potential for influencing audiences: 'Employees assigned to information programming areas are limited in engaging in political activity, as they have the potential to influence or appear to influence politically related programming.'[35]

The manual then recites part of the CBC's corporate bylaws, specifically forbidding newspeople from activism unless they have advance permission. They may not, 'take a position publicly in a referendum or plebiscite, actively support a political party or candidate, stand for nomination as a candidate and/or be a candidate for election to the House of Commons, a provincial legislature, the Councils of the Yukon or the Northwest Territories, or a municipal or civic office.'[36]

If they are elected federally or provincially, they are automatically out of the Corporation, though those elected to municipal or civic office may be permitted to keep their jobs.[37] None of this means that CBC newspeople are hindered from staying informed. The manual specifies they 'may attend political occasions as private-citizen members of a publicly-invited audience.' But if they want to be politically active they must request an unpaid leave of absence and agree to be re-assigned to another department when they return if their usefulness to the Corporation is deemed to be 'impaired.'[38]

The clear intention of all this is to keep CBC news staff absolutely neutral, so listeners and viewers can trust them – to adopt Andrew Barnes's terminology – as observers rather than advocates. It also gives a clear yardstick by which staff can judge and be judged. So CBC Winnipeg news anchor Mike McCourt probably recognized that he got off lightly when he was suspended for only a week for speaking up at a public meeting to protest high property taxes. His ability to report on that subject was thereafter impaired.[39] That incident was debated at a conference of the Canadian Association of Journalists in Winnipeg in 1990. Some speakers pointed out that journalists are bound to have opinions, and media managers, particularly some newspaper proprietors, are often highly political. But Southam columnist Don McGillivray put it well when he said journalists can let off steam in bylined columns, but they should not march for causes: 'The ultimate responsibility of the journalist is to his audience, not himself,' he said.[40]

The Goldhawk Affair

Another incident, which was the subject of widespread debate, involved a host of CBC's network radio phone-in show, *Cross-Country Check-Up*.[41]

Dale Goldhawk was, in addition to being a radio host, president of ACTRA, the Alliance of Canadian Cinema, Television and Radio Artists. ACTRA consistently opposed the contentious Free Trade Agreement being negotiated with the United States in 1988-9, and Goldhawk, as president, attacked the agreement in a strong article in the union newsletter *Actrascope*, shortly before the 1988 federal election. One union member, Southam columnist Charles Lynch, was upset by the article and criticized the CBC for letting Goldhawk host a current affairs show during an election campaign in which the Free Trade Agreement was a major element. When CBC management expressed concern to Goldhawk, he voluntarily withdrew from the program pending the election. After the election, the CBC decided Goldhawk could not be both ACTRA president and show host, and ordered him to choose. Goldhawk reluctantly stepped down from the presidency. A year later, the Canada Labour Relations Board found the CBC guilty of unfair practice in forcing Goldhawk to choose, and it ordered the CBC to permit him to serve with the union.

Journalist Bronwyn Drainie concluded that what the CBC wanted was eunuchs. 'A sweeping policy that denies journalists the right to express their own beliefs on important and controversial questions, either by writing about them independently of their jobs or by taking active part in pressure groups, essentially deprives them of rights other Canadians automatically take for granted.'[42]

To a degree, this tone of hurt surprise is misplaced precisely because the standards are so clearly set down in the policy manual. To put it colloquially, 'If you can't stand the heat, get out of the kitchen.' But as Drainie points out, the heat has been turned up, with revisions to the policy book. However, Goldhawk was already president of ACTRA when he was assigned to host *Cross-Country Check-Up*, so his affiliations and views should have been clear to his supervisors.

Furthermore, one wonders if the CBC would have ever mentioned the matter to Goldhawk if columnist Charles Lynch – not known for his left-wing sympathies – had not first raised the issue.[43]

The whole incident fits all-too-easily into the continuing pattern of attacks on the CBC by government and government supporters and spineless responses by nervous CBC managers (who evidently had much to be nervous about, judging by the multi-million-dollar cuts in CBC budgets in the early 1990s).

In the best-of-all-possible worlds, all CBC personnel associated with news and current affairs would demonstrate constant fairness and neutrality in public; in their private lives they would avoid all activities that could lead to a perception of bias in their journalism. But having said that, one must add that Trueman and Drainie are both right in asserting that good journalists are not powerless.[44] Dale Goldhawk behaved as he should have behaved, both as a host and as president of a major union in a unionized company. The CBC managers erred. When they considered Goldhawk for the hosting post, were they (to paraphrase the manual) 'sensitive to his personal involvements, associations and background'? If they determined there was no potential for conflict at that stage, they should have stuck by that decision; if, on the other hand, they felt that hosting a current affairs program and heading a high-profile union were inimical, then why did they appoint him?

In all this, we must not lose sight of the audience. How are they best served? Listeners and viewers must be able to trust CBC journalists, especially as many of them now rely almost exclusively on the corporation for their news. It may be unwise for a union official to thrust himself into a key post, at the centre of public debate during an election, even though he knows in his heart he is entirely fair. It is certainly unwise of the CBC not to stand up for its appointed staff when the slate is clean. And the public may not always see the nuances of such esoteric debates; they may not, for instance, take into account how easy it may be for the government to leak ideas to a newspaper columnist who is married to a government MP.

Being Seen to Be Clean

How far should a journalist's neutrality go? Mike Duffy, prominent Parliament Hill reporter, once said that to demonstrate his neutrality he had not even voted for the previous ten years: 'We as journalists can't take the same kind of role that we expect other citizens to take,' he remarked.[45] Probably very few reporters feel they need to go to such extremes. But very few reporters have such a potent role. The half-dozen senior parliamentary correspondents for CBC, CTV, and Global television between them reach a larger audience and therefore potentially wield more influence than most other Canadian journalists combined. What counts is not which way they vote, but the perception that they favour one party or person strongly enough to vote for them and against others. Any MP, being interviewed by a journalist who has been seen to cast a ballot, must entertain a nagging suspicion about that interviewer.

However, many journalists either have not felt so constrained or have simply been overwhelmed by events. CBC-TV anchor Stanley Burke became more and more appalled by the Biafra crisis (1967-70) and felt he *had* to get involved to stop the slaughter. As a result, he had to quit his post. Saskatchewan reporter John Twigg became a government information officer in British Columbia, but when he wanted to return to regular reporting he found it took him several years to recover his credibility as an objective writer. Ron Collister, a prominent CBC commentator in the 1960s and 1970s, tried for a Conservative seat and subsequently became a columnist with the *Calgary Sun*; Bruce Phillips was a senior Southam and CTV correspondent before becoming a federal government information officer; Tom Gould roved the world for CBC and was CTV's head of news before becoming media advisor to Brian Mulroney. All, having become somewhat politicized, would have difficulty getting back into news reporting.

The difficulty of re-establishing one's credentials of objectivity is often underestimated. Many Canadian journalists have 'gone political' and later spent years re-earning public trust. Tom Steve, who went from straight journalism to become a Saskatchewan government information officer before returning to objective journalism as news director at CKCK-radio in Regina, spoke later of having to undergo a 'cleansing process,' having to prove himself once again to his peers.[46] Bill Peterson, then credibility commissioner at the Saskatoon *Star-Phoenix* and subsequently publisher, used a similar metaphor. When his paper hired Paul Jackson, a respected journalist who had previously worked in Regina as advisor and speech writer to Premier Grant Devine, he said Jackson was put on the police beat as a process of 'laundering.'[47]

Taking 'political' positions should be understood in its widest sense, in this context. Issues such as abortion may well cross traditional party political boundaries, but nonetheless be highly contentious and therefore be something the writer must take care in expressing views on.[48] A young Kingston, Ontario, editor perhaps thought that participating in an anti-war demonstration during the 1990-1 Gulf crisis was safe enough. But Allan Antliff, from *Between the Lines*,[49] participated in tearing and burning the Canadian flag at the demonstration. A picture of him doing this appeared in the established local daily, the Kingston *Whig-Standard*. His little paper then received a number of threats, a rock was tossed through a window, and advertisers pulled their ads. Within weeks, the shoestring newspaper closed down. Was it unfair of the *Whig-Standard* to run the photo identifying the editor? A spokesperson for *Between the Lines* agreed that if *they* had had a picture of a *Whig-Standard* editor burning the flag, they would have run it and identified him.[50]

In Dispute: The Union

Sometimes journalists are tempted to make political statements en masse. Some years ago, unions at Pacific Press, which publishes the two Vancouver dailies, the *Sun* and the *Province*, refused to handle an advertisement that sought replacement workers for a Canada Post strike. On another occasion they refused to handle ads for the Famous Players cinema chain while its employees were locked out. While such decisions only affect the newsroom peripherally, journalists are among those represented by the Joint Council of Unions, and, as such, their solidarity with other labour activists can be assumed by the readers. Their ability to distance themselves from the story as reporters would therefore be seriously limited.

The decision was tougher, and closer to home, in June 1987 when the BC Federation of Labour called a twenty-four-hour work stoppage across the entire province of British Columbia to protest government actions. Pickets were thrown up around the Pacific Press building, and only 10 to 25 per cent of the work force went to work, so both papers missed one day. For the reporters, said then *Sun* Victoria bureau chief Gary Mason, this meant a lot of soul-searching:

By going out in opposition to Bill 19, I would have made a political statement ... There is a real perception problem here. I've questioned politicians all the time about the perception of conflict of interest. If I went out, I couldn't very well go up to a minister and question him about a perception of a conflict of interest.

I thought long and hard about coming to work. I'm a member of a trade union, and I'm also a journalist. But I should report the story and not be a part of it.[51]

Mason did not face a picket line at the legislature, unlike his colleagues at the Pacific Press building. More than half the news staff crossed the line, but they still could not get a paper out.

Of course, the other side of the coin may also be true: Journalists may on occasion be embarrassed by the position taken by their managers, as when it was learned in 1984 that Southam Inc., Thomson Newspapers, and BCTV had contributed to the Fraser Institute, often seen as a thoroughly right-wing think

tank.[52] But this pales by comparison with journalists at some US papers who have been ordered to slant stories in a particular political way.[53]

And as news workers may be embarrassed by the actions of management, so the reverse is true. In 1988, the Council of Newspaper Unions at the Sudbury, Ontario, *Star* voted to make a small monthly donation to local public health nurses who had been on strike for several months. As a result, publisher Maurice Switzer announced the reporters could no longer cover the nurses' strike, as their objectivity had been put in question: 'You don't publicly support political parties or one side in a labor dispute without jeopardizing your integrity,' he said.[54]

Such a contretemps is always risked in such 'joint council' operations where the journalists are in a minority and can easily be outvoted by classified ad clerks, press operators, and janitors. The public is not served well either by seeing the journalists on whom they rely, especially in a one-paper town like Sudbury, publicly avow their solidarity with labour or by seeing a publisher cut off a story.[55]

Using the Media for Personal Gain

One further form of potential conflict needs brief mention.

Powerlessness is frustrating to everyone without power, journalists included. There may well be occasions when a private citizen who is also a newsperson knows he will get better service or better bargains by mentioning that he works for *Such-and-Such News*. But the clout of the newsroom must not be employed for personal ends, even to correct perceived wrongs. The reporter, for instance, who buys a lemon instead of a car may be sorely tempted to let the dealership know that he works for the *News* and that his experience would make a fine front-page story.

But the reporter is only a typical citizen. Certainly, like any other citizen, he may report his complaint to the editor/news director as a possible story. But if a story transpires, he certainly should not write it himself.

Not many codes of ethics address this topic, but the *Windsor Star* spells it out effectively: 'Staff members may not use their positions directly or indirectly to obtain any benefit or advantage in commercial transactions not available to the general public. This specifically prohibits the use of *Star* letterhead-stationery for private business matters, letters of complaint or protest, or similar activities. Staffers should be careful not to identify themselves as such when dealing with outsiders on matters of a private or personal nature.'[56]

Thus, as the US journalism teacher Katherine McAdams argues, there are few guidelines in the news media which govern non-monetary conflicts of interest for journalists.[57] Specific, detailed rules may not be necessary, however, if the principles of conflict are understood and enforced. Newsrooms could do worse than incorporate in their codes a paraphrase of Andrew Barnes and Don McGillivray: 'The reader has a right to expect a news story to be told by an observer, not an advocate ... The ultimate responsibility of the journalist is to his audience, not himself.'

Such a sentiment could usefully be engraved in every newsroom, and especially in every press gallery. Political reporters are evidently far more vulnerable to perceptions of conflict than are reporters in other areas. However, such susceptibility is not limited to questions of conflict. In the next chapter, two further problems that political writers in particular face will be discussed: the obstacles entailed in pack journalism and in the cult of personality – the reporter as celebrity.

TOUGH CALLS

1   A respected local newsperson was hired by the Conservative provincial government to handle Cabinet public relations. After several years, the government is defeated and the PR person finds herself job-hunting. What are the issues?

2   One of your reporters – a family person with a home and a mortgage – is incensed about increases in property taxes, as are many other citizens. Does he have the right to speak out on the issue? Should he?

3   Your station manager asks you to develop a memo for news staff regarding freelancing. What does it say?

4   While shopping, an off-duty reporter finds what she suspects is a dead mouse in a bulk-food bin. She writes a third-person story – not naming the shopper – about the incident, which ends up on the top of the front page. What are the ethical issues, and what is the appropriate way to handle such an incident?

5   The publisher of your newspaper – whose policy manual forbids reporters from getting into conflict-of-interest situations – wants you to editorialize passionately in favour of a new expressway into downtown. The highway would significantly facilitate newspaper delivery. What do you write?

6 Pack Journalism and Celebrity Journalism

To the viewer watching the evening news, journalism must sometimes resemble some ancient blood sport, as the harried cabinet minister is cornered at the entrance to her lair by a pack of insatiable reporters in pursuit of the juicy quote. Why do the media sometimes feel constrained to swarm together, all after the same story at the same time? And why do some reporters break away from the pack, becoming lone wolves and, occasionally, becoming more well known than the celebrities they are supposedly reporting?

The two roles – pack reporter and celebrity – are related only by their mutual exclusivity. Pack journalism was defined neatly by the Royal Commission on Newspapers as 'the unimaginative pursuit and filing of essentially the same stories.'[1] A celebrity journalist, on the other hand, is one who is as famous – or even more famous – than the people she writes about.

Clearly, when a journalist has achieved celebrity status she has escaped the pack. It could be argued that by definition pack journalists will never achieve celebrity status because they are content to run with their peers rather than to be out ahead of them. And yet the journalist who foregoes the pack does not by any means automatically win adulation and honour, but sometimes risks danger and in many ways faces a much greater challenge.

The pack mentality is not limited to journalism. As Paul Rutherford remarks, 'Such rampant incest, of course, plagues virtually every profession.'[2] But pack journalism is frequently very visible to the community in the form of 'scrums' – clusters of journalists besieging a source. It looks undignified and aggressive, and it typifies pack journalism at its worst. Every reporter observes the same raw data at the same time and will likely produce basically the same story.[3]

Why does pack journalism occur in a field that is ostensibly highly competitive and individualistic? As Ottawa journalist John Sawatsky, who deplores pack journalism, colloquially puts it, 'It's a way for reporters to cover their arse.'[4] Anthony Bevins, discussing the British context, agrees as to the importance of the security factor: 'There are many forms of journalistic manipulation, but the most insidious of all is the herd instinct, the frontline reporter's cultivated craving for safety in numbers.'[5]

Another Ottawa journalist and critic of pack journalism, Peter Calamai of Southam News,[6] says there are several reasons for it, beyond security. It is easy ('Everyone else says there are 500 people in the audience: I'll say 500.'); it is induced by peer pressure ('Jeez, you were the only guy who led with that!'); it's fast (enabling the job to be done quickly and reporters to relax socially together afterwards); and it's self-confirming ('If they say it's a story, it must be a story'). Cynics might add one further reason: The need to be wrong in company, rather than wrong in isolation. Harris describes an incident during the Falklands War when five reporters arrived to cover the attack on Mount Kent. Based on a briefing, they had already written their reports and forwarded them to military censors aboard HMS *Fearless* for approval. Instead of the assault following a heavy bombardment, as they had been told, it was a silent, surprise attack: 'The journalists held a hurried meeting. Two of the reporters were unhappy, but the consensus was to let the inaccurate stories – by now on their way to *Fearless* for clearance – be transmitted unchanged.'[7] So the motivations here have much more to do with what's easiest and what's least embarrassing than with providing an accurate record.

Calamai says that sometimes the pack is not a bad thing. For novice reporters, there may be an element of apprentice-and-master: watching the more experienced journalists, who supposedly know the ropes. And sometimes it is unavoidable or necessary for sheer safety. The logistics of news conferences and of election campaigns force journalists to share facilities and sources, and covering dangerous situations – wars, floods, etc. – may well be safer in company.

Calamai divides pack journalism into the 'mechanical pack,' where logistics force reporters to behave in a similar way, and the 'mental pack,' where journalists choose to think the same way. It is the latter that is dangerous and avoidable.

All these add up to a self-protecting mechanism for those reporters who, necessarily, work far from their home newsroom. By definition, pack journalism only occurs when 'competing' reporters from different media all cover the same story and so are all away from their newsrooms and supervisors – at council meetings, legislative press galleries, and in sports press boxes. And it is precisely in this environment that the reporter is, in a sense, most insecure. Not only does he not have colleagues from his own office around him for consultation and reinforcement, but his supervisors, back at the newsroom, may be concerned about the beat reporter's ability to see 'everything' and get the 'whole' story.

From such a scenario developed the laconic telegraph message dreaded by field reporters of old : 'WHY WE NO HAVE?' Or, equally threatening, 'WHY GLOBE HAS?' Each message implicitly questions the judgment of the reporter at the scene: The editor is saying that the competition – such as the *Globe and Mail* – has a different story or angle on a story, and therefore the reporter must have missed something.

This struggle for 'matchers' – stories that match the competition's stories – is a perennial nightmare for the reporter on a complex beat. She may, for instance, attend a municipal council meeting with thirty items on the agenda, of which half-a-dozen seem newsworthy. But if (for reasons of time and space) she is only to write one story, which does she choose? And within a story, which 'key' quotes from sources does she select? Thus, inevitably, the novice reporter may be glad of leadership from old hands: She may discreetly watch colleagues (competitors) at the press table, to see which items on the agenda they are paying attention to and which they ignore, or, more specifically, she may watch which quotes the other reporters write down and which they do not.

Mark Fishman, in his brilliant *Manufacturing the News*, describes in detail two such incidents, in which all reporters 'agree' which items at council meetings are 'non-events' and therefore not reportable.[8]

Similarly, Sawatsky described being a young reporter covering Vancouver School Board meetings for the *Vancouver Sun* in the early 1970s. A veteran from a local radio station would 'choreograph' the four or five other reporters by actually giving a hand signal: 'Of 15 or 20 items on the agenda, you knew which to do. It made it simple, and you knew you were protected.'[9] From this initiation, Sawatsky quickly saw the attraction of the pack: 'The pack is a protection for the lazy journalist or the cautious journalist, because you know you are not going to be scooped.'[10]

In emergencies, this can also be enormously helpful. Sawatsky describes how once, as a cub reporter, he was sitting at a press table at a meeting of Delta, BC, town council. The media representatives were gossiping and suddenly found that a controversial alderman was in the process of announcing his resignation. The reporters pooled together what they had heard with half an ear and so were able to file full stories. Such mutual protection is reassuring but selfish:

It works in the reporter's own personal private interests, to have a pack ... But the problem is the public is not being served. The public gets less news: It becomes a de facto news monopoly ... That's why I say it's bad. In fact it's worse than bad, because it is insidious ... Before you realize what's happened, you're part of the pack, and it's far too comfortable. The overwhelming majority of reporters today practise it: The press gallery in Ottawa is the absolute king of pack journalism, because everybody can cover for everybody else. But it happens everywhere.[11]

Sawatsky describes the process in detail:

I don't know how many times this has happened with me. You attend a meeting in which there are 20 items on the agenda, and the press is all sitting at the press table, together, and they all say 'Oh I don't think that's worth a story, what do you think?' 'No I don't think that's worth doing.' 'Oh, yeah, I think this is a good story.' 'Yeah, I think that's not bad.' And you all sort of work this out. And suddenly you'll have the two radio stations and the one newspaper in that town all come out with the same story.

Well, that's very convenient for the reporters, because that means when one reporter goes back to the office he's not being upstaged by what somebody else has written. And city editors tend to be a bit unpredictable that way, and say, 'Well, So-and-So has this, why didn't you get it?' And of course *your* story doesn't carry any weight: They want to know why you didn't have the other one. The two stories ... there may be no difference between them: It's a very selective thing ...

It is extremely prevalent. It IS the norm, the way the media operate in this country. But it's really not a good way to go ...

Ottawa takes it a couple of steps further even, where basically the *Globe and Mail* determines what's in the news, and everybody follows the *Globe and Mail* ... Even the MPs follow the *Globe and Mail* ... Then it gets raised in the Question Period, and Question Period is the only thing in the House of Commons that the press covers anymore,[12] and all the press covers Question Period, and therefore that story in the *Globe and Mail* was the lead-off question, so the rest of the press runs with it, and it just goes into one circle ...[13]

The pack either comes in with a vengeance, or it stays out ... So a lot of this is done for the convenience of the press, rather than for the information of the public.[14]

David Taras confirms the *Globe and Mail*'s role as a key agenda-setter in Ottawa, with data from several sources, and quotes a number of journalists who confirm the importance of the pack in Ottawa.[15] Even the Kent Commission detected the pattern, noting that, 'The first item of the day's business in every radio and TV newsroom is the reading of newspapers, usually the *Globe and Mail* followed by the main regional newspapers, and the scanning of reports from CP, largely drawn from newspapers.'[16]

Calamai recalls another specific incident. He was among the herd of journalists covering the colourful Colin Thatcher murder trial, where acoustics were poor and none of the reporters took shorthand: 'At the various recesses you would see clusters of reporters, including me, gathered together, saying, "Now, what did they say then?" and we would be comparing quotes. And in fact we would be making up the quotes ... We would come up with one quote that we all agreed was probably the quote that was said.'[17]

In *Trials and Tribulations*, Calamai compares reporting of the court case with the official transcript of the trial, and concludes that pack journalism played

a key role. He summarized his findings in his talk to journalism students in Regina:

Some people have as high as 25 per cent wrong, of their quotes from the trial – the testimony. These are big name reporters, some of them even work for Southam News, [who] had the quotes wrong, of a murder trial. This is an important trial, and people could not get the quotes right. And one of the reasons they couldn't get it right is because they practised pack journalism. People would change their quotes to conform with other people's quotes, even though theirs were right, and the other person's was wrong, because they only worked for the *Winnipeg Free Press* [for instance], and the other person worked for Canadian Press, and they were worried that their editors would say 'C.P. says he said such-and-such, how come you say he says so-and-so?' ...

That's all that matters to an editor: It's not whether it's right or wrong that matters, but whether it's uniform ...

The perfect antidote to too much pack journalism is to realize that what you're doing is the better way of doing it.

It's when you start turning your brain off that you are engaged in the worst form of pack journalism.[18]

Calamai noted that pack journalism also occurs at management level, because editors also do it (though it may then be called agenda-setting) when they are influenced by other editors' decisions.[19] The 'Why We No Have' syndrome is based on the editor's fear of being different.

Calamai suggested that another form of pack journalism is manifested in the way in which many newsrooms tend to keep going back to the same sources. 'The same 40 people are always quoted locally.' Reporters start their research with the clippings file – and go back to the same sources who have proved reliable and quotable in the past. Or they may turn to senior colleagues in the newsroom and ask whom to talk to for stories. 'There's nothing wrong with doing that as long as you don't stop at that point. Ninety per cent of the people stop at that point. So the same people end up being quoted in the paper about the same story all the time ... You're safe; You've covered your butt. But you may not have talked to the best person.' Calamai's advice to young reporters: 'The key element

is break away from the pack. Use the pack to your own benefit as long as it's to your benefit. And always keep in your mind the idea of breaking loose at some point.'[20]

The pack can also be useful in playing continuo while the reporter plays solo. Young Bill Peterson, covering the Saskatchewan legislature for the Saskatoon *Star-Phoenix*, relied on the pack, particularly Canadian Press, to keep an eye on the government while he went off into the hinterland for a day or two each week. That way, he got both the day-to-day bureaucratic news and the unique stories. (And he made such a good reputation for himself, he was made publisher while still in his forties.)

At its worst, pack journalism can cause real damage. Calamai attributed the media's dislike of Joe Clark (as he rose from Opposition leader through external affairs minister to a brief stint as prime minister) largely to one columnist:

When it originally started out, only one person was writing that Joe Clark was a klutz, who couldn't rub his stomach and pat his head at the same time, and that was Allan Fotheringham, on Clark's round-the-world tour as Opposition leader. And when the tour ended three weeks later everybody on the tour was writing that story.

Part of it was peer pressure. Part of it was status, with Fotheringham writing it. Part of it was their editors saying, 'Well, Allan Fotheringham says Joe Clark is a klutz, how can you keep saying he's alright? He looks like a klutz to us.' All those aspects came into it.

There was the mechanical pack: They *had* to travel together; they *had* to go in the same airplane; they *had* to stay in the same hotels together; probably had to use the same filing facilities, same telexes, same copy-drops, all that stuff was forced upon them.

It became a mental pack as well: everyone agreeing, 'Yes, this guy is a klutz and shouldn't be Prime Minister. We'll just finish him off here, and put him out of his misery.'[21]

Television can be very potent in this relationship. When the premiers of all the Canadian provinces were called to a First Ministers' Conference in February 1985 by the new prime minister, Brian Mulroney, the entire event was watched by the media.[22] But as the sessions (held, incongruously, on the stage of the Centre of the

Arts in Regina, Saskatchewan) broke for lunch and at the end of the day, journalists were allowed onto a cordoned area at the front of the stage to try to reach the eleven leaders. So, as Mulroney swung the gavel, bedlam broke out with a hundred or more reporters, camera operators, and photographers surging onto the stage, calling out to ministers, or their aides, for an interview.

A few ministers quickly slipped out through the wings, but many responded, choosing whom they wished to talk to in the few minutes available. Typically, the most important or 'newsy' ministers (for instance, the late Richard Hatfield, premier of New Brunswick, who was concurrently embroiled in bizarre drug-possession allegations) would respond to the most 'important' journalists – the network television reporters.[23] Within moments, the melee resolved into a series of 'nodes,' at the centre of which was, for instance, Mike Duffy (then with CBC-Ottawa, commanding three million viewers with *The National*) questioning Hatfield, surrounded by twenty other reporters, cameras, and microphones – all getting the same story.

At another node, the CBC French reporter might be interviewing the Quebec premier, surrounded by francophones. At another, the Ottawa reporter for Global-TV, based in Toronto, might have captured the Ontario leader. Within minutes, these groups would break up and might regroup briefly for a second interview, but would then leave quickly for lunch or other events. The result was that, in effect, very few reporters would ask very few questions, with the answers heard by all the colleagues in their particular cluster.[24]

Pack Editing

Editors can themselves act as a pack in their choice of stories. Each night, as dozens of daily paper editors across the country plan their papers for the next day, Canadian Press distributes a series of items known colloquially as 'the fronts.' This comprises a list of the front-page stories on the first editions of tomorrow's *Globe and Mail, Toronto Star*, and several other major dailies. About the same time, CP lists the top items on the television network evening newscasts. Such material serves one primary purpose: reinforcement of the editors' own views. Of course, many editors and news directors do not need such confirmation, but the fact

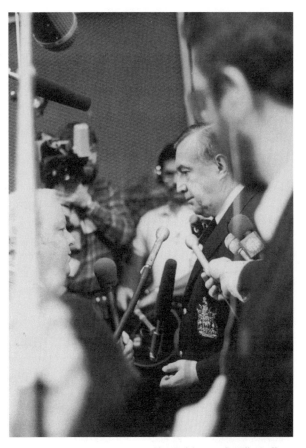

The pack in pursuit: Mike Duffy, then with CBC, questions New Brunswick Premier Richard Hatfield at a First Ministers' Conference in Regina, surrounded by a thicket of microphones and cameras.

that CP supplies the lists suggests that significant numbers of news supervisors have requested them.

In fact, a strong case could be made for describing Canadian Press itself as the archetype of pack journalism. As a cooperative news gathering agency, CP is wholly owned by its member papers and is devoted to exchanging the stories from each paper with all the others. When the *Toronto Star* obtained 'exclusive' photographs of the 'elephant boy' story (described in Chapter 4, 'The Media and Money'), Canadian Press castigated the *Star* for withholding them from the agency.[25] The Canadian Press mandate is not simply to supply news to individual papers, but to supply the *same* news to all members, and an editor would be justifiably indignant if his paper failed to receive a story that some other paper did get.[26]

Pack journalism is not, however, solely the creation of the journalists: undoubtedly the newsmakers have learned to manipulate the pack, particularly in the form of scrums, for their own ends. As has been suggested, the scrum is largely controlled by the source, or his handler, who can provide the opportunity for it to happen, can cut it off, and can control the questions. By having a scrum, the politician can more easily sidestep unwanted one-to-one interviews. And the scrum, because it makes 'good visuals' for television, will provide access to welcome exposure on the evening news for the aware politician who gives good twenty-second quotes for the cameras. Scrums used to emerge spontaneously; however, wily politicians (or their media handlers) now routinely *invite* the press to scrums, making a mockery of the concept. The scrum has simply become a corridor news conference.

So it is that some journalists, such as Peter Trueman, have welcomed television into the House of Commons: 'It has at least saved us from the nightly scrum, in which a mob of newsmen, waving a forest of notebooks and microphones, used to buttonhole the key figures outside the House when the debate was over. Before debates were televised, and clips from them were freely available, it was the only way to get the principals on film.'[27]

Two final incidents are worth describing. In the summer of 1990, Mohawks barricaded themselves on the Kahnawake reserve near Montreal and the Kanesatake reserve near Oka, Quebec, to publicize various grievances.[28] In the resulting standoff, some reporters were permitted through the barricades and others were not. The result was that *two* packs developed, one on each side, each arguably more loyal to 'their' side.[29] At one point, *Montreal Gazette* reporter Jeff Heinrich was ejected by the Natives; the other reporters decided to walk out in support of him but returned the next day: solidarity among the pack lasted only as long as they didn't lose out on the story.[30]

The second incident was a 'good news' story, involving the rescue of two grey whales trapped in the Arctic ice in October 1988.[31] The plight of the whales and attempts to rescue them made front-page news around the world for two weeks.[32] Yet there are an estimated 22,000 whales in that area each season, and their predicament was not unusual. What made this different? Concluded Ian Ball, writing in the London *Daily Telegraph* after the rescue: 'That the plight of the whales captured the world's attention and held it for so long is a tribute to the determination of Miss Cindi Lowry, the Alaskan field representative of Greenpeace. Almost single-handedly, she forced the Alaskan and then the federal government to intervene.'[33] Ultimately, a $1-million rescue was mounted involving Soviet navy, US army, oil companies, and Inuit whalers. And the media spent hundreds of thousands of dollars to get crews to this remote hole in the ice and then get pictures back, pictures that were mostly the same, night after night. Ball quoted a TV news editor: 'We dared not leave them off, even though the pictures we were getting were basically the same each day – whale comes up, whale wheezes, whale goes under the water.'[34] The whole event became a media merry-go-round that nobody dared get off. Lowry egged on the government, the media then further egged on the government, reporting the results. The story contained many journalistic cliches. It was a tearjerker and a cliff-hanger, with a romantic remoteness peopled by Inuit, and was coloured with 'Man rescues Animal' and 'Man against the Elements' heroism and the 'little guy' forcing the bureaucrats and the war machine to 'do something useful for a change.'

But whales were routinely hunted in the Arctic every year. And the Native village of Barrow, which hosted the media extravaganza, marked its end with a feast –

featuring whale meat. Even Lowry, who helped whip it all up, was quoted as saying, 'To be honest, there is no real ecological reason to save these whales.'[35] And Paul Watson, who has done his share of media manipulating over the years as founder of the Sea Shepherd Society, which grew out of Greenpeace, said, 'In the beginning I thought it was a worthwhile effort, but then the hypocrisy of what's going on started to bother me.'[36]

Watson labelled the whole incident 'a hypocritical "kitten-in-the-tree" media event.'[37] And perhaps he was right. The incident happened near Barrow, Alaska, which – with a population of 3,300 – happens to have a cable television system and two-way satellite facility. The event got onto the world news agenda because, for the local cable operator, it was a major event, so he taped it and offered it to an NBC affiliate in Anchorage. From there it was bounced into the networks and became a world story. A few years earlier, the electronics would not have been possible, and the local Inuit would probably have slaughtered the trapped whales for food, as usual. But once the story had made it onto the world's evening news, it could not just be abandoned or allowed to quietly fade away. There had to be an ending, and the audience – as even the White House and the Kremlin came to realize – wanted a *happy* ending, at any cost.

So Tom Rose is wrong to maintain that 'The Media Created the World's Greatest Non-Event' (to paraphrase the subtitle of his book on the subject). The media did not *create* anything. Technology permitted it to be beamed into the world's living rooms, and after that the authorities were at the mercy of the taxpayers. The media had to report the events as they unfolded, though there were many nights when there was little new to report. What the media generally failed to do was to put the beads on the string: to tell readers and viewers that there were better ways these vast sums of money could have been spent, even to protect whales in general, and to warn that the whales, when freed, had very little chance of survival.[38]

The Journalist as Star

When the First Ministers' Conference, referred to above, adjourned and the premiers responded to Mike Duffy's call for an interview, they were responding both to his

reach (three million viewers) and to his celebrity status. The round visage of the tireless reporter was as well known across the country as most provincial premiers, and considerably better known than some.

Jeffrey Olen, writing about the star quality of network news anchors such as Dan Rather, says this is not only due to the anchor being seen nightly across the country, and to the media sometimes fawning on such stars, but also to 'CBS's packaging of him as a star in order to keep the ratings up.'[39] Fortunately, so far, this manufacturing of stars out of anchors and reporters has not happened to any great degree in Canada. But that just gives the high-profile journalists a greater chance of exposure and fame.

In one sense, the University of Regina's Minifie Memorial Lecture series is all about this star quality. Each year, one top Canadian journalist is invited to give a keynote speech on journalism. The speakers generally draw an audience of a thousand or more, often in the depths of prairie winter. Who are these stars? They tend to be TV journalists, household names across the country. Admittedly there have been several print writers in the series' history (Alan Fotheringham, Charles Lynch, Clark Davey, William Stevenson, June Callwood) and one radio star – Peter Gzowski; but the others – starting with Knowlton Nash in 1981, and including Eric Malling, Patrick Watson, Ann Medina, Joe Schlesinger, Pamela Wallin, Helen Hutchinson, and Arthur Kent – have all been drawn from television. Furthermore, Stevenson is known primarily for his books (not newspaper work), while Fotheringham's fame is due in large part to several books, his magazine column for *Maclean's* magazine, and his role on the *Front Page Challenge* TV quiz show.[40] Perhaps only Callwood, Lynch, and Davey could be said to be exclusively print journalists, and they have done odd stints on television. By comparison, how many print writers have an opportunity to gain a national audience and national stature?

Even James M. ('Don') Minifie, after whom the series is named, though very much a print journalist, only won national acclaim when he became CBC's first Washington television correspondent.[41]

As early as 1977, journalist Nora Ephron, columnist and author, identified television as the cause of this celebrity status. She noted: 'Journalists are now celebrities. Part of this has been caused by the ability and willingness of journalists to promote themselves. Part of this has been caused by television: the television reporter is often more famous than anyone he interviews.'[42]

The creation of stars, particularly in television, has been encouraged by the media consultants who, during the 1970s and 1980s, encouraged newsrooms to package their news shows as entertainment.

Back in 1981, Knowlton Nash, then CBC key anchor and senior journalist, saw the whole concept as dangerous: 'Perhaps the most worrying cancer on journalism today is the idea that the news business is show business. It sure as hell is not. There is a role for "show biz" in news, but it is supplementary to the basic function.'[43]

However, while the cause of this phenomenon is not of direct concern to a debate on journalism ethics, the effects are important. In his Minifie lecture, Canadian columnist Charles Lynch emphasized the danger incurred when journalists become celebrities: 'The principal hazard of celebrity journalism is attracting more attention than the people being reported on ... being sought out and flattered by people who may want a mention, but have no tidings to impart. How many times did I see Don Minifie come into an election hall and attract more attention from the audience than the person who was there to campaign?'[44]

Lynch went on to suggest that with fame came a personality cult, typically as an opinionated columnist:

Personal journalism, on the other hand, has tremendous advantages for those of us who practise it. It means big bucks, which comes with big ratings, leading in many cases to big egos. Some say big influence comes with it, and I'm not sure about that. The danger is that the care and feeding of a national reputation takes over from the business of reporting on the story itself, and that's addictive. Like taking dope.[45]

Peter Desbarats, in his *Guide to Canadian News Media*, devotes a section specifically to 'The Print Journalist as Celebrity' but, oddly enough, does not acknowledge the impact of TV.[46] Commenting on Lynch's remarks, he notes,

The celebrity journalist who quickly earns a reputation through verbal pyrotechnics, astute self-promotion and fierce criticism of everyone and everything – often based on bias rather than sound research – may even hinder the development of journalistic professionalism by creating a set of false values and giving the public the impression that glibness mixed with cynicism deserves the biggest rewards.[47]

Walter Stewart, who has had a long and distinguished career as a Canadian journalist and editor, remarked once that celebrity status can have its bonuses – notably, people return your telephone calls. But this is offset by disadvantages: 'You're not invisible when you interview somebody. Dumb innocence is now something I can't use.'[48]

There are other disadvantages, particularly the danger of interfering with news events. As Olen points out, the presence of a 'star' reporter with a TV crew can change the nature of some events, and even turn a small demonstration into a large one.[49]

The advantages of celebrity status – fame, fortune, and returned phone calls – are primarily accrued only by the individuals involved (though the parent company may profit from the journalists' enhanced reputation). The disadvantages, however, tend to be industry-wide and affect both quality and credibility.

Knowlton Nash, brooding on this tension, concluded:

In news, the important must always take precedence over the merely interesting. Of course, a journalist must make certain the important is written and produced in as interesting, attractive and understandable a way as possible, without trivializing or distorting the story ...

Too often today, some news organizations and reporters give priority to theatricality over substance.

That's a particular danger for television and tabloids which too often surrender to their susceptibility to trash journalism in a frantic search for greater ratings and readership.

When 'show biz' takes over news, a totally different set of priorities results. The emphasis is on entertaining, not on informing and enlightening.[50]

Nash puts his finger on the key problem of celebrity journalism: It gets in the way of news. While there is no question that competition is built into Western, capitalist journalism, which means that there will always be a demand to increase audiences, what motivates the media accountants must not be allowed to motivate the newsroom. As Ann Medina optimistically says, 'News organizations aren't in the business to make money, and editorial desks, the ratings book and "sweeps week" don't determine where and what stories are ... yet.'[51]

Does credibility suffer with stardom? Olen suggests that it may, in fact, improve,[52] but he may be interpreting credibility in the narrow sense of 'believability.' The eminences grises of television journalism, such as Walter Cronkite, sometimes top the polls on trustworthiness,[53] but this may be at the expense of other news staff, who get lost in the shadow of the star, and of the whole news package, where style and stardom overwhelm content.

In this situation, the audience, once again, is the loser. The celebrity journalist rarely brings 'better' journalism to his audience because of his personal success. Many analysts have remarked on the way political reporting on television tends increasingly to degenerate into 'horse races' and coverage of the 'stars' (presidents, prime ministers, etc.), with a concomitant loss of the issues and platforms.[54] Similarly, journalism that emphasizes the anchors and the star reporters can easily lose sight of the information being conveyed. It is difficult to avoid because the newsroom may seem to bask in the aura of a celebrity on its staff and may, indeed, increase its audience. And although there is very little incentive for the individual journalist to avoid becoming a star (few can resist the trappings of stardom – fame and money) the reason to do so is unambiguous. By definition, journalists should be transparent, neutral observers, not participants, let alone the news itself. It is one of the ironies of the profession that the journalist, while constantly rubbing shoulders with the great, and constantly aware of their fallibility, must choose to remain in the shadows.

Pack journalism reduces the quality of journalism simply because it lessens the options. All stories – even from alleged competitors – may sound the same, with the same sources, the same angles, and the same quotations. Celebrity journalism, too, reduces the quality of journalism because it distracts from the story and

may even interfere with it. Both are unethical for the simple reason that ethical journalists aim to give audiences the best journalism.

Both phenomena tend to apply to the entire news industry, as indeed do all the ethical dilemmas discussed in this study. In the next chapter, we turn to specifics: ways in which the media can run into ethical problems peculiar to each medium.

TOUGH CALLS

1 As a new legislative reporter, you are invited to a government cocktail party. You are surprised to see a prominent woman cabinet minister smoking dope with an intimate male friend. When you start asking questions, your press gallery colleagues say they've seen it before, but it's a private matter, not for publication. Agreed?

2 The acoustics outside the Cabinet room were lousy. You believe the minister said, 'I'm resigning because I'm gay,' but the other reporters think he said, 'I'm resigning. Have a good day.' Which do you run?

3 Charles Lynch describes following British prime minister Winston Churchill as he led victorious troops into Germany. The well-lubricated leader stopped the convoy in order to urinate into the Rhine. The press turned a blind eye. Was that appropriate journalism? (This incident is further discussed in Chapter 8, 'To Press or to Suppress?')

4 You've finally made it to the top, with job offers from both the *Economist* and *Maclean's*. Is your choice influenced by the fact that all *Maclean's* articles are bylined, while nobody gets bylines at the *Economist*?

5 When a girl was found shot to death in a small Alberta town, the media from nearby Calgary swarmed all over the community, trying to get interviews with her family and friends. Their requests were refused, but the local weekly managed to get an interview by discreetly asking through an intermediary. The Calgary media were incensed and asked the paper for the family's unlisted phone number, but the editor declined. Shouldn't she have helped her colleagues?

Manipulating the Media

Withholding news goes against the journalist's grain. The folklore of journalism suggests that the first instinct of any writer worth her salt is to publish, to get the story out, and it is only with great reluctance that reporters and editors will withhold material.

However, sources put constant external pressure on the media to withhold news that they regard as negative to themselves. And there are constant pressures to publish 'non-news' – material that sources want aired as 'good news' about themselves.

Some of this pressure is subtle and difficult to identify. Some is transparently obvious. (The crudest method – actual payoffs from politicians to journalists – seems to be extremely rare in Canada today. The concept has been touched on in Chapter 5, 'Conflict of Interest.')

Overt Manipulation

Governments are the most frequent culprits when it comes to exerting pressure on the press.[1] It is a fundamental premise of those who govern that, once having won power, they want to keep it. As an earlier Canadian editor, Bob Edwards, wryly remarked back in 1915, 'In trying to get up in the world, politicians use newspapermen as step ladders.'[2] But the captains of industry, or more likely the faceless transnational megacorporations, also have their own agenda – and their own arsenal of weapons.

One crude strategy is to create laws specifically to muzzle the press. One of the most flagrant examples of this in Canada occurred in the 1970s, when revelations began to leak out about a federal government plot to increase the sale price of uranium. As *Montreal Gazette* reporter John Saunders reconstructed it, the government designed the *Regulations Respecting the Security of Uranium Information* specifically to hide details of a Canadian-sponsored cartel to rig world uranium prices.[3] 'So for a period of 13 months in 1976 and 1977 it was a federal offence for any person – a reporter, a conscience-stricken executive or anyone else – to reveal the contents of any note or document relating to any meeting or conversation about production, processing, ownership, sale or use of uranium between 1972 and 1975.'[4]

The effect of these simple regulations (authorized by a Cabinet meeting attended by only four ministers) was to put an entire topic off-limits, 'censoring a fact,' as one lawyer said.[5] Saunders points out that the penalty for infringement was up to $10,000 in fines or five years in jail. (The regulations were eased and then simply not enforced after some newspapers eventually called their bluff.)[6]

Much more common, in governmental attempts to suppress material, is that simplest of tools, the 'SECRET' stamp. Canada's national government has never been known for its openness, and even Freedom of Information laws have done little to liberate the federal files.[7]

Perhaps the bluntest instrument is the injunction.[8] In the news media context, the injunction is generally used as a muzzle, a form of prior restraint, to prevent the media from publishing something thought to be potentially damaging. In the right hands, it is not an unreasonable tool. If people learn they are about to be libelled and recognize that even if they win a subsequent legal action they may never recover their good names, then an injunction may help to protect them before the damage is done.[9]

However, such a scenario is very rare. Newsrooms cannot afford to lose major libel actions, so they generally play it safe. But when an injunction is issued, it is usually done in a rush, to stop a newsroom on the eve of publishing, and it is often issued ex parte, that is, the journalists are not present to defend themselves or to explain the nature of their intended publication. The judge will issue the restraining order having heard only one side of the story, based on allegations of a 'potential' libel. To soften the very one-sided nature of this, the judge usually issues the order only temporarily, pending further legal action. But even the threat of a legal action – delivered to the newsroom by a team of sombre, pin-striped lawyers – may well serve to chill the entire project.

A classic incident in 1974 demonstrated how effective this weapon can be. The CBC had prepared an hour-long radio documentary, entitled 'Dying of Lead,' to air 29 January on the *As It Happens* program. It was alleged in the program that two Toronto metal companies were causing lead poisoning. After the program had already been broadcast in eastern time zones, an injunction was delivered to the Toronto studios. Portions of the show were then deleted from the western broadcasts. However, a judge subsequently fined the producers, saying the entire program should have been postponed until it could be corrected. Ultimately, the injunction was extended so that the uncut documentary was never aired.[10]

A similar sort of injunction was used in British Columbia in 1993, but an overzealous lawyer and fearful client were too flagrant, and the weapon rebounded and injured the enjoiner more than the enjoined. The CBC television show *The Fifth Estate* was preparing a feature about a Vancouver stock promoter who had operated a Colorado mine that caused massive cyanide pollution. The man feared the program would also reveal his juvenile criminal record, and on that basis

his lawyer managed to get a blanket injunction that not only forbade the CBC from publishing the material but forbade *all* media from even revealing the nature of the ban itself. The media were so incensed by this vast restriction that they – particularly the CBC and the *Globe and Mail* – challenged it in court and ran almost-daily news stories describing the limits being imposed on freedom of the press. Ultimately, the courts threw out the ban on the eve of the show being aired, and the CBC – finally unmuzzled – was able to report that it had never intended to reveal the man's criminal record. As a result of the injunction, the plaintiff not only ran up substantial legal bills and attracted vastly inflated ratings for the show and the whole story, he also succeeded in getting most media to report the details of his youthful LSD dealing, which would otherwise never have been revealed. Score 1 for the media. Nonetheless, there does seem to have been a marked increase in the use of this particular weapon against the press in recent years, and newsrooms will constantly have to challenge such incursions, at considerable expense.

The Vulnerability of Broadcasters

Governments are fully aware of the power of the electronic media, especially television, and not unnaturally will try to get the most exposure from them that they can.

One technique is to demand free airtime for 'major' governmental pronouncements. In March 1990, Saskatchewan's premier Grant Devine asked for free time on local television stations. In retrospect, Frank Flegel, then news director of CKTV, is highly critical of the way the government manipulated the situation. The premier wanted to make a statement about the provincial economy, but in demanding the time, his aides would not reveal the contents, let alone the script, for the broadcast. The premier's videotape was delivered only forty-five minutes before airtime, at which point Flegel concluded that the content did not warrant free-time broadcast and should have been delivered via a news conference. But it was too late to cancel. He agreed with the free-time concept, to enable leaders to talk directly to the electorate occasionally. But while the media had a responsibility to provide some access for leaders, they also had the right to refuse access if it was going to be abused. In this instance, the government also refused to release advance copies of the address to Opposition leaders so they could make an informed analysis of it. 'We tried to get the government to give it to the Opposition in advance,' said Flegel. 'I think the government was patently unfair in not releasing it [to them].'[11] As a result, Opposition leaders could only make a knee-jerk response when asked for immediate reaction, attacking the man rather than the policy.

Flegel vowed to develop a newsroom policy for such requests that would require advance indications of the broadcast's content and its release to Opposition leaders 'at least half-an-hour before airtime.'

Similar use of timing to curtail criticism is described by Geoffrey Mungham in the US context. He cites a *Christian Science Monitor* conclusion that the US Administration favours holding news conferences in the evening, as 'the TV networks don't want to spend a lot of time on commentary in that prime time.'[12]

In Canada, control of broadcasting is a federal responsibility, hence provincial governments can do little to formally constrain electronic journalism. But Ottawa's power in this regard is formidable. The regulations appear to be administered at arm's length through the Canadian Radio-Television and Telecommunications Commission (CRTC), but the commission is, nonetheless, a creature of government, set up under the Broadcasting Act and comprising government appointees.

Peter Desbarats describes the CRTC's approach to policing journalistic standards as 'benign neglect' and 'something of a joke among broadcast journalists.'[13] The commission has only refused to renew broadcasting licences because of poor journalism three times out of several thousand applications, he notes. However, the power is there, and restrictions can be imposed without totally rejecting the licence application. For instance, alarmed by the amount of American news pouring north across the border, the commission renewed the licences of two Windsor, Ontario, stations with the proviso that, 'the licensee shall ... insure that a minimum of 45% of the news items broadcast ... have a Canadian orientation in that they must relate to

events taking place in Canada or the distinct Canadian involvement in international events.'[14] This is a clear intervention in newscast content and imposes a bizarre logistical burden on the newsrooms.

Changes to the Broadcasting Act, passed 5 December 1990, were also condemned as possibly permitting more parliamentary intrusion into broadcasting policy.[15]

Creery concludes that the planned changes are poorly motivated and could have dire consequences. 'The new broadcasting act is a lobbied law, representing a consensus of special interests, brokered by the politicians ... largely designed by cultural bureaucrats ... The public interest in freedom of broadcasting is forgotten.'[16]

The Boys and Girls on the Bus

If the electronic media are regarded as important by policymakers most of the time, this is magnified during election campaigns. The phenomenon has been widely examined in the US milieu,[17] and the Canadian experience seems – unfortunately – to ape the US practice. Peter Trueman, a Canadian television veteran, recalls a comment from a New Democratic Party official during one federal election campaign: 'Campaigning is now almost entirely devoted to producing a television show.'[18]

Clive Cocking, who emulated Crouse with his book *Following the Leaders*, quotes the communications manager for the federal Conservative party in Canada as saying in 1978, 'Television newscasts are by far the most important medium.' Concludes Cocking: 'What is new is the extent to which television has become the all-powerful god of election campaigns ... If this campaign demonstrated anything, it is that, while once preeminent, print journalism now follows television.'[19]

Even big turnouts at campaign meetings are not that important any more, says Patrick Gossage, Liberal party communications expert: 'It used to be that the aim was to draw 1,000 people out to hear the candidate. Now the crowds are almost incidental, except as props for television.'[20]

Inevitably, this leads to the manufacture of events on the campaign trail. David Bazay, then executive producer of the CBC's nightly TV news show *The National*, said this poses a constant problem. 'Staged events are the reality of modern political campaigns. If the Prime Minister is not accessible to the media, we leave it up to the viewers' intelligence to realize that he is being evasive.'[21] And this is echoed by colleague Nigel Gibson, a senior producer on *The National*. 'The staged photo opportunities and the attempts by political handlers to manipulate what we put on the air remains the greatest single problem we face in TV.'[22]

Yet despite recognizing the problem, journalists still have difficulty deciding how to deal with it. Television, particularly, is always hungry for good visual material, which staged events usually strive to provide, and there is always the nagging fear that if the event is boycotted, the competition may get something worthwhile. Wallace describes the soul-searching that went on behind the scenes at *The National* during the 1988 campaign over whether to use video clips that showed John Turner stumbling over his words. But despite the navel-gazing, the stumble got on air.[23]

The danger from all this is that the journalists lose control of the news. As George Bain, columnist and veteran journalist, puts it, campaign control 'is in the hands of the party, and the reporters become media pawns.'[24] The irritation engendered by such a relationship is voiced by Andy Moir, senior news editor for the CTV *National News*: 'On election campaigns, we are too tied to the damned leader. They have press planes, and we go on them. But in the process of agreeing to follow the leader's tour, you are agreeing to be manipulated ... You know damned well there are a lot of staged events you are expected to cover dutifully ... and it's not even a logical way to cover an election in the first place.'[25]

A further danger is that those 'on the bus' often find they can't help growing to like the candidate they must follow.[26] And, not unnaturally, they want 'their' candidate to win.

Making It Easy for the Media

Another way in which governments may overtly attempt to manipulate the news is by providing material to journalists in as accessible a form as possible. Several provincial governments (including British Columbia, Saskatchewan, Quebec, and Nova Scotia) have developed mechanisms for sending videotaped or audiotaped material to outlying broadcast newsrooms. Such items might, for instance, show a cabinet minister reading a news release as if for a news conference. Not unnaturally, she is well rehearsed and filmed under the most sympathetic studio conditions. Larger TV newsrooms, which could attend the actual news conference, would spurn such offerings, but smaller, more remote stations may appreciate them.[27]

Such a technique was brought to full flower in 1987 when the ruling Progressive Conservative party created the cleverly named Parliamentary News Service (PNS) in Ottawa to distribute similar material all over the country, absorbing the satellite transmission costs (estimated at $25 a minute).[28]

Throughout the Conservative government (defeated in 1993), this office recorded hallway interviews with ministers and Conservative MPs and distributed material localized to suit particular broadcast stations. It also provided hookups for local news anchors to interview Conservative spokespersons.

Some commentators simply labelled the PNS product as 'electronic press releases,' but it is clearly much more: it is localized, it can involve local media people, it is produced under optimum conditions (fine video and audio quality), it is fast, and it is ready to air. The psychological pressure to use such material in isolated communities must sometimes be considerable. From the Conservatives' point of view, it was evidently a success, and the PNS quickly added a parallel audio service for radio stations.[29]

Any illusion that this was a truly 'parliamentary' service was finally shattered when Parliament adjourned for the November 1988 election. The PNS service kept on producing audio clips from the campaign trail (the television unit did not go out in the field because of cost).[30] And any hope that journalists were just throwing out the tapes was shaken when the PNS claimed that between 100 and 150 radio stations were using them during the campaign.[31]

Ottawa Citizen reporter Greg Weston quotes an Ontario radio news director, Bob McIntyre of CKGB/CFTI: 'I think the general feeling among news directors is that we don't really care who shoves the microphone in a person's face, as long as we get the clip.'[32]

This was echoed by the then news director of MTN,

a radio and TV station in Portage la Prairie, Manitoba, in an interview with the CBC: 'I don't think that where the information comes from is the factor: It's the information itself. We're making sure that the information is reliable, it's credible, it's accurate. [pause] Does it really matter to the viewer where the information is from?'[33]

Of course the answer must be 'yes, it does matter,' even if the viewer does not know it matters. It matters considerably that such clips are groomed for quality, selected for political impact, and one-sided. The other parties did not provide balancing services. And how can a small newsroom, remote from Ottawa, without an Ottawa correspondent, 'make sure' that the information is accurate?[34]

Receiving the material does not compromise the journalist: editors must always be willing to examine any material that comes their way. But the president of the Radio Television News Directors Association, Eric Rothchild, argued in the same CBC program: 'As long as you maintain editorial control, then there's no compromise.'[35]

However, ideally, editorial control includes access to equal, balanced material. These neatly manicured clips ensure that the scales are tipped in favour of using Conservative propaganda. The news director simply does not have the facilities to air similar material from other political parties and may well forgo the extra trouble of identifying such clips as coming from the Conservative propaganda machine. Yet such material fails most of the tests of the five Ws of Ethics: *Who* benefits from use of PNS items? Only the Conservative party. *Who* loses? The other parties, but also the audience, who are unaware of the dynamics behind such material. *What* does it do to the newsroom's credibility? Among those who know and care, the credibility will suffer. *How* was the information gathered? It wasn't. It walked in the door. *How* was it corroborated for accuracy and fairness? That may be very difficult to achieve. *Why* do the sources do this? For political gain.

The opposition parties were horrified by the creation of the Parliamentary News Service, both for its overt propaganda and because they could not afford to compete.[36]

A cruder form of this exists with government elec-tronic systems. The Saskatchewan government, for instance, for years provided a teletype service to major newsrooms around the province, distributing press releases and similar government data. If journalists tired of the endless material churning out all day, they could turn off the machine ... but this triggered an alarm at the distribution centre, and somebody was sent round to turn it back on.[37]

The Ubiquitous Press Release

By comparison, such techniques make the press release seem a familiar and harmless public relations tool. Journalists have no illusions about the propagandist nature of releases, and yet they know they cannot ignore them, as they may contain the kernel of a news story.[38]

New technology has made things easier for the public relations people and, consequently, that much more challenging for the journalists. There's a psychological pressure that comes with a document delivered, for instance, by the Canada News-Wire: It looks like a news story. It feels like a news story. It's actually a press release.[39]

With the advent of computer-to-computer communications, it is now possible for public relations operatives to deliver messages to the editors' screens. Editors, hence, won't have the usual red flags of official envelopes and promotional letterhead and must prepare themselves psychologically for dealing with such very accessible material. For the editor working all day with a cathode ray tube, the screen *is* the news. The screen provides the window onto the newsroom's computer, which contains all the news gathered by reporters and input by wire services. The message flashed on the screen looks serious, and it may take a special effort to segregate the normal flow of news across that screen from the material provided by external public relations departments.[40]

Covert Methods

In September 1975, Jean Desrosiers, a Canadian Press reporter, interviewed one of the leaders at a strike at the huge E.B. Eddy Co. in Hull, Quebec. But there was never any news story. In reality, Desrosiers worked for the RCMP and had simply passed himself off as a CP reporter, accompanied by an RCMP photographer.

This was far from the first or the last time that police or others have used the press in this way. For instance, in June 1969, officers of the Quebec Provincial Police, in plain clothes, obtained press credentials to the convention of the Union Nationale political party in Quebec City.[41]

Police sometimes simply request reporters' cooperation. Kitty McKinsey, a reporter for the *Ottawa Citizen*, says she rejected a request by an RCMP officer in May 1977 for information about Soviet journalists accredited to the parliamentary press gallery.[42]

In 1988, Reid Morden, head of Canada's spy agency, the Canadian Security Intelligence Service, confirmed that his organization had asked Ottawa TV reporter Charlie Greenwell to 'spy' on two colleagues, one working for La Presse Canadienne (the French arm of Canadian Press) and another working for Radio-Canada (French CBC). Both men had written stories on the spy agency.[43] John Sawatsky notes that this is far from new. What is new is that Canadian journalists are now turning down such requests and talking about it. Why do the spy agencies do it? 'Journalists are valuable to the Security Service because their cover is almost perfect,' says Sawatsky. 'They can snoop around and ask questions without arousing suspicion.'[44]

In the case of spying on Soviet journalists, the justification – at least during the cold war – was that large numbers of USSR journalists were supposedly nothing more than spies in disguise, so they had to be spied on. In the past, both Soviet and US intelligence personnel have apparently used press credentials.[45] But this has been carried a step further by operatives actually employing journalistic techniques. Stein describes KGB officers disguised as journalists passing on 'tips' and even 'news stories' to 'fellow' Western journalists.[46] And J.E. Roper outlines provisions in US law authorizing government undercover agents to 'infiltrate any political, governmental, religious, or news organization.'[47]

Fortunately such ruses appear to be very rarely used in Canada. However, Canadians can be subjected to such harassment abroad. Cheryl Arvidson, Washington correspondent for Cox Newspapers, details attempts by FBI agents to intimidate respected Canadian journalist Donald Sellar in Washington.[48] The agent threatened Sellar with theft charges unless he revealed sources for a series of stories on the cruise missile. The matter was dropped when he refused to cooperate, but Sellar learned during the process that his stories were being read before they ever got to his Canadian office. Evidently, the telephone lines over which he transmitted stories from Washington to Ottawa were being regularly monitored.

What has all this to do with ethics? The answer lies in the reporter's reaction to such approaches and intimidations. Journalists must keep at arm's length from authorities, even when their patriotism is challenged. If Canada is involved directly in a major war, journalists' perspectives *may* be somewhat altered. But this must only happen after mature debate at the highest levels. To preserve their credibility, journalists must avoid at all costs any appearance that they are in collusion with authority.

Such covert activities emphasize the need for constant vigilance on the part of journalists. Not only must the material in front of them – the plain brown envelope – be examined for its news value, but its accuracy must be rigorously challenged and the motives of the senders must be questioned.

The Washington gadfly I.F. Stone once wrote that 'every government is run by liars, and nothing they say should be believed.'[49] While this may seem extreme, Anthony Marro, managing editor of *Newsday*, explains very effectively why governments lie: 'Once the [US] government began running covert operations it had to have cover stories to hide them, and that required government-sanctioned lies. The chief criterion thus was not truth, but just the opposite – developing lies that would be plausible enough to be accepted as truth.'[50]

Leaks and Trial Balloons
While the press release represents a direct, frontal attempt to access media space, leaks and trial balloons are far more devious. The motivation and methods of leakers are legion.[51] What can be safely said is that most people who leak stories to the news media do so to satisfy their own agenda: They may be interested in informing the public in a benevolent way, but they may also be driven by jealousy, anger, fear, or a need

to 'see justice done.' Journalists who receive plain brown envelopes (or any sort of leak) need to ascertain, as clearly as possible, what the leaker's motives are. Those who leak material are, by definition, anonymous, so it's the media – as messenger – who will suffer any consequences from wrong or unbalanced information.

Two examples will make the point. In 1985, Canadian Press distributed a story about Suzanne Blais-Grenier, the new and unpopular federal minister of the environment. Blais-Grenier, a political novice, in Cabinet for less than five months, had already approved major budget cuts to the Canadian Wildlife Service and suggested that services in national parks could be privatized; so it can be assumed that she had angered environmentalists and many of her own staff.

A news story headlined 'Records Show Minister Let Go for "Incompetence, Hysteria"' in the Kingston *Whig-Standard* described two private court cases in which Blais-Grenier was suing a former employer and others for damages following her sacking several years earlier.[52] The news story begins: 'Suzanne Blais-Grenier, in hot water almost from the day she was appointed environment minister, was abruptly fired from her last job and was unable to find other work in her field, court records show.' The story goes on: 'Court documents quote Blais-Grenier as saying she was accused of falsifying minutes of meetings, hysteria, incompetence and intellectual dishonesty.'

The use of the present tense here is revealing: 'Court records show' indicates a continuing event, and in the ninth paragraph of the ten-paragraph story, it is revealed that 'both cases ... were initiated in 1983.' There is, in fact, absolutely nothing new in this story. The court cases were started more than a year before she was appointed and still had not come to trial. Why, then, had the media suddenly reported this? Clearly, Blais-Grenier or her supporters would not suddenly release this material, as they would prefer to avoid such negative reports. It is more likely that her detractors – possibly even disgruntled civil servants in her department – brought this old court case to the media's attention feeling it would help discredit her.

The second incident involved the colourful premier of New Brunswick, Richard Hatfield. In 1984, security officials found a bag of marijuana in the outside pocket

of a suitcase with which he was travelling. News of the discovery was leaked to the media within hours, but Hatfield was not immediately charged. After three weeks, the press broke silence, reporting the find and the current investigation, and a week later he was charged with possession.[53] Some critics wondered whether the find was leaked to the media to ensure that the incident could not be hushed up.[54] Certainly, the media do not normally report that a drug has been found in someone's possession until *after* charges have been laid.[55]

George Bain cites another interesting anecdote in which the *Ottawa Citizen* published a leaked memorandum on the eve of a first ministers' conference on the Constitution.[56] The document implied that if the provincial premiers could not agree on patriating the Constitution (bringing it from London to Ottawa so that Canada would have full sovereignty), the federal government would go it alone. But is this a genuine leak? It might fit more comfortably under the label trial balloon, that species of 'information' beloved by Prime Minister John Diefenbaker. Peter Dempson, Ottawa bureau chief for the Toronto *Telegram*, recalls how he was invited to have tea with the prime minister every Friday afternoon, and 'Dief' would offer snippets of information, provided they were not attributed directly to him. Such material might include details of a proposed Cabinet shuffle, which Dempson would then print, and if public reaction was adverse, Diefenbaker simply dismissed it as press speculation.[57]

Likewise, the Bain example may well have served two covert purposes for the federal government: as a discreet threat to the premiers to persuade them to cooperate and as a way for the government to gauge the country's mood towards federal leadership on the issue. Rather than a leak from some disgruntled employee, it may have been deliberately planted by government.

Whatever the source and means, journalists must examine leaks from all angles, as the motivation of the leaker may be just as important as the content of the leak.

The Media Event

Increasingly, information officers recognize that in the fight for space in the news media their humble news releases get lost. To compensate, they put on an 'event'

– perhaps a modest news conference, but more frequently a happening of some sort.

The trouble with press conferences is that the sponsor is playing with loaded dice. She can choose the time and place for the event; she can select the source to face the media and thoroughly brief that source in advance; she can select whose questions will be answered, and she can shut down the whole event if things get tough.[58] For a participating journalist, all these factors are manipulative, and the situation is exacerbated by the complete lack of spontaneity or exclusivity. The answer to *his* perceptive question is heard by all the other journalists. This is particularly galling for the print reporter who has to wait till tomorrow to see his story published, while broadcasters have long since gone to air with the news revealed by his question.

But if this is not a level playing field, at least the journalists know the nature of the event and can weigh its news value by standard measures. More difficult is the event staged specifically for the media. When angry farmers, for instance, dump truckloads of manure on the legislature steps, it is difficult to ignore. If nothing else, it's good video: a lively thirty-second clip for the evening telecast.

Farmers had a particularly difficult time in Canada in the late 1980s, with economies of scale luring them to buy more land just before land values dropped, mortgage rates skyrocketed, and world wheat prices plummeted. Until then, they did not seem to be well organized to protest or fight back. However, the Canadian Agricultural Movement (CAM) changed all that. Led by Allen Wilford, an Ontario farmer and eventual author of *Farm Gate Defense*, CAM staged many high-profile events deliberately to catch the media's eye. Tom Nunn, then a farm writer for Regina's *Leader-Post*, described one incident in which CAM helped Russell Melnyk, a farmer in Swan Plain, Saskatchewan, who was close to bankruptcy. Publicity, they believed, would buy time, forcing bankers to postpone foreclosure.

CAM contacted reporters in every newsroom they could think of and told them Melnyk would shoot his cattle if bailiffs moved in.

Just imagine TV footage of an angry farmer, broke and crying, pumping bullets into his beloved cattle.

But it never happened. The cattle weren't shot, of course, but CAM had the news coverage it wanted.

We have no choice, us fish in the media. We can't refuse that kind of hook, and CAM's organizers know it, they've read Wilford's book. We're forced to go out there, even if the bailiff never shows up and Melnyk's cows are spared for another day.

But that was just the start. This saga at Swan Plain was pure theatre.

'As soon as the CBC came, they [the Melnyks] turned on the tears,' said one reporter who was on their farm last week. Then Russell Melnyk fumbled with his heart pills – just exactly what you'd expect to see when a farmer goes under.

'When the CBC left, the tears were turned off,' says the reporter. 'It makes you a little cynical.'[59]

Should the media refuse to attend? On the one hand, they suspect the event simply will not happen if the cameras don't show up.[60] On the other hand, they fear that opposition media will run a story, making it look as if they missed something.

Sometimes it is difficult to detect that the event has been manufactured specifically for the media. In 1983, the Canadian Football League championship was to be played in Vancouver, with the champions winning the Grey Cup. The huge silver trophy was duly flown to Vancouver, and the press were invited onto the airport tarmac to meet it as it was brought off a private jet by security guards. Only later did the media learn that the 'photo opportunity' had been manufactured: the cup had in fact arrived on a regular commercial flight two days before.

Sources Fight Back

The polishing of news releases and media events has been accompanied by a polishing of news sources. Increasingly, sources are being groomed to deal with the media so they can get their message across better.

At one level, this is undoubtedly a positive development. A business leader, for instance, may be an excellent money manager but may turn into a nervous wreck at the sight of a microphone. A cabinet minister may be an astute politician, but may be reduced to an incoherent babbler by a tough interviewer. So some intelligent help on how to handle interviews and how to perform in front of microphones and cameras under pressure may be to everyone's advantage.

Indeed, the media may have provoked this training themselves by overly aggressive interview techniques, high-handed editing of less articulate speakers, the sensationalization of material, or the taking of quotations out of context. However, the reverse side of the coin is that some sources have been trained to be even more aggressive and offensive than their interviewers, many of whom in reality are mild-mannered, polite, and inoffensive. An article in the *Globe and Mail Report on Business Magazine* summarized the role of media consultants: 'Consultants teach executives how to rephrase hostile questions, answer reporters in 30 seconds or less and project a trustworthy image.'[61] Such training typically includes mock interviews under hot lights and TV cameras, so the executive learns 'either to duck or to effectively fire back,' and that 'every negative has a positive lining.'[62]

Such training probably does not teach executives to be dishonest, but it certainly prepares them to block and distract questioners, enabling many interviewees to control interviews to a far greater extent than in the past.[63] Such preparation may lead to an escalation in interview-training for journalists, and a subtle dance between reporters and sources to establish at what level their exchange is being conducted.[64]

This process of helping sources deal with the press can be taken to depressing and fatuous extremes. The *UK Press Gazette* uncovered a London workshop for executives entitled 'How to get Press coverage for unnewsworthy products.'[65] The one-day event, costing £247.50 each (about $500), included 'How to make dull and uninteresting products appealing to the media,' and 'How to create news when there is no news.' It would be funny if it wasn't true, and it shows journalists must always be on their guard.

The vast armies of public relations and information officers are dedicated to one prime purpose: getting out positive material about their government, their company, or their client. Their techniques are becoming more sophisticated and their products more pervasive. For the journalist, this means ever-increasing scepticism and sensitivity. As some newspeople like to say, they need 'good bullshit detectors.'

But in addition to this constant vigilance against manipulation from 'the enemy without,' journalists also have to be wary of the enemy within. The next chapters examine ways in which journalists may themselves decide to withhold news as well as one other way news can be manipulated: the hoax.

TOUGH CALLS

1 Your town police chief is planning a major drug bust but needs to reinforce the credibility of his undercover agent. He promises you an exclusive story if your paper will publish a fake report that the agent has been charged with robbery and released on bail. How do you handle this?

2 A press release warns of a danger of high radon gas leakage in your community. Do you run the report? What are the considerations? Does it make a difference if the release comes from a company that makes radon gas detectors?

3 A local group decides to draw attention to poverty by holding a mock auction of the premier's home, complete with fast-talking auctioneer. It would make great video for your newscast tonight. How do you handle the event?

4 A Métis group calls your TV newsroom at noon to announce they will blockade an important highway to support various demands. You ask when this will happen. 'When can you get here?' replies the caller. How do you handle this?

8 To Press or to Suppress?

Erwin Krickhahn was dying of Lou Gehrig's disease when he decided to invite the media to watch him commit suicide. He hoped his gesture would help persuade Parliament to legalize assisted suicides. But for the media, it posed some fiendish questions. Would attending the event influence the event itself? Was it fair to assign a reporter/photographer to cover such an event? Would newspeople attending the event have any ethical requirement to stop the suicide? Would the presence of television cameras, lights, cables, photographers, tape recorders, trucks, reporters, and possibly even US network satellite transmitters turn the event into a media circus and devalue or even undermine the man's message? Would such a media circus sacrifice Krickhahn's dignity? Was Krickhahn acting in his own best interest, or was he being manipulated by the Right to Die Society of Canada?

In the end, only the *Toronto Sun* said it would assign a reporter to the suicide. The other media chose to abstain and said they would cover the story by assigning reporters to a 'deathwatch' outside Krickhahn's home. So for most journalists, the actual suicide was a story *not* to cover.[1]

Journalism is, in fact, partly an exercise in what to leave out, so the criteria for leaving things out are crucially important. Grounds for withholding material may include invading people's privacy, vulgar language, violence, nudity, and sexism (see subsequent chapters). Advertising may also be rejected on the grounds that it is offensive (X-rated movies) or destructive

(tobacco ads or 'happy hours' encouraging people to drink on their way home from work).[2] News stories are often omitted from the media simply for reasons of space. And it must be admitted that on occasion stories are simply missed: journalists do not stumble on them or sources shield them from the media.

A number of other situations can now be added to this list. However, it might first be useful to examine some terms. Even at this stage, it may be maintained by some that withholding material from the audience amounts to censorship and suppressing the news; that except in situations of mandatory withholding (what Lawrence Kohlberg would characterize as rule obedience, with respect to such laws as privacy, libel, and contempt of court), the media 'must' publish, and that to act otherwise is to set oneself up as a community censor, sanitizing the news and protecting the audience from reality.

Terms such as 'censor' and 'suppress' are, however, laden with emotional overtones – what S.I. Hayakawa would call 'snarl' words. Censorship involves the involuntary withholding of material in compliance with a powerful outside agency – typically government or a military regime.[3] Suppression can mean quelling, putting an end to something, again in a militaristic, involuntary sense. But it can also simply mean withholding or restraint, and it is in this spirit of *self*-restraint, or *self*-control that this topic is addressed. It is possible and sometimes desirable, it will be argued, for journalists to exercise restraint for their own or the public good.[4]

At the simplest level, the journalist already selects the elements of a news story based on a series of criteria (albeit ill-defined) that include such things as human interest, proximity, and immediacy. Therefore, by definition, the journalist 'withholds' material that is uninteresting, remote, or old. And in some media there are doubtless occasions when material is withheld from public consumption because of pressures brought on the newsroom by internal/external forces such as the proprietor (who may want to please a friend or placate an angry advertiser). In a more proactive sense, however, the following situations may lend themselves to restrained reporting:

1 Wartime
2 Civil emergencies
3 Where harm may result
4 Copycat crimes
5 How-to details of crimes
6 Government requests
7 Management requests
8 Embargoes
9 Privacy
10 The newsroom may be injured
11 Religious topics
12 Propaganda
13 Missed stories.

To explore these in some detail:

1 **Wartime.** The media react with differing degrees of patriotism to war. Large elements of the British press threw themselves into both the Falklands War and the Gulf War with a nationalistic zeal verging on jingoism.[5]

In Canada, there has been no media equivalent since the Second World War, although the coverage of the Vietnam War was coloured significantly by the supply of war news, predominantly via the Associated Press. However, during the Second World War there was considerable media support for the cause – mirroring popular support – which led to sympathetic treatment of the Allied side and willing acceptance of Allied reporting restrictions, such as troop movements and casualty scores.[6] This is neither necessarily wrong nor unexpected, but has to be taken into account when categorizing situations where news may be willingly withheld.

The closest that Canada has come to wartime since 1945 was during the FLQ Crisis of 1970. The Front de

Liberation du Québec was apparently staging an armed insurrection, and the government's response was to invoke the War Measures Act, which, among other things, imposed war-style censorship on the media. When the rebels issued a 'manifesto' of demands, the government ordered the media not to broadcast it.

2 **Civil emergencies.** Occasionally, when emergencies arise in a community, it may be in the public interest to temporarily withhold some details. This is likely to occur rarely, however. For instance, in 1985, the eleven-person police force of Chatham, New Brunswick, went on strike. The police chief and his deputy tried to control the town with the help of four security guards, but one Saturday night in June a mob began smashing windows. Photographers who tried taking pictures were turned on by the crowd – and by the police chief. 'These are tough but fun-loving people,' chief Dan Allen was quoted as saying, 'and you, all you news people, are starting the violence.'[7] Allen threatened to jail the media and confiscate photographic equipment. His own outburst certainly could not have endeared himself to the press, who may have grown all the more determined to cover the story. But did their presence alter the nature of the event? Did the cameras and lights provoke or aggravate the situation?

3 **Where harm may result.** The hostages in Tehran incident could be categorized, in a sense, as 'wartime' or as an 'emergency.' However, in no sense was Canada at war. The incident involved a number of US citizens sheltering in the Canadian embassy in Tehran and ultimately being smuggled out. One Canadian journalist, Gerard Pelletier, had details of the story weeks before the hostages escaped. He agreed to sit on the story until the group was safe, although his first journalistic instinct was to publish what was, perhaps, the scoop of a lifetime. But he recognized that revealing even his simple arithmetic – that seven Americans were unaccounted for after the Iranians stormed the US Embassy – would almost certainly jeopardize their escape if not their lives. This doubtless pleased the government, but it can scarcely be labelled censorship.

Events such as kidnappings, hostage-takings, and terrorism can be severely hampered by media activity. During a panel discussion on covering such events,

Global television's Peter Trueman commented: 'We have an obligation during a hostage-taking not to publish things which are of advantage to the terrorists.'[8] This was echoed by Mark Starowicz, producer of the CBC's *The Journal*. Starowicz made the point that the media should not aid the perpetrators of crimes to make a profit.[9]

A clear case of potential interference occurred years ago in Ontario. Joe Scanlon, then a Carleton University journalism professor, tells how a reporter phoned a hostage-taker *in medias res* and asked why he was asking only $10,000 in ransom. The thug decided to increase his demand, and although the incident was finally settled peacefully with no money changing hands, 'the conversation is still remembered in police circles as irresponsible, an example of unethical media interference in police operations.'[10] Scanlon also notes that reporters can interfere with ongoing events by tying up the telephone lines, trying to reach the protagonists.

After a kidnapping in Montreal, police thanked the media for sitting tight. A schoolgirl was kidnapped but subsequently rescued and a man was charged. Reporters knew about the ongoing drama but withheld all reports until the child was safe.[11]

In other situations, individuals may contact journalists to act as intermediaries – typically, during a prison riot or breakout. Presumably the journalist has been chosen because she is seen as 'objective' or even sympathetic to the cause, and she must then be careful to keep a distance from the criminals, yet still retain their trust. Scanlon, who has made a special study of hostage and terrorist situations, urges journalists to catechize themselves before becoming involved in such scenarios to identify the likely effects, both immediate and indirect.[12]

The potential for harm is sometimes difficult to assess. Does publishing a budget before it is officially released cause harm? Debate still rages over the April 1989 'Doug Small/Global incident,' in which a TV station acquired details of a budget designed to be released the following day and immediately broadcast them. Shortly after, in October 1989, another Ottawa station acquired a summary of the federal auditor-general's report before release, but decided to withhold it.

Why were the two incidents treated differently? In the first incident, Ottawa reporter Doug Small acquired a copy of the *Budget-in-Brief*, a pamphlet summarizing the following day's event. He gleefully waved the document on camera, revealing the contents in the belief that if *he* had a copy, others might too, and they might therefore be benefitting financially from this exclusive advance knowledge. Many people criticized Global TV for releasing the contents, rather than merely reporting that the pamphlet had been released and urging the finance minister to act quickly.[13] (Conceivably, the minister could have stood up in the Commons that evening and released the budget.) Anthony Westell, director of the Carleton University School of Journalism, wrote subsequently that journalists should keep secrets only in 'exceptional circumstances, when there is a clear public interest in keeping quiet.'[14] But this, surely, was an exceptional situation, possibly influencing stock markets and providing scofflaws with an opportunity to make a quick buck.

The second leak involved Carleton anthropology student Heather Waite, who rented a videotape player in Ottawa one weekend and found in it a tape summarizing the auditor-general's report, due for release in the House of Commons the following Tuesday. She contacted CJOH-TV, the local CTV affiliate. Managing editor Dave McGinn decided to withhold the material: 'It would have been a great scoop, but that's not how the world works,' he said. 'We considered it not necessarily to be in the public interest to release this early.'[15] After the report was read in Parliament, CJOH described the leak and showed a tape of Waite returning the videotape to the auditor-general. McGinn went on to differentiate the two incidents, on the basis of potential damage. Budget information could be used for personal gain, he said. But in both incidents, the real 'news' was the leak, not the contents of the documents.

4 **Situations potentially leading to copycat crimes.**[16] The Tylenol incident brought the media face-to-face with the problem of copycat crimes. In late 1982, seven people were killed in the Chicago area after taking the pain reliever, which had been laced with cyanide. Reports of murders cannot be suppressed, and there was clearly a need to alert other people in the community to the danger. But similar, subsequent incidents may well

have been inspired by reports of the first outbreak. The US Food and Drug Administration (FDA) found that reports of tampering more than doubled in the two months after the Chicago incident. And when four more deaths occurred in 1986, reports of tampering increased by thirteen-fold, causing $5-million worth of extra FDA investigations.[17] When another Tylenol death was widely reported in Nashville, Tennessee, police were so overwhelmed with further allegations of tampering that they threatened to give lie-detector tests to those complaining and to charge anybody suspected of making a false complaint. The complaints abruptly stopped – and the Nasville incident was found to be suicide.[18]

Similarly, reports of suicides, at least among juveniles, appear to lead to an outbreak of other teenage suicides. US sociologists Steven Stack and David Phillips conducted independent studies of suicide patterns in the United States and found significant copycat correlations. 'The imitative effect was most apparent among young males,' concluded Stack.[19]

Few newsrooms have firm guidelines on handling suicides, but even if they do, they will likely make exceptions. For instance, farmer suicides are seen as a serious reflection of the recession on the Canadian prairies and, therefore, may get reported where other deaths do not. Some newsrooms feel the solution is not to mention how the person died in news stories or obituaries – in effect 'laundering' the news and protecting the community from reality. Discussing the question in the *Washington Journalism Review*, two journalists, Jaben and Hill, cite the managing editor of the *Des Moines Register*, Arnold Garson: 'I've never believed that society cures its problems by sweeping them under the carpet. In fact, the only way to solve problems is to deal with them openly. If the cause of death is self-inflicted, that's what we say. The purpose of the obituary is to inform readers, not necessarily to make the families happy.'[20]

Even would-be suicides pose a problem. The media cannot pretend that nothing happened if a massive crowd has gathered downtown to watch a man threatening to jump off a high-rise parking building. But there could be a possibility of others doing the same thing just for publicity. If no charges are laid, this is not only a victimless crime – it's a crimeless crime. As a newspaper-of-record, the paper should resist the temptation to use numerous pictures of the man threatening to jump and of police talking him down and, instead, just run a couple of inches of copy explaining the traffic jam.

The trouble with reporting such incidents is that they may lead to others; the trouble with *not* reporting them, argues reporter Pamela Wallin, is that the public will then distrust the media. Wallin, then Ottawa reporter for CTV, said in an after-dinner speech that journalists have an obligation to report terrorist events, even if they inspire further terrorism. 'Friends, family and fellow human beings are involved,' she said. 'The need to know outweighs the dangers of selective silence. If we encourage them, it's unfortunately a sad commentary on our society.'[21] Wallin was referring to the recent hijacking of the cruise ship *Achille Lauro*, which would, indeed, have been difficult to keep quiet. But Wallin's argument, that journalists are only dealing with facts and 'We just take the snapshots' implies an unwillingness to take any responsibility for their actions. Once again, like many others taking this position, she overlooks the fact that those 'snapshots' are carefully selected every day. It's not a matter of *if* journalists leave out information; it's a question of Which and Why.

Less problematic are bomb threats. Most media simply ignore reports of bomb threats, especially those involving schools around examination time, as one report leads to a flurry of repetitions. After Regina's *Leader-Post* did a profile of the local bomb squad in the mid-1970s, a bomb turned up in a local school – the first in twenty years.[22]

And have razor blades ever been found on a waterslide? Word-of-mouth reports that razor blades have been placed on waterslides are almost as old as the slides themselves, taking on a folk mythology of their own. But media very wisely steer clear of ever reporting such tales.

On occasion, the media may decide to avoid a story because of some other potential harm. For instance, in the early 1980s, the Regina *Leader-Post* considered doing a feature on the local SWAT team but demurred – explained editorial writer Will Chabun – for fear that somebody might decide to 'take them on.'[23]

5 **How-to details of crimes.** The media would be ill-advised to run stories on how to commit crimes or perform antisocial acts. But they cannot be expected to decline to publish any details for fear that somebody, somewhere, might emulate them. However, a man who was convicted of ten trust company robberies told a British Columbia court he learned his particular method from a story in the *New York Times*.[24] (Perhaps the moral of this story is that the banking institutions should read the press to learn what sort of tricks to expect and to prepare for them.)

The media can hardly be blamed for reporting crimes, as long as they do not provide the recipe for success. But sometimes even the tone of a piece may be an incentive. For instance, a book review in the *Calgary Herald* some years ago might have given the impression that growing marijuana was now socially acceptable – although it remained a criminal offence. The writer cheerfully asserted 'grass has almost achieved respectability' and suggested that the problem of supply could be solved by growing one's own, with the help of the US publication *Indoor Marijuana Horticulture*. The writer quoted the head of the police drug squad as praising the book for its accuracy. He noted that cannabis 'is no more difficult to grow than tomatoes or carrots,' had a high street value, and that local courts were lenient with offenders. He listed the equipment necessary and where it could be purchased locally.[25] The tone of the whole article, therefore, was somewhat laudatory, appearing to condone or even encourage flouting the law. While it certainly would not make law-breakers out of people who did not wish to break the law, it might give enough impetus to those who would like to grow their own drugs but had always assumed there were too many obstacles. (After all, the Calgary climate is scarcely equatorial, and the average apartment is not a logical place to grow six-foot plants.) This does not mean the article should not have been written, but editors might have questioned whether the tone was suitable and whether the benefits would outweigh the loss of respect accruing from such an approach.[26]

6 **Government requests.** The authorities frequently have two requests for the media, involving either withholding or revealing material: 'Would you please leave out some information that you have?' or 'Would you please give us some information that you have?' It is vitally important that the media keep a distance from authority figures such as government and police, and they must consider very carefully the implications of complying with either request. (On the second question, involving revealing information to authorities, especially names of sources, see Chapter 12, 'Naming Names and Revealing Sources.')

Authorities will have varying reasons for wanting material withheld, ranging from protecting themselves because of reprehensible activity to a genuine fear that premature publicity will damage an important activity, such as acquiring a block of land for a major development. All must be measured by the journalists in terms of what will best serve the community in the long run, rather than what will serve the source in the short run.

Typically, for instance, law enforcement agencies are more comfortable giving than receiving criticism (giving speeding tickets or arresting a murderer is all about criticizing antisocial behaviour). But the police have to recognize that their own activity must withstand the spotlight of publicity and even robust criticism. Both the public *and* the police were furious at revelations of RCMP barn burning and burglaries. In 1989, when the *Winnipeg Free Press* covered the Manitoba Native Justice Inquiry, which revealed considerable racial discrimination by the police against the Native population, the newspaper was flooded with complaints blaming the reporters for the contents of the story.

Much more insidious was an incident some twenty years ago when the city of Kitchener decided to redevelop its historic downtown core. The council took the media into their confidence, urging them to sit on the story until it was virtually signed and sealed. Concluded Hugh Winsor, *Globe and Mail* reporter: 'The burghers were able to operate this way because Kitchener's only newspaper, the *Kitchener-Waterloo Record*, and the city's radio and television stations opted to be "good corporate citizens," rather than news operations and withheld all news of the development until the deal had been approved at a secret meeting of council.'[27] (On the positive side, several years later the *Record* ran some pictures implying police brutality – pictures the police department definitely did not want published.)[28]

7 **Management requests.** There is little hard evidence that media proprietors interfere with newsroom decisions.[29] But the CIJ *Bulletin* alleged that Norman Klenman, co-owner of CKVU-TV in Vancouver, ordered his newsroom to ignore two days of court hearings regarding ownership of the station, resulting in one journalist resigning in protest.[30]

In general, the media are very slow to report on themselves. For instance, the meetings of the Canadian Daily Newspaper Publishers Association were closed to the press until the 1980s. But media are big business – major corporations, many listed on the stock markets, with a huge labour force. The news organizations should be seen to be as newsworthy as any other large and influential unit in society.

8 **Embargoes.** The media generally respect embargoes – release times imposed by news sources – in order to retain the sources' cooperation[31] and because of the feeling that the embargo gives everyone equal treatment. However, the equality is only within specific media. An embargo of 6 P.M. today is equally fair to two competing morning papers – but it gives radio the edge (for a 6 P.M. newscast), and even television gets a better break than the morning papers. It becomes increasingly apparent that embargoes are self-serving, used by politicians, for instance, to control the media's ability to get reaction to a story (see Chapter 9, 'Playing Fast and Loose with the Truth').

9 **Privacy.** Invasion of privacy, which will be explored in Chapter 11, often involves conscious withholding of information, such as the identification of individuals in the news. One such incident, for instance, occurred in 1989 when media in Wilmette, a Chicago suburb, learned that a child with AIDS was in a local school. The journalists agreed to protect the child's identity so he could remain in school without hysterical public reaction (as happened in some other communities), and they did so until after he died.[32] The media also tend to respect privacy in such matters as divorce cases.

Another form of protecting individual privacy can occur if the press decides to protect 'public' individuals out of a sense of respect. It may be, with the current climate of 'disrespect' for leaders, that this will not recur. However, Ottawa columnist Charles Lynch tells two anecdotes that illustrate the point. In one, he describes Winston Churchill leading the armies of liberation into Germany and urinating into the Rhine as a victory gesture.[33] The incident was not reported. 'There was a reverence, in those days, for Churchill and Roosevelt,' he said in an interview.[34] Lynch also told the interviewer he regretted the media did not write sooner about the breakdown of Prime Minister Trudeau's marriage. The reason the story was withheld, he said, was, 'A sense of propriety. A sense of disbelief.'[35] In retrospect, he felt uncomfortable covering up a story that everybody was talking about on Parliament Hill.

Generally, today, however, the media are no respecters of persons, and as a result a lot more gets into the press than some public people would prefer. This is probably all to the good, as politicians should not be dictating what goes in the press. The journalists must never abrogate that responsibility. But the rallying cry of 'We're in the business of disclosure; we're not censors' may just muddy the waters.[36]

10 **The newsroom may be injured.** It is not unnatural for journalists to want to withhold stories that show them in a questionable light. When a young woman was arrested at a prairie airport for joking that she had a bomb in her bag, the news director of the local television station said, 'Run the story!' – although the girl was his daughter. Some editors might have chosen otherwise.

One weekly newspaper editor decided he was going to 'suppress' his local MLA. Frank Wilson, publisher of the Watrous, Saskatchewan, *Manitou*, ruled that MLA Eric Upshall was using his weekly newspaper column for purely political purposes. Wilson maintained that the columns simply repeated material already covered in the media, and that they were produced by the Opposition party office, not by Upshall. He therefore decided the columns should not be given a 'high priority.' Many weekly papers across the country routinely run such columns by MLAs and MPs, believing it is important for elected officials to report to their constituencies on their activities. But the space is not theirs by right, and if the politicians abuse the privilege, as many do, the publishers have every right to cut them off. Upshall resorted to buying advertisements in the *Manitou* to get his message across, but evidently had not learnt the lesson, as the ads contained vitriolic attacks on the government, instead of reports of his own activity.

11 **Religious topics.** It's far from an iron-clad rule, but traditionally many newspeople have avoided church-related topics, knowing that they are controversial. Church news often remains under-reported, and only one or two Canadian newsrooms have reporters assigned to extensive coverage of the religion beat. Few editorials are written on religion-oriented topics, and very little investigative journalism touches this rich field. It is possible that the Mt. Cashel incident is related to this. When charges of sexual assault were brought against several lay-brothers who ran the Mt. Cashel Orphanage in Newfoundland, it emerged that there had been a widespread cover-up of the incidents over many years. Commented Kevin Fox, the *Globe and Mail's* Atlantic bureau chief: 'For more than 14 years the media of St. John's allowed the sickening physical and sexual abuse suffered by the boys at Mount Cashel orphanage to be the best known secret in Newfoundland.'[37]

Fox points out that evidence emerged during the 1990 public inquiry that at least one local news manager had been aware of the events but preferred to let the church solve the problems 'internally,' without publicity. Fox concluded: 'The challenge for the Newfoundland media now is to prove that the era of shameful silence is finally behind them.'[38]

12 **Propaganda.** Journalists have to make ongoing decisions about news that 'walks in the door.' They must avoid missing stories, especially if the competition has them, but must also guard against being 'used' by propagandists. Thus when a citizen called ITV news in Edmonton in 1988 to call a news conference to denounce French-Canadians ('We're being taken over by the Frenchies!'), the decision was made to ignore the 'event' (see next chapter).

13 **Missed stories.** For more than a decade, a team of news watchers in the United States have gathered an annual list of stories overlooked by the media, under the rubric of 'Project Censored.'[39]

The title is perhaps a little unfair – loaded words, again – as it implies that all the stories listed have been deliberately suppressed, presumably for the wrong rea-

sons. But the listing has made people, especially journalists, aware of how vulnerable they are, how easy it is to make a poor judgment call on a story or to play follow-the-leader, relying on somebody else to set the news agenda (see previous chapter). The founder of Project Censored, communications professor Carl Jensen, concluded that at least 250 major stories had been missed by the US news media during the first ten years of the project's existence.[40] What sort of stories?

- Risk of nuclear disaster with the space shuttle carrying radioactive plutonium.
- The dangers of food irradiation, despite US plans to make it widely available within ten years.
- Acid rain as a threat to human life as well as crops, trees, and fish.
- CIA payments to at least fifteen Honduran journalists and eight Costa Rican journalists to provide biased reports in favour of the Contras.
- Nerve gas being manufactured in at least forty-six US communities, even though the military was ordered to dispose of the materials.
- The apparent increase in the number of newborn babies with serious abnormalities in the US.
- The genocide of up to 200,000 people in East Timor (one-third of the population) as a result of Indonesian policy.

Jensen reported that many explanations for missing the stories were offered by journalists, including:

- The source is not reliable.
- The story is still continuing and so can't be written yet.
- It is not timely.
- It is expensive. Investigative journalism is costly, and so are libel suits.
- It is not in the nation's best interest.
- It is too complex for the public.

Jensen concluded that the big stories are missed not because of any vast media conspiracy but because of ineptitude, second-guessing, and nervousness.[41]

Cooperating with Authority

The other side of the coin, however, is that while government and law-enforcement agencies may well ask the media to withhold material, they may on other occasions demand the cooperation of the press, especially in surrendering material – reporters' notes, videotape, etc. Frequently, this is achieved by 'force' – the use of search warrants. Such pressure is very difficult to withstand, and the media that have opposed this, such as the *Edmonton Journal* and the *Ottawa Citizen*, are to be commended for their spirited fight. It is expensive and intimidating to take on the full weight of the federal government (which is what the papers have done by challenging newsroom searches all the way to the Supreme Court), but both the community and the media will benefit from such challenges.[42]

During the 1970s, there was a spate of such direct newsroom interventions by law or para-law agencies.[43] Creation of the 1982 Charter of Rights, which formally enunciated freedom of the press, gave pause to some of the activities but certainly has not stopped them.[44] (Similar pressure is evident in Great Britain.)[45]

The evidence suggests, therefore, that some elements of the law enforcement field feel that the news media have a role – as the British police put it – in 'helping with our inquiries.' But journalists do not exist to make the work of the police easier. Certainly they should not *obstruct* police work, but it would be highly detrimental for the media to be seen as an arm of the law, ready accomplices of authority against non-conforming elements in society. It may be necessary to refuse even the simplest police requests to avoid such a perception.

However, two elements should be taken into account. If the police simply require copies of, say, a videotape that has already been aired or a story that has already been printed, the media are in no way compromising themselves by cooperating. They would do the same for any citizen. It is the other material that is so vulnerable – video 'outs' and reporters' notebooks and address books. Once again, such decisions can be facilitated by consulting the five *W*s of ethics, particularly asking the question: 'Who stands to benefit the most?'

Challenging search warrants is more difficult but is, nonetheless, necessary. Newsrooms may just have to budget for this as a cost of doing business. Fortunately, more heavy-handed actions are relatively rare in Canada – the tactics of subordinates rather than the conscious plan of policymakers trying to restrain news flow. When autocrats want to muzzle the press, they are more likely to use the injunction as their tool.

TOUGH CALLS

1 Three freight cars have been derailed on a CN spur line three kilometres from town. The RCMP ask you, as local radio station news director, to withhold the story as the tanks contain liquified ammonia gas. The gas can burn flesh and cause blindness, and they do not want onlookers attracted to the site. What questions should you ask the police? What will you likely decide? If there are homes in the area of the accident, will it make a difference to your decision?

2 The *New York Times*' motto is All the News That's Fit to Print. Is this ethical?

3 When Harvey Southam, scion of the Southam family, died in Toronto, many papers, including his 'hometown' paper, the *Vancouver Sun*, declined, out of respect for the family, to report that he had committed suicide. Was that an appropriate decision?

4 A local man is killed in a highway accident. As a daily paper reporter, you recall that the man was in and out of jail, once was charged after barricading himself in his home against police, and regularly flew a swastika flag outside his home. You mention all this in your news story, but several readers are outraged at your disrespect for the dead. How should the story have been handled?

5 You learn of a hostage-taking from your police scanner. When you arrive, you find that the wild, screaming gunman is demanding to talk to a reporter. The chief negotiator asks for your press card and notebook. Using your card and posing as a reporter, the negotiator goes in, persuades the gunman to come down to 'the newsroom' for an interview, and the man is then safely disarmed and arrested. Two days later, you try to interview the gunman's wife, but she refuses, asking, 'How do I know you're even a newspaper reporter?' The journalists' association subsequently condemns your action as 'deplorable.' Did you make the right decision?

Playing Fast and Loose with the Truth

Truth itself is a slippery subject. I have suggested that deciding which elements of truth are 'newsworthy' is often difficult and that ascertaining what is true is complex. This is aggravated by pressure from some interest groups to leave things out (to avoid offending some readers) or put things in (to satisfy the curiosity of others), and by the pressures of authorities or public relations operatives to leave things out (to protect the community or particular clients) or put things in (to make their clients look good).

So the pressures on the press are considerable. The journalist is virtually besieged with complex decisions, made all the more difficult by an increasing penchant on the part of some governments to lie. Truth may be further compromised by deliberate attempts to trick the media. It can also be jeopardized by several newsroom-driven activities: the re-creating of news events (so-called docudramas or simulations) to make the news more 'entertaining'; dubious reporting techniques (such as lying to obtain information, which can be driven by desperation or competition); and even by the theft of words – plagiarism.

Hoaxing the Media

Over the past few decades, many people have reported seeing flying saucers, and the news media have treated such reports with healthy scepticism. Occasionally, citizens have produced pictures of strange flying objects, and the news media have printed them, with carefully worded captions using terms such as 'claimed.'

But a sighting near Atlanta, Georgia, in 1953 was different. Not only were there *two* witnesses, but when the craft landed the men managed to shoot one of the aliens, retrieve the body, and rush it – with great presence of mind – to the newspaper office. The *Atlanta Constitution*'s front-page headline next morning was riveting: **Hairless Critter Killed, 2 'Escape.'** There was only one problem. The whole thing was a hoax. The 'hairless critter' was simply a pet rhesus monkey that had been shot, shaved, and had its tail cut off.[1] The motivation for this little jape was nothing more than a bar room bet. One man bet his friends that he could get his name on the front page of the local daily. In retrospect, it is very easy to laugh at the newspaper's gullibility in this incident. Could they really not tell the difference between a monkey and a Martian? But the point, for succeeding generations of journalists, is that there is a perpetual procession of people who would like to hoax the media, or hoax the public through the media, and they must be permanently on guard – not cynical, but sceptical, especially of the bizarre, the unlikely, or the incredible. This does not mean journalists must simply disbelieve everything they encounter; they must call on more sources, find more experts.

Some more examples:

1970: A pet shop owner in England finally succeeded in cross-breeding dogs and cats. Pictures of the cute offspring – called dats – were distributed by the Reuter news agency and were carried prominently across North America. 'Just joking!' said Roy Tutt later about his perfectly normal mongrel pups.[2]

1972: The carcass of the fabled Loch Ness washed ashore and was pictured in many North American newspapers. April Fool's![3]

1972: Reuters carried several stories about a wild girl running with the kangaroos on the plains of western Australian ... including the final revelation that the tale and pictures were cooked up in a remote bar.[4]

1972: Associated Press reported that a Los Angeles police officer was injured when he was 'bombed' from an upstairs window with a fifty-one-pound water-melon. But the melon, which the officers told news-people was being held as evidence, was actually just a police station snack.[5]

1981: A scientist announced in New York that he had developed allergy pills made from crushed cock-roaches. The story ran in 100 US dailies and was only revealed as a hoax two months later.[6]

Arch-villain in many such incidents in the United States is Joey Skaggs, a communications teacher at the School of Visual Arts in New York. Skaggs apparently feels he has a vocation to hoax the media and does it with great regularity.[7] Skaggs claims part of his moti-vation is to persuade the media to check their sources more thoroughly,[8] though there is some evidence he revels in the media attention and gets lucrative speak-ing engagements from the activities.[9]

Sometimes the hoaxer's motivation is a bet; at other times some wily citizen sees this as a good way to make some quick money from the media. Whatever the rea-son, hoaxes are apparently widespread enough to fill an entire book.[10]

In the Canadian context, four incidents stand out, illustrating several different aspects of the phenomenon.

During the FLQ crisis of 1970, in which the War Measures Act was invoked because of threats of armed insurrection, a woman in Hull, Quebec, was tortured by the dissidents, who released her with an awful mes-sage that topped the Saturday *Vancouver Sun*: New FLQ Warning: 'Women and Children Next' Hull Torture 'Message to PM.' It was a fearful development at a time of high tension.[11] It was also a fabrication. Several days later, a tiny story well inside the paper said the torture marks were apparently self-inflicted.

A 1981 incident began as a small prank by an

Ontario university student. Victor Notaro, nineteen, went from Welland, Ontario, to Western Michigan University to play university soccer. From there he phoned his hometown paper, the *Welland Tribune*, with a fictitious report that he had been selected for a (non-existent) Canadian junior soccer team, training in Michigan. The story ran. Notaro wrote another. And very soon he was filing regular reports of the team's success – with him as star player – culminating a year later in an illusory World Cup tournament in Australia. The reports were picked up by Canadian Press and distributed widely, until a *Toronto Star* sports writer got suspicious and uncovered the hoax.[12]

In 1985, the *Toronto Star* was the victim, conned by another teenager who sold the paper a picture of a tor-nado that swept through central Ontario. The twister was real enough – but the 14-year-old had simply rephotographed a picture in the *Barrie Examiner* of a tornado that had occurred earlier in the US.[13]

In the same year, a bizarre incident rocked the *Edmonton Journal*. The front page on Tuesday 10 September had a scarlet streamer headline across the entire top: Dead Mouse in the Dog Biscuits Stuns Shopper. The story reported that a woman 'who didn't wish to be identi-fied' had found a shrivelled, dead mouse in a bulk food store bin and implied that ants were to be found in other products from other bulk food stores.[14]

The story caused consternation among bulk food shop operators in the community (one of whom was a major advertiser). A smaller story on Wednesday reported that the dead mouse was probably dried veg-etable matter, and the anonymous woman was the bylined reporter. A Thursday story, headlined '*Journal* rouses anger with its handling of false story,' con-firmed the 'mouse' was inanimate, included a full apology to readers and shops, and announced that the reporter had been fired.[15]

The whole incident is curious because it was not intended as a hoax. The reporter evidently believed she'd found a dead mouse in a food bin and felt that it should be reported, but that it was inappropriate to write about the experience in the first person.

These four incidents are remarkably different. In the FLQ case, the hoaxer is perhaps motivated by her own psychological problems and is attempting to attract attention by going to police and thus, unwittingly, the press. The press get drawn into such hoaxes willy-nilly. If the sources (here, the police) accept the story at face value, it gains in authenticity when passed on by them to the media.

Such fakery is difficult to guard against, however sceptical journalists may be. Even the fake soccer tournament and the fake tornado photo are tricky to spot as fakes before publication. Should the *Toronto Star* picture editor have recognized the boy's tornado shot as being lifted from the *Barrie Examiner* or remembered it from the earlier wire photo? Most tornados look much alike. Certainly there were suspicious elements in the soccer story, as the series developed.

The mouse incident had the imprimatur of a colleague. It was not a hoax, yet the story that appeared gave a seriously distorted picture of the bulk food industry. When a staff reporter writes something, desk editors will assume they can trust his or her judgment. But it's awfully easy for there to be a breakdown in communication on deadline. The reporter subsequently sued the newspaper for libel, and the *Journal* settled out of court. The implication is that some of those five Ws didn't get asked, either by the reporter *or* the desk, in the rush to publish a good story. *Where* should the story appear? (Did it really rate the top of page 1?) *When* should it be published? (Couldn't the story have waited till the next day, in order to authenticate the claims?) *How* was the story corroborated? (Was the reporter herself an expert, or were other experts consulted to confirm her suspicions?) (That writer was unfortunate in that her story came fairly soon after the Janet Cooke incident at the *Washington Post*, which will remain as a cautionary tale in North American newsrooms for decades to come.)[16]

In terms of determined jokers or pathological liars, there are generally few things the media can do to totally protect themselves. It may help to put two reporters onto sensitive stories, to back each other up and check each other; it may help to tape sensitive interviews and recheck facts again and again.[17]

But bogus submissions are even harder to check, as there is such a vast flow of material into newsrooms, particularly in the vulnerable areas of letters-to-the-editor, obituaries, and announcements of marriage, birth, or engagement. Random checks and a sixth sense amongst editors may help. Letter writers should be required to give their name, address, and phone number, and their authenticity should be checked by phone. Obituaries should be checked if they do not come directly from a trusted funeral home. Birth announcements should be checked with the hospital. Weddings can be confirmed with the minister. It is time-consuming and expensive, but it may save considerable embarrassment later.

The 'all-news' concept may increase the danger of hoaxes on the media. The insatiable hunger for material, to feed the gaping maw of twenty-four-hours-a-day news, can make the media vulnerable. This may be further aggravated by improved technology. CNN, the American all-news network, has made it clear it will buy amateur video, which would have been unthinkable a decade ago.

So scepticism – especially around April 1st – may be increasingly necessary in newsrooms, along with a willingness to admit errors.

Hoaxes by the Media

Hoaxes by journalists themselves have a long – if not honourable – history, and so perhaps journalists are to blame for the whole game. Among the first in North America was the entirely fictitious New York Zoo disaster of 1844.[18]

Orson Welles's 'War of the Worlds' broadcast as war was breaking out in Europe was one of the most celebrated and horrific examples in this century. But by far the most popular excuse for a little knavery is April Fool's Day.[19]

Many Canadian media have played jokes on April 1st, with mixed results. In Western journalistic folklore, for instance, there are tales of the CBC announcing that Mt. Blackstrap, Saskatchewan (a tiny manmade ski hill in the middle of the prairies), had suffered a volcanic eruption; and of Vancouver CBC revealing that a smugglers' tunnel had been discovered under the Fraser River in British Columbia.

Among Canada's most enjoyable news stories were two 1960s Canadian Press features on the hard-drinking, hard-swearing Carcross Parrot, and its subsequent demise (just before the television cameras arrived). It

Back in the 1970s, an exuberant Campbell River *Upper Islander* liked to entertain its audience. One spoof, printed on pink paper, was a 'pink tea edition' to illustrate how boring a paper would be if it only reported 'good' news; another, shown above, on yellow newsprint, illustrated the possibilities of 'yellow journalism,' by finding Hitler attending a high school basketball game. The high jinks were clearly labelled as such.

The *Weekly World News*, a supermarket tabloid, routinely finds Hitler, Elvis, or Martians but never suggests it's less than the whole truth. Do such revelations lower the public's trust of media in general?

certainly must have been a remarkable bird, according to the description.[20]

Some newsrooms have not waited for April 1st to run spoofs. In the 1960s, for instance, the small British Columbia town of Campbell River (population then about 12,000) had three competing weekly papers. The rambunctious *Upper Islander*, edited by ex-Fleet Streeter Tony Simnett, was on occasion accused of sensationalism, so answered the charge with a 'pink tea' edition printed on pink paper full of nice stories about the nice community.[21] This was followed by a 'yellow journalism' issue printed on yellow paper, with suitably sensational headlines[22]

Such spoofs work best when clearly labelled as such (like the *Upper Islander*'s), and to succeed they must be quite harmless. Some incidents in the United States have been more malicious and have caused serious loss of credibility for the media.[23] If the answer to 'Who gets hurt?' is *anyone*, then the joke should not be played. And always the media must remember that credibility is fragile and much more easily damaged than repaired. At the same time, human credulity seems to be high (some people will believe anything), and people generally resent being tricked.

Of course, a few publications thrive on that appetite for bogus revelation. The US supermarket tabloids are largely fictional or wildly distorted, and yet enjoy huge circulations. (See, for instance, the very different Hitler story below the one in the *Upper Islander*.) How much of their nonsense is believed is unclear, but there is a real danger that segments of the audience are not sophisticated enough to discriminate between these publications and mainstream newspapers.[24]

First You Don't See It, Then You Do

Simulations, re-creations, re-enactments, dramatizations ... They have a host of names, but they all mean that what the audience is seeing is not what actually happened. Perhaps the delicious oxymoron 'creative non-fiction' is more appropriate?

When the press photographer is told to take a picture of the poor kitty stuck up a tree and finds the cat has safely escaped, there may be a temptation to stick the beast back up the tree again to get a photo. Certainly the photographer who arrives late at the wedding for the cake-cutting may have little compunction about asking the bride to do it again, and though the guests know it's fake, they are happy to be part of the conspiracy. But harmless as this may seem, the crowds around are different, the lighting is perhaps different, and above all, the onlookers know what they have seen: the media massaging the message. If, they may well dimly wonder, the media are so high-handed with history here, what else do they simulate or re-create?

The genre seemed to climax in the late 1980s with a number of US television programs, including *America's Most Wanted*, *A Current Affair*, *Crimewatch Tonight*, *The Reporters*, *Prime Time Live*, *Hard Copy*, and *Yesterday Today and Tomorrow*, all thriving on reconstructing history.[25] This is not the exclusive perquisite of 'entertainment' shows such as those re-creating famous crimes but has spilled over into current affairs programming such as 'Saturday Night With Connie Chung,' which routinely re-created recent history.

Television news, having a high entertainment quotient, feels it, too, should use the technique. The incident that brought the debate into the public forum was the 1989 ABC News treatment of US diplomat Felix Bloch, who was accused of spying for the Soviet Union. As Peter Jennings, anchoring the 21 July *World News Tonight*, described Bloch being secretly videotaped handing over a briefcase to a Soviet agent, viewers saw grainy black-and-white video complete with digital countdown of one man secretly passing a briefcase to another. The image included the word 'simulation' in the corner, but many journalists seemed deeply disturbed by the trend.[26]

But such reconstructions have been around for some years.[27] Among formidable Canadian examples were the 1986 CBC one-hour docudrama in which an actor re-enacted Nelson Mandela's five-hour speech in court before his life jail sentence, and the CBC's thirty-eight-minute re-creation of the 1986 Commonwealth leaders' conference in London in 1989. They were both said to be based on transcripts.[28]

Both of these were produced by Tony Burman, who explained to a 1990 conference of the Canadian Association of Journalists (CAJ), formerly the Centre for Investigative Journalism (CIJ), the raison d'etre for the Commonwealth conference show: 'It was *The Journal*'s decision (in this case in league with Grenada), that ... the journalistic motives here over-rode the natural journalistic timidity about doing that. In terms of the [Mandela] programme, it was our goal in '86 to make accessible in a public, broad sense the mystique of Mandela which at that point was not known and not appreciated.'[29]

Burman repeated that 'if the motive is valid and over-riding,' the technique was justified. He noted that the CBC manual on journalistic policy cautioned against dramatizations:[30] 'It is CBC policy not to use re-enactments on newscasts, and that I personally agree with. It is the CBC policy to be incredibly careful about such use. But I think that for us to, in a sense, cave in to what would be the widespread kind of alarm, particularly in print circles, towards the use of this kind of thing in television, is wrong, because the credibility of television is a far more complicated thing.'[31]

Burman estimated that these techniques had been used on only four or five occasions out of perhaps 1,000 documentaries done for *The Journal*.

Mark Starowicz, executive producer of *The Journal*, then the CBC's flagship current affairs show, was quoted by the *Globe and Mail* as subscribing to a similar rationale: 'We use it when there is no other way to convey a reality which we consider journalistically important ... If there isn't a transcript, we shouldn't be doing it ... Unless you have journalistic standards and motives, you're confusing people and doing damage to journalism.'[32]

There is little doubt, in terms of the CBC ventures into this genre, that the motivation is pure. The producers have no intention of misleading the audience but simply of making accessible something that would otherwise be beyond their experience. But for the viewers, the motives are unimportant. The key questions must be, did they realize they were not seeing the 'real thing'? and does viewing this distort their perception of reality? A lot more research is needed in this area.

If the TV managers are to be believed, the genre will not expand in Canada. The *Globe and Mail*'s John Haslett Cuff and journalism teacher Ross Perigoe quote senior executives.

• Peter Rehak, executive producer of CTV's *W5* believes firmly that re-creations should not be used in news:

'Reality is what separates us from entertainment ... The viewer expects to see the actual event.'[33]

- Kelly Crichton, executive producer of CBC's *The Fifth Estate*: 'When your very criterion is what will sell an audience, then you've abandoned your journalistic responsibility.'[34]
- John Owen, area head of news for CBC television: 'They're so slickly done. The more I see of it [re-creation], the more I get upset. Unless we hold to our standards, the public can't distinguish [between news and] quasi, pseudo journalism.'[35]
- Eric Morrison, CTV's executive producer of news, was asked if he would re-create: 'No, I don't think so, because so much of this has to do with inflection, tone and look, and I don't think you can faithfully re-create that. I don't think we are in the business of drama.'[36]

Despite this unanimity, the stern admonishments of head office may not filter down to the bright and enterprising staff in the regions. In about 1988, the deputy police chief of Saskatoon was alleged to have patronized a prostitute. The local CBC-TV newsroom re-created the story by acquiring a vehicle similar to the officer's and showing it cruising through hooker territory in the city. A super saying 'dramatization' showed through the re-created sequence.

In another incident, the same station described a local poet losing a briefcase full of his poems. It showed his wife answering the phone as a man called to say he had found them. But the story neglected to identify this phone call as a 're-creation.'[37]

In one situation, the name was different but the technique was much the same. On 21 January 1990, the network CBC radio show *Sunday Morning* carried an item on 'senior abuse.' Listeners heard an elderly woman called Rose describe how her husband, Albert, had died and how she had gone to live with her daughter and son-in-law; she lent them all her savings, handed over all her pension cheques, and became the house drudge in return for 'free' board. Only at the end of the pathetic recital was the piece described as a 'composite story.' (The same term, it will be recalled, was used to describe Janet Cooke's story of the child heroin addict.) The listener who caught that tag may have been left wondering, did Rose exist? Did any one person suffer all the tribulations ascribed to Rose? If

so, why not just say that her identity had been changed to protect her from reprisals? If 'Rose' was manufactured, why was it necessary? Was it – the listener may finally wonder – because the makers of the item could not find a real person who was a victim of senior abuse? Thus, the credibility of the entire package comes tumbling down.

Certainly the immense furor that greeted the CBC series 'The Valour and the Horror' suggests that the audience is uncomfortable with anything other than pure *documentation* of events in news or current affairs documentaries. The makers of that show approached their subject with a determination to 'balance' what they saw as a hitherto jingoistic view of Canada's role in the Second World War. But the series appeared, to the casual viewer, to be presented as a three-part documentary describing Canada's role in the war, which it certainly was not.

A new 'genre' has appeared on Canada's television screens recently to further muddy the waters. This is the promotional video, such as shows about the making of *Miss Saigon* and *Show Boat*. If such programs are underwritten by the promoters of the original shows, and those promoters have any control over the content, then they cease to be documentaries. The *Globe and Mail*'s Liam Lacey remarked, 'They are, essentially, good-looking hour-long commercials.'[38] Perhaps we need a new label for them, such as 'documercials,' and each should have a disclaimer describing its origins.

Special Techniques

Some TV techniques, such as the 'double-ender,' can easily be abused. With this process, the reporter or anchor typically sits in the Toronto studio facing a camera and interviews a source sitting in similar conditions in a studio in Rome, Winnipeg, or Whitehorse. The technique is invaluable, especially in a country the size of Canada. But the audience of, say, *The Journal,* may well have been unaware that this was *not* a face-to-face interview, that it was *not* live as it appeared, and indeed that anchor Barbara Frum may not even have conducted the interview: another reporter may have done the research and the double-ended interview even before Frum got to work that day, and the popular anchor then later asked the same questions, which were skilfully edited together with the answers.[39]

Television reporter Ann Medina, discussing the credibility of TV news, says that the public is becoming increasingly restless as they discover such tricks being played on them. For instance, many such tricks were publicly revealed during General Westmoreland's libel suit against CBS.[40] Said Medina: 'People who call themselves reporters really aren't ... programs that appear to be live are really pre-taped. Or reporters who appear to be reporting from a specific country really aren't there ... We can't play around with trust. If you cut a corner here and cut a corner there, the square disappears.'[41]

Are such images qualitatively different from artist's sketches representing the jury in secret conclave? Are they substantively distanced from Janet Cooke's 'composite' of the child drug addict or from the Toronto *Telegram*'s coverage of Marilyn Bell's 1954 swim across Lake Ontario, culminating with Bell's first-person account of the swim? (The story, under the enormous headline 'MARILYN'S STORY. I FELT I WAS SWIMMING FOREVER' was in fact written by a *Tely* staffer, though it bore Marilyn Bell's signature.)[42]

It may be argued that docudramas are just as accurate as newspaper stories, written by journalists trying to reconstruct events after they are over, and to a measure this is true. But the honest reporter who was not actually at the event will attribute his report to witnesses who were there, rather than trying to convince

the audience this was his own observation. There will be grave cause for concern if newspapers attempt to pass off news descriptions of 'second-hand' events as first-person reports.[43]

For all of these, a crucial issue is the difference between a newscast and a news-magazine-type show, between a print news story and a feature. In 'hard' news reporting, the audience must know that what they 'see' is real, and not a facsimile. As Perigoe concludes, 'One thing everyone seems to agree on is that news, the simple factual telling of events that go on in the world, has no business in the re-creation game.'[44] If re-creations are deemed essential to describe an event in a 'softer' feature environment, the makers must make absolutely certain that the audience will not believe they are seeing reality.

Subterfuge: Reporter as Sleuth

News gathering offers a number of situations in which the reporter may be tempted to dissemble or use clandestine methods. Indeed, some stories may never be told if the journalist does not employ some 'undercover' techniques. When radio CKNW in New Westminster, BC, for instance, became aware of a racket involving tow-truck companies in the 1970s, they concluded that standard up-front reporting techniques (asking the operators about it) simply would not work. So reporter George Garrett resurrected his middle name and managed to get a job driving tow

---

Television viewers saw the truck explode into flame when a car crashed into its side. What they did not see, until later, was that the demonstration was rigged to 'prove' the danger of side-mounted gas tanks. NBC later apologized to General Motors for the item. The TV producers believed the gas tanks posed a danger and wanted to demonstrate it. Is that quantitively different from wanting to demonstrate that Canadian soldiers were sacrificed in the Second War War, or wanting to show an event on screen although TV cameras were not actually there?

A determined mom wins bitter victory over GM

JIM AUCHMUTEY
Cox News Service

Atlanta

When Shannon Moseley died in the flaming wreck of his pickup truck, his mother set aside her grief and guilt and embarked on a five-year quest to discover who was really to blame

NBC apologized after admitting it rigged this crash demonstration

Tom Moseley grew up in the Chevrolet faith. He was confirmed at 16 when he got his first car, a '63 Impala with a big V-8 engine perfect for gunning the streets around Towers High School. A few years later, he married his teenage sweetheart, Elaine, and they started their life together with a '70 Chevy II. After a hitch in the Army, he took his place in the family fence business, tooling from job to job in a Chevy station wagon.

Given his loyalties, there was little question what make of vehicle Moseley would buy for his son Shannon when he turned 16. It was there on the birthday cake: a General Motors pickup sketched in festive red icing.

Late last month, a snapshot of that happy occasion was exhibited in a sombre chamber in Fulton County State Court. Three years after Shannon's truck ignited in a blind-side collision, a jury held General Motors liable for his death, finding that the corporation knowingly used a defective gas tank design. It upheld the $105.2 million award would be the largest in the history of the automobile industry.

But don't look for silver-haired celebration at the end of the suburban Snellville cul-de-sac where Tom and Elaine Moseley live with their second son, 17-year-old Tracey. Almost five years after they bought that truck, Shannon's parents are still sorting out the pain and anger and frustration and guilt in court and can dispel.

"We put our son in the truck that killed

him," Moseley, 44, says softly as he sits at the kitchen table across from his wife, who's stubbing out cigarette after cigarette. He stares vacantly ahead in silence before forcing out the rest of the thought. "You're just not supposed to outlive your children."

It has been a tough two weeks since the verdict. First there was the commotion of winning and so many strangers calling with congratulations that the Moseleys had to get an unlisted phone number. Then came NBC's startling admission that it had rigged crash demonstrations for a *Dateline NBC* segment that focused on Shannon's death.

The Moseleys are plainly irritated that NBC screwed up and allowed GM to shift public attention so dramatically from pickup safety to journalistic ethics.

"What NBC did was stupid and dishonest," the couple's lawyers said in a written statement. "But it is beside the point. It was irrelevant to the Moseley verdict; it is irrelevant to the real issue."

That, the Moseleys believe, is the safety of five million full-size GM pickups pro-

"There was a lot of tension between (the Moseleys). It was an indictment everytime Elaine talked about the case in front of Tom. That was the truck he put his son in."
— lawyer James Butler Jr

duced from 1973 to 1987 with dual gas tanks placed outside the main frame, which auto safety groups say makes the trucks more likely to catch fire when struck on the side. Federal investigators are considering whether to order GM to recall them.

• • •

Whatever the decision, Elaine Moseley, the 42-year-old daughter of a Baptist minister, sees a greater hand in her family's tragedy. "The Lord does not make mistakes. I believe there was some purpose for what happened to our son. We were supposed to go to court."

Shannon Christopher Moseley was 17 when he died. A junior at Brookwood High, he was a handsome, popular honors student who planned to pursue engineering at Georgia Tech. When he wasn't swimming, lifting weights or playing football, he was earning money doing yards or working at Pike Nurseries.

"He worked hard, he deserved a truck," his mother says. "Tom mentioned something about getting a smaller one, maybe an S-10, and I said, 'No, I want a big truck.' Bigger's better. Bigger's safer."

Her husband shopped for weeks before hearing that a local lumberyard wanted to sell its fleet. It was a great deal — $3,120 for a red '85 GMC Sierra V-6 pickup with 75,000 miles on it. Moseley customized it with chrome trim and turned it over to his son.

Oct. 21, 1989, was a Friday night. Shannon's new girlfriend, Gretchen Roberts, came over to meet his parents and watch movies. Shortly after 11, he left to take her home. It was no night to stay out late; they were supposed to take their first college board exam early Saturday morning.

Please see VICTORY/G2

trucks. He did not exactly lie, but he certainly did not reveal that he worked for CKNW. The result was a splendid series taking the lid off a scandal and resulting in the situation being cleaned up.

Such journalistic posing is widespread and often appears to be the only way to get the story. It may also appeal to the reporter's romantic side. It represents the cloak-and-dagger role that cinematic representations of the press always highlight. The 'watchdogs' of society pursue the 'bad guys' – and all's fair in love and war. Some other examples:

- CBC produced a major, half-a-million-dollar, two-part series on the mafia in Canada, in the late 1970s, called 'Connections.'[45] In the process of making it, they set up an elaborate fake company, with fake offices, phones, and business cards. They then sent a reporter with fake ID down to Atlantic City, New Jersey, to discuss buying property with people believed to be involved in laundering 'dirty' money through Canada. During that scene and others, the team used hidden cameras, body-pack tape recorders, and other surveillance techniques. (For a full description of the entire project, see Wade Rowland's *Making Connections*.)[46]
- The *Chicago Sun-Times* was concerned about corruption among city officials, such as health inspectors, and so purchased an old tavern. Reporters and photographers staffed the pub, appropriately renamed The Mirage, for six months, under cover, then closed it and wrote a stunning series resulting in more than 100 prosecutions, firings, and a general cleanup. The project was so successful it was nominated for a Pulitzer Prize, but the prize committee rejected it on the grounds that it was entrapment. The committee maintained that the journalistic enterprise had altered reality.[47]
- A *Toronto Sun* reporter and two members of the Fund for Animals posed as husbandry students to research an article on local slaughterhouses.[48]
- The Nashville *Tennessean* was concerned that the Ku Klux Klan was on the rise in the early 1980s. Reporter Jerry Thompson used an alias for thirteen months as an active member of the white supremacist group, before writing a major exposé.[49]
- Several waterbed shops closed in Ontario in 1989, and an angry citizen complained to the *Hamilton Spectator*

that he had apparently lost his $300 deposit on a bed. A reporter, posing as a customer, called the company headquarters and got information that she subsequently included in the story.[50]

- Val Sears nostalgically recalls 'picture pick-ups,' when, as a cub reporter for the Toronto *Telegram*, he was ordered to get photos of people who had recently been killed: 'We had to lie, cry, sometimes get down on our knees and pray with the family in return for a blurred photograph ... On one occasion, I had to tell the mother of a young girl, stabbed by her boyfriend in a schoolyard, that we had a revealing picture of her daughter taken at the beach that we would have to use unless she gave us another. She did. I felt rotten.'[51]

What all these anecdotes add up to is the sense among journalists that there *are* occasions when the ends do justify the means.

Yet the craft is by no means as permissive as it used to be. Increasingly, such activities are firmly rejected. The Code of Conduct of the National Union of Journalists, for instance, says: 'A journalist shall obtain information, photographs and illustrations only by straight-forward means. The use of other means can be justified only by over-riding considerations of the public interest. The journalist is entitled to exercise a personal conscientious objection to the use of such means.'[52] The CBC *Journalistic Standards and Practices* manual says: 'Deception must not be used to gain information. CBC employees, therefore, should not misrepresent themselves or their purposes to gain it.'[53] But, significantly, after that ringing caveat, the CBC manual continues: 'However, there may be occasions when it serves a legitimate program purpose for a journalist not to declare his or her profession but to seek information as an ordinary member of the public.'[54]

Such clandestine methods are not usually warranted in day-to-day news reporting, but they do occur in 'investigative' journalism – the harder-hitting, more massive journalistic projects usually involving 'uncovering' something that somebody would prefer to keep covered. This adversarial quality means the journalist is far less likely to get the cooperation of sources through conventional means.

Using Lawrence Kohlberg's schema (see Chapter 1), we can identify the pressures at play in such situations.

The journalist, tempted to lie or secretly tape-record to get a story, fears public condemnation for employing the very tactics that she opposes (lying). She recognizes that scriptural law forbids such activities ('Thou shalt not steal, bear false witness, etc.'), that statute law similarly forbids misrepresentation, bugging telephones, withholding sources, etc., and probably that a newsroom rule forbids such subterfuge. Thus 'rule obedience' would suggest she keep her hands clean by not employing such methods (and hence abandoning the story). But she recognizes that the disapprobation she faces may be offset by the wider benefits to the community at large. It may even be the journalist's *duty* to break the law.

As Louis Hodges, one of the seminal thinkers on journalism ethics, puts it, evaluating the Mirage incident: 'Obviously more people were being hurt by corrupt officials than by the *Sun-Times*' deception. Moreover, they were being hurt more seriously. Since people (perhaps especially journalists) have a moral duty to prevent harm to innocent citizens, the *Sun-Times* had a moral duty to get that story.'[55]

So the issues have been placed on the scales, and the advantages to the community of using the covert methods are found to outweigh the disadvantages accruing to the newsroom. It is the Pulitzer committee, here, which gets stuck at the level of rule obedience and is unwilling to accept the stronger call of journalistic duty and public benefit.

A key element that must be placed on the scales is *necessity*. The devious methods must be necessary, based on the over-riding importance of the story to the community *and* on the lack of alternative methods. The journalist must first exhaust all traditional, socially acceptable methods of investigation before resorting to the clandestine.

Deception may range from adopting a complete persona and lying to sustain it (as in the 'Connections' series) to the restaurant reviewer who insists on anonymity to ensure he does not get special treatment. In the latter case, nobody suffers from the duplicity, whereas the audience might well get a distorted view of the restaurant if the technique were *not* used. One test might be to insist that the covert methods used to get the story be described *in* the story. If the journalist can

comfortably confess her techniques to the audience, and if the audience can comfortably accept those techniques, then the end probably does justify the means. This test indicates clearly to the audience (and to oneself) that journalists do not have special privileges or rights. Where it may be satisfying to ride a white charger in pursuit of the forces of evil, journalists must sometimes remind themselves that they are neither in the law enforcement business, nor are they above the law.[56]

One thing is all too clear. The audience will not necessarily appreciate the techniques used or the motivation at work. New York journalist Nancy Palmer describes a fifty-two-year-old New York TV reporter who spent five days drifting as a bag lady in the city, only to be accused by some of 'exploiting the homeless as a ratings gimmick.'[57]

Getting It Taped

The laws regarding tape-recording conversations are fairly clear, and so may seem to exonerate the journalist from ethical dilemmas. But though it is quite legal in Canada to secretly tape one's conversation or interview with somebody else, even on the telephone, this does not, in itself, sanction the practice.[58]

What is wrong with secretly tape-recording an interview? Words like 'secretly,' 'surreptitiously,' or 'covertly' tend to muddy the debate. The process involves ensuring that the reporter gets an accurate record of his conversation. Does anybody advocate that a reporter should ask a source at the outset of an interview 'Do you mind if I take notes?' And yet the tape recorder is simply a more accurate way of taking notes for those who have not mastered shorthand. It is another reporting tool, just as the pencil and notebook are tools that are taken for granted. Indeed the reporter who does *not* take notes is highly suspect: she is very likely *not* going to be accurate. Conversely, the reporter who slavishly follows the *Globe and Mail*'s narrow rule ('if a conversation is being tape-recorded, let the person being interviewed know that a record of the conversation is being kept')[59] may find this inhibits the normal interview process.

Why, then, do some newsrooms ban unannounced taping? Theodore Glasser summarizes some of the resistance neatly, noting that secret taping suggests entrapment and FBI-style surveillance: 'Indeed, it may be the case that surreptitious recordings are thought of as unethical not because they are themselves *prima facie* wrong but because they are associated with what is ordinarily thought of as wrongful conduct.'[60]

In a similar review of taping ethics, Frederick Talbott, a Virginia lawyer and journalism teacher, cites several editors who condemn unannounced taping. He quotes Arthur Ochs Sulzberger, publisher of the *New York Times*, in a 1984 staff directive forbidding such taping on the grounds of 'common sense and courtesy ... We wish to conduct our business only in a highly ethical way.'[61] But beyond such abstractions, Sulzberger advances no reasons. Talbott also cites James Squires, editor of the *Chicago Tribune*, as equating unannounced taping with eavesdropping, warning that 'we are going to become evidence gatherers for the government, and that is not the role of the press.'[62]

Some of this resistance may stem from dealing with both telephone interviews and face-to-face interviews in the same breath. Simply taping a telephone conversation for accuracy is quite different from actively hiding a tape recorder in a pocket or purse for an interview face to face. The motivations may be quite different. And the presence of even a tiny tape machine on the table may intimidate a few sources. But the tape recorder is not a weapon (though it can be a blessed shield in a libel suit). The reporter must be sensitive to the source's comfort level, and just as she might say lightly, while pulling a notebook out of her briefcase, 'You don't mind if I take notes, do you?,' so she might say while sliding a tape recorder onto the table, 'You don't mind if I tape this, to make sure I'm accurate, do you?'

The real problem comes with *deliberately* taping an interview in secret, using bugs or hidden tape machines. This deliberate technique is clearly designed to mislead the source, so it must be treated quite differently from normal, daily interviewing.

Stolen Words: Accident or Capital Crime?

Plagiarism has been variously called 'the skeleton in journalism's closet,' 'the cancer that destroys the soul of journalism,' and 'the canker at the core of journalism.'[63]

Such venom may be justified, but three points need to be made early in any debate. Genuine plagiarism is theft, and so indefensible; serious incidents of plagiarism happen very rarely; and there is a difference between plagiarism and lack of attribution.

Admittedly, some instances of plagiarism probably escape undetected. But readers are apparently both vigilant and catholic in their reading. For instance, fragments of an article in a small Toronto magazine were recognized by a reader when they turned up in a Saskatoon newspaper.[64] And a reader of the *Chicago Tribune* spotted something lifted from the *Jerusalem Post*.[65]

Is plagiarism rare? David Shaw, investigating it for the *Los Angeles Times* in 1984, felt it was getting worse: 'Plagiarism is a growing problem in newspapers today – a problem of far greater dimensions than most editors and reporters realise.'[66] But he adds, in the same article, 'such incidents are rare.'[67] Indeed, there does not seem to be a lot of evidence to suggest it is increasing in Canada. An indication of how *rarely* this happens is the uproar that ensues when it is uncovered. In a small spate of incidents in Canada in 1989, one writer was fired and another committed suicide. And that – the firing, at least – is as it should be. Plagiarism would disappear if (a) it was clearly defined and banned by newsroom codes[68] and (b) it was denounced loudly and heavily punished when it did occur.[69]

The theft of other people's words is most likely to occur under three conditions: laziness, desperation, or accident.[70] The lazy writer will take other people's sentences or paragraphs and incorporate them because they are easily available. It saves research and it saves writing. Such thefts are usually palpable because the writing style is different and the material may well not fit smoothly with the writer's own work.

Desperation might be the result of such journalistic nightmares as missing the campaign bus or being too drunk to think. These are not excuses, but they may be explanations. Accidents may seem less likely. Many journalists might say it is impossible to 'accidentally' quote somebody else's words. But Don McGillivray, a respected Ottawa columnist for Southam News, has written engagingly of what he calls 'unconscious memory': 'Is plagiarism really foreign to journalism? I think we swim in it every day. We pick up facts from each other and use them without attribution. We follow time-worn styles of writing borrowed from others. If anyone invents a spicy way of saying something, he or she can expect to find it picked up and used as the common coin of journalism. When we write, we snap together modular phrases from our memory. And that memory is stored with the things other people have written.'[71]

This is a disarmingly honest picture of daily reality in newsrooms, and McGillivray goes on to point out that plagiarism is neither a new nor a journalistic prerogative. Poets, playwrights, and politicians have indulged in it for centuries. McGillivray urges newsroom managers – and peers – to 'go easy' on people found to have plagiarized, to concentrate on identifying the psychology that led to it: 'Goodness knows, writing under a byline for the public is sometimes like tightrope walking. Is [plagiarism] a cry for help?'[72]

What about recycling phrases from news sources? Incorporating a few felicitous words from a press release is scarcely grand larceny. For a news writer to co-opt a press release sentence that says, 'The 33rd Scout Troop will hold a rubber duck race on May Day' is perhaps technically plagiarism, but realistically it may be practical, deadline journalism. That may be the best way of saying it. Does anybody get hurt? The writer of the press release will be both delighted and flattered, unlike the writer of some original journalism, whose material then reappears under somebody else's byline without attribution. The conscientious journalist will always try to write material that is better than the press release. At the very least she will want it to be different so it does not resemble similar stories based on the same material in other media. But it would be bizarre to give attribution for such phrases: 'A news release from the 33rd Scout Troop says the group will "hold a rubber duck race on May Day."' Or, 'The 33rd Scout Troop will hold a rubber duck race on May Day, according to a news release dated 17 April, from scout headquarters.' Such exaggerated attributions are patently absurd and serve neither the media nor the public.

Copyright law – and plagiarism is all about the right to copy – makes it clear that there is no copyright of an idea. The news itself cannot be copyrighted, only the writing thereof. But small amounts of other people's work may be used, if appropriate attribution is given.

(There is honour among thieves.) Adopting longer chunks of other people's original writing and passing them off as one's own to colleagues, editors, and the general public is theft, but it is much worse: It is deliberately misleading and hence threatens the very foundation of trust on which the relationship between journalists and news consumers is based.

It is for this reason that writers have castigated plagiarism as 'cancer' and a 'canker.' Whether, as Roy Peter Clark of the Poynter Institute maintains, plagiarism leads to wholesale fabrication, is a matter for psychologists and other researchers.[73] But it is easy for journalists to give credit where it is due. And it is essential that they never pass off any significant material as their own.

For these reasons, newsrooms have been taking an increasingly hard line on plagiarism in recent years, even insisting on publicly admitting their guilt. The *Toronto Star* policy manual specifies that a single proven case of plagiarism could result in suspension or dismissal, and incidents must always be reported to the readers, with an apology. The *Ottawa Citizen* echoes this, saying plagiarism can bring dismissal. 'Where the *Citizen* concludes that plagiarism has occurred that is serious enough to warrant suspension or dismissal, the newspaper is obligated to report the instance publicly and with apology to the original author and the readers who were misled.'[74]

After Errors: Who's Sorry Now?

Hoaxes, dissembling reporters, reconstructed stories – there are many ways for the news media to give the audience an erroneous picture. The 'daily miracle' is perhaps more miraculous for paucity of errors (one or two in tens of thousands of words each day) than for their frequency.

However, each error or bad judgment whittles away at audience trust, and it is important for the news media to expeditiously admit they erred.

Twenty years ago, it was common practice for Canadian media to refuse to apologize or issue a correction unless forced to by imminent legal action. (A full apology can mitigate legal damages in some libel actions.) Such an attitude was probably based on the assumption that an admission of error would show that the media were vulnerable, that they could err and, therefore, might not be wholly trustworthy. In addition, as US columnist Russell Baker put it, 'The presumption of most newspapers, based on two centuries of applying the marketplace test to human nature, is that the great public wants to know who pulled this afternoon's stickups, not who was victimized by yesterday's newspapers.'[75]

Today, the opposite position seems to be true. Many media rush to correct themselves, in the belief that credibility will be *enhanced* by an admission of error. Furthermore, those media, particularly newspapers, which see themselves as forming part of the fabric of history ('newspapers of record') recognize that any error must be quickly corrected in order to set that record straight. Future historians looking to a newspaper to find what happened on a particular date must also turn to the *next* day's issue in order to find how history was rewritten.

Few newsroom manuals give much space to handling errors, and those that do may be difficult to interpret. The CBC policy manual, for instance, says this: 'The CBC will not hesitate to admit a material error when it is established that one has been made. To do otherwise ... would lead inevitably to loss of credibility by the CBC. Errors of fact must be corrected clearly and promptly in order to maintain the principles of accuracy and fairness.'[76] But there is much room for manoeuvre with issues such as whether an error is 'material' and whether this has been 'established.'[77]

The Canadian Press *Stylebook* is perhaps a little stricter: 'Accuracy is fundamental. Discovery of a mistake calls for immediate correction. Corrections to stories already published or broadcast must not be grudging or stingy. They must be written in a spirit of genuinely wanting to right a wrong in the fairest and fullest manner.'[78]

Failure to correct errors is frequently cited in credibility surveys as a major cause of dissatisfaction with the news media, and as a result many major dailies now routinely run boxes with standing headlines such as 'Our Mistake.'[79] (The advantage of displaying such a correction box prominently in the same place, typically, pages 2 or 3, is that readers know where to find it and will be less inclined to accuse the newspaper of 'hiding' the correction.)

Journalists' worst fears are realized, however, when the paper's main front-page story is found to be materially wrong. Very few papers will give equal prominence in such a case. But that it can be done was bravely demonstrated by the *New York Times*, which played a correction as its lead story during the Iran-Contra affair with the headline: **A Correction: Times Was in Error On North's Secret-Fund Testimony**. The admission was made after *Times'* staffers read the verbatim transcripts of the Oliver North hearing. The editors felt their version of the proceedings was not supported by the transcript and hence 're-wrote' it, even though they had received no complaints.[81]

Even the correction will quickly pass into history, and that, too, can be a danger. Newsrooms would be wise to ensure that corrections are filed in the newspaper library with the original story, so that future references do not repeat the error.[82] Some newsrooms go a step further and also record corrections in the guilty reporter's personnel file. Several of those could make a serious difference during performance reviews.[83]

With most corrections, the error is minor and the journalists – wanting to maintain their audience's trust – will simply admit the mistake. Nobody is perfect, and almost all errors of fact are the result of accidents – haste or carelessness. But the media's credibility can be eroded in many other ways. The next chapters will explore some of the specific situations that journalists may encounter that can undermine public trust.

TOUGH CALLS

1 A major daily does a piece on children and horror movies, using staged pictures with child models. Is that acceptable? How else can such a story be illustrated?

2 A TV station learns that a poltergeist is disrupting a local house. The newsroom gets some fine video of a flying telephone and other paranormal phenomena. How should the story be handled?

3 A radio station reports – in a regular Christmas Eve newscast – that Santa's sleigh and reindeer have been spotted, heading south. Is that a hoax? Are such things acceptable in the news media?

4 You learn that your newsroom was royally hoaxed by a local liar two years ago. Do you keep quiet? Excoriate the perpetrator? Grovel?

PART 3

Specifics

10 The Media and Violence

The eager young freelancer rushed to the scene of a terrible highway accident. Gagging, he took pictures of everything he saw, including a severed head rolling on the road like a bowling ball. One editor to whom he offered the pictures was appalled that the reporter had even taken them. Another editor paid him well.

Such scenarios are not uncommon, though the mainstream media generally protect their audiences from the most ghastly scenes their news staffs routinely experience. But each poses a question: How far should the public be protected? Part of the audience cries 'Sensationalism!' at the sight of blood, while part of the audience cries 'More!'

It is at this point that newspeople face what British columnist Katharine Whitehorn calls, 'the tension that exists between the journalist as a pro and the journalist as a citizen ... What it comes down to is that your professional ethic may require you to do something from which as a citizen you would recoil.'[1]

The journalist must recognize the realities of the competitive marketplace and give audiences exciting and eye-catching information in a palatable form; yet this may seem to involve a steady diet of doom and disaster. Look, for instance, at these headlines:

Initial Death Toll Set at 51 as Major Quake Hits Manila

Bombs Kill 43 in Pakistan

Traffickers Cited as 51 Die in Colombia

N.Z. Woman Charged with Stabbing 4 Children

Seven Blacks Dead after Explosions Rock South Africa

The headlines are all from one edition of the *Vancouver Sun* – a typical day.[2] It sometimes seems as if we're under siege: Earthquake ... bomb ... crash ... hockey fight ... mudslide ... chain-saw video ... volcanic eruption ... wrestling ... bus plunge ... There is so much violence around.

But the problem is not that it is getting worse. What could be worse than throwing Christians to the lions in front of a cheering crowd? What could be worse than being hanged till nearly dead, then dragged round town behind a horse, and finally hacked into quarters? Is 'necklacing' someone with a burning tire any worse than burning someone alive at the stake?

The public generally complains about violence in the media only when it involves human beings. When the BBC series *Trials of Life* shows jackals closing in on an antelope and then tearing it to pieces, that merely reinforces our suspicion that nature really is red in tooth and claw, which in turn implies the inherent superiority of civilized humans. But when violence involves people against people, it challenges that view, raising doubts about the separation between humans and beasts.

Certainly violence is nothing new in Canadian society. Paul Rutherford, tracing the history of Canadian media, found nineteenth-century papers teeming with murder and mayhem.[3] Indeed, violence in the media seems to have waned even over the last forty years. A *Detroit News* editor, James Vessely, who headed a committee that studied violent pictures for the

Associated Press Managing Editors' Association, summarized the trend in a Canadian Press interview: 'Reader reaction to sudden, instant visual death seems to be so strong that editors seem to be much more cautious than they used to be ... cautious in the sense of shocking readers for no apparent reason.'[4]

HERMAN®

"Go and watch some lunatic behavior on TV. You're not old enough for this stuff."

This sense of irritation on the part of news consumers is reflected in contemporary cartoons, which often satirize a perceived penchant for 'bad' news. What is different, in modern 'civilized' times, is not that there is more violence, but that the 'bad' news travels so fast. Before modern media developed, one had either to eyewitness the violent act (as the crowds did around the guillotine), or rely on gossip and itinerant news bearers, such as wandering minstrels. Today, a state official has only to shoot himself at a news conference, and video is instantly available via satellite in almost every newsroom around the globe. There is a story that a remote African tribe had to be relocated because of drought, but they delayed the move until the current season of *Dallas* was over. This may be apocryphal, but it certainly suggests that media are now almost all-pervasive.

The on-camera assassinations of John F. Kennedy, Lee Harvey Oswald, and Robert Kennedy, followed by the atrocities of the Vietnam War, probably brought this most dramatically into people's consciousness: violence, live, over breakfast, with the Wheaties. Especially with respect to the war, such an invasion of the home was resented by many, especially advocates of US involvement in Vietnam, thus invoking the Cleopatra syndrome – the messenger, the bearer of the bad news, was blamed. The media have been increasingly accused of venality, cashing in on pain and death, to sell newspapers or boost the ratings.[5]

The question that is implied by this criticism is *Why?*

For Better or For Worse
by Lynn Johnston

Why do the media run violent pictures or stories? And the innuendo is that they are doing this only for their own profit. The question is not unfair, and it is one that journalists themselves ought to ask a little more often. An editor may be tempted to justify running a gory picture on the grounds that it is news. But that really begs the question. It might be more truthful to respond: 'It's a dramatic picture,' 'It's fabulous photography,' 'It tells the audience more than a thousand words could.'

In a newspaper, space is dictated largely by the amount of advertising available. But there is some flexibility. More pages *can* occasionally be added for major events such as the Calgary Olympics, as long as it balances out over the month or the quarter. With TV, there is *no* flexibility. In order to coordinate with network programming, the news show cannot run over more than fractions of a second. A typical commercial TV station might have a thirty-minute newscast, but in reality this includes news, sports, weather, and commercial breaks. The actual 'newshole' may be little more than half that. James McLean, then senior news producer of CKTV, Regina, said:

16 minutes and 30 seconds is carved in stone. Television is the only medium that I know of where the parameters, for the length of time that you have to fill, aren't negotiable.

You can get around it in newspapers by printing fewer pages, you can get around it in radio by reading more slowly or by cutting out stories. It is a lot easier to do in radio, because there is a wealth of information available for a very short period of time.

With TV there is no way out. So automatically there is a pressure on the assignment editor. The assignment editor has to get the goods to fill the time slot.[6]

This tiny time frame (the equivalent of perhaps 2,000 words) can probably accommodate only ten or twenty stories. If video is included (and pictures are paramount on TV), then there will be fewer stories; each might average ninety seconds. As McLean points out, the assignment editor seeks visual images ('viz' as it's often known in newsrooms), rather than relying on the 'talking head' of an anchorperson simply reading

the news. But the editor has to rely on the journalists and story producers in the field, each of whom is eager to 'sell' his or her story. So a bidding war may emerge. The reporter on the scene of, say, a bomb blast in Belfast may well emphasize the dramatic possibilities of *his* story – his 'viz' may include sixty people dead, where somebody else's disaster story has only a few bodies. The conversation may go like this:

Editor: Have you got pictures?
Reporter: Yes, we have pictures.
Editor: How are they?
Reporter: They're great. We've got bodies lying on the ground. We've got babies burned, being carried off. It's mayhem.
Editor: Great stuff. Give us a minute-30.

But the assignment editor still has not seen the footage, and she does not see it until it is transmitted to her newsroom later, probably at a pre-arranged time, via satellite, maybe only minutes before show time. And perhaps, in the cold light of downtown Sudbury or Halifax or Burnaby, she will see the pictures that were described from the battle zone as 'great' and will find them offensive. But the ninety seconds are committed. It may be difficult or impossible at this stage to substitute some more mundane material. And the editor's ulcers, her wish to get away for the weekend, and possibly some deadening of sensitivities from seeing thousands of such pictures over the years – all of these may conspire to force her into a 'publish and be damned' situation.

For the print media, similar issues are at stake. There is a not-unreasonable rule that 'every page needs a picture' – but there is not always a calm, effective picture to fill that hole. Furthermore, the art editor will be remembering that television may well have pictures of the same events – colourful, moving pictures. And the editors may well – as mature, world-worn adults who have thought about violence, war, and human iniquity – feel that a picture is 'important' or 'useful,' where a more vulnerable audience may just find it offensive. 'You don't have to show dead bodies to prove that people have died,' succinctly remarked Ron Neil, deputy director of BBC news and current affairs.[7]

So why do journalists apparently 'like' violent pictures, and why does the public apparently dislike such images? And indeed, if this is so, why do the media persist?

What sort of images do audiences decry? Are they just those of death and dying? Some images are horrific even though their final message is in fact 'happy.' The child impaled on a fence spike or the bus passenger with a steel pipe through his chest (see 'Tough Calls') who survives to tell the tale are, in the end, 'good' news stories.

Are dead bodies, per se, images that editors should reject? Even this is not quite that simple. Look at the body of the dead sailor found by archaeologists. And are there occasionally overpowering reasons for showing pictures of bodies? Again, the answer must be yes. The world *had* to be shown pictures from Auschwitz after the Second World War, as well as photographs of some of the worst atrocities from Vietnam, such as the naked child fleeing her napalmed village, the monk burning himself to death in protest, or the cold-blooded shooting of a Viet Cong prisoner. These images are etched into people's memory. The viewers and readers, especially in the United States, needed to be shown the reality of war, a reality that the Pentagon wanted to sanitize precisely because of its enormity. It is for this reason that the thoughtful UK Sunday paper, the *Observer*, ran a horrifying picture of a dead Iraqi towards the end of the Gulf War. The picture was headlined, 'The real face of war,' and the cutline said, 'Price of victory: The charred head of an Iraqi soldier leans through the windscreen of his burnt-out vehicle, attacked during the retreat from Kuwait.' The British were at war, though a remote, senseless, and unnecessary war, and the editors evidently felt that their particular readers could cope with facing that stupid brutality. When we complain about violent images in the Canadian media, we should remember there are far worse shots, such as this, which editors generally protect us from.[8]

There are other issues, too:

- Is there a difference between violence committed by others and violence committed by oneself – murder or suicide?
- Is a picture of a dead body acceptable if it is covered up by a blanket?
- Is there a difference between pictures of the dead and pictures of those about to die?
- Can words be as offensive as pictures?
- Is repetition of images an issue?

Critics of the press often ask petulantly why the media exhibit so much violence, or they simply dismiss the perceived trend as exploitation. But clearly there is a paradox here. The law of supply and demand

This picture of a burned Iraqi war victim was given 14 x 8 inches on a section front in the thoughtful British Sunday broadsheet, the *Observer* (3 March 1991). No Canadian paper would dare publish such a horrific shot, but perhaps readers need to know the horrors of a war in which they are participating, although it is thousands of miles away. The headline says it all.

suggests that if the audience did not like violence then the media would not carry it. As Rutherford, quoted above, suggests, it is the fulcrum where democracy and free enterprise meet. In other words, the consumers police the media with their pocketbook. If they do not like the product, they cease to buy it, and that ultimate weapon keeps the media in line, preventing excesses.

This is equally true of similar transgressions, such as sexism and vulgar language in the press. Yet evidently some people, judging by letters to the editors, are not persuaded. However conservative a newsroom may be, there is probably someone out there who is more conservative. As the early American publisher Ben Franklin wrote, 'If all Printers were determin'd not to print any thing till they were sure it would offend no body, there would be very little printed.'[9] And the reasoning behind the public protests is as basic now as it was then. In the words of the BBC's Ron Neil: 'Viewers write to me and protest they don't want to see the violence of the world because they don't want it to intrude into the normality of their lives.'[10] Unfortunately, it is not that simple. We cannot pretend – ostrichlike – that things did not happen because we did not see them. Life cannot be laundered, so no one is hurt or hungry.

Rational media watchers recognize that it is unrealistic to expect the media to clean up the world. And the more robust members of the audience may ask why the media should cut out the nasty bits just because they would offend very puritanical people.

Meanwhile, *The Return of the Chainsaw Murderer, Part 9* plays to packed crowds at a cinema near you, or on late-night TV.

Is the world made up of voyeurs and anti-voyeurs? (The voyeurs are those who slow down to stare as they pass a highway accident, or who clog the roads to the airport when they hear there is a crash. The anti-voyeurs are those who view the world through rose-tinted glasses, who are, perhaps, squeamish, who would impose their blinkered Pollyanna view of the world on others.) On our left we see the crowd at the boxing match, jeering fear and cheering on the blood lust; on our right we have the evangelical lobby who see Satan in rock music and want the media to sanitize the world. Perhaps Ben Franklin was right.

But back to news. The difference between the fans of the chainsaw movies and the critics of the violence in news is the element of volunteerism. Nobody forces us to see blood-curdling horror movies, but in a sense they do force us when those violent scenes are played out in the TV newscast or on the front page. We 'have' to watch/read and listen to the news to stay informed and be good citizens, but is this grim procession of vile images a necessary price?

It can be argued that it is sufficient to 'tell' the audience about violence, without showing it to them. Ron Neil found that the BBC could tell the horror of the Lockerbie air crash quite effectively 'by showing scenes of devastation and rescue,' rather than bits and pieces of bodies. And Knowlton Nash, CBC news anchor, 'told' the story of the Pennsylvania treasurer's suicide to news viewers without showing footage.

Many viewers find themselves uncomfortable in the role of voyeurs, taken to the scene of agony by satellite. And of course they fault the media for voyeurism. Perhaps even before the editor asks herself, 'Is this image too shocking to show?' she should be asking about the very nature of news. If conflict is news (and of course the wars of the Roses or of Vietnam or of the Gulf *are* news), then does that necessarily mean ALL conflict is news?

This does not mean that we should eliminate conflict from the news menu or pretend it does not happen. The pacifists may wish that, but hiding it doesn't make it go away: 'There is a deeply ingrained attitude in the media which hooks into conflict as the major angle for any copy, and if possible makes that conflict larger than life,' claims Alan Morrsion, a spokesman for the Avon Peace Foundation.[11] Hopefully, the media do not really react with such a knee-jerk response and do not sensationalize in this way. Morrison maintains that journalists perceive the world as a violent place and deliberately choose bellicose vocabulary, such as 'lashed out,' 'hits back,' 'slammed,' 'axed,' 'chopped,' and 'smashed,' to tell even the most passive tales. He makes an interesting point. A story may well seem to be 'brightened' and dramatized by the use of such images even in non-warlike situations. Typically, elections, polls, and even parliamentary debates may be dressed up with such metaphors. (Sports reporting certainly uses such terms with relish.) Each may be colourful and justified, but does the sheer volume of such images reinforce the news consumer's feeling that the media only report the bad news?

Without question, some of the violent pictures could be avoided. The bloody body of Benigno Aquino's alleged assassin on the tarmac at Manila airport in *Maclean's*, the charred body in a Brazilian gasoline explosion in the Saskatoon *Star-Phoenix*, the picture of a dead NBC soundman being dragged away from the scene of a failed coup in Thailand in Regina's *Leader-Post*, the photographer dead in the street after being caught in crossfire in Beirut in the *Toronto Star* – all are probably unnecessary beyond the (valid) argument that every page needs a picture. Words could tell each of these stories, without the brutal images.

Others are more difficult. A series that was used in dozens of Canadian dailies during the FLQ crisis showed a Canadian army engineer trying to defuse a bomb placed in a Montreal mailbox. In the final picture, he is lying in the street dying. The pictures, in my view, had to be used, bringing home to people in the remotest corners of the country the true nature of the insurrection. During the Vietnam War, *Time* magazine ran a shot of a smiling soldier brandishing the severed heads of two enemy soldiers, which certainly said something about the war. A picture in the *Vancouver Sun* of two dead children in a Beirut refugee camp is sickening but proves the slaughter *did* occur, despite claims to the contrary. The horrifying pile of bodies on the front of *Time* magazine brings home man's inhumanity to man – even at a soccer match. (But the same argument was doubtless used half a century ago when the Yellow Press ran streams of cadaver pictures – such as a ghastly 1950 *Chicago Daily News* shot of dozens of burned bodies packed like cordwood in a burned-out subway car.[12]

Less convincing is the 'educational' rationale for accident pictures. A boy is killed by a train after being trapped on a railway bridge. One full-colour picture of the dead child partially under a blanket and another of an injured friend dominate the top half of the *Calgary Herald*'s front page. Will it deter other children from playing on the bridge? A child is hit by a dump truck near a construction site and gets on the colourful front page of the *Oakville Beaver*. Will that discourage other youngsters from playing in the street? Assistant editor Rod Jarred later told this writer that the paper was 'inundated with phone calls' complaining about the picture, but 'some people said they showed it to their kids as a warning.'[13]

If that argument holds, why, then, did Regina's *Leader-Post* choose *not* to run a picture of a dead child pulled from the frozen river after he played too close to the edge of the ice? (Instead they ran a shot of police divers at the scene.) Perhaps the *Leader-Post* chose not to further upset the grieving family, recognizing that a picture of the dead four-year-old would not deter other four-year-olds from playing on the ice. But perhaps a newspaper picture might deter twelve-year-olds from playing chicken on a railway bridge? Or the authorities might be forced to do something (what *can* they do?) to prevent this happening again?

Some of the five Ws help focus the debate.

Who benefits/loses? Perhaps with the dead child on the bridge the family suffers more because of the picture, but they may also feel the picture might help prevent it happening to other children. And if the publicity stimulates the authorities to do something that prevents further incidents (e.g., a warning sign to train drivers or for children, a separate footbridge close by), then everyone benefits. But is that not the role of the *editorial* page?

What is normal procedure? Many newsrooms have a standing rule, No Dead Bodies. If that is so, then there must be an over-riding reason to break the rule, and presumably the decision must be made by a senior manager (managing editor, news director). *What* does it do to newsroom credibility? If publishing this picture will damage the newsroom's reputation, it may not be worth the risk.[14] And there may well be situations – like the Pennsylvania suicide – where the newsroom may actually gain credibility by withholding offensive material.

Where should the picture go? Is it so important that it deserves to be above the fold on page 1, and is it worth the inevitable charge that the paper is sensationalizing to sell papers? *Why* run the picture? Is the newsroom doing this, as Ann Medina says, 'in order to'? Should the newsroom's agenda go beyond informing the audience? It may seem commendable to be

Most of the *Calgary Herald*'s
front page was devoted to stories
and colour pictures after one
child died and another was
injured on a local railway bridge.
The bottom picture showed a
body covered by a blanket.

After the *Oakville Beaver* ran a
picture of a local traffic fatality,
they received — and published —
dozens of letters from upset
readers. Yet only a sneaker was
visible, protruding from under
the blanket.

running a picture such as the soccer game massacre to
shock people out of their complacency, but are newspeople comfortable taking on the role of public conscience? Would such a picture be more appropriate,
for instance, on the editorial page? With all the news
that is happening in the world, is there not something,
somewhere, of greater importance than the death of
one child on a rail bridge? To what extent are decisions
like this influenced by the – very real – fear of being
scooped by the opposition, in this case, the *Calgary
Sun*, which could be expected to run similar pictures?
And finally, *how* might the editors feel if the reversibility rule were invoked: if it were *their* child or mother
or themselves in the picture?

Those are a lot of questions. What they amount to is
a sense of discomfort with the rationale for such shots.
Editors – and readers – need to be convinced that the
motivation for running such pictures is adequate. If the
bottom line is 'run it because it might boost ratings,'
then it should not be run; if the reason is somewhat
more benevolent ('because the audience needs this
information; because this picture may help get the situation rectified'), then the risk may be worth taking.
And sometimes the pictures may be so brilliant that
this alone justifies the ensuing ruckus.

So we might develop a short checklist of possible
motives for running a debatable picture:

- Is it to provide audience thrills?
- To boost circulation?
- To communicate some social message?
- To show off an outstanding picture?
- Or is it simply because the picture has indisputable,
  intrinsic news value?

The Many Forms of Violence

Violence in the media takes many other forms, some
of which require different responses.

Dead bodies. Among the most profoundly disturb-
ing images in Canadian media recently have been the
pictures from the Montreal massacre of 6 December
1989. When a deranged man shot fourteen women students and injured thirteen others at the University of
Montreal shortly before Christmas, the media
descended on the scene, as they must. Two of the pictures caused a furore. One showed a dead student

slumped in a cafeteria chair, the other showed a woman on a stretcher, oxygen mask on her face, and part of one breast exposed. Complaints about the first of these two pictures are understandable, but nonetheless I believe it was necessary to run it. The second picture should not have run.

Was the story newsworthy? Of course; it was enormously important. This was one of the worst incidents in modern Canadian history, and many people felt the sexist nature of the crime indicated some terrible

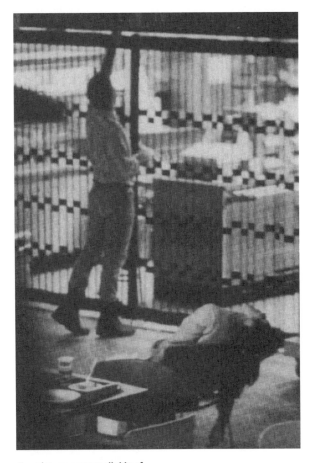

Few pictures were available of the massacre of students at the University of Montreal. One enterprising photographer got this shot through a window, showing a dead woman slumped in a chair, with a guard taking down Christmas decorations in the background. Many readers complained.

things about contemporary society. It was an overwhelmingly important story, one of the two or three most important Canadian news stories of the year. Could all that have been told in words? Yes. But a story that is going to be the top story on every front page in the country must have pictures. And the reason that this picture is so powerful is *not* the body in the foreground, but the activity in the background. Cutlines clearly described it. A plainclothes police officer was taking down a colourful banner proclaiming 'Bonne Année' – Happy New Year. Perhaps the man is feeling helpless in the aftermath, and he is offended at the grim irony of the holiday sign at the scene of carnage. The action underlines the grief, the bitterness, the sadness. Crop him out of the picture, and the shot becomes just another prurient body picture.

Who gets hurt by this picture? One might be tempted to answer that the dead girl's family would be hurt, but she cannot be recognized from the picture. (Four different families telephoned the *Montreal Gazette* to say the girl was their daughter.)[15] Who benefits? The audience does. The need-to-know over-rides the issue of privacy here. What does it do to the newsroom's credibility? The newsroom does not lose significant amounts of audience trust by running this. Some readers will be upset, but that may be the price of good reporting. What is normal practice? 'No dead bodies,' but this is not normal. The city editor of the *Montreal Gazette*, Ray Brassard, remarked that the story was of such magnitude, a lot of rules were broken. Commented *Ottawa Citizen* night news editor Sharon Burnside, 'Normality did not apply.'[16]

Like many papers, the *Gazette* – the hometown paper – used the colour picture on its front page, and was rewarded with some 300 telephoned complaints and 100 angry letters. Explained *Gazette* editor Norman Webster:

We try hard not to offend people needlessly. Anyone who reads the *Gazette* regularly knows we don't publish that kind of picture often.

But the picture we used was not gratuitous, not violence for the sake of violence. It was shocking, but this was one of the most shocking stories I've covered in my entire career – perhaps the most shocking.

We had a photo that, I felt, conveyed as nothing else in the paper could the real horror of the massacre.[17]

The answer to the question why is therefore one of overwhelming newsworthiness. The picture told, grimly and instantly, the whole stark horror of the tragedy. It is justifiable because of the content and composition – foreground and background – and would have been purely offensive without the background activity.

On that basis, the argument that pictures of disasters must be run 'because they happened' is a classic cop-out. Said Murray Ball, acting managing editor of the *Calgary Herald*, in a Southam survey: 'We cannot deny the event and have a responsibility to our readers to tell and show them what happened. Certainly people have been offended and I am truly sorry for that. But the offence was not ours. The offence occurred in the University of Montreal engineering classrooms.'

This just doesn't stand up to close scrutiny. Newsrooms constantly police themselves and do not simply hold up a mirror to society, warts and all. If they did, then there would be a steady stream of bloody pictures on every page, every day. This argument would justify running hundreds of pictures that editors now decline to run because they feel they are unsuitable: mutilated bodies and gore from wars, train, car, and plane accidents, murders and suicide – the list is endless. And clearly there is an appetite for such things among a segment of the audience, otherwise *Hallo Police* and *Le Journal de Québec* would not thrive as they do. Fortunately, most of the mainstream news media do not pander to this.

Another factor in the body-in-the-cafeteria debate is external to the picture itself. The event was so enormously important that the same pictures were used in every paper and on every television newscast. The public is thus overwhelmed and repelled by the sheer repetition.[18] Editors polled by Southam's in-house newsletter *Moving Up* clearly had thought carefully before running the picture, which they knew would offend some of the audience. That polarization was highlighted when the picture was subsequently honoured as the best spot-news photo of the year by Canadian Press and in the National Newspaper Awards.

The second picture – of the girl on the stretcher – is much less defensible and a much greater invasion of privacy, even if she, too, was unrecognizable. In defence of the editors who did approve using the picture, however, is the fact that the image was very confused and busy, and some editors said they simply were unaware that the girl's breast was partly exposed.

How dead is dead? In the photograph on this page, we have a partly decomposed body exhumed from burial, and yet most people will probably regard the image as inoffensive, because the cutline tells readers the body is 140 years old and has been dug up by archaeologists. Contrast the different impact the same picture would have if the cutline said, 'Murder victim John Hartnell was discovered Tuesday, under fresh cement in the basement of an Ottawa home. His landlord has been charged with murder.' Same picture, but it is the reader's imagination that makes the difference.

Death-about-to-happen. The dramatic image that comes to mind is the *Challenger* space-shuttle explosion. These and similar pictures will be discussed fur-

2 shipmates on 1845 trip likely starved

Canadian Press
EDMONTON

Canadian and U.S. scientists performed autopsies this summer on two more crewmen from the doomed 1845 Franklin expedition to find the Northwest Passage.

Despite earlier evidence of cannibalism among the 129 men who perished in the expedition, X-ray analysis showed the two crewmen died of natural causes — probably a combination of tuberculosis and starvation.

Owen Beattie, a University of Alberta anthropologist who has been studying the lost expedition since 1981, held a news conference in Edmonton yesterday to discuss the team's findings.

Mr. Beattie led a team to the site where he uncovered the perfectly preserved remains of Petty Officer John Torrington in 1984.

The two latest bodies exhumed by the team, those of Able Seaman John Hartnell, 25, and Royal Marine William Braine, 33, had partly decomposed.

The bodies were encased in ice for 140 years, but bad weather likely forced fellow crewmen to keep the bodies aboard one of Franklin's two ships for as much as a week before burial.

Still, Mr. Beattie said, exhuming the bodies was "a remarkable experience."

Mr. Beattie said medical evidence shows the two were very thin, but it is unclear if they starved to death. The expedition had taken a three years' supply of food.

The research team also found evidence of tuberculosis, but there was no sign of scurvy, a disease common to sailors and caused by a lack of vitamin C.

However, scurvy likely played a greater role in the deaths of other crewmen as supplies dwindled, said Mr. Beattie. Evidence of lead in the crewmen's remains also suggests ...

John Hartnell's body: crewman with doomed 1845 Franklin expedition.

Generally, television stations and newspapers don't show dead bodies in the news. But many papers, such as the *Globe and Mail*, made an exception for one that had been buried in Arctic ice for more than a century. Anthropologist Owen Beattie felt it was important to respect the deceased crewman from the ill-fated Franklin expedition, but he found that not all media shared his view. The *Weekly World News* used the picture to report an iceman had been revived after 100 years!

ther in the chapter on privacy. But certainly a picture of somebody who you know is about to die is almost as offensive as a picture of the dead body. If the story had a happy ending (if, say, the *Challenger* crew had bailed out in an emergency module and landed safely in a trampoline), then the same image would be not merely acceptable but admirable.

Self-inflicted death. Many newsrooms have a standing rule against covering suicides, partly because there is some evidence that reports of one suicide lead to others, although that rule gets broken fairly frequently.[19] But no rule could cover the enormity of Budd Dwyer's suicide. The Pennsylvania state treasurer had been convicted of taking bribes and faced up to fifty-five years in jail. He called a press conference and, after reading a rambling statement, drew a revolver from a manila envelope, stuck it in his mouth, and pulled the trigger. Cameras rolling. This certainly fits into the category of 'public' suicides, and Dwyer was a high public official. But the rules were not made for people who invite the TV cameras to record them blowing their heads off. Sickened camera operators, photographers, and reporters found themselves competing with each other – and with deadlines – with some repellant pictures.

How was it handled? At least one Pennsylvania station ran video of the entire event. Further afield, CFTO in Toronto ran the first few seconds up to Dwyer putting the gun in his mouth, then went to black, with the sound still running. None of the Canadian TV networks – CTV, CBC, or Global – ran the video, though news anchor Knowlton Nash told the 10 P.M. audience his newsroom had the footage but was suppressing it.[20] Global's senior producer, Eddie Taylor, said the images were of questionable news value and to run the video for shock value would be 'almost despicable.'[21] Global did not even report the incident on the evening news.

In print, many Canadian dailies ran the gun-in-mouth still picture, some on page 1.[22] Gary Hall, associate editor of the *Hamilton Spectator*, which ran the picture on page 1, told *Media File*, the CBC program which usefully explored Canadian journalism, 'This one was a tough one.'[23] But Hall was sure the story was newsworthy. 'If the *story* is newsworthy, so is the *picture*,' he argued.

That is an interesting point, but Hall did not get a chance to explain it. If we grant that the story was newsworthy (and just how newsworthy is arguable, in a foreign country, hundreds or thousands of miles away), must the picture also be run? Making one decision (about the value of the word-story) does not exempt the editors from making the second decision (about the value of the picture). If only it were that easy. But that way lie all those other body pictures – child on the road, child in the river, headless car-accident victim. Each may be news somewhere, but the picture has to be evaluated separately. (Hall's argument certainly was not universally accepted. The *Vancouver Sun*, for instance, ran a brief story, but no pictures.)

In the Pennsylvania case, the decision was aggravated because editors had three or more photographs; when this happens, there may well be a subconscious feeling that one has to choose *which*, not *whether*. And always nagging in the back of those print editors' minds is the sure knowledge that 'TV will have it.'

Media File program host, Vince Carlin, stepped out of his usually neutral role to lambaste those who ran the suicide pictures. 'There might be some excuse in Pennsylvania,' he said. 'But in Canada it's exploitation, pure and simple.'[24]

The bottom line? Pictures were not necessary to tell this story in Canada. Even if television lives and dies by visuals, it is not necessary to broadcast everything you have. Value judgments must still be made, and news personnel have to decide if the information contained in the pictures outweighs the shock of such images (for children home at lunch break and for people eating dinner, for instance), and the inevitable complaints. In this case, it doesn't.

Violence without death. Occasionally, a picture comes along that is so gruesome it can be classed as violent even without the presence of dead bodies or blood. Does the fact that it lacks these ingredients make it acceptable?

Two images come to mind: The boy on the fence spike and the man on the bus. Julio Castillo, aged fifteen, was trying to retrieve a ball on Saturday, 12 July 1989, near his home in Queens, New York, when he slipped on a six-foot iron fence, driving a picket spike

R. Budd Dwyer moments before killing himself.

Pennsylvania official

The media had great difficulty deciding how to deal with pictures of the Pennsylvania state treasurer who called a news conference and blew out his brains. Some television stations ran the whole video, while others ran none. Some papers printed all four stills taken from the video. The *Globe and Mail* ran the first picture, shown above, on the comics page.

The image of the New York teenager impaled on a fence-spike is shocking and irresistible, and the drama is emphasized by the fire-fighter wielding an oxy-acetylene torch in the foreground. Many papers rejected the picture; some used it, and many readers protested that their Sunday breakfast was ruined by the picture. Does it make a difference to know that the boy was released from hospital within two weeks — and citizens in many communities got fence-spikes removed after the incident?

through his jaw and out of his mouth. Many papers ran the picture of the impaled boy as firemen fought to cut him free. Thousands of readers across the continent protested. But the picture is riveting, the tortured boy in the centre, while a man with a welding torch works in the foreground. The picture is also sickening. Would a story suffice, without the picture? Not at all. A words-only story would not make it across town, let alone across the continent. Kids get in all manner of scrapes each day, but these do not normally rate photos.

What sort of emotion is provoked by the picture? 'Good lord: Poor kid! That must be the ultimate nightmare!' might be the readers' reaction. Could such a picture act as a deterrent? In several communities, efforts have been made to get such fences 'debarbed' since the picture ran. The child or his family would not likely be hurt by the picture any more than by the event itself. But it does not need to run on page 1. The shot is just too gut-wrenching for that sort of shock, perhaps particularly as it ran in many papers on a Sunday morning.

Does the child's ultimate fate make any difference? Emphatically, yes: He was out of hospital in two weeks. If he had died, the picture would have been unusable. So, such a riveting picture has intrinsic merit, and might lead to protecting other youngsters in the future: Run it, inside.

Egregious violence. Just before Christmas 1986, *Maclean's* magazine ran a cover story on violent toys. The cover art, of jolly old Saint Nick with a camouflage shirt and machine gun, roused enormous hostility from readers. Editors quickly found that Santa Claus – like the RCMP – is sacred, an innocent image of childhood that readers simply could not bear to see perverted.

The picture was, nonetheless, clever and eye-catching. But is that enough justification for offending readers? The editors' purpose was both to attract attention (inevitable but realistic) and to shock readers into reading about a phenomenon: the intolerable number of violent toys on the market for Christmas, led by the Rambo craze. As such, the story was justified and important.

Who gets hurt by such a cover? The argument that 'we had to hide your magazine from the children' does not carry a lot of weight. *Maclean's* has never appealed to children, especially those who still believe in Santa. If a

INSIDE: THE WHITE HOUSE SCANDAL DEEPENS

Maclean's
DECEMBER 15, 1986   CANADA'S WEEKLY NEWSMAGAZINE $1.75

WARFARE IN TOYLAND

Barbie vs. Rambo:
Battling for the
Holiday Millions

'Warfare in Toyland' was a suitably graphic headline for a
cover featuring the influence of
Rambo on Christmas gifts. But
readers weren't amused.

child sees such a picture she is likely to ask her parent about it, which would provide an excellent opportunity to discuss violence, commercialism, and Christmas. The likelihood of some little tyke getting nightmares about Santa Claus because of this picture is remote.

Certainly the magazine cover is an eye-catcher and it may offend some readers. But it is a deliberate editorial comment designed to provoke discussion among a fairly discerning readership. Beneath the complaints is, once again, the Cleopatra syndrome: an unwillingness to face the unpleasant message that Christmas, as a Christian family festival, has itself been debased. But the target for protest, if any, should be toy manufacturers and retailers, and the best antidote would be a good family environment.

When Words Suffice

When sickening sex-killer Ted Bundy finally went to the electric chair after fighting execution for eleven years, crowds gathered outside the Florida jail to cheer – and the media had a field day. The *Globe and Mail* alone ran stories for three days on his execution, including a description of how the 'charismatic' Bundy, with one leg 'shaved and greased with conducting gel,' was led to the oak chair known as 'old Sparky,' where 'two thousand volts of electricity caused Mr. Bundy's body to tense against the restraining buckles and straps of the electric chair at precisely 7:16 A.M.' Surely this oversteps the line between what the reader needs to know and what the voyeur will enjoy? (But this fades into nothing compared to stories in supermarket tabloids such as the *Weekly World News*. Under the headline 'Woman Dies in Her Own Oven,' for instance, the paper reported, 'In one of the most horrifying deaths imaginable, a woman accidentally tipped an oven over her head while cleaning it – and was broiled like a sirloin steak. "You could say she was well done," said ...'[25]

Such grotesque news judgment makes the average Canadian family newspaper look like a Bambi or Snow White story.[26]

But certainly papers can pander to readers' prurience with words alone. For instance, when a sordid murder, laced with homosexuality, transvestism, decapitation, and hints of Satanism, occurred in

Corner Brook, Newfoundland, the local weekly paper went to town. Over the three-week trial, the paper ran some five-and-a-half, full, broadsheet pages of copy, much of it verbatim. At the start, reporter Brian Basiia asked the defence lawyer why a crowd of citizens attended the trial: '"It is really quite simple why they are interested: It's their basic human curiosity. They want to come and sniff the victim, in a sense," he explained.'[27]

The reporter and editor obligingly helped people who could not get to court by providing column after column of squalid detail, so that they, too, could 'sniff the victim.' How far the media should go in helping with this desire to sniff is not clear. What is clear is that every situation is unique, which makes it perpetually difficult for editors and TV producers trying to fill newsholes with lively, colourful images.

'It's constantly a case of judgment calls,' said Barry Gray, a photo editor at the *Toronto Sun*, in an interview with *Content* magazine. However, his solution does not work. He continues: 'But you can't censor yourself. Every photograph will offend somebody. Of course you don't want to upset your readers, but you have to get the news across. Or get a point across.'[28] Every sentence here begs for debate. Evidently, what is meant by the word 'censor' is editorial discrimination – and editors exercise some form of such self-control *all the time* and would be seriously remiss if they did not. And of course most pictures do *not* offend somebody. And very few pictures are justified solely on the basis of 'getting your point across' – journalism 'in order to.' They need much stronger justification if the audiences are to stomach them or the news managers are to weather the complaints.

A similar scenario was played out in *Saturday Night* magazine in July/August 1993. The cover story was a long piece by veteran journalist Peter Worthington about Clifford Olson. Or was it? Even the cover picture was of Worthington rather than Olson (which can be defended on the grounds that putting Olson on the cover would just glorify the serial murderer). Yet when does the mere scribe become the star, worthy of the front cover? The cover blurb explains. 'The Journalist and the Killer,' says the scarlet headline and continues: 'Peter Worthington's Chilling, and Unauthorized,

Encounters with Serial Murderer Clifford Olson.' So the editors see this as being as much about Worthington's escapades as about Olson. In the eleven-page, first-person article, the former *Toronto Sun* editor-in-chief then describes how he slipped into the jail for a series of interviews. Although he goes to great lengths to criticize Olson, and ends by saying he, himself, would gladly 'pull the switch that would end Olson's life,' he displays a fascination with the child rapist/murderer. The piece is bulked out with italicized quotes from Olson, describing his unspeakable acts.

If Olson invited *me* in for interviews, wouldn't I take the opportunity and be delighted to write a *Saturday Night* cover story? The temptation is obvious. But it is Olson who is setting the agenda: Olson gets Worthington into the jail; Olson controls the interviews by talking endlessly about himself to the rapt reporter; Olson gets his adored publicity. Worthington quotes the jail warden calling Olson an 'unrepentant attention-seeker,' and says himself: 'Olson's ego and vanity know no bounds,' he's a 'highly manipulative liar,' he's 'incessantly looking for ways to manipulate,' and 'In our relationship he has lied, exaggerated, fabricated.'[29] The article is fascinating, as a cobra is fascinating, but it provides little useful insight for the general reader. The transcripts of the interviews, however, might usefully be turned over to experts in sex-killer psychology.

Nobody said journalism was easy. However, one old journalistic axiom is appropriate here. If in doubt, leave it out. It is often not a difficult decision simply to omit the potentially offensive words, pictures, or even an entire article. Unfortunately, such an easy solution is not always appropriate in cases involving a closely related topic, and the subject of our next chapter: 'Privacy.'

TOUGH CALLS

1   On 7 April 1986, the *Globe and Mail* ran a story and two pictures on page 1 describing an accident in which a bus carrying forty Americans to the Toronto Zoo careered off the road. Thirty feet of fence rail pierced the windshield, impaling two passengers. One 15-column-inch picture showed David Roberts sitting on a stretcher after being sawn free, pipe sticking out of his chest and his back. What are the issues? How is the picture similar and dissimilar from the boy-on-the-fence-spike shot?

2   A man is horribly mutilated by a pit bull terrier. He believes the public should know the danger of the dogs, so he holds a news conference and invites the media to take pictures. He has lost his nose, part of his lips, and much of his facial skin. His local daily (the *Lincolnshire Echo* of England) ran the picture on page 1. Was that the best response?

3   A New York man starts several fires in his mother's twenty-storey apartment building, then climbs to the roof, strips, and jumps to his death. Two pictures are available. What are the pros and cons?

4   Two thousand Croatians demonstrate outside the US Consulate in Toronto. One burns himself to death, and the picture takes about a quarter of page 1 in the *Globe and Mail*. What are the arguments in favour of running this picture?

5   Canada is participating in a UN peacekeeping force that is trying to restore democracy to Haiti. The Haitian justice minister is gunned down in the street, and Reuters distributes a colour picture of his grief-stricken wife beside the bloodied body. Should Reuters have taken the picture? Distributed it? Should papers have used it? Was the *Ottawa Citizen* right to have used it on page 1, as it did?

The bus passenger was an innocent bystander, thrust into the public spotlight by a freak accident in which a pipe from a bridge railing speared through the length of the bus, pinning him to his seat. He was pictured in the *Globe and Mail*.

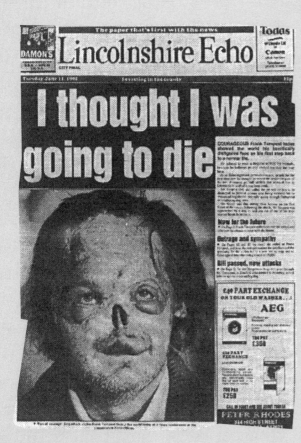

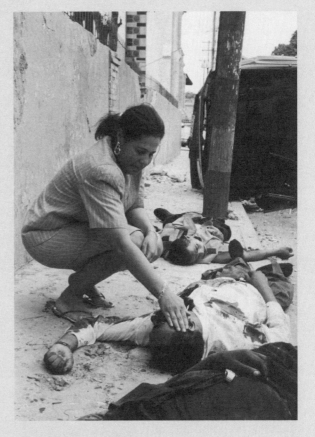

Several North Americans have
been badly mauled by pit bull
terriers. But it's unlikely that
any newspaper is ready (or
feels it's audience is ready) for
a picture such as this British
newspaper ran. The victim,
who lost much of his face,
agreed to the pictures, and the
paper received only two complaints, but was flooded with
offers of money and help. The
picture was picked up by most
of Britain's 'national' dailies.

Haiti may seem a long way
away from Canada, but when
Canadians were involved in a
United Nations peace-keeping
effort there in October 1993, it
seemed closer. During the ini-
tiative, gunmen assassinated
the Haitian justice minister on
the street. The *Ottawa Citizen*
chose to run the picture of his
grief-stricken wife beside the
blood-soaked body in full
colour on page 1.

Privacy

When a man is trapped in a bus accident, with a fence rail spearing him to his seat, he is a victim of accidental violence, and editors must decide if the subsequent pictures are too upsetting for readers to face over breakfast. But they must also ask themselves another question. Does that freak accident mean the victim loses the right to the privacy normally afforded private citizens?

The reporting of violence frequently involves situations that may be seen as invading individual privacy. Many of the occurrences of violence examined in the preceding chapter involve people in embarrassing or humiliating situations, and usually not of their own volition (suicides are obviously an exception). And frequently the violence, which attracts the media, results in grief to parents, children, or spouses caught up in some tragedy not of their own making. Why, then, must the media arrive, cameras rolling?

First, a definition. Privacy is the right *not* to be in the public eye, the individual's need for and right to be withdrawn from society, from public interest, and therefore from media scrutiny. This is not, however, entirely one-sided. The community has rights, too, particularly the right to know a good deal about the people it elects and appoints to govern it. The chairman of the British Press Council, Louis Blom-Cooper, calls this 'legitimate public interest.' Speaking in London, Blom-Cooper, a respected British lawyer, defined it as follows: 'A public interest instantly arises by reason of some public office or position that an individual is holding; or by reason of his conduct in the public domain; or by reason of his involvement in a public event.'[1]

In terms of privacy, most people are born roughly equal. The wealthy may be able to buy more privacy than others, but they also attract more public attention.[2] Individuals lose increments of that privacy as they emerge from childhood onto the public stage – playing on the school football team, working in an office, using public resources (such as courts or police), fighting city hall, or becoming vulnerable to public events (an accident victim, a robbery witness, a protester in a parade). Sometimes people lose more of that protective cloak when they are thrust into the public spotlight by events outside their control. The public has a right to know a limited amount about the bus passenger injured in a dreadful highway accident. The amount of public-ness is increased by the involvement of public transport on a public highway, with use of public rescue facilities and public hospitals.

People forfeit much more of that cloak when they propel themselves into the public eye – the man who becomes a movie idol, the woman who runs for office.

So there is far more to privacy than merely how accidents or other violent events are handled, though these will need further exploration. Coming under the same heading are such issues as:

- Scenes of grief: Should the media leave sufferers alone?
- How private are the lives of public people? (Gary Hart's bid for the US presidency collapsed in spring 1987 on this very issue.)

- Exactly who is fair game – only the famous, or spouses, offspring, uncles, and aunts? (Is a prime minister's wife a subject for legitimate public interest?)
- What of people swept up in incidents – the citizen who neglects to pay a parking ticket and is suddenly named in a city hall crackdown on offenders?
- History: Can people who have become public figures by criminal acts (murderers, rapists, etc.) earn back their anonymity, or are they always to be haunted by the past?
- To what extent does the 'how' effect the debate? Does the situation alter if the reporter *steals* the photograph or the magazine gets its information from somebody's garbage? Does the 'news' remain the same, whatever means are used to collect it?
- What, indeed, is 'news' when it comes to privacy? If the premier has an affair with a cabinet minister, does that mar her ability to perform her job? Many people have committed such indiscretions, yet they have still been reasonably good leaders, so perhaps it doesn't make any difference?

In judging issues of privacy, the reversibility rule is often particularly appropriate. When the writer/editor asks herself if the story should be treated the same if *she* were the central figure, does she flinch, or does she want the story treated differently?

Scenes of Grief

It has already been suggested that the bus accident victim was, willy-nilly, subject to news coverage. Although the incident is horrifying and bizarre, the community has a right to know of such incidents. If the story was not published, then commuters who saw the accident while driving by would be confused and might well distrust the media ('Why are they covering that up?'), and rumours – many wrong and exaggerated – would fly. There is also some validity to the argument that publicity for such an accident would lead to measures being taken to ensure it didn't happen again. Running through the five *W*s outlined in Chapter 1 in connection with this picture produces fairly predictable results. But 'where' does force one to wonder if the picture really deserved page 1 play. Perhaps it was a slow news day.

The same argument (that conditions might be improved) can be advanced for the Boston fire-escape picture. But there is one profound difference in this situation. The woman in the picture is about to die. The photographer knew almost instantly that she was dead. Certainly editors knew it when they selected the picture, and the audience knew it as soon as they read the caption beneath the picture. And surely death is the most private of all private moments? (Again, public suicide excepted.) Does the 'in-order-to' argument justify running the picture, knowing this? If the woman had survived unharmed, there would be no complaints. The picture would be acclaimed as a brilliant piece of photography, and a beautiful moment – 'good' news. And for just this reason, the photographer *had* to keep his motorized camera shooting. By all means *take* the pictures, as nobody can predict the outcome, but just because they have been taken – because they exist – is not sufficient reason to publish them.

Can a grim picture be justified purely on the grounds of artistic merit? A babysitter, fleeing a Boston tenement fire, died when the fire-escape collapsed. There was no dead body in the picture — but hundreds of readers complained anyway.

But Norah Ephron may be right in her argument that the central picture in the series should have been published for another reason: simply because it is a brilliant picture.[3] Ephron concludes that the quality of a photograph may occasionally be sufficient to justify running it. With this raw evaluation, the editor now has to decide whether the picture is worth the inevitable public wrath. The bold editor may well say, 'Yes. Publish and be damned,' and can be praised for not hiding behind an entirely hypothetical 'in-order-to' rationalization.

It will be readily recognized that such an argument will not, however, justify running the picture of the bus passenger with the pipe through his chest (referred to in the previous chapter). It is not intrinsically a fine photograph. Nor will it justify the Montreal massacre picture or the *Challenger* explosion photograph. Each of these has other overwhelming merits.

So often, it seems, the victims of violence are ordinary, defenceless citizens, even children. An interesting example of a child being caught up in a web such as this involved a small boy abducted from outside a swimming pool in Moose Jaw, Saskatchewan, and taken on a hair-raising cross-country ride by a man with a long and sordid record. The event was given large coverage by the south Saskatchewan media – the disappearance, the cross-country pursuit, the arrest, the child's release, and the final court conviction. Newspapers gave the story huge, front-page coverage, but surely this is justified as a 'good' news story, as it had a happy ending? Certainly the entire community was deeply concerned, rooting for the child and fiercely condemnatory of the abductor. By and large the press left the child alone once he was recovered. Yet the boy was merely an innocent victim, not in any sense having pushed himself into the limelight.

There is one justification. The story had to be written as a warning to parents never to relax their vigilance. The initial story about a child disappearing *had* to be written, and after that, it could scarcely be abandoned. The family or the little boy were probably not further harmed by the coverage, and the community got an all-too-rare 'good news' story.

Should media leave sufferers alone? The lift-off of the *Challenger* space shuttle was a major news event, so the subsequent, ghastly explosion was seen live, worldwide. Probably the images that stuck most in people's memories were that of the swirling smoke trail after the shuttle broke up, and that of Christa McAuliffe's family, watching as the disaster unfolded.

The first of these two obviously had to be run. The second was such a harrowing picture, apparently showing a mother watching her astronaut-daughter die, that it disturbed many people.[4] Typical captions under that Associated Press picture read, 'The family of Christa McAuliffe, scheduled to be America's first teacher in space, realize the horror after the space shuttle *Challenger* blew apart shortly after takeoff from Cape Canaveral. McAuliffe's sister Betsy, left, and parents Grace and Ed Corrigan console each other.'

Is such a picture an invasion of privacy, although there are, in fact, no dead bodies nor people about to die? The picture ran front-page on hundreds of dailies across North America, and some papers got complaints, saying that this was a private moment of grief. But the picture *had* to be used. The family ceased to be ordinary citizens once McAuliffe volunteered to be the world's first school teacher in space.

It is interesting to note, once again, the extent to which the cutline affects the readers' response to this picture. It was subsequently revealed that this picture was not taken *after* the *Challenger* had exploded but *before*, and it simply showed the family's awe and anticipation as the spacecraft blasted off the launchpad. It then takes on quite a different impact. The words make all the difference to what one sees in the picture.[5]

Funerals, of course, bring out similar relationships – Mme. Lévesque paying her respects at Quebec premier René Lévesque's catafalque ... the Kennedy family at John F. Kennedy's funeral, with the small boy saluting. Are these legitimate public events? Does the public have a right to know? The status of these people is derived only from their connections, on the basis of other people's achievements. Must they, too, pay the price?

But such moments are not limited to the rich and famous. Sometimes ordinary people are just as photogenic. A *Toronto Sun* cover shows a man who went out to buy an ice cream – and came back to find his entire family murdered. The public's interest is undeniable, and it fits Blom-Cooper's definition of 'involvement in a public event' in the sense that no multiple slaying can be viewed as purely private. The public has a right to know about a crime of such magnitude, the authorities may be seeking witnesses, and the event will likely end in the court system. Will the picture hurt the man? The hurt is already done. A picture is now more likely to arouse sympathy and help.

Often, grieving relatives gather at an accident scene. A picture showing a child dying in the street after a bicycle accident, with mother stricken with grief, was shown to editors gathered at an ethics symposium and produced some interesting reactions.[6] Some editors said they wouldn't run it. But Bill Dunfield, editor of the *Kitchener-Waterloo Record*, which ran the picture originally, explained: 'It's a dramatic moment captured on film ... Perhaps there's a safety lesson in there somewhere.' Dunfield said boosting circulation was irrelevant: 'Some of our critics accused us of running it to sell papers which is a non-argument as far as anybody in the business is concerned. We sold absolutely no more [papers] than we would normally have sold.'[7] The editor of the Regina *Leader-Post*, John Swan, added: 'I think that would *lose* readers,'[8] but suggested he might consider such a picture if it happened at the start of the school year – 'in order to.'

Another example of a family grieving over a dead child was used by the *Bakersfield Californian* newspaper – which received an astronomical 500 letters of complaints. The justification for the picture given by editors was that it might stop other small children from swimming alone. Professor Jennifer Brown concludes, 'Editors felt that [the] photograph was too powerful to be ignored.'[9]

But once again the argument is weak. Just because the photograph existed does not mean it had to be printed. The picture was, indeed, powerful, but dozens of such pictures are available every day across the continent, and hundreds of photographers daily *decline* to take others.

Another element to take into account here is the 'viewfinder effect.' The composition of this picture is too intimate. It might be more telling if taken at a greater distance, showing rescue vehicles and helpless paramedics all around. As it is, it lacks context and has a sense of looking through a keyhole. The 'how' of that

The explosion of the space shuttle *Challenger* was particularly shocking, as millions watched it live on television.

So the subsequent use of the same images in daily papers and then news magazines seemed to make it worse.

When a Toronto man returned home from the corner store, he found his whole family dead. Leaning on a police car, he weeps. Grief is private, but can such a moment remain private when five people are dead and the street is a chaos of screaming sirens, ambulances, police cars, and gawping neighbours? Instead, could such a picture in fact provoke sympathy and support for the griever?

This photograph of a family surrounding a drowned child provoked a storm of protest from readers.

An RCMP constable consoles a man whose brother has just died in a motorcycle accident. This beautifully composed shot seems less intrusive than some, both because no body is actually visible, and because the man's face is also invisible.

particular picture is, in fact, instructive. The photographer, using a twenty-four-millimetre lens, shot eight pictures from a distance of about four feet. Four feet – he was virtually in the centre of this tormented group. Generally, it may be best for the photographer to take the pictures first and decide later whether to use them,[10] but in this case the photographer really has interfered with the family's privacy.

A former editor, discussing similar incidents, echoes this sentiment: 'The picture which creates in the beholder the feeling of intrusion upon grief of private anguish, the feeling of "here I should not be," ought never to be taken.'[11] The other reason that many people react against such a shot is the reversibility factor. For most parents, if that was their child lying there, they would be consumed with grief and guilt, and would be mortified and infuriated to have a camera stuck in their face. But to feel 'there but for the grace of God go I' is very different from feeling 'that is private grief and should not be invaded.' On balance, then, this picture might prevent other drownings and *might* arouse public sympathy and support; but these are not public people and this should be treated as a wholly private moment.

Grief is not only associated with death. Some years ago, the Canadian Press news agency ran a picture of an elderly woman weeping, leaning on the door of her house, from which she had just been evicted. It was a beautiful, moving picture, and a thousand words couldn't have said it as well as that little shrunken woman with carpet slippers and a bag, wondering what to do. From such moments the reader learns a lot about politicians and the economic system, and such a picture may arouse sympathy, and bring support from the community.

Private Lives and Public People

Is that cloak of privacy completely torn away when someone steps voluntarily under the spotlight – the entertainer, the politician, the star running-back, the TV evangelist? By forcing themselves into the spotlight of public attention, do they stand, as it were, naked?

Not quite naked, perhaps, but they must recognize that they are indeed submitting themselves to public scrutiny – and not just the best bits. They will quickly find, once in the glare of publicity, that they cannot turn it off when it suits them. The public become passionately interested in their every move and every moment. Unintentionally, and sometimes to their consternation, they suddenly find they have acquired new responsibilities as role models. US president Thomas Jefferson once said, 'When a man assumes a public trust, he should consider himself as public property.'[12] He was not, perhaps, aware of the things the press might print – or of the private peccadilloes to which public figures might stoop.

The law does little to help either Joe Citizen or the celebrity. *Toronto Star* writer Val Sears, surveying the scene, concluded: 'There are about a dozen sections of the common law ranging from trespass to wilful infliction of nervous suffering that do bear on privacy, but they have failed to create a "right" to privacy.'[13]

Some provinces have invasion of privacy acts, but they tend to concentrate on such issues as the use of people's names for advertising purposes or bugging telephones. There is little or no redress under law for public figures simply photographed in public. Libel laws, for instance, won't protect the fat woman in shorts waddling down the street from an unkind photographer – unless he identifies her and says in the caption that she resembles two kids fighting under a blanket.

Generally, the mainstream news media, which excludes media such as the *National Enquirer*, are far more protective of people. The CBC's *Journalistic Standards and Practices*, for instance, says this: 'An individual's right to privacy is cherished in Canada ... The invasion of an individual's privacy is repugnant. Privacy in its broadest sense means being left alone. It means protecting an individual's personal and private life from intrusion or exposure to the public view.' Breaching this is acceptable only 'when the individual's private life impinges on or becomes part of the person's public life or becomes a matter of legitimate public concern.'[14] Inevitably, such statements are difficult to word, and such vagueness is open to interpretation or even abuse.

People in general, of course, resent being found out. For a priest, for instance, it is embarrassing to have the world discover that he, too, is susceptible to the sins of the flesh. But is it news? People don't want to be seen in a bad light, especially if they are considered community role models, so they may resent it when the bad news leaks out – that their marriage is on the rocks or they have a drinking problem. Are the media goaded to be super-critical by pressure groups such as the moral majority and the fundamentalist movement? There's certainly a puritan streak in North America, and some pressure groups can be very loud and outspoken and can imply to the media that they are missing the views of a segment of their audience. But this runs in total opposition to another North American trait. As US press critic A.J. Liebling said once, 'There's almost no circumstance under which Americans don't like to be interviewed.'[15]

Community Attitudes

Community attitudes also vary with respect to different human weaknesses. The public (and the press) may be more willing to forgive a drunk than a sexual molester or a murderer. Nora Beloff describes how the British press turned a blind eye when George Brown, Labour foreign secretary, got drunk, until the weakness was mentioned in a *New York Times* profile and the London *Observer* then ran the *Times* article.[16]

Similarly, the inebriation of a member of the British Columbia legislature in the 1970s was never mentioned in the press. Perhaps if a backbencher arrives a little the worse for wear and sleeps it off during debate, no harm is done. But what if he wakes to vote? And his vote breaks a tie? And what if he rises to speak? Usually little harm is done. If it recurs, the confused speech might deserve reporting verbatim, without comment, on, say, the editorial page. If, however, the speaker was a cabinet minister, it would fit well within the Blom-Cooper definition of 'legitimate public interest' and deserve to be reported.

Was such an interest justified in the private life of Gary Hart, US presidential candidate? Hart, it will be recalled, was a strong contender for the Democratic nomination in 1987, until the media reported evidence that he was cheating on his wife. It was subsequently argued by some that his bedroom activities had no bearing on his presidential calibre, and that some former presidents had had liaisons that had not affected their ability as leaders. But Hart made one serious mistake – or perhaps two. Hart, or Hart's campaign team, had described the candidate as a fine family man. Reporters, believing otherwise, had asked Hart about this. 'Follow me around,' he challenged. 'I don't care. I'm serious. If anybody wants to put a tail on me, go ahead.'[17] So they did.

From such a challenge and such activities, the journalist can quite fairly construe a legitimate public interest 'by reason of his conduct in the public domain.'[18] Gary Hart proved to be a liar, and if even his wife couldn't trust him, who could? What clout can someone have in the league of nations when he's a proven liar? So in a sense what he does in bed isn't the issue, it is the fact that he couldn't be trusted. If he will lie about that – the argument goes – he may lie about other, more important, things too.

As the *New York Times* concluded:

Reporters once treated candidates' 'personal' indiscretions discreetly. No longer, and that's to the good. Beyond the proper, debatable bounds of privacy, the public needs to know as much about a candidate as possible. It is, after all, the person whom the voters elect to be president, not a set of policies. Once in office, the policies may change, but the person's intellect, judgment and character will not. Mr. Hart's judgment was already in doubt. This new episode deepens those doubts.[19]

Unfortunately, in such a process the community may lose some capable potential leaders – people who simply refuse to submit themselves to such rigorous examination. It may be healthy to recognize that even though presidents and prime ministers are role models, they are just as fragile as the rest of us. And there seems to be little evidence that puritanism is a prerequisite for good leadership.

Prime Minister Pierre Trudeau is credited with the statement 'The press has no place in the bedrooms of the nation.' But he may be in the minority on this. After all, bedroom antics may reflect something of the nature of the people involved. As Ottawa journalist Val Sears irreverently put it in his memoirs: 'I came to believe the press has business in the bedrooms of the political establishment. What a man is doing to his mistress at night, he is likely to do to the country in the morning. And for the same reason – for personal satisfaction.'[20]

But is that true of other people as well, or only of elected people? Does a movie star have privacy? She is not an elected official, she is still a human being, a private person. What about Colin Thatcher, the prairie cabinet minister who murdered his wife? Or Clifford Olson, the British Columbia mass murderer? They threw themselves into the public light, Olson by committing murder, Thatcher by being a politician *and* committing murder.

When the lover of a Canadian cabinet minister, Francis Fox, became pregnant, he accompanied her to hospital for an abortion in January 1978 and signed her husband's name to get that operation. He was solicitor-general at the time, and forgery is not really a role-model activity for a minister of the Crown. But does that make him unsuitable for the job, or for any portfolio? Doubtless he rationalized this two-second crime as being for the best. Canadian society allows a woman to have an abortion. Fox admitted it, apologized, and resigned. Interestingly enough, like British cabinet minister Cecil Parkinson in a similar situation, he re-emerged following a federal election a year later as minister of communications.

The extent to which 'stars' retain a modicum of privacy was illustrated nicely in an incident at a hockey game in Winnipeg in 1986. Edmonton's brilliant Wayne Gretzky was leading the Oilers against the Jets. In the crowd was another star, one-legged runner Steve Fonyo, not to mention the usual number of reporters. When Fonyo got in line for a hot dog during the second intermission, he found himself chatting to a reporter. And next morning (7 February 1986) he found himself quoted across the nation with headlines such as, 'Gretzky's a Wimp,' Says Fonyo. Fonyo subsequently denied the quote and said he was a Gretzky fan. But even if he did say it, was it news? The reporter has a right to record (accurately) most of the things he hears for *possible* later use. But the decision about whether it is published is based on several of the five *W*s: Who cares? What does it do for the reporter's credibility? (Certainly Fonyo's credibility as a fund-raiser may have suffered.) What's the motivation for airing it? How would you feel if the roles were reversed and *you* were reported saying this? As one local columnist remarked, Fonyo often made gaffes: 'Such remarks haven't been reported because they are silly. If questioned, Fonyo would have withdrawn them.'[21]

But most important, how was it obtained? Whether or not the young and naive Fonyo – who was running across Canada to raise funds for cancer research after losing a leg to the disease – knew that the man he spoke to was a reporter, did he know he was 'on the record'? It would be unrealistic to demand that every reporter ask every source before every interview if the event is for the record, but to someone who is patently not media-wise, a casual conversation in a hot-dog queue may well not be intended for posterity. The reporter should have assessed that. His desk editors should have assessed that. The editors across the nation, seeing the Canadian Press report, should have assessed that.

Are Relatives and Ordinary Citizens Fair Game?

How far does the cloak of anonymity stretch? Are relatives of the star players open to equal scrutiny, to limited protection, or to the same protection as other private citizens?

Should the press have reported Margaret Trudeau's pre-occupation with the Rolling Stones rock band? Her unconventional behaviour may well have upset the prime minister, and so the media were probably justified in reporting it. But according to Ottawa journalist Walter Stewart, the press was aware of the fact that she experimented with marijuana but declined to report that.[22] Similarly, if a prime minister's wife chooses to go sunbathing on a Caribbean Island in the buff, this fails the Blom-Cooper test of conduct in the public domain or involvement in a public event.

A touching picture ran on the front page of the Saskatoon *Star Phoenix* during the hugely publicized Colin Thatcher trial. The picture was, in fact, taken by a photographer for the *Toronto Star*. Each day the defendant's daughter was taken to sit in the court, drawn inexorably into the turmoil. She is pictured – despite this – being a 'normal' little girl, stopping at a newsstand on her way to court. As such it is a useful and legitimate picture.

Would it make any difference if the photographer

Stephanie Thatcher was only ten years old when her father, former cabinet minister Colin Thatcher, was charged with murdering her mother. Her grandmother took her to court each day, but occasionally she took a break at a hotel newsstand.

had earlier given the child a couple of dollars to buy a comic book, so that she would go in and look at the pictures and he could call out 'Stephanie!' so she'd turn her head? Under these conditions, the 'how' overwhelms the value of the picture: It is, in effect, set up, composed by the photographer.

Another Canadian Press wire story several years ago began, 'TORONTO (CP) – The uncle of comedian Eddie Murphy has been charged with sexual assault in the rape of an 18-year-old Toronto woman in a midtown hotel last week,' and got such headlines as, **Comedian's Uncle Charged in Sex Assault.** What claim to fame did Raymond Murphy, fifty-two, have? Only that he looked after his actor-nephew's security. Apart from that he was a nobody. A common sexual assault does not rate national news distribution, and that is all this was. If it had been Eddie Murphy, that would have been a different story. Even using Blom-Cooper's criteria, there is little legitimate public interest here.

Ordinary citizens are often swept up by events. In the autumn of 1985, CBC-TV's *The National* ran an item about the city of Edmonton cracking down on unpaid traffic tickets. The network showed police arresting a man at his home for not paying a $15 jaywalking ticket.

People don't usually get on the national news for not paying a $15 ticket, and this individual was upset to face a TV crew as he was marched to the waiting police car. Was this unfair? Should his face have been masked out so he wasn't recognizable? Senior Southam journalist Peter Calamai raised the incident while discussing ethics with journalism students and concluded: 'I didn't like the piece because I could see myself in it.'[23] So for him, the reversibility rule meant the item was unacceptable. But although it might be humiliating to find yourself faced by police and a TV camera, there is an 'in-order-to' element here that is worth considering. Isn't the embarrassment primarily caused by the presence of the *police*, perhaps exacerbated by the camera, but certainly not caused by it? And isn't the embarrassment suffered by that one individual outweighed by the public's need to know about the police crackdown? In the long run, the embarrassment at city hall, for such petty bureaucratic vindictiveness, might be far greater, precisely because the media have shown how private individuals have been humiliated. In that light, the man being hustled away by police takes on an almost heroic quality as a victim of city hall insensitivity.

Other cities, aggravated by a backlog of unpaid fines, have tended to send police after only the major violators. The Regina *Leader-Post* went a step further, running a list of all the people owing more than $100. Is that really the press's job? Even if we agree that the media have a role in preserving the rule of law, they are not an agency of law enforcement. The newsroom may be risking its credibility here by being seen to ally itself too closely with the Establishment. Certainly it is news if the city announces a crackdown on unpaid fines. But there's a holier-than-thou element to running the list – unless the editor's name is on there, too.[24]

Publishing the names of businesspeople owing thousands of dollars in city taxes may be more justifiable. Not only is paying taxes a part of doing business, but in many cases the violators may delay paying as a financial tactic, and such manipulation does, of course, cost the 'honest' taxpayers money. In such a situation, which of the five *W*s are helpful? Who gets hurt? Those who haven't paid their taxes. There is a danger that innocent people may be caught up – perhaps people who have been jinxed by the computer – but the media cannot be blamed for this. Most could have avoided the hurt by paying, though the sudden publicity may be an unwelcome double jeopardy. Who gains? All the law-abiding citizens who have paid may be pleased at the others being caught: The system is vindicated. When to publish? Well after the deadline – giving non-payers ample opportunity to pay up. Why publish? It is unquestionably of interest. The audience want to know if their social system works. How was the information gathered? It is important that the *newsroom* initiate such a project rather than city hall, and the newsroom must be satisfied as to the accuracy and fairness of the list. The reversibility rule? While the reporter, too, might be embarrassed if her name were published for non-payment of thousands of dollars of city taxes, it would still be fair to publish it.

Can criminals ever clean the slate? When a former teacher ran for a seat on the Catholic school board in Regina, the news would normally have rated an inch or two: 'Another candidate has thrown his hat into the ring,' etc. But the headline on this announcement was a little different: **Man Convicted of Sex Offences Seeks Election to School Board**. The story began: 'A former Regina separate school teacher, convicted of sexual offences involving members of the girls' basketball team he coached, is seeking election.'[25]

The man had served a jail sentence for assault after a team member became pregnant, some five years earlier. He was quoted as saying, 'I've served my time, I've paid my debt.' So now, he felt, society should forgive and forget. But opposition was vocal, and he was soundly defeated. The headline is somewhat too colourful, but the electors had a right to know the story.

The Brampton, Ontario, *Times* was called to account before the Ontario Press Council after it ran a story titled 'Molester now priest at Brampton church,' about the appointment of a Roman Catholic priest in the community. But the press council concluded that the paper was justified in revealing that the pastor had served time after being convicted for the sexual assault of a seventeen-year-old in Newfoundland, 'in light of the refusal of local church authorities to discuss the affair,' and because he would continue to have contact with young people.[26] The parish priest had declined to tell parishioners about their associate pastor's past, although he had been in the town for more than a year. Was it therefore the paper's duty to reveal this in order to alert parishioners of a possible danger? Clearly, the pastor, still undergoing counselling, would be seriously hurt by the revelation. Was a year long enough to wait? How would the newsroom staff feel if they withheld the story, and the priest committed another offence? But if we accept that the motivation for this story is, indeed, 'in order to' (to prevent a recurrence), are there better ways of doing this? Would it be valid, for instance, for the editor to discuss the situation privately with the parish priest, and agree to withhold a story if he was convinced the man was rehabilitated and no longer a danger? But journalists are traditionally uncomfortable with such pro-active roles and tend to say, 'We're in the publishing business, not the secrets business.'

Here, for instance, is Paul Sullivan, then editor of the *Winnipeg Sun*, discussing a hypothetical case in which his paper breaks the law to get a story: 'My job is to print things. My job is not to set up an investigative service. My job is not to be some kind of policeman. And what I do is print things. And that is precisely what I would do under these circumstances.'[27]

A Dirty Job: Does Somebody Have to Do It?

Sometimes HOW the reporter gets the story may actually BE the story. Does the news remain the same, whatever means are used to gather it? Enterprising journalists have used an astonishing variety of means to acquire information over the years. Perhaps the best – and worst – example is the old tradition of 'pickups,' stealing, if necessary, photographs of the deceased 'as seen in happier times.' As the right to privacy has long been recognized, so the illegitimacy of some news-gathering techniques has also been recognized, though not often articulated in writing. One example, however, is the *Rule Book* of Britain's National Union of Journalists: 'A journalist shall obtain information, photographs and illustrations by straightforward means. The use of other means can be justified only by over-riding considerations of the public interest. The journalist is entitled to exercise a personal conscientious objection to the use of such means.'[28]

Those 'over-riding considerations' can, as with the CBC policy manual cited above, be stretched to fit almost any circumstance, and the British tabloid press are certainly less respectful of privacy than their Canadian counterparts.

What other techniques have been used? The range of incidents in recent years includes: digging through dustbins, eavesdropping on private conversations, persuading people to wear hidden microphones, dressing up as doctors, using long camera lenses, appropriating forgotten papers, listening through hotel walls, and monitoring cellular phones.[29]

ITEM. When Governor General Jeanne Sauvé was in hospital with a respiratory virus, she asked for no publicity. If anything, this piqued the curiosity of journalists. Phones rang throughout the night in the hospital, 'and a crew of journalism students were found roaming the hospital's halls with cameras in search of Sauvé,' according to the *Ottawa Citizen*.[30] (In Paris, three men – one unemployed reporter and two journalism students – ended up with jail sentences after they donned white doctors' coats to enter the hospital room of a comatose soap opera star.)[31]

ITEM. In November 1984, an Ontario radio station received an audiotape in the normal line of business and found on the end of the tape the voice of External Affairs Minister Joe Clark dictating letters regarding Canada's embassy in Nicaragua. The St. Catharines station broadcast some of the audio clips. This just added fuel to the Clark-as-Klutz image, but of course the error was probably made by a staff member.

ITEM. In the early 1970s, a Hamilton, Ontario, TV camera operator was filming federal finance minister Marc Lalonde in his office and got close-ups of the budget, open on his desk. The issue here is the premature disclosure of matter scheduled for later release.[32] This is not that remote from learning to read upside down, a skill taken for granted by every enterprising reporter a few decades ago. Is peering through the keyhole or listening through a thin wall any worse?

ITEM. The *Globe and Mail* set out to test Ontario budget secrecy, found copies of the budget in a printer's garbage bin, and revealed the contents on the front page.[33] It is useful to know there has been a leak and that an opportunist *could* take advantage of it, but releasing the contents early may well not be in the public interest. The news story *began* by telling readers the size of the provincial deficit and of an increase in insurance rates. The printers subsequently sued for damages and settled out of court.

ITEM. Ambush Journalism: The Enter, Cameras Rolling Interview. In a celebrated 'interview' for the old CBC-TV program *This Hour Has Seven Days*, Larry Zolf went to Cabinet Minister Pierre Sevigny's house and knocked on the door, cameras rolling. All he got for an answer was a crack over the head with Sevigny's cane. Good visuals; unhelpful journalism?

ITEM. In Vancouver, a report turned up before the Expo 86 fair showing there were problems in getting everything ready on time. The *Province* in Vancouver reported that the confidential papers were 'found in some trash.'[34] Is the story in the public interest? Should the reporter steal, trespass, lie, use duplicity in pursuit of some hypothetical 'greater good'? Is trash on the street fair game, but not trash in the disposal bin?

ITEM. Occasionally, the garbage is thought to be worth writing about *as* garbage. The London *Sunday Times* magazine ran a feature titled 'Inside Some Very Famous Dustbins,' picturing the dross culled from bins behind the homes of the Reagans, Brigitte Bardot, Clint Eastwood, and others. Who needs or even wants to know if Liz Taylor has thrown out an unused chequebook or that Mrs. Reagan has tossed away a worn brassiere? Does the audience need to know who has haemorrhoids, who uses contraceptives, or the private phone numbers and bank-account numbers of the rich and wasteful? They were all revealed. (That piece of 'research' was also based on a wholly erroneous premise: that everything in a specific garbage bin was thrown out by the 'star' living there. What about staff, relatives, and house guests?)[35]

ITEM. Does privacy vary with the clock? The reporter who makes very late-night phone calls needs to gauge the importance of the question he or she is asking and the ability of the person to answer it. Even cabinet ministers deserve *not* to be grilled at 5 A.M.

Is death news, per se? Mostly not. It depends on the person or the circumstances. When a child drowned at a water slide in Regina in March 1988, it was news because of the place. (But not everyone agreed. A CBC reporter, Gordon Steinke, was sent to the scene and was berated and browbeaten by a crowd who had gathered.)[36]

In fact, reporters often have to ask unpleasant questions and expose themselves to unpleasant situations. This is part of the job description. Sometimes the questions themselves can be downright embarrassing. One prairie TV reporter knew he would have difficulty with a question he felt needed asking. The question involved the sexual orientation of a provincial cabinet minister. Ordinarily this would not be news, but shortly before, leading New Democratic MP Svend Robinson had chosen to 'come out of the closet' on network television. The reporter knew that his minister – who had just announced his retirement – had had a distinguished career, but the reporter had heard rumours about his sexual orientation. The reporter saw one last chance to ask his question. And so, despite being advised not to by his assignment editor, he drew the minister aside after a final news conference and asked him, in front of his camera the following: 'There was some talk a while ago about Svend Robinson declaring himself as being gay some time ago. Are you, Sir, gay?'

'How dare you!' spluttered the outraged minister, who then marched off. The footage did not amount to much, and when the reporter got back to the office and showed it to his superiors, they had one response. They fired him.

Certainly the question was a provocative one. And asking it in a public hallway was ill-considered and insensitive. But should he have been fired for that? (The reporter was ultimately reinstated after filing a grievance.)[37] Why ask the question? The reporter had wondered if his source might choose to 'spill the beans,' perhaps describing a life of misery as a senior public official, or speaking proudly of overcoming obstacles to become a role model for other undeclared gay politicians. The minister was most unlikely to *initiate* such a revelation, so asking the question was the only way to find out. The man was offended by the question, but, *so far*, what harm has been done? Cabinet ministers do not and should not choose the questions they face, and they may well field worse than this during a long career.[38] Editors can only decide whether to *use* the interview when they've *got* the interview. Who was worse offended – the minister by the personal question, or the news director by the perceived insubordination and the boat-rocking?

In the final analysis, tough questions, even unpleasant questions, are sometimes necessary. The answers do not have to be published. News managers must not be intimidated by sources, and reporters must not second guess their supervisors and launder questions to avoid offending their own managements.

Covering Suicides

There's just one other facet of violent reporting that needs touching on here. Are suicides news by their very nature? And if so, to what degree do the media invade privacy by covering them?

The privacy aspect is limited, for a dead person has no privacy to protect. Certainly his or her relatives may have, and they may be embarrassed to be drawn into the resulting publicity. But generally speaking the media have a simple rule: 'No suicides. Except.' And of course the exceptions are difficult to define. (The issues were explored in Chapter 8, 'To Press or to Suppress?')

Generally, it is the *cause* of the suicide that leads to the debate about privacy rather than the death itself. If a teacher is charged with sexually assaulting students, he may commit suicide. For the news media in such an inflammatory situation, the story is clearly news; the ethical dilemma is whether to name the man and, hence, risk identifying his victims.

But that's the subject of the next chapter, 'Naming Names and Revealing Sources.'

TOUGH CALLS

1   A CBC camera operator was covering the murder of an Anglican priest in Maple Ridge, BC. He managed to get shots of bloodstains on the victim's office carpet by shooting through the mail slot. Good journalism?

2   Is it news if the police chief is caught drunk-driving? What if it's his daughter who is arrested? Or a hydro meter reader's daughter?

3   As a TV journalist, you are doing a piece about unemployment insurance. To illustrate it, you shoot some footage of a typical UIC lineup. Are the people in that queue fair game?

4   In 1984, Finance Minister Michael Wilson made a visit to Winnipeg and accidentally left a file of private briefing papers in a hotel lobby. Inevitably, they quickly fell into the hands of a reporter and made the top headline in the *Winnipeg Free Press* the next day.[39] If you were the editor, how would you have handled the material?

5   A Newfoundland lawyer is pregnant, and the media discover that former Canadian prime minister Pierre Trudeau is the father. Is the baby's parentage newsworthy?

6   Two people die in a house fire. A freelance photographer gets a picture of a firefighter carrying a child to safety. In the background is the boy's older brother, who has heroically helped in the rescue. He is standing in the snow in just his jockey shorts, and is visibly distraught by the deaths of another brother and their grandfather. Do you buy the picture? How do you use it?

The hero of the house fire was distraught and dressed only in his undershorts when he was caught by a photographer. Should photographers not take such pictures? Should editors not run them? Many readers felt it infringed upon the young man's privacy.

12 Naming Names and Revealing Sources

Police arrest a teacher and charge him with assaulting boys. He commits suicide. Should the media report the events and name the man?

A journalist reports that a terrorist group plans to bomb an Air Canada plane. The police want to know who told him. Should he say?

Discussion of such situations tends to concentrate on protecting the privacy of citizens, whether they are on the public stage through some public-spirited role such as politics or whether they happen into the spotlight by some misfortune such as involvement in an accident.

However, even people who behave antisocially, such as criminals, presumably deserve a modicum of privacy. Is it fair to reveal the names of people only *suspected* of crimes? Is it just bad luck if a newsroom names somebody who consequently commits suicide? And to what degree should reporters protect the confidentiality of sources, if, for instance, the sources are criminals?

The primary argument in favour of naming citizens who run up against the law is the fundamental tenet of Common Law, that justice should not only be done, but should be seen to be done. If, it is claimed, the media decline to name people facing the due process of law, then the law itself may be abused. Conceivably, it would be possible for a judge or court clerk to ensure that a case involving a friend be held in secret

or even quietly dropped, or for malevolent police to hold citizens incommunicado or detain them without charge. Furthermore, it can be argued, if criminals are not named, then the legal process loses part of its punitive and deterrent effect. It is much more embarrassing for Jane Doe, managing director, to be jailed for stealing her company's money than for Ms. X to be so punished. And it is much more salutary to learn that Mr. Klaus Kugelschreiber down the street has been fined for cheating on his income tax than to learn that a remote Mr. X has been so punished.

The community has, after all, developed a process for the apprehension and punishment of those who offend communal norms. Why, then, should citizens not see that process in operation? There is a public need, and right, to know that justice is being done. The glare of publicity is part of the punishment. This glare is multiplied as media multiply, but before people were embarrassed publicly in print they were embarrassed publicly in the stocks.

Furthermore, if the media decline to report specific courts or specific individuals, it may appear as if they, too, have been suborned and are in collusion with the defendants, reinforcing the suspicion that the old saw is true: There is freedom of the press for everyone who owns one. Finally, naming specific names silences the rumour mill. It may be better that one specific teacher, charged with assault, be embarrassed by publicity than having all male teachers in the community under suspicion.

However, the arguments against these rationales are simple. The media are not, per se, part of the judicial process and should not be expected to publish news reports as if they were a punitive agency. The community already has police, judges, juries, and jails to protect them, so why should the media arrogate that responsibility? The decision whether to run a particular story must be based on the intrinsic newsworthiness of the event, not on some quasi-punitive, 'in-order-to' motivation. And defendants are not guilty until so proved by the courts. Police may have arrested the wrong person, a witness may have misidentified someone, or a person may be 'framed.' But by the time Jane Doe has been found *not* guilty, her reputation is irreparably tarnished.[1] If the public want to see justice being done, they may do so, simply by attending courts, almost all of which are always open to spectators.

It is easy for the media to 'lose' somebody in the court system. Once a person has been reported as charged with, say, robbery, the newsroom then needs, in the interests of fairness, to track that individual through the maze of preliminary hearings, lower courts, higher courts, and appeals. It may, conceivably, be years before the defendant is finally found not guilty – years during which court reporters and editors have changed and initial interest in the case may have waned.[2] Furthermore, the media that decide to name names must get them right and fully identify the individuals. There may not be a lot of John Does around, but there are John Browns and Jane Smiths aplenty. The *Moncton Times-Transcript*, for instance, has a policy of naming everyone before the courts, but in 1992 one citizen went so far as to complain to the Atlantic Press Council when the newspaper reported that someone else with the same name was in court. Because there was no identification beyond the name, he said he was widely mistaken for the accused and wanted the council to help set the record straight.[3]

Another concern is the varying views that society seems to have of different crimes. Someone charged with a parking violation or even killing her husband may be viewed far more sympathetically than somebody accused of rape or molesting children. 'Equal' treatment by the press would result in far more opprobrium for some defendants than for others.

Is there a potential for interference in justice? With revisions to the *Criminal Code*, Canada now has clear regulations controlling contempt of court and permitting a judge to ban publication of details from pretrial hearings, which should in most cases respond to this concern. It might be a mistake to extend the law to always forbid such coverage. Inevitably, there will be extreme cases where banning publication of a defendant's name – such as in the Colin Thatcher murder trial in Saskatchewan – would be akin to trying to stop the tide with your toe.

Many jurisdictions have tried different approaches to this dilemma, ranging from an 'open season' approach, reporting all details of all charges (from speeding tickets to murder) to naming no names at any level.[4] The Canadian solution seems to be a typical compromise. The law says media may not identify juveniles in court and are restricted in reporting preliminary hearings – the first step before trial. Many newsrooms voluntarily decline to name people involved in minor offences, such as speeding or jaywalking, but such rules are often broken, depending on the nature of the incident or the prominence of the defendant. For instance, a man charged with exposing himself in the park would very likely not get reported. But when police round up several men in a public washroom, it may well get large headlines, such as **War Graves Commission Chief Charged in Ottawa Vice Ring**. This *Ottawa Citizen* story from 12 March 1975 would likely be handled very differently today.[5] Is the job of one of the defendants relevant to the story? Was it just chance that the police named defendants over a period of several days, giving the media new material for further stories day by day? One of the defendants in that case committed suicide after being named in the newspaper, and his lawyer subsequently maintained the man believed he had no chance of a fair trial because of the publicity. It is easy to condemn the press for sensationally reporting a sordid story that perhaps did not deserve reporting at all. But it is worth remembering that during revelations in 1990 about repeated sexual assaults on children in a Newfoundland orphanage by the lay-brothers who ran the place in the 1970s, it became clear the media had decided *not* to report the original offences, which subsequently continued for several years. Perhaps it would have been too risky, in terms of libel, to write the story, but there is a lingering suspicion that if the media had decided to pursue the allegations, the subsequent cover-up would not have occurred and the incidents would have stopped years sooner.[6]

A similar value judgment is necessary in cases such as prostitution. Traditionally, the media have declined to name customers of prostitutes (sometimes seen as a male conspiracy), though often naming the hookers (for punitive reasons?). When the federal government decided in 1986 to crack down on prostitution across the country, newsrooms were challenged with how to handle subsequent charges. The authorities urgently wanted names to be named as a deterrent, and so offered them to the media. Rod Goodman, ombudsperson of the *Toronto Star*, reported that there was a fierce debate in his newsroom, some people urging *Star* editors to break a long-standing rule not to name people accused of lesser offences.[7] The paper stuck to its rule in this instance, but Goodman asked some other newsrooms their policy and found that the *Vancouver Sun*, the *Halifax Chronicle-Herald*, and Toronto radio station CFRB would publish such names, though the *Montreal Gazette* would not.

Linda Hughes, editor of the *Edmonton Journal*, was faced with the same debate in 1990 when the city police specifically asked her paper to name 'Johns' as a deterrent. 'If there is a feeling there isn't enough deterrence in current sentencing procedures,' she responded in a newspaper column, 'surely the laws should be changed to provide stiffer penalties. I'm sure judges would rather change the sentencing guidelines than start depending on outside agencies, over which they have no control, to carry out part of the sentence.'[8]

In March 1993, police near Ottawa urged the media to publish information about a convicted pedophile who was being released on parole after serving time in jail. But here again the motivation is at issue. The police – perhaps dissatisfied with a short sentence and worried in case the man might commit another crime after being released – are driving the event. But the real question is not whether this particular criminal should be named or will offend again. The real issue, which the media should examine much more closely, is

whether parole is working properly and whether treatment of prisoners is effective. Certainly the man's neighbours might like to know they have a former pedophile in their midst. But if the system is working properly, he should have been adequately punished and cured and now have the right to be rehabilitated as a full citizen. If the media believe the system is not working, they should investigate, reveal, and editorialize to get the system changed.

One further example will serve to show how the media must keep control of the agenda rather than letting outside pressure groups dictate the news. On 10 October 1990, a Winnipeg police officer called a *Winnipeg Free Press* reporter at home to tell him a prominent local lawyer was about to be arrested for sexual assault. Not surprisingly, the reporter alerted a photographer to cover the event, and thus began a nightmare for the lawyer. Two months later, the case fell apart in court, but the lawyer's life continued to be haunted by the incident as an inquiry investigated police procedures.[9] Obviously, the case was newsworthy, but considerable evidence emerged later that the police were out to 'get' the lawyer, and the media, by maximizing their coverage, played into police hands.

Journalists joining this debate will often respond vigorously, 'We're not in the cover-up business.' But this presupposes that all those charged are guilty. And the thin end of the wedge was inserted long ago. A classic case of *commendable* 'covering up' occurred in the late 1970s, when a child in Houston, Texas, was diagnosed as having severe combined immune deficiency syndrome. This meant he would always have to live in a completely sterile environment. The boy was a medical rarity and became known in the news media as 'the boy in the bubble,' as he lived in a sealed room without even being able to touch his mother. The child lived in his 'bubble' to the age of twelve, and only after his death did the media identify the child, his family, and his home. The decision by all media to protect him from becoming a curiosity, pointed out by tour-bus operators, was entirely and only in the family's interest. The news stories over the years were no less effective, and the media must have won some community respect for their action. There would have been *no* gainers if some competitive reporter had decided to break this self-imposed restraint. A much more recent case in Canada involved the woman known only as Nancy B. The totally disabled woman wanted to be allowed to die with dignity and sought court permission to have life-support systems turned off. At her request, the media did not identify her until after her death. So the principle is clearly established: the media sometimes choose *not* to name names.

Similarly, the media today, quite rightly, almost always respect the privacy of rape victims by not naming them, though the identification may be easily available to them.

At the other end of the spectrum, Canadian society seems to demand the right to know who are its most antisocial members. It is inconceivable, for instance, that Canadians would have tolerated not being told the identify of Clifford Olson during his trial and jailing for the murders of at least a dozen British Columbia children in the 1980s.

The issue, therefore, appears to be not whether all names should be named, but where the line should be drawn. It is interesting, however, that the courts themselves seem to lean heavily towards permitting full disclosure. Judges, facing requests for a ban on publicity of a case, frequently quote precedents going back to the eighteenth century.[10] This freedom given by the courts, however, was not intended to hurt the innocent, and, as has been argued before, just because a particular action is *permitted* by law does not mean it should be carried out.[11]

The concept of 'victimless crimes' might be useful to mention here. This is not an easy term to define but generally implies that where no personal injury occurs – such as in the cases of tax-evasion or speeding – the offence is less antisocial. Such crimes might be reported without naming the defendant. Where individuals are injured – rape, child molestation, manslaughter – the defendant might be named as a deterrent and to show that justice is being done.[12] But in neither case is it necessary to name individuals before a final guilty verdict is reached, unless prominent public figures are involved.

In any event, newsrooms need to develop internal guidelines for handling names, based on giving the community the maximum amount of information commensurate with a fair trial and fair treatment. Is that the motivation inherent in the *Ottawa Citizen*'s guidelines, for instance? The *Citizen* names all adults charged by police. 'Naming the accused in any crime story is part of a long-established, fundamental principle of open criminal proceedings that guards against arbitrary arrest and detention.'[13]

Unfortunately, however long-standing that rule may be, it does more to save editors from making value judgments than it does to protect citizens, and it does *nothing* to guard against the irreparable damage done to somebody's reputation if the case is eventually thrown out.

A rule against naming defendants until they're found guilty can contain an 'unless' clause (stipulating that names won't be named *unless* the citizen is overwhelmingly important or there are other significant factors), which permits some flexibility. But this needs to be interpreted by senior newsroom personnel, such as an editor or news director, rather than by a reporter in the field.

If this is too restrictive, then newsrooms might, at least, rule against publishing names of defendants *before* their trial. Until that is done, people possibly facing a future trial will also face public ostracism just because, as *Globe and Mail* reporter Kirk Makin puts it, 'one or two police officers thought they had sufficient evidence to warrant a criminal charge.'[14]

Another issue, though not directly related to the subject of naming names, involves a basic question: Do the media overemphasize crime news? If one subscribes to Ericson's view of journalism, there is an unwarranted penchant in the media for crime news.[15] The clear implication is that the media should decrease the amount of space devoted to crime reporting, despite the public appetite for it. If newsrooms reduced the space given to minor and victimless crime, there might well be less demand for anonymity of defendants.

Edmonton Journal editor Linda Hughes argues persuasively for a worthier use of limited media space: 'Better to give good coverage to the most important and newsworthy cases and to go beyond that and write in-depth stories about the underlying causes and possible solutions to crime problems in the community.'[16]

When Courts Demand Sources

The corollary to the problem of when to withhold names in court stories is the problem of when to *reveal* names, when ordered by a court to do so.

Unlike their US counterparts, Canadian journalists have no special recognition under the Constitution and are accorded no shield laws. This means journalists who are requested in court to reveal information are given no special status (unlike lawyers), and are – rightly – treated as 'ordinary' citizens. It is generally preferable for journalists to be seen as ordinary citizens rather than as privileged and set apart from the community on which they report.[17]

Eugene Goodwin, author of *Groping For Ethics in Journalism*, quotes approvingly Robert W. Greene, assistant managing editor of *Newsday*, on the subject: 'To say that we will not cooperate when we have seen a crime committed, that because we're reporters we don't have to testify, is to say that we're not citizens, that we're privileged people.' And Goodwin urges reporters to avoid becoming such a 'despised privileged class.'[18] However, over the years Canadian courts have generally treated journalists in a benevolent way, permitting them to maintain confidentiality of sources by seeking other means of finding the required information. Only on rare occasions have reporters been fined or jailed for refusing to cooperate.

Without debating the legal ramifications, the principles involved are simple. Journalists should not interfere with the course of justice, and journalists should not break trust with their sources. Where these issues collide, the journalist must weigh the following:

- Can the court be persuaded to elicit the information through some other route?
- Was a promise of confidentiality freely given to the source?
- If confidentiality was guaranteed, what will breaking that promise do to the reputation of the reporter and the newsroom?
- Does a decision to refuse to cooperate with the court stem from loyalty to the source, or from a wish to be a martyr and get a look 'inside'?
- Are the authorities who want the information merely on a 'fishing trip' to establish if the information actually exists?

Unfortunately, attempts to 'use' reporters as information sources seem to have spread in recent years from the courts to quasi-judicial units such as Combines investigators and fire commissioners. Many media see this as a serious threat to press freedom, and believe it should be vigorously opposed through the courts.

However, one of the difficulties with revealing sources seems to stem from a lack of understanding of the initial arrangement between reporter and source. It is vitally important for the reporter to establish, at the outset, the nature of the relationship. Do both parties mean the same thing by 'off the record' (i.e., not to be used at all, not to be attributed to the source, or only to be used for background?)[19] The Canadian Press *Stylebook* sensibly points out that guarantees of anonymity can be overturned in court, and that sources should be told that reporters must identify their sources to their supervisors.[20]

Another difficulty arises with manipulative and lying sources. Reporters (who may, themselves, misjudge or misunderstand) are sometimes 'used' by sources. Increasingly, newsrooms wisely insist that it is not sufficient for an individual reporter to be convinced of the reliability of her source: She must share that identification with at least one other senior newsroom manager. One of the best-known cases of this was, of course, the Watergate story, where nervous *Washington Post* managers insisted that every new revelation be corroborated by three or more sources, and that they, at least, know the identity of 'Deep Throat.' The CBC's *Journalistic Standards and Practices* now insists that the reliability of sources be checked and information corroborated elsewhere. Also, 'The identity and *bona fides* of a confidential source must be made known prior to broadcast to at least one senior editorial supervisor.'[21]

Too often, a promise of confidentiality may be made hastily, without appropriate thought. The following points need to be considered *before* that commitment is made:

1 Can I get this information any other way, even though it may be more difficult, expensive, or time-consuming? (In other words, am I cutting corners?)[22]
2 Will my editor/news director support this commitment through thick and thin (including paying for expensive legal advice in court)?

3 Is this information essential to my story?

4 Having got this information, will I publish it, or do I simply want it for my own use or benefit?

5 Why does the source want confidentiality? Is his or her motivation questionable?

6 If I am ultimately forced by the courts to reveal my source, where will I stand in relation to this source, other sources, and my own credibility?[23]

Such considerations have led a few journalists to conclude that accepting *any* information off-the-record is unacceptable. Ottawa journalist and author John Sawatsky was asked by journalism students whether they should go off-the-record: 'No, never. Ever. You're violating your duty as a journalist if you take off-the-record information. Your duty as a journalist is to inform the public, and if you take off-the-record information, you can't inform the public because you are being prohibited from passing on that information, and you are then abusing the trust that is in you.'[24]

Few journalists are that firm. However, Gordon Fisher announced, when he was appointed editor of the *Ottawa Citizen* in 1989, that his paper would cease to use unnamed sources because it 'gives these people too much rein in determining coverage without having the courage to identify themselves.'[25]

The *Miami Herald*, despite a reputation for tough investigative journalism, tries to avoid all unnamed sources. Associate editor Gene Miller explained in an interview with the *Columbia Journalism Review*: '[It] is an invitation to exaggerate, embroider, embellish, slant. Or to take the cheap shot. This is true for the reporter, as well as the source. It is a bad habit and it is getting worse ... In the end, the reader is cheated.'[26]

Increasingly, other newsrooms are insisting reporters consult with supervisors before making any off-the-record deals. (On the same basis, the *Washington Post* now bans staff from attending 'background briefings' with officials.) More than a decade ago, Associated Press staff were instructed to cut down on the routine use of nameless spokespeople. 'As a basic practice from now on, let's name the spokesman or representative or company official or whoever, unless there are legitimate circumstances that dictate otherwise,' said executive editor Louis D. Boccardi. Boccardi allowed that confidentiality was sometimes necessary, but, if so, the

reasons should be explained in the story. 'Too much anonymity when it's not necessary hurts credibility and puts in a bad light the occasions when ... sources cannot be identified.'[27]

Similarly, the Canadian Press *Stylebook* urges staff to avoid unnamed sources and to use them only if: '(a) The information is of genuine public interest; (b) The information can be verified from at least one other source, even if unnamed; (c) The source is known to them; (d) There is no real possibility that the source is using CP for selfish purposes; (e) Normal standards of fairness and balance are followed.'[28]

Two Important Cases

Several cases of particular interest in these areas have emerged in recent years, notably the BCTV-Oakalla incident.

Terry Hall was among thirteen men who escaped from the grim old Oakalla prison outside Vancouver, British Columbia, after a prison riot at New Year's, 1987. Hall called BCTV, the largest television newsroom in the province, and arranged to meet a reporter to talk about prison conditions.

The interview was aired by the TV station and Hall was later recaptured. The TV station was bitterly criticized by Attorney-General Brian Smith for interviewing a jail escapee instead of helping police to arrest him. However, the arguments on both sides were weak. Smith (in an interview with the CBC current affairs show *The Journal*) damned the TV station for giving a criminal media time and for making a deal with a criminal who might have committed another crime while on the run.[29] Yet how else could the media get the story of prison conditions, as jail officials had adamantly refused to let journalists examine conditions for themselves? News director Cameron Bell insisted (in the same program) that Hall had agreed to surrender and that 'we helped him go back.' But Bell said his reporter had agreed with the escapee not to reveal his whereabouts. 'It is not our responsibility to assist in the recapture when to do so requires us to betray the undertaking we have given,' he said. This poses an interesting dilemma. Which is most important – the promise to the criminal, required in order to get the interview? Or the need to uphold law and order and perhaps protect citizens from further crimes? In a nutshell: justice or journalism? One can only speculate what would have happened if the escapee had committed a major crime after being interviewed. But the key questions have to be: Was the promise essential to getting the story? Was the story more important than the respect for law? In other words, was the net benefit for the community (information about prison conditions) great enough to risk the resulting accusations of sensationalism?

Bell denied that the scoop mentality or ratings were considerations in the matter. But the audience may have seen it differently. Certainly, to break faith with the source after making such a commitment would mean that the newsroom would lose the trust of future informants. Lawrence Kohlberg (cited in Chapter 1) asserts that breaking the law may, indeed, occasionally be necessary for the greater good. Were Hall's revelations in this instance of such over-riding importance?[30]

In the second case, CBC journalists in Edmonton suspected that a significant number of people were driving despite having lost their licences. Their investigation led to a dramatic network story on 13 September 1993. But the police – who were, by implication, criticized for failing to catch the suspended drivers – were bitterly critical of the journalists for not reporting the incidents to police, so that the suspended drivers could be caught in flagrante delicto. The CBC rejected the suggestion, saying, quite rightly, that it was up to the police to catch the criminals, not up to the journalists. But the police demanded the video 'outs' – the original, unedited tapes – and CBC staff expected to find themselves called as witnesses in subsequent prosecutions based on the program. Clearly, journalists must not be seen to be doing the police's work, but they don't cease to be citizens just because they are reporters; so if they witness a crime during their research, why not report it, even anonymously? If one of these drivers had subsequently killed someone, after being filmed driving illegally, that would have weighed heavily on the journalists' consciences.

Should Journalists Protect Their Friends?

In May 1987, the cosy relationship between newspeople and some sources was brought into question. Reporters at the British Columbia legislature were

chatting with a colourful cabinet minister, Stephen Rogers, outside the legislative chamber in an area that the speaker of the House had said was not to be used for interviewing. Rogers made some controversial remarks while one CBC reporter had his tape recorder discreetly running. The CBC reporter chose to ignore the comments (describing Britain's unemployed as 'poor white trash') as casual banter. But another reporter who heard it chose to report the comment.[31]

Rogers, who was seriously embarrassed – not least because he at first denied making the remark – commented later on the incestuous relationship between politicians and reporters. 'It's like a cruise ship at anchor, here. We all know each other very well. We know when someone buys a new suit. We know when somebody gets a new tie. Everybody knows each other and there's things that are said that are for public consumption and things that are said off the cuff and off the record.'[32]

This relationship puts a considerable strain on reporters, who have to be careful how intimate they become with sources[33] (see also Chapter 5, 'Conflict of Interest'). The friendships developed between press and politicians in the BC legislature were even further strained, subsequently, when an affair between a minister and a reporter became public knowledge.

This raises a further question: Just how far can the media go in writing about people's sex lives? This will be explored in the next chapter.

Tough Calls

1 A teacher in Sooke, BC, is charged with four counts of sexual assault, and the court agrees to a ban on publication of his identity at a preliminary hearing. The media unsuccessfully fight the ban on the grounds the community is tiny and rumours are rife. A local radio station identifies the man, who immediately commits suicide. Was defying the court order justified? Are the media to blame for his death?

2 Two Swift Current, Saskatchewan, hockey players are charged with sexual assault. During the trial, the charges are dropped and a charge of mischief is laid against the complainant. Should your newsroom name the defendants? Are they treated fairly?

3 During a robbery at a Saskatoon service station, the attendant behaved heroically in fighting off the raider. Your local TV crew interviewed him and got some nice quotes. As you were leaving, the attendant called you back nervously and begged you to kill the interview, in case it provoked the robber to come back and take revenge. Do you run the footage, which he originally freely gave? Run a story about an anonymous hero? Kill the item?

4 The Alberta Teachers' Association is calling for an automatic ban on naming teachers accused of sexual assault because the charge itself can ruin a teacher's reputation. 'For the number of charges laid, a large percentage have not led to conviction,' argues a spokesperson. If you are writing an editorial for a local daily, what's your position?

The Media and Sex

The trial involves a school teacher who has attempted to fondle a woman applying for a teaching job. The reporter reports what he hears: vivid, specific language of intimate sexual activity. As surrogate for the public at open trial, does he have the responsibility to describe the event? Or must he sanitize, protecting both the audience and the defendant?

The difficulty of how to handle sex in the news media is very like the problems encountered while handling violence and issues of privacy, and the audience certainly sees them all as symptoms of media greed. To sell more newspapers or boost ratings – they complain – the media sensationalize violence, invade privacy, and exploit sex.[1]

Yet the issues are vastly different. There is an appetite for 'private' information about 'public' people, at least among some segments of the public, which the media have to resist. The public may feel overdosed with violence and may criticize the messenger for bearing bad news, but they would quickly rebel at a sanitized view of the world, demanding knowledge of an explosion in Chernobyl, a shoot-out at Waco, Texas, starvation in Eritrea, an airplane crash over Lockerbie, a slaughter in Beijing, or mass murder in Montreal. So a balance is struck, giving the public some of what it really needs and would quickly demand. It can readily be argued that the audience needs to know about Chernobyl, for instance, because of the implications for world radiation fallout and the safety ramifications at other nuclear power plants.

World aid for the Eritreans was only mobilized after the media highlighted the disaster. And news reports of the Montreal university murders helped bring changes to gun laws.

By contrast, 'Newfoundland Priest Charged with Fondling Choirboys' may rate very low on a 'need-to-know meter' in Victoria or Oshawa, though it may well get high readership. Though the audience may not 'need' such a story in order to live a full and happy life, they may 'want' a lot of stories about sex. Ample proof is provided by the very high sales of publications such as *Penthouse* magazine or the London *Sport* 'newspaper.'

Sex is undeniably a primal force and a powerful factor in human relations. It is sometimes embarrassing, frequently ridiculous, and occasionally hilarious. Above all, it absorbs a lot of attention. But for journalists, the perennial question is just how much attention *they* should give this pervasive subject.

In the context of media ethics, we can define sexist journalism as primarily involving the demeaning use and abuse of the human body, especially that of women. It will be evident that it appears in many forms in the news media.

Nudity in the News
The naked body is largely banned from Canadian news.[2] Full frontal nudity is virtually never shown on television newscasts, in family dailies, or in weeklies. Exceptions are very rare and are based on extreme news value, such as the Vietnamese child fleeing from

Pictures of streakers, jiggling naked down Canada's main streets, had the potential to be quite vulgar, but some papers — during the shortlived fad — found tasteful but entertaining shots. The composition of this picture — shot at a British soccer game — is brilliant.

British cricket fans take their sport seriously, so when one player was suspended in 1986 for smoking marijuana, protesters quickly mobilized. A topless woman interrupted play, flourishing a banner. Was it newsworthy?

her village after a napalm attack during the Vietnam War. This picture was widely used in North American media as it embodies the stupid ghastliness of war in a few column inches. Hundreds of North American dailies ran the picture, but probably few people complained about sensationalism. Almost certainly this would not have been acceptable if the child had been older.

On rare occasions, the media will *hint* at total nudity. The photographs at left are both from British sports events, and both were widely distributed by the wire services in North America and given wide news play. They are acceptable in part because they are not explicitly sexual and offer entertainment value.

The first shot illustrates 'streaking' (a short-lived phenomenon in the early 1970s), in which people, mostly young males, ran naked through populated areas. Such activities caused consternation in some quarters and, consequently, yielded many pictures of naked runners – some of which made it into print. It would be easy for such pictures to be sexually explicit and offensive. But the picture of a streaker being escorted off the field at an international soccer match in England is neither. One English police officer is 'helping' the streaker with his helmet, while another resourceful official runs up behind with a raincoat. It is a delicious shot for the sports page, but would be inoffensive even for the front page, although its only claim to news value is its bizarre character. In the second picture, a young woman makes a game-stopping protest at a cricket match by running topless across the pitch. Neither picture shows genitals, and both are more likely to provoke a wry smile than a salacious drool.

Readers can get a harmless smile out of such pictures – a smile at the bizarre behaviour of humankind. Such pictures are neither chauvinist nor sexist and are ex-tremely unlikely to provoke complaints.

Even in public places, some nudity may be tolerated.[3] For instance, late-night Canadian television may briefly show a woman topless, and urban film theatres (especially drive-ins) may show fairly explicit love scenes. In urban centres, 'adults-only' video shops readily rent pornographic films for home-viewing. The criterion is one of 'invitation' – how much the viewer initiates and can control the exposure.

The media have to adjust to such values. The difficulty of making this judgment is evident in the instruction on taste in the CBC *Journalistic Standards and Practices* manual: 'CBC programs should be in good taste, that is to say, they should respect and reflect the generally accepted values in society regarding such matters as vulgarity, profanity, or sexual behaviour.'[4] But measuring 'generally accepted values' is difficult, and there is a real danger that those who must measure will either use their personal values as the criteria, or will be swayed by which ever lobby is loudest. This, in a nutshell, points up the difficulty in the fascinating 'existentialist' thesis proposed by a respected US journalism teacher, John Merrill.[5] Merrill argues that the ideal journalist would be autonomous, with self-determined values: 'The only valid ethics is that which is within each person,' he concludes.[6] But if, as he maintains, the existential journalist does not give in to external pressures and does not conform, then he must surely thumb his nose at community values and tastes. Merrill clearly has no time for codes such as the CBC's, but his perfect reporter would be in constant conflict with his audience in Smalltown, Canada, and with his more sensitive superiors.

The incidents of 'sexy' materials in the news media can be seen as falling into six other categories. The most obvious form is sexually exploitive material in the news pages, such as the *Toronto Sun*'s page 3 'SUNshine Girl.' Other incarnations include sexist language, the depiction of erotica from the public domain (such as art shows), the use of sex in advertising, sexually explicit text, and various forms of vulgarity such as a picture of someone 'giving the finger.'

People as Sex Objects

The images above can hardly be interpreted as exploitative. But in the next examples, the human body is more obviously being treated as a sex object. To a degree, as with television and videos, the readers of daily newspapers can consciously select the paper they believe they can trust to meet their standards. If the reader is offended by 'SUNshine Girls,' she can buy the *Toronto Star* or the *Globe and Mail.* (When feminists protested to the *Sun* about the SUNshine pictures, the paper's response was to offer 'fair play' – the SUNshine Boy.) But in communities where there is little or no choice of dailies – and today that is most communities in North America— the 'family newspaper' has to meet the 'house rules.' Readers are quick to telephone their displeasure, prefaced with such remarks as 'I had to hide the paper from the children today.'

By contrast, television is very ephemeral: The viewer wonders if she really *did* see that bit of nudity, but it is gone into the ether, not to be recalled (except by those who had the videotape machine turned on). Meanwhile, the newspaper sits, reproachful, on the coffee table, and with weekly newspapers, it sits there for a week.

Hence few mainstream Canadian dailies emulate the *Sun*'s chauvinistic approach to people-as-decoration (apart from its sister *Sun*s in Edmonton, Ottawa, and Calgary). And unlike the London *Sun*, which the Toronto paper unashamedly copied, the *Sun* does not exhibit full female toplessness, even on page 3. (The Ontario Press Council has upheld at least one complaint about the SUNshine Girls, but apparently the nay-sayers are still outnumbered by the yay-sayers.)[7]

Occasionally these pictures even creep onto page 1. It may be argued that this is news. The young person had, after all, just won second place in an international competition: local person wins fame. Even better, she was a former *Toronto Sun* SUNshine Girl. But page 1? Must have been a slow news day!

If such a scantily clad female appeared in the *Cape Breton Post* or the *Vernon News*, the papers would be besieged with complaints. Even if the picture had a newshook, there would be complaints. When topless dancing arrived in western Canada some twenty years ago, a weekly newspaper, the Richmond, British Columbia, *Review*, noted its arrival in that community with a picture of the dancer, which did not show anything more than one sees on the beach every day. Yet there was a keyhole quality to the shot (she was shown covering her breasts with hands), and the cutline went far beyond simply giving readers the information they *needed*. Apparently Ms. Jill Jacks, did not mind being seen as a sex object; but the newspaper was – back then – clearly contributing to the general view of women as sex objects.

If the newshook for that seems fairly insubstantial, that merely bears out a common view of the press. And at first glance, the bikini-clad sunbather who appeared

The *Toronto Sun* was fiercely criticized for its daily 'SUNshine Girls' — so responded by introducing a 'SUNshine Boy.'

in the *Medicine Hat News* falls into the same category. The wire photo vividly tells that it is absurdly warm in Toronto for February. (Extreme cynics will ask whether Andrea Desroches was a professional model.)

In British papers, the genre is known colloquially as 'tits-and-bums' journalism – and some London tabloids are significantly more explicit than their Canadian counterparts. (The urban market, it has already been suggested, may be far more tolerant than the small town, and the experience of British newspapers implies that competition can be the enemy of responsible journalism.)

Some of these pictures may be described as 'cheesecake' photographs, a genre that now occurs far less frequently in the Canadian mainstream media than it did twenty or thirty years ago. Newsrooms, once the bastions of old male editors, have changed very markedly in the last few decades, both with many bright women moving up the career ladder and males who are becoming sensitized to feminism.[8] But they have not *all* changed, nor has all the audience.

Does publishing these pictures reinforce – add credibility to – sexist values? Perhaps the *Sun* is reaching an audience of people who might not read any paper otherwise? Surely that is its right in a capitalist environment?

In Canada's free-enterprise climate, SUNshine Girls are acceptable cannon fodder in the circulation wars. Is the *Sun* using women as sex objects? The media are generally proud to resist the pressure of fundamentalists regarding abortion or politicians regarding political criticism, so why should they listen to the anti-SUNshine Girl lobby? The dilemma is clear: The newspapers have a tiger by the tail. They must decide, themselves, to eschew images that reinforce old sexual stereotypes, without appearing to be caving in to lobbyists, but they quite legitimately fear the cost, possibly losing thousands of readers and therefore *hundreds* of thousands of dollars in advertising revenue.

There are other examples of material that might be construed as sexist, including the weekly newsmagazine, *Maclean's*, which has run a 'People' page for years, containing snippets of gossip about the rich and famous. Generally, the page carries two or three pictures. Typically, at least one of those pictures every week is of an attractive young woman with few clothes – a minor actor or a beauty-pageant winner.[9]

Tastes change, over time. Occasionally the *Toronto Sun*'s 'SUNshine' girls have spilled from page 3 to the front page. This young person — a former SUNshiner — was named Miss World Canada and then won second place in the Miss World contest in 1984. Today,

Managing Editor Mike Strobel comments, "I think that was the easy way out.... I can't remember the last time we had a SUNshine girl on the front. Those sorts of things we don't do anymore. We might sell a few newspapers, but news sells."

Normally, bikini-clad sunbathers get short shrift in Canadian family newspapers. But the date and the place put a novel spin on this picture: She's on the beach in Toronto — in February.

MACLEAN'S

A DAY OF RECKONING FOR PRINCIPAL

ABORTION ON TRIAL

New Rulings Intensify The Raging Debate

Barbara Dodd's Change Of Heart

BARBARA DODD

A pretty woman with a problem makes the cover of *Maclean's*. Abortion is a difficult subject to illustrate, and her boyfriend, trying to prevent her having an abortion, was less photogenic.

Ship shape
Models Kathy Lloyd (right) and Andrea Kovic pose during the launch of the 1988 Lamb's Navy Rum Calendar, one of the most famous in the world.

Distributors of Lamb's Navy Rum were doubtless pleased when pictures — distributed with a press release announcing their new calendar — were used by newspapers. The balancing act between informing and entertaining readers is sometimes difficult to maintain.

The same magazine did a cover story on abortion, which was highly topical. The eye-catching cover showed a scantily-clad Barbara Dodd, an unfortunate young woman caught up in a court case when a former lover wanted to prevent her from having an abortion. The story does describe her trial and tribulation, but the cover gives the distinct impression that Dodd, who was vulnerable and far from media-wise, was being 'used' to sell magazines. But what better, more topical, way was there to illustrate the subject?

Public relations representatives for a large distillery distributed pictures from their forthcoming calendar to the media. Some papers actually ran the photographs of young women in swimsuits. The 'news value' is explained in the caption: 'Models ... pose during the launch of the 1988 Lamb's Navy Rum Calendar, one of the most famous in the world.'

Some sports departments retain vestiges of old male chauvinist attitudes. One writer, doing advance copy for a bobsledding contest called the North American and World Invitational Skeleton Championships, found his eye caught by one competitor:

Sweet Sue's Got the Key to Skeleton
Sue Calvert is a happily battered woman. The blonde bachelorette is learning, if ever so quickly, that her shapely 28-year-old anatomical lines are not fully protected in a skin-tight skeleton suit.

At least, not when she caroms head first down the Canada Olympic Park bobsled run on a 65-pound sled at speeds in excess of 110 kilometres per hour.[10]

The *Calgary Sun* piece dwelt on the competitor's bruises for another three paragraphs, as if being a battered woman was funny, before turning to her career, ending, 'But one of these sunny days, she's going to put on a bikini and tan those bruises.' The patronizing tone of this piece is positively embarrassing. 'Gee, fellas,' it implies, 'lookee here at this *woman* trying to do a guy's job.'

These examples raise a simple question: Would the items have been treated in the same way if the gender of the protagonists had been different?

The Canadian Press *Stylebook* has a long and useful section on the issue of sexism, notably: 'The test always is: Would this information be used if the subject were a man? ... Never suggest surprise that a woman has talent ... Avoid stereotyping jobs and careers.'[11] Imagine the piece above, running like this:

Sam Calvert is a happily battered man. The blond bachelor is learning, if ever so quickly, that his well-proportioned 28-year-old anatomical lines are not fully protected in a skin-tight skeleton suit ...

Somehow it seems likely that the copy desk just may not be impressed.

The CP directive contrasts sharply with a story distributed by CP in 1984, describing the vicissitudes of women sailors:

HALIFAX (CP) – There is more to life than cooking and cleaning for most female crew members on the tall ships – there are sails to be hoisted, lines to be taken in and watches to be kept ... [The] women, for the most part, match the men in enthusiasm and elbow grease.

This sense of patronizing surprise can easily be aggravated by the choice of headline. Here's one example: **Female Crew Members Do Their Share of Work**.[12] Is that really *news*? Obviously, progress *has* been made in sensitizing newsrooms, even in the last decade.

Sexist Language
Sexist attitudes lead, of course, to sexist language.

Here's the CP *Stylebook*, again: 'Referring to a woman gratuitously as *attractive, leggy* or *bosomy* is as inappropriate as describing a man as *a hunk, hairy-chested,* or *having great buns.*'[13]

A great deal has already been written about the way sexist stereotypes can be reinforced by the conscious or unconscious use of language. Since the Ontario Press Council first produced its booklet, *Sexism and the Newspapers*, with a chapter on terminology, this battle has been largely fought and won.[14]

The booklet recommends banning such terms as 'gals,' 'the weaker sex,' 'Jewess,' and 'manpower,' and it is refreshing and encouraging to realize that no self-respecting newsroom in the country would today permit such terms in its columns. Similarly, considerable progress is being made with gender-specific terms such

as 'fireman,' 'stewardess,' and with constructions such as 'An MP can expect his salary to ...,' which implies that all MPs are male.[15]

Doubtless it is too soon to be complacent, but the flood of women into newsrooms has unquestionably helped arouse consciousness on this front, in addition to feminist complaints and critiques such as the press council booklet.[16]

Erotica in the Community
The news media have to face some awkward decisions when erotica occurs in some form – typically in an art show – in the community.

The journalists must be sensitive to community standards and decide (a) what is necessary, and (b) what is acceptable. It may be, for instance, that the community will tolerate an art show of erotica in a private club but not in a public gallery. Or the gallery may be acceptable – but not the newspaper.

The Regina *Leader-Post* seriously misjudged when it covered a St. Valentine's Day show titled 'Erotica.' The entertainment-page review was illustrated with four pictures that contained – at least for the reader who stared hard enough – depictions of people actually coupling, and at least one erection. Those who complained argued that people who were genuinely interested in the show could go to see it; meantime, *they* had to hide the paper from the children. The paper, invited by unsuspecting citizens into their homes, had broken the 'house rules.'

Did the show deserve a newspaper review? Unquestionably. In a small city, any innovative art event deserves notice. But the reviewer must remember she is not writing exclusively from her own perspective as an aficionado of the art community; she has to act as surrogate for her audience. While she may be a well-travelled intellectual imbued in the arts, her readers may be significantly more conservative.[17] Her role, certainly, includes 'educating' her readers, so they will be more critical and demand ever-better art, but the revolution does not happen overnight. Virtually every newspaper page needs artwork, and it is entirely logical for an entertainment page editor to want to illustrate a discussion of art *with* some of that art. But it is naive to assume that whatever is acceptable to those people who decide to attend the show is also acceptable on the coffee tables of the entire community. Were there no less provocative pictures? And if not, was it necessary to run four of them?

None of this criticism implies that the news media should grovel to every complaining reader or viewer. The media have an educational role that includes developing awareness among the audience in order to make the community a better place to live. This may include offering robust criticism of the arts and ruffling feathers among the conservatives. But this must be done consciously rather than unconsciously.

Critic John Bentley Mays described the content of some pictures in a controversial touring exhibition in Cincinnati by the American photographer Robert Mapplethorpe: 'Among the topics depicted in these pictures: a man's arm rammed, up to the forearm, into the rectum of another man; a man urinating into the mouth of another; a man with a finger thrust into his erect penis, and so forth.'[18]

Mays says that other pictures concentrate on children's genitals but adds that he cannot even describe some of the 'most gruesome' photos in the paper. This verbal detail is repugnant, but it is essential. Mays subsequently describes Mapplethorpe, in a long and thoughtful essay on public galleries and obscenity, as

It may have been buried on page 17, but the Regina *Leader-Post*'s spread on a Valentine's Day art show, titled 'Erotica,' provoked howls from readers. One picture showed large erections, and two others depicted copulating couples. The art gallery was packed, but Regina readers weren't ready for the show in the paper.

having 'a manifest hatred of innocence, the longing to defile loveliness ... a breathtaking malice toward life itself.'[19] But such a condemnation would be difficult for readers to understand or accept without having some images in their mind's eye.

What about hiding it from the children? The fine print on the arts page of the *Globe and Mail* is much less likely to catch the eye of the average impressionable child than the vivid pictures in the *Leader-Post*.

Ads that Provoke

Advertising is not strictly the concern of the newsroom, whether it be TV commercials or newspaper ads. But the tone set by ads is bound to affect the credibility of the newsroom. If, say, a newspaper routinely accepts sexist advertisements, it will be assumed by critics that the paper *is* a sexist newspaper. If a paper is prepared to accept money from advertisers of questionable products, so the paper will be thought of as merely operating on capitalist greed, rather than having the interests of the community at heart. And when people complain, they do not necessarily distinguish one department from another – they will complain to whoever answers the telephone.

In fact, most newspapers have developed internal guidelines to prevent unacceptable advertisements getting into the paper. But occasionally, risqué ads have got through anyway, resulting in some amusing antics by newspapers as they try to avoid offending reader sensibilities. Tastes have changed, but years ago one of the Vancouver dailies ran an ad for the film *The Killing of Sister George*, which included a sketch of a faintly visible naked breast; between editions, a crude attempt was made to airbrush it out. And in an advertisement for an innocuous film called *A Married Couple*, the two parents and child, sitting naked and facing the camera, suffered the indignities of airbrush, scissors, and felt pen. In one edition, a neat little maple leaf was placed over the child's genitals. In yet another example, a nurse portrayed in an ad for the film *Nurses Report* was successively given a lacy brassiere and even a tank top over a period of several days.

If newspapers think it is morally acceptable to run ads for dirty films, then why do they think they should airbrush out details in the ads? If they feel it is acceptable to take money from the people putting on these films, then why should they think the ads will offend the public? Increasingly in Canada, however, newspapers have decided to refuse advertising for products of which they disapprove.[20] Though this may be a considerable expense, it does provide the freedom to editorialize on the topics – such as the evils of tobacco or pornography – without loss of credibility. Thus a paper can freely say it believes a particular film is good or that the dangers of secondhand smoke are not proven, without being accused of hypocrisy.

The counterargument – that our right to free speech means we have a right to advertise any product – does not hold up under close scrutiny. It might appear that anyone marketing a product – as long as it is legal – should be permitted to advertise that product. But nobody has the 'right' to place an advertisement in the media. The media have won (and retained through the courts) the right to refuse advertising they feel is unacceptable to their audience. This is realistic, though they should provide space to as wide a spectrum of opinion as possible to protect freedom of speech.

One incident illustrating this situation occurred in 1984, when many Canadian dailies ran an ad that featured a provocative model for *Penthouse* magazine. The ad upset a lot of readers, although other papers refused to run it. When *Penthouse* fought back at the criticism with a second ad (dominated by a swastika and ostensibly defending free speech on behalf of a mythical periodical publishers group), many more papers refused that ad, too.

Media managers also have to adjust, as tastes change over time. Only a couple of decades ago, a few papers were still airbrushing navels out of news pictures, as if human beings really were delivered by storks. A palpably sexist PR picture that somehow got onto the Associated Press wire in the early 1970s certainly would not make it today: The picture showed identical twin females, discreetly nude, one in an antique tin bathtub and one in a modern bath, promoting a London homes show. It is probably safe to say that if the picture had featured a pair of *male* twins in the bathtubs, instead of females – or no people at all – it would never have made it on the wire even then.

Words Alone

In some cases, leaving out the pictures and just running words might appear to be the answer. But words themselves can, of course, be highly offensive. Just how much graphic detail is needed, especially in court reporting?

Here is a sample from *Western Report*, a prairie weekly newsmagazine, describing the trial of a school principal for harassing a nineteen-year-old whom he invited to his apartment for a 'job interview':

[He] started to massage her shoulders. She protested when he touched her chest. He stopped, then asked about her sex life, suggesting she 'go to bed with someone experienced.' A few moments later he led her by the arm to a sleeping bag and placed her face down on it ... Then [the man], who remained clothed, raised her sweater and undid her brassiere. When he began massaging her buttocks, she protested, and he instead rubbed her feet and legs. He then tried to remove her panties, but she told him to stop. He rubbed himself against her legs and attempted to fondle her. She fled to the washroom ...[21]

Not much is left to the imagination. Doubtless it was all submitted as evidence in open court. But does that mean it should be published? Is such graphic detail necessary for readers to make up their minds on the case? Is this designed to inform, to educate – or merely to titillate? Could there be some other agenda here, of an editor either wanting to show how wicked teachers can be (though the man has already been jailed) or being desperate for copy to fill an entire page (vividly titled 'Crime and Calamity')? The story could have been written much more tightly, without such detail, yet still conveying the information about a teacher abusing his position and facing the obloquy of his small town and of the courts.[22]

Sometimes the urban dailies offer similar detail. The following is taken from a report of a judge's decision in another case: 'MacIntyre said the obstetrician's evidence left doubt in his mind. The doctor testified that the girl's mature sexual development meant she most likely engaged in frequent intercourse. MacIntyre noted that the doctor could not say for certain that her abnormally-large vagina resulted from her allegations against her step-father.'[23]

Certainly, in a rough-and-tumble world, the media can not protect audiences from unpleasantness all the time, and justice must be seen to be done; but on the need-to-know meter, such anatomic detail rates pretty low.

The community weeklies are rarely so rash, and one green reporter found out why when he used very similar courtroom detail in a story for the *Cariboo Observer* of Quesnel, British Columbia. The small-town paper vividly reported the trial of a local man, charged with gross indecency towards two young girls. As the Vancouver *Province* subsequently reported, in a story headlined 'Story Sparks Uproar in Town,' the daily quoted local officials: '"It's the talk of the town – my understanding is that there's quite an uproar over it," Mayor Mike Pearce said Wednesday. Pearce said that the article concerned him because there are "certain things that go in a newspaper and there are certain things that don't belong there."'[24] He could have been more specific, but it's clearly the sexual details that offended citizens.

Such detail may occasionally be necessary but can be treated less directly. The *Province* itself was much more subtle years ago when it described a furore over an innovative nightclub stripper. The woman is described by her manager as being 'like a nun.' 'Mitzi used various props, including ping-pong balls and a flute, in imaginative ways for her show,' the paper solemnly reported. Later, the bar manager is quoted as saying, 'She's not a drinker, she doesn't do drugs. All she does is shoot ping-pong balls and send half her money home to her mother.'[25] It would be very difficult for anyone to complain about this, without revealing a vivid imagination. Should such a story be hidden from the children?

Reporting Vulgarity

Occasionally, the media are faced with reporting or picturing some very public vulgarity. Such things are probably best ignored. Jerry Rubin and other rebels leading street demonstrations in the US in the late 1960s found they could get TV cameras switched off very easily – if they so wished – by raising a middle finger to them, or shouting four-letter words. The media simply felt they could not carry such a message.

More recently, this attitude has softened. Prime Minister Pierre Elliott Trudeau, roused by hecklers at a rally in British Columbia one day, was reported as having given one the finger. And at least two incidents in the United States resulted in newspaper pictures. In one, Vice-President Nelson Rockefeller gestured with his middle finger to hecklers, and the media judged the prominence of the person involved justified running the picture. In the second, which aroused widespread complaints, the fingerer is a convicted double murderer being led out of court. Many readers of the Wilmington, Delaware, *Morning News* were not persuaded that the prisoner was important enough or that the gesture was socially significant enough to run the image in their family newspaper. More recently, Calgary mayor Ralph Klein was caught with a finger raised at the camera.

In conclusion, it can be said that the public view of how sex and sexism should be handled in the media is rapidly evolving. Journalists have to be sensitive to the nuances of what the community is ready for, recognizing that what may be acceptable in downtown Toronto may not be acceptable in Peggy's Cove, Nova Scotia. (The liberated young journalism school graduate may have a much different view from her grand-parents of what is appropriate in the news media. And that graduate, fresh from the city, may find her first job in Melita, Manitoba.) This is not to say that the media must be constantly apprehensive of popular disapproval, never daring to challenge communal values, but that this must be done consciously and with appropriate debate, rather than accidentally or with a desire to shock.

Use of vulgar language, to be debated next, can be approached in much the same manner.

Tough Calls

1 Your photographer, covering a car show, produces an eye-catching shot of a souped-up vintage car with a shapely model called Sandra in cowpoke clothes draped over the hood. Would you run it? If it's the only picture you have for the page? Would your decision be different if Sandra was Samuel?

2 Engineering students at the local university decide to have a 'Lady Godiva Day' and hire a model to ride nude through campus on a white horse. Do you send a TV crew to cover the event, and, if so, what do you show?

3 Your daily paper has run a classified ad offering abortion services across the border in the US. When the advertising manager decides to cancel it, some feminists in the newsroom complain. Should the managing editor approach the publisher on the subject? Does it make any difference whether or not there have been complaints from the public about the ad or about its cancellation? Does it matter if this is a one-paper town? Does it make a difference if this is Kimberley, British Columbia, or Windsor, Ontario?

'Shoe'   **By Jeff MacNelly**

The media have often been criticized for allegedly caring more about sex than 'real' issues. When there was a push to enforce women's equality in the United States with the Equal Rights Amendment in the early 1980s, demonstrations in support were not considered vary 'newsy' — unless there was some novel angle.

Hide the Paper:
Here Come the Kids

How should a journalist spell the most controversial four-letter words?

The dilemma that journalists face with vulgar language is somewhat akin to that faced with provocative pictures, but there are additional puzzles because of the different standards for different media. For instance, what is regarded as acceptable in a Canadian movie theatre is quite different from what may be accepted in a community newspaper. And there are words that can be heard on the street, but will not likely be heard on the CBC's *Prime Time News*.

Which words are on the blacklist? The CBC, like many newsrooms, balks at even making a list for staff: 'As a general rule, profanity or expressions which would give offense to a considerable number of the audience must not be used. It is not practicable to prescribe a list of words and phrases which could not be broadcast in any circumstances, as public acceptance in this area is always changing. However, shock value is not a permissible criterion.'[1]

Tastes are, indeed, always changing, and, as will be seen, there are different levels of acceptance even within the CBC. However, it is difficult to enforce a rule that is so circumlocutory. The US Federal Communications Commission is less coy, issuing a formal codex of banned words: shit, fuck, cocksucker, motherfucker, piss, cunt, and tit.[2]

This list is far from exhaustive, as there are many street vulgarities that would doubtless also provoke repercussions if anyone was naive enough to try to use them in a newscast or newspaper. As with attitudes towards sex, the public's pain threshold appears to be ever-shifting. The word 'tit,' for instance, would probably not cause a great stir on most metro radio stations. In the late 1970s, merely hinting at the word 'fuck' (while discussing curious car registration numbers) was a firing offence at a Vancouver station, but by the '90s the word had turned up fairly frequently on network television newscasts.[3]

Print vs. Broadcast

A single vulgar word on radio can, however, slip by in a millisecond, leaving the listener wondering if she actually heard it. On television, it may be somewhat confirmed if the viewer also sees it mouthed, or accompanied by a matching gesture. In print, such words seem to leap off the page, assaulting the reader.

The decision on whether to use it, then, will be based partly on normal newsroom practice, which in turn is largely based on previous public response to the use of vulgarities and the sensibilities of the newsroom personnel themselves – presumably an older, fundamentalist news director will be less permissive than a bright young party-lover, particularly with regard to profanities that seem commonplace, such as 'goddam.' Radio stations aimed at a youth audience will nonetheless recognize that adults sometimes listen and feel the need to protect their offspring. (The firing incident in Vancouver occurred after a parent accidentally heard a rock-music disc jockey using – or hinting at – the word 'fuck.') Ironically, some of the music currently played on teenage rock stations, particularly American rap, is repeatedly vulgar, virtually using 'fuck' instead of punctuation. But news staff have to recognize that such permissiveness does not apply equally to the newsroom.

The CBC would virtually never permit most of the FCC words in newscasts, and yet they may occupy centre stage in a more erudite environment. When the *Ideas* radio program did a series on the *Oxford English Dictionary*, scholarly interviewees discussed the book's evolving attitude towards vulgarity. Sir Randolph Quirk noted the following about founding editor Sir James Murray:

Murray ... excluded words that were taboo words. With those, he had a certain amount of difficulty because some of them were in the *Bible* and in early good texts, you know, like Chaucer and Shakespeare, so that words like 'shit' and 'piss,' which are also shunned in polite conversation, as it were, were in the dictionary, but 'cunt' and 'fuck,' that's about it really, are not.

[The OED] really needs to have the historical record going back because 'cunt' and 'fuck' are for a long time. 'Cunt' certainly has been in the language since before Chaucer's time.[4]

So the erudite discussion of language is certainly one place where such words are perfectly permissible: impressionable children are unlikely to be listening, anyway. And the precedent has even been created in the printed media. The London *Guardian*, for instance, was reviewing the OED *Supplement* twenty years ago and noted, 'For the first time in any Oxford dictionary, "fuck" is there, and this word and its derivatives is supported by 64 quotations, from Dunbar in 1503 to the underground magazine *Ink* in 1971.'[5]

In a similar intellectual vein, the *Guardian* discussed the *Oxford Advanced Learners Dictionary* in 1974 and used an illustration from the book, which included 'bloody hell,' 'sodding hell,' and 'fucking hell.'[6] Discussion of language itself will become very coy if it doesn't actually name the words, so British columnist John Crosby took the direct approach twenty years ago in the London *Observer*, while discussing the ideology

of review writers: 'You might call it the New Puritanism of the Left. You can say "fuck" on the stage but you shouldn't suggest that a duke's daughter might be more toothsome than a working girl.'[7]

However, if this seems unadventurous by contemporary standards, it should be remembered that even the dictionaries have only accepted four-letter words recently. In a thorough exploration of the subject, R.W. Burchfield noted that the *Penguin English Dictionary* was the first general English dictionary ever to include 'fuck' and 'cunt' (and then only with three-word definitions each), and that was not until 1965.[8]

In each of the preceding newspaper examples, the topic is fairly esoteric and is unlikely to catch the attention of children – but the print examples are largely limited to the superior British press. Canadian dailies will rarely venture into such rarefied topics, so the occasion for vulgarity may not arise. However, it clearly does arise when major newsmakers use vulgar or profane language. The quandary for the media is then whether this justifies publication. The celebrated Trudeau quote of 'fuddle duddle!' in House of Commons debate is an example. These were clearly not the words actually used, but the prime minister himself said later that this was all he said, and the media were almost all content to publish that (the *Globe and Mail* may have been the only paper that spelled out 'Fuck off!').

In the United States, the dilemma was even more acute with the Earl Butz incident. The US secretary of agriculture was chatting informally on a plane with several people when he was asked why the Republican party could not attract more black members. 'I'll tell you why you can't attract coloreds,' he said. 'Because coloreds only want three things. You know what they want? I'll tell you what coloreds want. It's three things: First, a tight pussy; second, loose shoes; and third, a warm place to shit. That's all.' The major US wire services picked up the story because of its clearly racist tone. It revealed a great deal about a senior member of President Gerald Ford's cabinet. Eugene Goodwin describes how the Associated Press distributed two versions of the story, one with the quote verbatim and one – which was almost universally preferred by editors – which reported simply that Butz discussed in derogatory terms what he said were blacks' sexual, dress, and bathroom preferences. Some papers ran the bowdlerized version but also offered to make the verbatim text available to interested readers; 350 people turned up at one Texas daily, and some 3,000 wrote to the San Diego *Evening Tribune* asking for the transcript.[9] Evidently, the public interest – or curiosity – was there. Following the revelation, President Ford fired Butz, so it can be strongly argued that there was a 'need to know.' The electors needed to know the attitudes of the public official, and he needed to be disciplined, which might only have happened if it became publicly known. However, to have published the entire text might well have been seen as catering to prejudice and publicizing a racist 'joke.' The community benefitted by knowing *about* the incident but would have benefitted very little more by knowing the exact words used.

Which Words Offend?

As recently as 1984, an unscientific survey of twenty-nine US daily paper editors found four editors who banned the words 'hell' and 'damn.'[10] And the CTV public affairs interviewer Helen Hutchinson once recalled that the word 'contraceptive' had been banned by the CBC up until about twenty years ago.[11] Other words are more generally 'red-flagged.'

In a light-hearted commentary on the FCC regulation, Washington columnist Russell Baker pointed out that long Latinate terms such as 'micturition' or 'defecation' or even 'fellatio' were generally acceptable in the media, but the short Anglo-Saxon versions were forbidden.[12] He makes an interesting point, but even some of the longer words give pause. For instance, here's a discussion, on the *Globe and Mail* entertainment page, of advertising on the British subway system: 'Even those unremittingly provocative Underground advertisements, which reduced otherwise sensible gentlemen into frothing rakes as they descended on the long escalators at Leicester Square station past two dozen minimally covered, overtly isolated pudenda, are gone.'[13]

Considerably less technical was the term emphasized in a light Canadian Press feature: 'EDMONTON (CP) – Zookeeper Maureen Anderson hands over two slim cylinders for foreman Dean Treichel to inspect.

"Elephant snot," Treichel says cheerfully, nodding to the containers. "The elephants have been kind of mucousy so we're having them checked out."'[14] If *that* didn't give the reader a slight jar, the headline in at least one paper probably did: Elephant Snot All in a Day's Work.[15]

Other bodily parts and functions that sometimes give offence, though not on the FCC list, include 'crap' and 'piss.' Thomas Crapper, perfecter of the flushing toilet, is often thought of in connection with the former, but the word has Middle English roots, meaning the waste from fat-boiling. It has acquired a sense of faeces latterly and thus is now a taboo word. Hence when it crept into a *New York Times* article in a direct quotation,[16] the newsroom staff bulletin sternly admonished: 'Many plain-spoken sources use vulgar language in every-day conversations with reporters. But *The Times*, having chosen a standard of taste that bars vulgarity, does not quote such passages every day or even every year. It does so only when the offending language makes a point of overwhelming importance, one that cannot be made as clearly and forcefully through paraphrase. The May 11 passage did not meet either test.'[17]

While 'piss' would not likely occur very often in the news as a noun, it may occur in other forms. A Canadian Press story about racial tensions in Manitoba included this direct quote: 'They cause a lot of their own problems because they piss away their money on booze,' bitterly remarked the man behind the bar, who refused to give his name.'[18] When the *Edmonton Journal* used the expression 'pissed off' in an editorial, they received two dozen complaints, including six cancellations.[19]

Occasionally, foreign language expressions may provide similar pitfalls. The *New York Times* encountered this with a word quite commonly heard in that city and ingenuously reported by a staffer: 'Recalling an incident at an exclusive Los Angeles restaurant, Smith adds: "He once told the parking attendant at Chasen's what a schmuck Tisch was."'[20] (But, as the newsroom bulletin subsequently pointed out, 'schmuck' is Yiddish slang for male genitals and is therefore no more acceptable in the newspaper than English slang of the same nature.)

Editors of the *Globe and Mail* were probably taken by surprise when they received a complaint in 1990 from one reader who objected to a politician being quoted as saying someone had been 'gypped.' This, said the caller, was derogatory to gypsies. But there is no etymological connection. The Oxford dictionaries trace the word 'perhaps' to 'gippo' – a scullion.

It would be less surprising to get complaints for using the words 'fag' or 'faggot.' These are clearly regarded as derogatory terms in the homosexual community, but their use was justified by the *Los Angeles Times* when a local judge used them pejoratively.[21]

Some dictionaries now carry a full range of street language, and an increasing number of novels and plays use such vocabulary for authenticity. This does not justify their use in the media. One difference is that the book or play is selected. The reader usually has a sense of what to expect and will normally buy the book for personal use, rather than pass it round the family. Nobody is forced to read a newspaper, but there may be a choice of only one in a community, and many readers buy it by subscription or at least as a matter of habit. There are clearly communities in which the majority of adult readers do not want to encounter four-letter words in their newspaper, and the news worker has to be sensitive to the tolerance level of her particular audience.

So, in general, offensive language is undesirable in the news media, yet occasionally it may be necessary. There are situations when such words should be used or can be used. Of course, different words have different levels of acceptance, and these are constantly evolving. The word 'bugger,' for instance, was totally unacceptable in Great Britain a generation ago and would not have appeared in newspapers at all. It is appearing now, almost as a term of endearment. But many Canadian dailies still ban the word, remembering that buggery remains a serious offence under the Criminal Code.

Printing the Unprintable

There are a variety of ways of dealing with these situations. The writer can simply omit the word entirely without hinting it was used. The writer can leave the word blank, as in 'Witness said the defendant told him to "---- off."' Or the writer can hint even more obviously at the omitted term, as the *Globe and Mail* did in

reporting tape transcripts presented at a trial involving bombs and bikers: 'They f---ing put the cops on me and it's the other bikers that's doing it, it's not my club. It's the Outlaws and the Choice that are f---ing doing it, right, and meanwhile them ----suckers, they blew up a house in the north end. I was right there, I f---ing seen them do it.'[22]

This is particularly interesting in that it not only 'hints' at the missing elements by giving one dash for each missing letter, but it also captures with great care the slang and bad grammar. This is most unusual, serving to make this witness look ignorant and vulgar. Readers all know what the words are, and they can count the number of dashes if they are doubtful, then fill in the gaps. (The *Toronto Star* sometimes uses a similar 'crossword' technique.)[23]

In another story, about a staffing dispute at CTV, the *Globe and Mail* quoted an angry anonymous source: '"We have had a lot of anxiety and stress because of this and the biggest horror of all is that they might offer us our jobs back. But I don't want to work for these ass----s."'[24] This example is curious because it leaves 'ass' but omits 'hole.' This seems to contradict the general advice on vulgarity in the *Globe and Mail*'s own style book, current at the time. Editor Ed Phelan wrote: 'Generally speaking, rather than print "f--- off" or even " ---- off" I would prefer to skip the indecency entirely.'[25] But the evolution of taste is indicated by the 1990 revision of the *Globe*'s manual:

The fact that an obscenity is spoken in public does not constitute justification for including it in a story in any section of the newspaper, even in a sanitized form such as 'f--- off.' There must be some overriding consideration that makes the obscenity news in itself, as in the Trudeau-era fuddle-duddle controversy in the Commons ... In such cases, the decision rests with the editor, associate editor ... On those rare occasions when senior editors determine that use of the expression is warranted, we do not use a sanitized version, but rather spell it out in full.[26]

The *Globe* stylebook continues with several thoughtful paragraphs on the difficulty of deciding what constitutes obscene language. The public expects, it suggests, 'the courtesy of being considered capable of being offended by vulgarity.' The manual notes that it's usually sufficient to say that the 'crowd shouted obscenities, or that a speech featured salty, ribald or coarse language,' and recommends omitting the vulgarity: 'Few stories lose by the deletion of such expressions.'[27]

In one more example, the *Sunday Times* of London was describing demonstrations regarding redundancies in the printing industry as the new technology took hold. Two militants are disputing angrily: '"But first," she yells, "you've got to win the hearts and minds of the workers, you c--t!"'[28]

Yet doesn't substituting dashes, asterisks, or ellipses merely serve to draw attention to the situation, titillating the reader? Does anybody who is ABLE to read not instantly know what the words are? Does this, therefore, protect the young and impressionable as it is presumably supposed to?

The 'expletive deleted' technique was widely used during the aftermath of the Watergate story – tapes of President Richard Nixon's Oval Office conversations were peppered with obscenities. The approach was used during a *Toronto Star* story, which relied heavily on transcripts, re-creating a nightmarish plane flight in which the crew battled to save a crippled DC-10 high over Iowa: 'They pleaded with it – "Come on, baby! Come on baby!" – then cursed, calling it "a son of a (expletive)"..."I'll tell you what," Fitch said. "We'll have a beer when this is all done." Responded Haynes, "Well, I don't drink, but I'll sure as (expletive) have one."... "Now the God (expletive) elevator doesn't want to work."'[29]

Given some of the other words readily heard on the street, 'bitch,' 'hell,' and 'damn' seem very innocuous. Their omission here seems unnecessarily prudish and shatters the flow of this dramatic story.

Another method may involve using words that resemble the banned words, but which are not themselves directly offensive. The quality London dailies have a particular facility for this. For instance, the *Guardian*, reporting that the editor of the *Independent* had requested fewer vulgarities in the paper, commented puckishly: 'It stems from a recent day when the organ was peppered with effing quotes, including one on the front page about effing rabbits.'[30] On another occasion, a writer in the same paper, talking

nostalgically of the old 'hot-metal' days in Fleet Street, recalled encountering a harassed Linotype operator in the back shop: 'I once came upon him hacking his boots at the legs of a Lino and asked him cheerily what was up. In broad Lancs he snapped, "The phooking-phooker's-phooking-phooked."'[31]

Such verve and originality lift this beyond mere obscenity with humour and sympathy. Yet there is little doubt what the camouflaged words are, though they may not seriously pollute the children.

Again, the Canadian Press *Stylebook* offers a sensible yardstick:

Normally, disregard casual obscenities and vulgarities in reporting conversations, as you do other verbal mannerisms. On the other hand, so-called four-letter words are reported in compelling circumstances, such as the prime minister's use of an obscenity in Commons debate.

The recording of mild profanities is sometimes justified, though their overuse lowers the tone of the news report.

When an obscenity or vulgarity must be reported, do not use the prissy device of replacing some letters of the offensive words with hyphens.[32]

This is a very pragmatic approach to the subject: Do not use naughty words, but if you must, then spell them out.

The bowdlerizing, or cute hinting, cited above is not limited to newsrooms and can sometimes have bizarre results. In the 1970s, 'bugger' began to turn up occasionally in syndicated US comic strips, and sometimes slipped through.[33] But a 'Wizard of Id' cartoon caused anguish in some papers with the expression 'The little bugger keeps lapping me,' which occurred in dialogue about a foot race. At the *Calgary Herald* it was artfully changed to 'little beggar.'

The question remains though, should the news media be leading the way on this, holding back and reflecting the way society is today, or should it be even more conservative than society? Certainly street language may incorporate many such words, but most family newspapers would not regard that as a justification for putting them in the paper. In many radio and TV stations, the use of such words remains a firing offence. Yet they routinely turn up in the movie theatre and, quite often, on late-night TV. It is sometimes said that the media's role is to hold a mirror up to society, but in this case the magic mirror tends to erase many of the warts and pimples. It seems to be tacitly agreed, partly as a result of pressure from citizen groups, that at least the media should not be leading the way, embracing new words and popular street words to show their freedom from restraint.

For parents and the protectors of communal purity, things become particularly difficult with television. Parents cannot realistically tell children, for instance, that they must not watch Channel 4 because it sometimes uses naughty words. So TV is somewhat like a newspaper, in that it has to be *wholly* acceptable. However, tastes change with the time of day. Some things are acceptable at 11 o'clock at night that are not acceptable at 4 o'clock in the afternoon. On the other hand, newspapers have a longer shelf life, staying around the central traffic areas of the home for a day or a week, until the next issue comes in. Television, by contrast, is gone in a microsecond. Unless the kids have managed to videotape it, they cannot call in all the neighbouring urchins to ogle at, say, the news source saying 'shit' on air.

Taking the Name in Vain

Blasphemy, defined as offensive language concerning God or sacred things, continues to give offence in some quarters. In routine interviews, most reporters and editors omit phrases like 'for god's sake,' as they do not contribute to the story. But sometimes such phrases are felt to be integral to the story. For instance, in a court report involving violence in a senior citizens' home, the *Toronto Star* ran this: 'Roswell said Thibault twice threatened to kill "the whole God-damned Carr family" during alcohol-induced rages.'[34] The phrase here helps communicate vividly the relationship between the individuals involved.

AIDS: Communicating the Unmentionable

As suggested earlier, even the word 'contraceptive' was regarded as anathema a few decades ago. Today, it is routinely used, and words such as condom have appeared regularly, particularly in conjunction with discussions of AIDS. There are, however, street words that the news media never use to describe the transmission of this disease. Should the media be protecting the sensibilities of a sensitive audience, declining to use words like 'safe' in the newspaper because, for many people, it is not acceptable in conversation? Or should the media use such vocabulary because those are the words people understand?

How many youngsters in inner-city slums, for instance, know what a contraceptive is? (But they may be familiar with safes, having used them for water bombs.) If journalists are trying to help people at that

The Halifax daily was heavily criticized for this inflammatory headline. A few years earlier, AIDS was simply not discussed in the media, but by 1988 editors were somewhat more sensitized.

level of education by explaining how to prevent the spread of AIDS, which is the better word to use?

The same goes for formal terms such as 'anal intercourse' and 'semen' – cruder words are readily available, but very few newspapers anywhere dare use them. The exceptions are one or two papers in communities where the incidence of AIDS is very high, notably Los Angeles, where writers have felt they must be more explicit. The schizophrenia among newspeople is evidenced by two small US dailies. In a careful feature on AIDS, the New Bedford, Massachusetts, *Standard-Times* described semen-to-blood transmission of the AIDS virus and how the lining of the rectum differed from the lining of the vagina. By contrast, the editor of the Saginaw, Michigan, *News* said: 'We are a general circulation newspaper and that type of information would be highly offensive to the majority of our readers ... That type of information is widely available from other sources.'[35]

Is it the media's responsibility to inform and warn? Or is that the role of the medical authorities? And how do the authorities get their message across? With ads? Are things acceptable in ads but not in the newshole? Many newspaper editors may well feel that if their readers are literate enough to read the papers, they will understand the more acceptable terms. But there remain strong arguments in favour of special media – popular radio stations reaching ghetto audiences, for instance – using slang terminology for constructive information on this subject.

The media cannot slough off entirely the responsibility to protect or educate people, especially where schools, churches, and families fail to meet this need.

Drawing the Line

The sheer variety of 'red flag' words makes writing rules difficult, especially as situations differ with time, place, and medium. The basic issue remains one of offending the audience. Will the word offend a lot of people, and, if so, can it nonetheless be justified?

The CBC manual defines it like this:

As a general rule, profanity or expressions which would give offense to a considerable number of the audience must not be used ... However, shock value is not a permissible criterion.

There are occasions when the broadcast of an expression normally considered offensive may be justified. The validity of such language within the context of the program must be evaluated. Furthermore, it must be apparent that editing out the expression would impair the integrity and significance of the information which is in itself important enough to justify broadcast.[36]

This is effective, if 'considerable number' can be gauged. The 'elimination' test is constructive. Cut out the flagged word and evaluate the efficacy of the story without it. If the story is then seriously weakened, the word may be necessary.

But what do you do about *new* vulgar words? In 1993, an Ontario weekly, the *Napanee Beaver*, ran a picture of a demonstrator carrying a poster for the Ontario Public Service Employees Union. Boldly above the fold, the sign said, 'Boinked by Bob.'[37] The insult was aimed at Premier Bob Rae's budget restraints, but were some readers offended by 'boink'? Though the word could be said to be a simile for 'screwed' in the sense of 'abused,' it also has the Australian/English sense of copulate. British tabloids relish the word, as it still hasn't made it into most dictionaries and so is not officially designated an obscenity. However, dictionaries of slang do carry 'nooky,' so it was disarming to find that word in type an inch high in Saskatoon's *Star-Phoenix*. 'Narc Nabbed for Nooky?' the headline asked. The context made the sexual nature of the act very clear.[38] Both the OPSEU sign writer and the Saskatoon copy editor, doubtless on deadline, seem to have yielded to the appeal of alliteration.

The newsrooms of the nation have to observe that ever-shifting line between paternalism (protecting their audience for fear of isolated complaints)[39] and aggressive 'leadership' in introducing, accepting, or popularizing questionable language. Despite such maxims as All the News that's Fit to Print (the *New York Times* motto), deciding what is fit is often difficult, and once again it is clear that journalism is often all about leaving things out.

SEPTEMBER 8, 1993   51¢ + GST = 55¢

Students could find chaos as school begins

"As much as possible we need to continue to do our jobs and not let the children suffer."
— Barbara Sargent

By Michael Jiggins
Beaver Staff Reporter

Students and teachers face larger class sizes and confusion this fall as a result of the NDP's social contract, says Barbara Sargent, president of the Federation of Women Teachers' Associations of Ontario.

Sargent made the comments while addressing a crowd of public employees — including members of FWATO and the English Catholic Teachers Association — at Friday's noonhour protest in front of Frontenac High School in Kingston.

"Schools open on Tuesday (yesterday) and the education system is in chaos," shouted Sargent.

Interviewed later, Sargent said the outlook for education in Ontario over the next three years (the lifespan of the social contract) "doesn't look good."

She said unions expect a 4.75 per cent reduction in the number of teachers during the period which will raise student/teacher ratios to ever higher levels.

"It's creating a lot of stress and a lot of anger," admitted Sargent. "As much as possible we need to continue to do our jobs and not let the children suffer."

Lennox and Addington Women Teachers president Peggy Rice, also in attendance at

See **Students**, pg. 20

Sending a message — Val Lang listens intently to a speech by OPSEU president Fred Upshaw during Friday's noonhour protest.

The English language is constantly evolving, and what is vulgar for one individual may not be for another. Some readers might have been taken aback at seeing 'boink' on the front page of the community weekly, the *Napanee Beaver*, on 8 September 1993.

Narc nabbed for nooky?

SALT LAKE CITY (AP) — For six years, Kevin Carter repeated the final year of high school. Always the slow-looking new kid, he made friends, scored drugs from other students.

Was it naive to run a headline using the word 'nooky' across five columns in the Saskatoon *Star-Phoenix* , or is 'nooky' an acceptable word? The

Associated Press story says the undercover cop was charged with 'messing around with teenage girls.'

TOUGH CALLS

1 A well-known, colourful local lawyer has just lost a major murder case. As a TV reporter, you politely ask his reaction on the courthouse steps. 'Fuck off!' he replies, cameras rolling. Do you run the clip? Why? Does it matter which community this is?

2 Stalin's daughter, Svetlana, moved to the United States to raise a family, then suddenly moved back to the Soviet Union. A TV crew located her on a Moscow street, and the reporter called out, 'Lana, why have you come back to Moscow?' She turned and snapped, 'It's none of your bloody, fucking business!' And then she continued down the street. CBC's nightly newscast, *The National*, used the videotape. What are the arguments in favour and against running it?

3 Your paper is anxious to win young readers, and the youth-page editor has been urged to tackle important issues. A reporter has written a frank and lively piece about birth control, including a 'glossary' sidebar, defining terms like 'safe,' 'ejaculate,' and 'blow job.' As managing editor, do you approve?

4 A reader has written a letter to the editor that has an important message but is semi-illiterate. What do you do? Does it make any difference if the writer is a prominent local politician?

5 A reader, writing to the New York *Village Voice,* once suggested journalists should show their draft stories to sources so the interviewees could reformulate their words or retract things they felt foolish about having said. 'The idea of journalism is not to catch people out, or to hold them to their words ... but to try to represent their thoughts and feelings accurately and fairly.' Does this argument hold water given the reality of journalism?

Different Media: Different Problems

If it's a slow news day and there is really nothing earth-shattering happening, what does the newspaper editor use for that day's 'top' story? Should a TV station give prime time to a convicted murderer to proclaim his innocence? Is a gruesome picture better than no picture at all? Does the presence of a TV camera alter an event? These are the sorts of dilemmas news managers face each day.

The preceding chapters have concentrated on generic ethical problems, which can be encountered in any newsroom. However, a number of media face dilemmas peculiar to them: the nature of the medium itself exacerbates or even creates ethical questions. Some of these problems are specific to particular media.

News Agencies
By definition, Canadian Press is a cooperative news distribution agency. The 'pack' effect of this has been touched upon in Chapter 6.

By its nature, CP, and its subsidiary, Broadcast News, have a homogenizing effect. A Canadian Press writer or editor is, in effect, working for about 110 newspapers. Rarely does he or she handle anything for a specific newsroom but more generally serves all Canadian dailies, and/or particular geographic regions – all Prairie dailies or all dailies in the Maritimes, etc. While few papers have strong individual writing or editing styles, the CP staffer is writing for them all, which must have a dulling effect.[1] Three Canadian academics are all rather critical of this influence. Desbarats refers to a 'dispas-

sionate and "objective" style of reporting.'[2] Rutherford refers to what he calls 'factual, often bland, reports so as not to upset the editorial proclivities of client newspapers.'[3] David Taras, describing the history of objective journalism in Canada, is even more outspoken: 'The CP "sausage machine" relentlessly stripped away local flavour, colourful language, and political rhetoric.'[4]

Furthermore, because CP writers are, in effect, employed by dailies from coast to coast, they must be sensitive to six different time zones. As most dailies have deadlines spread over the day (usually starting with the opinion pages, and always ending with page 1), somebody, somewhere, is on deadline at almost any hour of the day or night. This means that there is considerable pressure on the CP writer and editor to work fast at all times. Although staff are urged to be accurate, and although CP is the only national wire service in Canada, publishers do carp at the network, and this is aggravated by the vast volume of material handled by CP staff. There is a demand for speed that militates against thoughtful evaluation of the effects of a story and against – as Helen Hutchinson phrases it – 'putting the beads on the string.'[5] This is aggravated at Broadcast News, where staff are serving newsrooms with news shows at every hour of the day and night.

Print Media
Before exploring problems peculiar to dailies, weeklies, or magazines, it would be useful to explore a few ethical problems applicable to all print media.

Several of these have been touched on in preceding chapters. For instance, the amount of space available for the newsroom will vary dramatically from issue to issue, bearing no relationship to the amount of news material on hand. Advertising rules. If it is midweek, there will likely be a lot of grocery advertisements. If it is August, there will be a rush of 'back-to-school' ads. Similarly, Christmas, travel planning, and the new car season may all influence the size of publications. And yet the flow of news works on entirely different cycles, more likely influenced by government activity (elections, House recessed for the summer), sports (a lot on Saturday), and business (little on Sunday). The best newspapers and magazines allow their newsrooms considerable flexibility over the amount of space they may employ, averaging it over long periods, and permitting additional pages when conditions warrant, even if there is insufficient advertising to support them.[6]

Shelf life is also an important consideration for print journalists. They can 'get away with' unethical behaviour more easily on the daily paper simply because the paper is so short-lived. If readers spend half-an-hour with their paper, editors consider themselves lucky, and almost nothing gets read twice. So the journalistic lapse is perhaps sooner forgotten than in the magazine, which can last a week or a month.

Newsprint: The Dwindling Resource
The newspaper is almost the ultimate ephemera. Nobody reads it all, and it is disposed of within hours or even minutes. Indeed, some controlled-circulation (free) papers are often thrown out immediately on receipt.

Despite concerted efforts by newsprint manufacturers and users, there is still limited recycling of newsprint worldwide, and there are few viable substitutes for wood pulp.[7] Meanwhile, there is clearly a growing concern about newspapers' contribution to pollution. While preaching responsible environmentalism, newspapers themselves have a constant and insatiable appetite, impinging all too visibly on the environment, with thousands of acres of clearcut logging and thousands of tons of waste newspaper. The environmental beat was popular in the 1970s and 1980s, usefully arousing public awareness about the

planet, but, ironically, this very awareness has likely contributed to a sense of guilt among newspaper readers. As they scan their two-pound Sunday paper, they have become increasingly conscious of how little of it they read and how little of it they need.

Economics is having some effect. With newsprint costing about US $700 a ton in North America, newspapers, which use hundreds of tons a day, are trying increasingly to conserve and to recycle. In the 1980s, many newspapers shrank their broadsheet format slightly and used narrower margins: conserving half-an-inch of paper can save hundreds of thousands of dollars over time.

What More Can Newspapers Do?
• They can promote community recycling, even if it is of no direct, immediate benefit to themselves.
• They can use less. Many papers are already trimming back, with shorter articles and fewer pages.
• They can use recycled newsprint.
• They can encourage development of wood substitutes, and use them where available.
• They can pursue the possibility of audience section-selection. The marriage of computers and demographics means it is increasingly possible to deliver a more personalized paper to consumers, instead of using the scatter-shot approach. In the past, every reader has received the same paper. But the Scarborough reader may not want Etobicoke or Oshawa news in her *Toronto Star*. Readers' time is limited, and they should not be forced to search through material they do not want to find 'news they can use.' With increasing emphasis on the 'use-paper,' newspaper producers must take the note lest they be dismissed as the 'useless paper.'

Some of these activities do not have any direct financial benefit. But wasting paper is poor PR.

Pictures
Newspapers need pictures. Television, of course, also needs pictures, but generally speaking the dailies and weeklies feel they need at least some artwork on every page to break up the monotony of grey type. Such a hunger is hard to satisfy.

So the editors producing, say, a fifty-six-page newspaper tonight have to find several dozen pictures. Even with no pictures on all-ad pages like the classifieds, they may need forty or more photographs suitable to run in each day's paper. Some sports, some entertainment, some international news, some local.

Why not just run stories? The newspaper, after all, is supposed to be *news*. The audience can turn to television to see pictures. But if every daily resembled the *Wall Street Journal*, there would be few dailies. It is said that the *Wall Street Journal* has only once had a photograph on the front page. It has small line drawings and graphs, but no pictures. It can get away with solid slabs of grey type (actually very carefully and creatively used) because its audience is devoted to it: The *Journal* contains information that the readers urgently want. Few editors elsewhere can command such loyalty, and few readers are prepared to work that hard.

In an age of uncertain literacy and passive entertainment on television, it is already difficult to win and keep newspaper readers. If, on opening the daily, the reader is faced by two big pages of solid grey type, she will be quickly put off. It is much more interesting to turn on the TV news or the movie of the week and be entertained passively than to have to *work* at reading. So there is an insatiable demand in newsrooms for pictures – pictures that go with the stories and match the hole available. Consequently, borderline pictures, which might be labelled risqué or sexist or free advertising, will sometimes get into the paper, although they are really not legitimate hard news.

Editors thus face a painful and perpetual balancing act. Do they risk criticism for a picture that is sexist or sensational? Or do they risk losing readers with a dull, grey page?

Headlines

As every page needs a picture, so every story needs some form of headline. Moreover, long experience has shown editors that headlines do much more than merely summarize the story: They also dress up a page visually (providing patches of black and white amongst the grey type); they titillate readers, to encourage them to try this particular item; and they help guide readers round the page, showing the comparative importance of each story.

But headlines must also fit: no headline can be

longer than the space allotted, and the headline that is very short looks as if something fell off the page before it was printed. The result is another challenge to editors: to write dozens of headlines that satisfy all these criteria, in a matter of hours or even minutes.

But picture headlines and captions (cutlines) need to be honest, despite the pressures. The preceding comments about the hunger for pictures and the difficulty of writing headlines indicate, on occasion, that corners will be cut. The two pictures from one issue of the British newspaper *Today* will suffice to illustrate the point.

On page 1, the paper runs an abysmal rearview picture to illustrate the Queen Mother's eighty-eighth birthday, under the headline 'Di Can't Resist Stealing the Show.' Perhaps the photographer arrived at Clarence House late and found the royal party already leaving. In desperation, he calls out 'Diana!' and she turns her head. Click! The resulting headline, if this scenario is indeed what happened, is blatantly unfair, implying that the princess is initiating some sort of show-stealing.[8]

The second picture is headlined 'Safety Last for the Dashing Duchess.' It shows the Duchess of Westminster trying out a new toy – a motorcycle given her by her husband. What the story neglects to say is (*a*) how far they travelled on the driveway outside Eaton Hall (ten metres? ten kilometres?); (*b*) how fast they travelled (the camera is being panned with the bike, but even so there is little blurring); (*c*) why the children were on board? (Could the photographer have suggested it? Evidently he told them all to look at the camera.) But the writer does go to the trouble of phoning the automobile association to ask – perhaps hypothetically – how they felt about someone not wearing a helmet and taking two passengers on a motorbike, with the predictable result (they said motorbike riders should wear crash helmets and should not take two passengers).

Too much weight should not be given to these two small examples, but they do imply that editors need to ask why more often. Why did the princess turn her head? Why did the duchess give her children a ride? (Why, indeed, does the reader need to be told how big their estate is or how much money her husband has in

DI CAN'T RESIST STEALING THE SHOW

IT was the Queen Mother's big day, but one backward glance from Princess

Safety last for the dashing Duchess

Are royals and titled folks fair game? An unscrupulous photographer or editor can use the caption to turn a harmless picture into something controversial.

the bank, unfair as it may seem? The reader already knows that wealth is not distributed fairly.)

What is clear is that captions can make a major difference to a reader's understanding, and value judgments can be easily transmitted. The caption for a picture of a wall spray-painted by vandals, for instance, can make it look clever, funny, or destructive.[9]

Meanwhile, there are some things print does well. The US journalism teacher John Hohenberg makes the point that the press has a special societal role, to examine, explain, and interpret: 'Moreover, because so much of the broadcast media is given over to entertainment, it falls to newspapers to provide their communities with an open forum for ideas, popular or not, and for the presentation of conflicting points of view.'[10]

This responsibility becomes even greater as the variety of voices diminishes. The shrinking and rationalizing of dailies across North America seems to have bottomed out, but only because most communities are now left with only one newspaper. Whether it is only one daily or only one weekly, the importance of it as a public forum cannot be overstated. This must go far beyond the letters page: news and features must strive, too, to cover the widest possible spectrum of interests and opinions.

Photojournalism can pose other problems too. For instance, it may be necessary to pose individual subjects for 'portraits' for publications (though it can be argued that spontaneity will produce much better photographs). But when *events* are posed, the readers need to be told. Thus, if for some reason the photographer fails to find a working prostitute to illustrate a story on prostitution, he should inform the reader that he got a reporter to pose instead. If he cannot find an addict injecting drugs for an addiction feature and so sets up a model, the cutline should say so.

Changing technology is also posing a whole new cluster of dilemmas for journalists. Photographers have long cropped, filtered, dodged, bleached, or 'burnt' pictures in the darkroom for dramatic or poetic effect.[11] Mostly, this is designed simply to enhance the photograph, rather than to cheat the viewer. However, the invention of the electronic darkroom or digital image processing (DIP) has seen the advent of the 'rubber picture.' It is now possible to stretch or distort pictures, to marry images together, to change the composition, to massage colours, and to eliminate details so that the result bears little resemblance to the original image or images.

The issue has raised a lot of hackles in recent years. Two incidents in the United States – where the expensive electronic darkrooms were first introduced – have particularly exercised members of the National Press Photographers' Association.

The debate first emerged when *National Geographic* moved a pyramid: the horizontal composition of the picture, used on the cover of the May 1984 issue, did not suit the vertical shape of the page, so one pyramid was simply moved a little closer to the others. Readers were unaware of the subtle change, but thoughtful photographers and editors were concerned. (The incident drew so much criticism that *National Geographic* now refuses to allow re-printing of the picture in texts such as this.)

In the second, a Diet Coke can was removed. The picture – a posed shot in the *St. Louis Post-Dispatch* – included a cola can in the foreground that distracted from the main image, and so it was electronically excised.

Neither incident appears to have been malicious or deliberately misleading, and, as such, each is forgivable. But the subsequent breast-beating has led to revelations that the practice is a lot more widespread than suspected.[12] This, as it becomes more widely known, will in turn lead to some loss of credibility, for at present the general audience probably still believes that the camera does not lie.

In either of the two cases, similar 'editing' could have been done before the picture was taken – the photographer in Egypt could have changed his angle, the photographer in St. Louis could have reached over and removed the cola. The massaging becomes more problematic when the motives are questionable and the result distorts reality.[13] Rogers says that since the pyramid incident, many news media have implemented written policies to prevent such activities.[14] Journalism student Kevin McGran's useful survey of the Canadian scene makes no mention of similar policies in Canada, probably because the equipment is only recently available to most newspaper editors. But nonetheless, McGran cites a fascinating example

involving the use of digital image processing for a shot of Senator Keith Davey, chair of the senate committee on news media, for the cover of the austere *Saturday Night*: "'At the shoot,' says Bruce Ramsay, *Saturday Night*'s art director, "the makeup was too heavy-handed. The lip gloss looked stupid. DIP plowed away the makeup, letting Davey look more natural."'[15] The media watchdog may have looked more natural, but the process may well have told the senator things about the news media he did not wish to know.

In an effort to clear the air, Michael Evans, picture editor of the Atlanta *Journal/Constitution*, proposes that some activities (which he carefully defines) should be acceptable, including 'image enhancement,' 'image alteration,' and 'an accurate image.' But he rates 'image manipulation' as unethical, as the aim is to deceive the viewer. He gives as examples the removal of an image element, addition of a new image element, or movement of elements within the image. These definitions may help, but ultimately the journalists must ask, once again, Why? Or, to be more specific, 'Are we deceiving the viewer?'[16]

The Weeklies

The community press has some ethical problems that are uniquely its own, largely stemming from a sense of loyalty – the need to support the town. The issue of newsroom personnel running for office has already been fully discussed under the heading of conflict of interest. However, it can be noted that the weekly editor/publisher is particularly vulnerable to this pressure because he or she so often puts down deep roots in a community and has a stake in its future.

The weeklies are also more prone to pressure from the community because they are so accessible and frequently rely on just a few major advertisers. So the editor cannot expect to 'hide' if he expresses unpopular views, unlike the metropolitan daily editor, who may rarely venture onto the street and can be shielded by staff. And there is less protection from pressure groups. If the Chamber of Commerce wants to turn Sleepy Hollow into Bingo Heaven or decides the Victorian city hall should make way for a supermarket, it can marshal considerable forces, probably including most of the major advertisers. The forces of 'progress' expect the newspaper to be 'on side,' supporting development and expansion, although the editor may recognize such trends will destroy the town he loves.

The community may also expect the editor to show she is truly loyal to her community by reflecting a rose-coloured version of it in the paper. Not only is she expected to respect the privacy of citizens, but she may be expected to protect the sensitivities of the bereaved and the disturbed. For instance, when Bruce Penton, editor of the Saskatchewan weekly, the *Moosomin World-Spectator*, heard that a local man had burnt himself to death in his car, he knew that everybody knew but felt obliged to report the suicide as an accidental death.[17]

Broadcasting

There are still areas of broadcasting that perceive a conflict – or at least a separation – between news and current affairs (or public affairs), though no such division impels the print media. Yet why should such an artificial partition occur? And – more to the point – in what way does this benefit the audience?

At best, such a separation is unnatural, with the two departments having to communicate on which subjects they are approaching and how. At worst, there will be duplication (e.g., the news program covers a subject and then the current affairs program goes over identical ground) or total omission of subjects. There may also be duplication of effort, as well as equipment that could be better deployed. Logic suggests that all the staff of a particular medium should be working towards a common goal (better programming), rather than competing internally with each other. The divisions go back several decades and are now entrenched, with separate news and current affairs crews protecting their particular turf, perhaps losing sight of their overriding mandate.[18]

The demarcation between current affairs and news is difficult to define. The 1988 CBC staff handbook *Journalistic Policy* obliquely defined it thus: 'News programs must follow the same journalistic principles as current and public affairs programs, but unlike the latter, they cannot be expected to explore with the same comprehensiveness the issues and choices confronting Canadians. Indeed, the basic purpose of radio and

television news broadcasts is to report on events, to be a fair witness to the reality of the day.'[19] However, this division seems to have disappeared in the 1993 revision, *Journalistic Standards and Practices*.

Yet no such division is imposed in newspaper newsrooms. Print journalists *can* 'be expected to explore' complex subjects as well as to report on events, because precisely the same skills are needed for both processes. Certainly a thirty-second item cannot explain the importance of the Brazilian rain forests or the impact of the Chernobyl explosion on Welsh sheep, but why shouldn't the same teams of information people (reporters, editors, camera operators, producers, etc.) work together on the summary and the explication?

Some issues:

- *Fewer rules: less news?* A brief article by Cia Curtis in the *Ryerson Review of Journalism* suggests that deregulation of broadcasting in the United States has meant a reduction in the amount of time radio and television devotes to news.[20] Curtis, a Ryerson Journalism student, goes on to offer some evidence that there has been a slight shrinkage in Canada and to warn that the trend may continue.[21]

  This seems to have come to pass, and it clearly bodes ill both for journalists and for consumers. Although the number of radio and television channels may continue to increase, the consumer can only monitor one at a time, and he or she may only catch one or two newscasts each day. Even if there are 100 television stations offering news simultaneously by satellite, if the actual length of those newscasts is reduced, the viewers are the losers. The world cannot be summarized in a three-minute newscast. If the entire program is to be so short, then it should be billed as headlines, with reference to fuller news reports at other times.

- *That's the answer, but what was the question?* Often the *context* of an answer is provided by the nature of the question asked, and yet the question is rarely cited in broadcast news. The journalist needs to analyze why the source answered the way she did. Was the question provocative or loaded? Should the question therefore be cited as well as the response?

- *The sound bite.* This, too, has been touched on above but can be repeated here. Both radio and TV need actual quotations from sources, rather than reporters paraphrasing those sources. The never-ending problem (given that stories may only be twenty to forty seconds long) is context. Due to the brevity of broadcast stories, it is rarely possible for the broadcast reporter to put a speaker's words into the context in which they were spoken, and so the speaker often feels ill-used. The corollary of this is that media manipulators – especially those who advise politicians – will pander to this demand for the quotable quote, feeding bon mots to those they advise to ensure they get on the evening news. David Taras touches on the phenomenon: 'Parties use television's own requirements and characteristics as their main weapons in getting their message on the news. Television journalists are trapped into reporting the party's pre-packaged news because their own medium demands dramatic visuals, leaders in conflict, and highly charged sound bites or clips.'[22]

• *Secret taping*. There may be more incentive for the broadcast reporter to secretly tape-record interviews than for the print interviewer to do so.

The celebrated 'de Jong incident' highlighted the difficulties. Simon de Jong, a veteran New Democratic Party MP, agreed with a CBC request to wear a 'hidden' microphone throughout a national party leadership convention in Winnipeg, 2 December 1989, so the television newsroom could do an in-depth documentary on the backroom dealing at such events. The scheme backfired horribly for de Jong, who emerged looking naive and self-serving. De Jong maintained later that he had agreed on the condition that the microphone be *visible*, and that he could turn it off at 'private' moments. But the thimble-sized microphone was pinned behind his tie, and in the heat of the event, he evidently forgot to turn it off. The subsequent furore obfuscated the issue, which is relevant here.

Was it appropriate for the nation (courtesy of CBC-TV) to be eavesdropping on patently private conversations between one MP and others negotiating the leadership and possible shadow cabinet positions? It was certainly titillating for the viewers, who had a keyhole look at the horse-trading. But it was unquestionably an invasion of the privacy of the other participants, who were quite unaware they were on 'candid camera.' Were the revelations sufficient justification for the

cloak-and-dagger journalism? The subsequent outcry was highly critical of the media for employing such tactics.[23] It also contravened the 1988 CBC *Journalistic Policy*, then in force: 'The information gained [by secret taping] must serve an important purpose, must be indispensible to that purpose and must be unobtainable by more open means.'[24]

The de Jong incident simply does not meet the first of these three tests, and it probably does not meet the other two. But even if it could be said to meet the letter of these 'laws,' the incident clearly breaks the spirit of the policy: The section, titled 'Clandestine Methods,' begins, 'As a general rule, journalism should be conducted in the open. The credibility and trust placed in the CBC's journalistic programming by the public depends largely on confidence in the ethical and professional standards of its practitioners.'[25] Evidently, management was not amused at the outcry. That section of the policy was substantially expanded in the 1993 revisions and now includes the remark, 'Even when it is justified, covert recording risks damaging the public's trust in the CBC ... prior authorization must be obtained from the Senior Vice-President ... it must concern illegal, anti-social or fraudulent activities or clear and significant abuses of public trust.'[26] That might cover the 'Connections' TV series, discussed on page 96 in Chapter 9 of this book, but it surely wouldn't include taping an MP at a political convention.

Television

Technically, television consists of moving pictures, so its ethical dilemmas are largely provoked by the endless demand for images and action. Issues include:

• *The viewfinder effect*. The television camera has an uncanny ability to shoot close-ups. The camera operator, seeking the action through his viewfinder, will – not unnaturally – tend to focus on where the action is. The camera does not lie, but it can lack context – the perspective of the small demonstration in the big, peaceful street. James McLean, a Regina television producer, first became aware of it with footage from street clashes in Belfast:

Instead of taking the establishing shot, a longer shot, to establish what is going on in a wide field of action, cameramen started taking closer pictures, so that on your set the field of view might be only as wide as a room, whereas before you could encompass down the street.

Now, what happens is that you can compress activity into a very small area and it looks like it is bigger than it is.

You see the same thing happening when a camera goes to cover a parade. If the camera goes and edits or shoots in editable sequences, a mass of people on every corner, you cut them together, and it looks like there are 200,000 people there. There may have only been 200, but it looks like 200,000.[27]

There is an element of thoughtless dishonesty in such activity. The camera operator is 'willing' her story to be more important than it is; the video editor is trying to 'make the most of' or 'get the best out of' the footage she is given. But each is sensationalizing, exaggerating the story. Television stories have grown shorter in recent years,[28] and if one of the results is the elimination of the establishing shot, this may seriously distort the total effect.

Respected TV anchor Knowlton Nash pointed out another dilemma: 'The media hold a mirror up to society but do so selectively. We have to recognize the very raising of the mirror will change the character of the event or issue by intensifying it or glamorizing it or denigrating it.'[29] Although he was not speaking here specifically of television, clearly the comment is particularly applicable to that medium.

- *The demand for action.* When Ernst Zundel went to court each day, facing charges of distributing hate literature, the cameras faithfully recorded his arrival.[30] Why? Because he marched to the courthouse in central Toronto wearing a bright red or blue construction helmet and surrounded by supporters also wearing hard hats, ostensibly to protect Zundel from possible attack by undefined enemies. The parade was pure theatre, designed to get sympathy and publicity, and it worked – on the network news, night after night.[31] Less imaginative defendants arrive at court in their hundreds each day, but the cameras do not follow them. The hunger for colourful action on television news can easily distort news judgments.
- *'TV likes the person, hates the policy.'* The origin of this piece of newsroom lore is lost, but the philosophy

remains. TV news concentrates on events (usually involving people) and the people themselves: 'Talking heads,' expounding complex ideas, are anathema. Discussing television specifically, Taras says succinctly: 'Drama is the prime ingredient of most news stories.'[32] He expounds at length on the importance of conflict in TV news.[33] And he remarks, 'In most other aspects, television news thrives on personalities ... The social and economic forces that propel events are seldom credited with being as important as the actions of powerful individuals, in fact, social and economic forces are rarely touched upon at all ... An offshoot of this is the tendency in journalism to tell a story through a person ... The story is thus humanized and made more understandable and graspable for the audience.'[34]

Eric Malling has dubbed the phenomenon 'the tyranny of pictures.'[35] 'Politicians and protests are easy to shoot. Thinking is not. A plane does a belly landing in Denver: It'll be on every newscast although no one is injured. Hundreds die every day because we don't require airbags in cars, but it's not news.'[36] Like Helen Hutchinson,[37] Malling called on the media, particularly television, to put the beads on the string so that Canadians can, as he put it, 'make smart choices.'[38] 'Historically the media has failed woefully to report the ideas and trends which are ultimately far more important than most events ... or pseudo-events like the latest vacuous political non-statement, or another threat from some crusader who's probably funded by the government anyway.'[39] This is a tall order, especially for television, but it's the difference between knee-jerk reporting and worthwhile journalism.

- *The presence of the camera.* There is clear evidence that the presence of a television camera (especially accompanied by a marked vehicle) changes the nature of events.[40] The CBC newsroom manual *Journalistic Standards and Practices* warns: 'In some cases of riots or civil disorder, it is clear that the presence of cameras has provoked violence ... Every precaution should be taken to ensure that the presence of CBC journalists, cameras or microphones is not a provocation.'[41]

The introduction of the camera into courts and legislatures has also inevitably changed the nature of the events and the perceptions of those events.[42]

- *Enter, cameras rolling.* Ambush journalism – taking interviewees by surprise – has long been a stock-in-trade for television journalists. It is a much more telling weapon for TV, where the viewer can see the body language of the ambushee. But it also shows people at their most vulnerable: the source is metaphorically naked, facing the aggressive interviewer. Brian McKenna, veteran of many dramatic documentaries for CBC, says the technique is now frowned on: 'We wouldn't do that now. There's a growing feeling that it's being abused. You're dealing with an incredible piece of weaponry.'[43] And he's right: the purpose of the ambush is to catch people out, when they are unprepared and defenceless. While journalists must not become ethical wimps, too afraid of offending people to do a good job, they must not adopt the role of aggressive inquisitor. The ambush may occasionally be the only way to get someone in front of the camera,[44] but if all they do is mouth obscenities or are struck speechless, the clip may well be scrapped. However, ambush journalism seems to have become a staple of the American 'tabloid' TV shows.
- *Made for TV.* Because television reaches so many people, it is increasingly being seen as the most important medium and is therefore the main target for those wanting media exposure. 'Media events' and 'sound bites' (discussed in Chapter 7, 'Manipulating the Media') are the inevitable result.
- *Logistics.* A variety of purely mechanical considerations impinge on journalistic decisions, particularly in television. The reporter out on a remote shoot (getting a story outside the office) has to consider communication facilities such as whether she can get a portable video unit to the site, whether power and light are available or whether battery packs and lights must be hauled in, whether a satellite transmitter must be taken to the site, and the availability and cost of satellite time.

  Knowlton Nash recalls James M. Minifie, the CBC's first television reporter in Washington, describing the way the medium dominates the message: 'He had worked for so many years in radio and print, and the new medium seemed alien to him. "They tell you to be natural ... be relaxed," he told me. "And yet there are all those lights pouring down on you, cameramen looking at you, soundmen checking you, someone screaming time cues in your earplug, and the bloody producer telling you what to do when he doesn't know a damn thing about the story. It's not natural at all. The whole thing is, in fact, an unnatural act."'[45]

- *Ratings.* If a search for higher ratings reduces the quality of journalism in any way, then the newsroom must re-examine its soul. There may well be a tendency to 'save up' blockbuster investigations (plus big promotion budgets) for 'sweeps week,' when audiences are being counted. This is similar to devoting substantial resources to a major newsroom project aimed at winning awards in the annual Radio and Television News Directors Association competition. In both cases the motives are inappropriate, and the newsroom must ask if the audience is being well served.
- *Time-slot controls content.* Television, particularly, has to recognize that the timing of some news shows will influence the content, particularly in terms of explicit violence and gore. Noon and 6 P.M. shows are often watched while eating. As the CFPL newsroom manual advises: 'As a general rule, we do not show dead bodies and excessive gore, especially on our noon and 6:00 P.M. broadcasts. At 11:00 P.M., discretion is still advised, but Final Editions cater to an adult audience that is not eating at the time.'[46]
- *Logistics vs. news judgment.* This may occur more often on screen than in print because of the logistics. It is much easier to dispatch a reporter with a notebook than a camera crew. John Owen, chief news editor of the CBC-TV national news, cited a producer with ABC television as saying that 80 per cent of their newscast material could be described as planned.[47] Typically, the assignment editor begins the day by consulting the newsroom diary and then assigns people to scheduled events. Little airtime is then left for the unexpected or spontaneous.
- *Visibility as a disadvantage.* Does the very bulk of a TV news unit (at least a reporter, camera operator, and video-camera, but often including lights, satellite dish, and marked vehicle) make it difficult to be invisible? Katharine Whitehorn makes the point that a print reporter can slip into, say, a school to do a story without being easily spotted. The TV crew knows it need not even try: 'A full-scale TV crew is going to have to deal with authorities to get into the place at all – in

itself that can be a distortion.'[48] This problem should shrink as the equipment shrinks.

- *The camera cannot lie, Part 2.* The television camera may not be able to distort images to quite such an extent as digital imaging can in print – yet. But the audience can be deliberately misled by other means. Ann Medina (quoted in Chapter 9) described some of the tricks. Do television news managers worry about what happens when viewers become aware of these 'tricks'? Do they deliberately conceal such techniques? Would it be practical to inform viewers when special effects are being employed? It may not be useful to have a super (text superimposed on the image) saying 'double-ender' on the screen, but it is helpful, when the anchor does such an interview, if the viewer sees her looking at a monitor labelled 'Montreal.' Similarly, viewers may well be helped by supers saying 'pre-taped' or 'reporting from Baghdad.'

Radio

News on radio is beset by the need for speed and the insatiable demand for more, and new, information. Issues include:

- *Every hour a deadline.* Radio news, particularly, devours information. And this voracity is nothing compared to that of the all-news format. Some metropolitan radio news shows air every hour for fourteen or eighteen hours a day. Although listeners appear to dip in and out, a significant proportion keep a radio on in the background for hours at a time. On this basis, the same news story is rarely aired more than once. The *data* may remain the same, but the wording will be subtly refreshed to make the item sound different each time. The process can be observed on the Broadcast News wire service, where hourly newscasts are carefully rewritten, with more major news stories reappearing in four, five, or even six consecutive news roundups, rephrased, though the basic story remains unchanged.
- *The thirty-second clip.* The need for tight quote-clips of twelve to thirty seconds has been explored above. It should be added, here, that the responsible radio journalist also retains the order of the original speaker's quotes, rather than re-ordering them. Similarly, composite questions-and-answers should not be used:

where possible, the original integrity of question and answer should be retained, if there is any danger of the listener misunderstanding.

- *Sticking a mike up his left nostril.* This vivid phrase is occasionally used to describe the behaviour of some radio reporters. The scramble for news against competition and relentless deadlines sometimes drives reporters to be too aggressive in their pursuit of news. Even if they are unconcerned about their own dignity or the dignity of their broadcast station, they have to allow the sources themselves to retain some vestiges of decorum. Such assertive reporting may dovetail with the growing sense of personal disrespect that some reporters evince for politicians. As Eric Malling points out, Canadian reporters have gone from one extreme to another: from 'being routinely obsequious toward the powerful, some became routinely contemptuous.'[49] Such an attitude can quickly lead to using the microphone like a weapon, thrusting it at the interviewee so that the inexperienced source either reels back or, if she's very unlucky, finds herself surrounded by these threatening spikes, for all the world like Archbishop Thomas à Becket cowering before his murderers on the altar steps. The radio reporter has to be somewhat more sensitive to sources – not least because television viewers may be watching.
- *Editing the incoherent.* John Forsyth, writing in the *British Journalism Review*, describes radio editors proudly cutting audiotape so that it looks 'like a lace doily.'[50] But what does that lacework do for the audience? Few speakers are eternally honey-tongued, without hesitation or repetition. Removing small glitches may aid the audience, who must absorb the radio message through only one of the five senses. (Television viewers can lip-read and watch body language; even print readers can be helped with adverbs.) But as CBC policy asserts, 'The editing process must result in a true reflection of what was originally seen and heard ... a slice of reality – which must nonetheless reflect the essential truth without distortion.'[51] If the interviewee is inarticulate or stammers seriously, the reporter needs to paraphrase.[52]
- *Taping off the telephone.* It is perfectly legal in Canada to tape-record a telephone conversation with a second party, without that party's consent. (It is not legal to

tape the telephone conversation of two other people, without either party's consent.) The law does insist that if a recording is to be *broadcast*, however, then the interviewee must first give permission. It would hamper journalists unreasonably if they were forced to ask permission all the time, just as it would if they had to ask permission to take notes during a telephone interview. It can be assumed, if the reporter introduces herself adequately as a working reporter, that she will be making a record of the interview in some form, be it tape or written notes.

- *Giving prejudice a platform.* While philosophical debate may be inimical to television (or at least difficult), radio *is* talk. Radio delights in controversy, strong views, and outrageous opinion. However, the fact that someone has said something colourful does not automatically earn it a place on news or current affairs programming.[53]

The 1991 Broadcasting Act requires broadcasters to respect freedom of expression as guaranteed under the Charter of Rights, but it also demands variety and balance. This is interpreted in the CRTC Regulations: 'Personal attacks on individuals or groups, unresearched and inaccurate reporting and failure to meet professional standards are examples of failure to meet the high standard of programming required of each licensee.'[54]

These guidelines deserve to be pinned on every newsroom studio wall, as they throw some light on some of the more controversial broadcasting incidents in recent years. They cast light on, for instance, a resurfacing of Colin Thatcher. The lurid 1984 trial of the former Saskatchewan cabinet minister for the murder of his estranged wife shocked the province, and his subsequent attempts to get an appeal attracted enormous publicity. When he was finally locked away for life, the public assumed his days in the public spotlight were ended. However, in 1990, as he tried to launch a new appeal in light of alleged new evidence, a Saskatchewan television station got permission to interview Thatcher in jail and, as a result, aired a one-hour piece with the man. The item was little more than a platform for the wily politician to spout his views. Any form of 'balance' would have been difficult normally, and with a new appeal threatened it was out of the question.

While this unquestionably pandered to those mesmerized by the aura surrounding the murderous millionaire, and while it pleased Thatcher supporters, it ignores the spirit of the policy cited above and of the CBC *Journalistic Standards and Practices* manual itself. Such a platform was *not* in the public interest (although 'interesting') and was *not* balanced, and attempts to defend it on the grounds of freedom of speech abuse that concept.

Radio and television regulations ban racism, yet the media continue to be used as a platform for prejudice. Consider the following:

- Professor Philip Rushton, who gained some notoriety in 1989 for claiming he had proved blacks, Orientals, and Caucasians had different cerebral and sexual capacities, has a right to those views and to voice them on a soapbox in the park. But he has no *right* to airtime.
- Malcolm Ross, who in the late 1980s was claiming the Holocaust was a hoax and was promoting the 'Jewish conspiracy' theory, had a right to those views, but not to airtime.
- Terry Long, who fathered the white-supremacist Aryan Nations organization, has similar rights.

Each of these people has become a household name largely because of the media time provided by producers and editors. Discussing the issues at a conference of CBC producers, Michael Enright, a senior radio producer, remarked, 'Sometimes it's absolutely necessary to put hate on the radio. It's the way we do it that's all-important ... We make programs, not platforms.'[55]

Broadcasters do not have to protect the public from extremist views, but they must ensure they are not being used by bigots, who want to use the airwaves as a bullhorn to reach a vast audience. Controversial issues *must* be explored. The informal contract between broadcasters and audience requires consumers to trust broadcasters, but broadcasters have to earn that trust by being fair, accurate, and balanced. Waving the flags of objectivity and free speech is easy. But balance does not simply mean letting one bigot spout his views and perhaps letting somebody else try to debunk them. It is far easier to claim there is a Jewish conspiracy to rule the world than to prove there is not; it is far easier to claim that whites are superior to blacks than to prove otherwise. Balance is a wonderful concept, but it does not exonerate journalists from following the precept of the Broadcasting Act, that is, that broadcasters 'have a responsibility for programs they broadcast.'[56] Stewardship of the airwaves is an awesome responsibility.

Nobody – prime minister, company president, or propagandist – has an automatic right of access to the media. And yet even common citizens often feel they should be granted 'equal time' or some right of reply. How this need can be addressed is explored in the next chapter, under the heading of 'Righting Writing Wrongs.'

TOUGH CALLS

1 You have a TV crew in a remote Newfoundland community doing a piece on a country fiddler. Invited to his home for some homemade blueberry wine, you find a party developing ... and some of the best country fiddling you ever heard. But your producer says if you break out the cameras and lights, it will change the event. Do you?

2 Your weekly paper has long advocated press freedom, naming names, and not being influenced by outside forces. The son of a nice local family has returned home – to die of AIDS. Do you report?

3 You've located a suspected former Nazi in your community. You want to film him being confronted by an articulate old Auschwitz survivor. You figure that the only way to get the Nazi in the open is to tell a 'little white lie' – inviting him to a local beer festival to 'talk about Slovakia.' Do you?

4 Your 'teen' page is doing a major piece on teen drug use but can't get pictures of youngsters shooting up. The page needs art. Do you get a model to pose?

5 The sports page has a good three-column soccer picture, but only a *two*-column hole. It would be very quick and simple to improve the composition by moving the soccer ball (in the electronic darkroom) and making the picture fit the space. Do you?

16 Righting Writing Wrongs

The media are quick to point out other people's errors, but who is watching the watchdogs? Increasingly, news consumers are demanding access to the media in order to 'talk back' to them and express their views. And they are demanding some sort of accountability by the media, which have been perceived as physically and psychologically remote. If, the audience may ask, the media are part of the commercial, big-business, free enterprise complex, how can they freely investigate and objectively report *on* that complex?

It is not that the media are necessarily 'bad,' but why should the audience expect them to be better than anyone else? The suspicion was summarized neatly by London columnist Katharine Whitehorn: 'I don't think there is any group anywhere that can be counted on to behave well if no-one is watching.'[1]

The media play an important role as protectors of the people, 'comforting the afflicted and afflicting the comfortable.' But this sense of detachment, deus ex machina, may isolate them. Consumers of news are bound to ask how they can best express their views of the news media, and how the media make themselves more accessible, more user-friendly.

Although the majority of any newshole is dedicated to straight reporting, and most reporters would describe themselves as fair and balanced, nonetheless, there is a clear perception that the news media are 'critical' of society. Criticism is often direct and outspoken in editorials, reviews, bylined columns, and backgrounders, and it is sometimes implicit in the display of stories (story selection, headline wording, or juxtaposition of a story with a bold picture). So an us/them antagonism emerges. The media (the audience feels) carp: who gave *them* the right to criticize *us*? And – worse – the media have in the past often refused to admit error and appear to resent any criticism of themselves. Jim Stott, ombudsperson for the *Calgary Herald*, once put it this way: 'The news business has a curious reluctance to talk about itself and then we wonder why readers are sometimes mystified by how we go about our business.'[2]

When a government is overwhelmingly strong and the Opposition weak, the media may see their watchdog role as all the more important. Hence the occasional label, the 'unofficial Opposition.' There are three main players in this relationship – the government, the electorate, and the news media – held in balance by both tension and cooperation, and creating a symbiotic triangle:

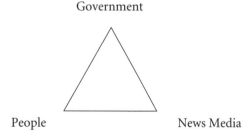

Nobody is at the top or the bottom here; rather, there is equilibrium. The government needs people to justify its existence; the government needs the media to reach the people (to stay elected); people need the media to assess the efficacy of government (and maintain democracy); people need government to ensure order and provide services; the media need the government for social stability (anarchy is bad for circulation); and the media need people for revenue.

Ever since Cleopatra criticized the messenger who brought bad news (or since Shakespeare's dramatization of the tale), news consumers have looked critically at both the message and the messenger. Many in the media have seemed remote and omniscient, many have often been highly judgmental about the community in which they function, and many are obviously just as human and vulnerable as other humans. They *can* tell lies, fake stories, make mistakes; they can be ignorant of the law and break it purposely or accidentally.

One problem, of course, is that when they make those mistakes, they do it in a very public way. As the saying goes, a doctor buries his mistakes and a journalist puts his on the front page. That can have a lot of impact. The word 'not,' missed from a sentence, can ruin a reputation. Put it incorrectly in a headline and it can do serious injury or injustice. So when a news operation loses a particularly large libel suit – and Peter Desbarats notes that settlements in the US now average more than $5-million each[3] – there may well be a gleeful sense of 'Serves 'em right!' among readers.

Increasingly the public is demanding media accountability.[4] Audiences demand explanations for media decisions; they demand access (an opportunity to voice opinions contrary to those expressed by the media themselves). Readers may not want to snuggle up to editors, but they do want them to be less remote, less apparently motivated by profit.

What can be done? There are a surprisingly large number of ways for the public to get access to the media, to 'get back' at the media, or for the media to make themselves more accessible. Some of these techniques are initiated by the community – the media users – themselves. Some come from within the newsrooms, driven by sensitivity to criticism, worry over faltering audience numbers, or genuine concern for the public weal. And much of this follows audience surveys – discreet readership polls conducted by pro-

fessional pollsters to assess reader/listener needs, or very public surveys conducted within the pages of the newspapers themselves. Several Canadian dailies have used their pages to ask readers' views on their own (the paper's) behaviour and values, and have published the results, as we will see later in this chapter.

The public seems to respond enthusiastically to such an opportunity, perhaps enjoying the challenge of being 'editor for a day' and the opportunity to tell the paper their views. It is healthy for the public to realize that the decisions facing journalists are not all black and white, that it is not all easy. But there remains the perception that the media are mostly money-driven, that they have to make a profit, and survive in a competitive society, and therefore must at all times strive for bigger circulation or higher ratings. And so people remain suspicious.

Everyone knows somebody who has had a bad experience with the news media. The error may have been minuscule; maybe it was a nephew's wedding announcement with a name misspelled, or an accident report that said three people were hurt and it was clear to a spectator that four people were taken off in the ambulance. But the spectator was there, she knew what really happened, and from that she extrapolated the general rule: you cannot trust the media.

So what chance does the public have of getting its own back? What avenues do laypersons have to get their two cents' worth, or to get revenge, to get inaccuracy corrected? Foremost, yet least visible, is the conscience of the story-handlers. But for the news consumers, there is a surprisingly wide range of options they themselves can initiate or at least participate in. They can, for instance:

1 Write letters to the editor
2 Resort to the courts
3 Lobby newsrooms
4 Cancel subscriptions/switch channels
5 Seek government intervention
6 Appeal to quasi-government bodies, e.g., the CRTC
7 Appeal to other media
8 Print their own
9 Buy an ad to express dissent.

The media themselves can do a lot to improve their rapport with consumers. They can:

1 Initiate internal programs (staff workshops, policy manuals)
2 Write for and support media reviews
3 Conduct media critiques (e.g., CBC's *Media File*)
4 Conduct surveys
5 Apply peer pressure
6 'Beckon' audiences by outreach activities.

Ways the Public Can Seek Redress

So the news consumer who is aware of how the media work and what her rights are has many ways of getting back at perceived inaccuracies or injustices. Yet each of these is limited or seriously flawed. They are worth detailed examination.

1 **Letters.** Editors have finite space. In smaller papers, local weeklies, for instance, every letter is appreciated and every word may be published, libel laws permitting. But few of the bigger daily papers can publish all the letters they receive, though they strive to publish most of them and most of their contents. Huge numbers of letters are sent to some newspapers. The *New York Times* gets about 40,000 letters a year[5] but can only publish 10 per cent of them.[6] Thus they turn away nine out of ten of the writers who submit their views. How do the editors decide? They may say 'We heard from this person seven times this year: we do not want to run another of her letters.' Or, on the other hand, 'We have got all these opinions in favour of this issue; is there a letter here against it so we can balance the coverage?'[7]

Sometimes, when editors receive many letters on the same topic, they will pick bits out of a number of them and package them as a unit. But while this may establish the tenor of many letters, it almost certainly does not satisfy the individual writers.

Does the reader have any 'right' of reply? Few democratic environments legislate a reader's right to space in a paper: it is unquestionably not the law in Canada, and very few newsrooms articulate any such right. The CBC's news manual, for instance, notes, 'The right of reply does not exist in law. It follows, however, from the journalistic principle of fairness that a need for remedial action will be recognized if it has been established that significant unfairness has occurred.'[8] But who establishes such a 'need'? What may seem like 'significant unfairness' to a homemaker in Blue River, BC, may not seem like it to a network producer in Toronto.

Any lingering doubt about such 'rights' was laid to rest by Patrick O'Callaghan while he was publisher of the *Calgary Herald*. Beset by a prolific anti-abortionist who churned out letters to the editor, O'Callaghan finally banned his fellow Roman Catholic from the paper entirely: 'He is a nuisance. He does not believe that there is a limit to the amount of publicity that even an organization of that sort rates.'[9] Doubtless, the irritating writer felt this was unjust and that he was being picked on. Obviously it is the publisher's final, desperate weapon. But no writer has a right to space, and few readers want to read the same predictable, repetitive views from the same person ad nauseam.

Abortion is an issue that brings out more polemicists than most. But politics, in general, stir many letter-writers to try to use the letters page as a platform. The Yakima, Washington, *Herald-Republic* got so tired of being 'used' in this way that in 1984 the publisher instituted a charge of ten cents a word for letters endorsing particular candidates – and was astonished to generate $2,400 in revenue during the next election.[10] The publisher remarked that politicians' campaign managers had been using the letters columns for free publicity, while spending their advertising dollars on television. Now the letters columns could be separated from the political rhetoric, and freed for their original purpose.

Editing readers' letters is itself a test in sensitivity and craftsmanship. Editors must keep the flavour of the original while eliminating libel (it is the paper that gets sued) and bad spelling and grammar (because they feel they are not in the business of holding readers up to ridicule), and probably cutting drastically for space (to allow other readers a say, too), though the writer probably feels every word is vital. Editors may call the process 'polishing' letters, but the writers may call it meddling and slanting. Of course, some letters have to be left out entirely because they are libellous, fake, or irredeemably illiterate.

Certainly editors do not have to polish every letter, but some people simply cannot put words on paper. And that suggests another problem: in general, the illiterate, by definition, are denied access to letters columns.

One solution is the telephone-answering machine. A few newspapers now have installed tape machines to encourage readers who are uncomfortable with words on paper – or who do not want to bother, or who cannot afford the stamp, or who are too handicapped to write – to express their views orally. (However, there may be a whole other set of problems in editing oral text for publication.)

The hope is that people who are not used to dealing with the newspaper or writing opinions on paper might much prefer to get on a toll-free phone and 'tell' their opinion, rather than write a letter to the editor.

Some papers are making their letters columns accessible by personal computer, but that helps the hackers more than the semi-illiterate.

The habit of publishing editors' replies to general letters to the editor has pretty well died out.[11] It can be abused by editors who insist on having the last word or who snidely put down their correspondents, but the idea is still valid when the topic is the newspaper itself. Readers sometimes demand an explanation or a public apology, and a diplomatic response may pacify them.[12] It is quite likely that many correspondents who write to newsrooms do not expect the letter to be published – but do expect a reply. Elizabeth Franklin, a former editor of the *Dallas Morning News*, in an enlightening examination of the ways the media can improve their manners, found that many managers, such as sports editors, are too busy to respond to requests for an old score or an obscure record. But being too busy just will not satisfy the customer.[13]

Letters pages have other limitations: they are rarely illustrated and often letters are not even given individual headlines. The result is that some letters sections are the dullest looking pages in the paper: just a series of little grey slabs bracketed by Dear Sir and Yours Truly.

Also, editors have traditionally declined to run letters on page 1 because this gives far too dramatic a platform to writers: everyone with an axe to grind would want similar treatment – with sixty-point headlines to boot! However, there may be exceptional circumstances. A Vermont editor received a letter from a rape victim that he found so dramatic and important he played the letter as the top front-page story.[14] His enterprise was doubtless greeted with cries of 'sensationalism!'

Increasingly, papers are dressing up the letters page, and trying to attract a diversity of opinion. The much-maligned *USA Today*, for instance, works hard at this. It is fashionable to dismiss it as the 'MacPaper,' filled with 'MacNuggets' of news. But among its innovations has been an opinion page dedicated to one theme each day, for example, working mothers. Views are solicited from specialists and laypersons representing all sides, with representation of appropriate constituencies – geographic, age, gender, etc. And readers are urged in advance to write in on selected topics.[15]

The *Washington Post* has introduced a Saturday page called 'Free For All' to display the most outspoken views of readers and writers, in addition to its regular letters pages.[16] Writers are positively urged to vent their spleen against the newspaper. One response: 'What in God's name was that swill masquerading as the lead editorial the other day?' Other editors promote 'guest columns,' which provide a forum for views opposite to those of the editorial writers. How this can best be achieved was raised by the Davey Commission on Mass Media in 1969, and Ivor Williams, then president of the Canadian Managing Editors' Conference, and managing editor of the *London Free Press*, responded: 'On our own newspaper, we seek other opinions for our editorial page. When we are presenting one point of view, we try and get the other side. If we are covering a labour dispute, we make sure we get labour and management sides.'[17]

It takes a special determination on the part of letters editors to boldly display critical mail. But it is important to do so. When the *Vancouver Sun* was roundly criticized for its coverage of a Solidarity rally, for instance, the letters editor ran seventeen letters and four pictures, under a forty-two-point, five-column headline: 'Coverage Grossly Misrepresented Solidarity rally.'[18] This was much more space than the original story received, and a fair attempt to redress the balance.

Elizabeth Franklin found some publishers who insisted on a fast reply to criticism, demanding that all letters about the paper not only be answered, but be answered within twenty-four hours.[19]

Letters are even more ineffectual in the broadcast field. Networks and network shows are perceived – quite rightly – as being remote and unreachable. (Not merely letters: anyone who has tried to phone a local CBC station in the evening to complain about the national news being pre-empted for some trivial event knows the frustration of trying to express *any* opinion to networks.)

Some broadcasters recognize that talking back to your TV is pretty unrewarding, and various programs attempt to solve this in various ways. Some shows, such as CBS's *60 Minutes*, devote a small segment to viewers, putting fragments of letters on the screen. One US program – NBC's *Today* show – has even experimented with sending a camera crew to the home of a letter writer and inviting him to speak his opinion, perhaps sitting on his tractor in the back-forty.[20] Obviously this is horrendously expensive, especially as seven or eight clips were used in each show. Even so, at five minutes every second week, that is only about two hours *per year*.[21]

One Prairie cable TV operator (Saskatoon Cable 10) introduced a show in which the manager listened to viewers' complaints and discussed them (for half an hour every second Wednesday evening) in front of a TV camera. But such 'talking heads' do not make good television.[22]

Phone-in talk shows permit the public to sound off, but the topics are rarely journalistic – they are more likely to concentrate on issues of more general public concern, such as capital punishment or cat bylaws. And such shows are easily dominated by the same habitual callers and by lobby groups deliberately plugging the lines. Yet programs such as CBC's *Cross-Country Check-Up* are to be commended for their conscientious efforts to give all Canadians a voice on issues of national concern. This is a very healthy antidote to the perennial accusation that the media only ever consult 'experts.' But even this is not a cross-section of Canadians. W. Brian Stewart analyzed audiences and concluded: 'CBC radio audiences are heavily skewed towards the older and more highly educated groups.'[23]

Surprisingly, some newspaper publishers are actually resorting to writing letters to their own newspaper. Rolf Rykken, a staff writer for the US editors' magazine *presstime*, describes several situations where US publishers felt a need to talk to their readers and so wrote open letters.[24]

Finally, on a parallel issue, how well do newsrooms respond to telephoned complaints? Franklin notes one study that suggests many people who sue for libel first telephone the newsroom with their complaint – 'and that the majority of them [go] away mad.'[25] The implication is that the simple expedient of ensuring phones are politely answered and complainers are listened to sympathetically could save a newsroom thousands of dollars. She adds: 'To hear newspapers' top brass talk, it's as important for the current crop of editors and reporters to graduate from charm school as from J-school.'[26]

2 **The courts.** It may seem satisfying to win a law suit against the news media, but taking a newspaper or broadcast station to court is a very limited solution. It works only when the law has been infringed (such as libel or invasion of privacy), and so may well be useless in cases of hurt feelings, bias, sarcasm, political prejudice, etc. Furthermore, a court action tends to be expensive for the plaintiff, it risks the paper dragging up even more 'dirt' on him/her, it further publicizes the original offence, and, oddly enough, few people are even aware of their rights to challenge a newsroom for invading their privacy or impugning their character. Even winning a libel suit is often a Pyrrhic victory. The verdict: this is not a very useful stick with which to beat the media, though some nervous newsrooms will capitulate at the first wave of a writ.[27]

Even less useful to individuals are other laws that constrain news media activities, such as legislation regarding dishonest advertising or election reporting. By and large, these affect a large number of people rather than select individuals and, as such, prosecutions are brought by the authorities, rather than by lay members of the audience. But the individual can, nonetheless, file a complaint regarding, for instance, misleading advertising with the appropriate government watchdog department. But this is an unsatisfying process. The department may choose to ignore the complaint, and they routinely refuse to divulge the results of their investigations.[28]

3 **Lobbying.** Any reader can telephone an editor or news director and express criticism and demand reparation. But one call does not carry a lot of weight, and editors quickly get hardened to the idiot fringe calling to express indignation about fad topics. There is also a

steady stream of people visiting and lunching editors, usually with some political or commercial axe to grind. However, when there are twenty or fifty calls, they listen, because they know that for every one who bothers to call, ten more agree but are not so articulate or motivated. And the appearance of a delegation in the newsroom – or, worse still, a banner-waving mob outside the building, attracting the attention of other media – can be downright embarrassing.

Editors do not, of course, want to appear to be easily manipulable, but delegations by B'nai Brith to various newsrooms after the Zundel trial and in preparation for the Keegstra trial seem to have had some impact.[29]

Occasionally, readers take things into their own hands. When reporters of the Hartford, Connecticut, *Courant* reported that some state legislators were driving cars with expired emission-control stickers, members of the capitol staff began checking reporters' cars and found *they* had expired stickers – which led to a nice follow-up story by the paper.[30]

The personal visit to an editor may, therefore, have some effect, at least in terms of the reader having a chance to express his feelings. Hence, it is important that senior management people ensure that they are accessible – that overzealous staff do not 'protect' them from citizens. As in all these things, if the complainer does not get satisfaction at one level – the newsroom receptionist, say – he or she can demand to speak to the editor, and if the editor will not bend, he or she can try the publisher.

But marching down to pound on the editor's desk is only an option for those who live within range. Most readers of Thomson newspapers, for instance, will never get within 100 kilometres of a Thomson, and most CBC and CTV audience members would not even know where to start looking for the top management of those networks. The bigger the organization, the harder it is to penetrate.

4 **Cancelling your subscription:** This is a grandiose gesture and makes one feel good for a while – phoning the newsroom and telling them in which orifice to insert their publication. In a sense, one can do the same thing on radio and television by switching the dial, and telling them what to do with their show. But who suffers most? No newsroom will worry about losing one audience member, especially if it has a circulation of 50,000 (a medium-sized daily), or 500,000 (the *Toronto Star*), or up to a million (*Prime Time News* on CBC). The newspaper reader who protests a story by cancelling her subscription forfeits not merely the item at which she took umbrage, but also the TV listings, the grocery specials, the comics, the NHL scores, and the business section. So readers tend to drift back, even if only by buying the paper from vendor boxes instead of subscribing.

5 **Government intervention.** On the face of it, occasional inquiries like the Davey Commission, the Kent Commission, and the Caplan-Sauvageau Commission seem to make waves for a short while, but end up merely gathering dust on bookshelves. However, even if the law is not immediately changed or the overt goal is not immediately achieved, there may well be spin-off long-term results.

Senator Keith Davey, for instance, tabled the report of his special senate committee on the mass media in 1970, and few of its suggestions were ever acted on. (Though Income Tax Act loopholes were eventually closed, at his urging, about five years later, allowing a vibrant Canadian magazine industry to emerge.) However, the intense spotlight on the media was extremely valuable in informing the general public. And, subsequently, more journalism schools were founded, organizations of journalists were formed (the Centre for Investigative Journalism and others), *Content* magazine for journalists began, annual media conferences were instituted (evolving into the CIJ annual conference), press councils were formed, and the Canadian Daily Newspaper Publishers Association became much more pro-active and more concerned with quality rather than merely profit. Probably, in few, if any, of these instances did someone say, 'The Davey Report suggested ... and therefore let us ...' But the consciousness-raising of the report helped create the climate for developments that Davey recommended.

Tom Kent's Royal Commission on Newspapers created a less positive climate, being greeted with howls of horror and derision by newspaper managements. Some recommendations were, indeed, pretty unrealistic (editors on contract, advisory committees for chain newspapers, and creation of a Press Rights Panel of federal Cabinet appointees, operating under the umbrella of the Human Rights Commission). But the report alerted Canadians to the ever-increasing trend to newspaper chain ownership and may have given chain owners pause before further reducing competition – though the trend certainly has not stopped, as the Southam, Thomson, and Hollinger groups have continued to grow.[31]

The *Report of the Task Force on Broadcasting Policy* called for more Canadian content and creation of another CBC-TV network, among other things. Most of its demands seem to have fallen on deaf ears (perhaps because of the estimated price tag of $175-million to $270 million a year), though CBC has since instituted its all-news channel.

But the private citizen does not get a federal commission set up on his behalf. Such moves follow widespread unrest and political lobbying. At best, the individual can make a presentation to a commission – if one happens to be currently open for business.

6 **Appeal to quasi-judicial bodies.** The Canadian Radio-television and Telecommunications Commission polices broadcasting and hence has the power to suspend a broadcast station's licence, putting it out of business for unacceptable behaviour.

In practice, this very rarely happens, though station operators can be harassed by critics during hearings for licence renewals. And occasionally complaints are so loud as to lead to public censure by the commission. Thus columnist and commentator Doug Collins was blasted by the commission in August 1983 for offensive remarks on CKVU-TV, Vancouver, about Media Watch, a watchdog group devoted to media issues.[32] And in November 1985, open-liner Gary Bannerman was condemned for 'racially offensive' remarks on CKNW radio, New Westminster, BC.[33] But whether such censure makes any real difference is hard to assess. It may simply boost ratings ('any publicity is good publicity'). Or it may make the commission a little more demanding the next time a licence hearing comes around.

Very occasionally, broadcast outlets end up in court for infractions of the Broadcasting Act. In 1977, a Regina radio station was charged with broadcasting a racist poem attacking Pakistani immigrants and fined

$5,000 following an appeal.[34] And in 1988, a Saint John, New Brunswick, station was fined $5,000 for allowing Aryan Nations leader Terry Long to express white supremacist views on an open-line show.[35]

There is, of course, no print equivalent of the CRTC, despite occasional calls for such a body. For broadcasting, such an agency is necessary if only to prevent anarchy of the air – a thousand competing broadcasters on every frequency. The economics of the marketplace prevent such chaos in the print medium. Anyone can try her hand at publishing – and at losing a few million dollars. And as long as 'news' is the primary constituent of newspapers, Canadians will demand a high proportion of Canadian (even local) news. So the need for controls over 'Canadian content' are less obvious (though arguable).

7 **Appeal to other media.** While journalists may stick together in pack situations, the competitive instinct can come out when there is a negative story about the opposition media. So an angry citizen can, on occasion, complain to one newsroom about the performance of another, and this may then be reported as a news story.

8 **Print your own.** As an extreme solution to complaints about the media, an entrepreneur can set up in opposition. This has happened in the past and becomes increasingly possible with modern technology.[36] Where one could start a newspaper a century ago with just 'a shirttail full of type,' today one can start with an Apple MacIntosh computer on the kitchen table. To most citizens, however, this is more masochistic than practical.

Grassroots publications such as *Monday* (Victoria), *New Maritimes* (Halifax), and *Briarpatch* (Regina) do get started and survive, and they do provide a useful alternative voice. But starting up a new publication is expensive, even with desktop publishing, and needs a high degree of organization in terms of regular publication and distribution. Few new publishers discover they have a licence to print money. After all, if there is a niche to be filled and money to be made, some entrepreneur has usually got there first with a commercial rather than a polemical motivation. Apart from making a profit – or *not* making a profit – the danger with starting an 'opposition' paper is that it may be driven by ideology, which is a poor basis on which to win circulation. Such a perception makes it difficult to sell advertising, especially in a community where the established media are presumably already selling ads as aggressively as they can. The advertising pie is finite.

All this is also true for broadcasting and is exacerbated by the extreme difficulty of getting a broadcast licence in the first place, and meeting the rigorous operating criteria demanded by the CRTC.

9 **Buy an advertisement.** A dramatic way for a dissatisfied reader to voice her dissent is to buy an advertisement in the paper, outlining the complaint. There is no regulation forcing newspapers to carry such ads, but responsible papers lean over backwards to carry ads representing a range of opinions, rather than strictly one view; indeed, many papers will take the money and smile all the way to the bank. But there lies the deterrent. It is costly to express views boldly (perhaps $500 to $3,000 for a full page, depending on the size of the paper), and who wants to give that sort of money to a newspaper you are angry with? It may be more appealing to patronize the opposition.

In rare instances, even the newsroom staff have disagreed with a management policy strongly enough to buy an ad in their own paper to challenge it.[37]

Ways the Media Can Reach Out

As suggested earlier, each of these approaches has limitations. But that does not mean the effort is wasted or that the public should not bother. Intelligent editors and news directors recognize that anyone initiating dialogue with his or her newsroom is a potential ally, and such communication is infinitely more to be desired than a cancelled subscription.

The editors and news directors can also reach out to the community, by, for instance, actively encouraging letters and displaying them well, rather than burying them among the truss ads.

The news staff can also be educated – sensitized – to the need to be accessible to the public, responding positively to questions and complaints, rather than turning them away. However, the truly concerned news manager will seek ways to actively initiate improvement. Techniques might include the following:

1 **Initiating internal programs.** There are many ways newsrooms can improve their relationship with audiences internally. After all, if credibility is critical, then the better the news product itself, the better the audience trust. So, many newsrooms now conduct workshops on topics such as writing, editing, and ethics, often bringing in outside coaches to help out.[38] Some operations have espoused California-style 'Quality Improvement' programs, which seek ways to encourage pride in work throughout the media operation: The fewer the typos – the argument goes – the better the credibility.[39]

In some newsrooms, senior journalists are also encouraged to critique the work of juniors, or to develop newsletters to brief staff on writing and editing pitfalls. Such leaflets as the *New York Times*' 'Winners & Sinners' have contributed significantly to keeping news staff on their toes (both finding fault and offering praise), and so can be good for both morale and quality.

In the long haul, some newsrooms have developed staff manuals, offering guidelines on writing and behaviour. These may range from fat 'stylebooks,' like those produced by the *Toronto Star*, *Globe and Mail*, *Windsor Star*, CFPL-TV, CBC, and Canadian Press, to looseleaf binders or occasional memoranda.

The way in which newsroom discipline is conducted clearly sends signals to staff and the public about the nature of the news organization. A paper that instantly sacks a reporter for blatant plagiarism (as did the Saskatoon *Star-Phoenix* in 1989, see Chapter 9) is telling the audience that it cares about honesty and credibility. When the sports editor of *La Presse* offered to resign after it was revealed he had been paid substantial sums to help bring a big boxing event to Montreal, it was only healthy that management accepted. (But that clear signal to the public was somewhat muddied when he was subsequently reinstated.) (See discussion in Chapter 5, 'Conflict of Interest.') Firings for infringements of ethics are rare in Canadian newsrooms, partly because ethical standards are often not clearly spelled out, partly because codes are so difficult to interpret and apply to specific incidents (see Chapter 17, 'Codes of Conduct'), and partly because – in some cases – strong newsroom unions will defend personnel being punished for purely 'philosophical' sins. Punishment for ethical violations appears to be more common in the United States. A 1986 survey by the ethics committee of the American Society of Newspaper Editors got responses from 225 papers, which reported thirty print journalists had been suspended and forty-eight fired in the previous three years.[40]

2 **Writing for and supporting media reviews.** The media do not write much about themselves, but there are a few arm's-length publications devoted to critiquing the media. Notable in Canada is the CIJ/CAJ *Bulletin* and *Content* magazine (absorbed by the *Bulletin* in 1993). These are the closest equivalents to the established and respected US journals the *Columbia Journalism Review* and the *Washington Journalism Review*.

Content was founded in 1970 by Dick MacDonald as a non-academic journalists' journal. Despite ups and downs, it survived more than two decades and might have continued longer if the *Bulletin* had not moved into its territory and they had not both ended up under the roof of the Carleton University journalism school.[41] The *Bulletin* is the publication of the Canadian Association of Journalists (formerly the Centre for Investigative Journalism). It was started by Henry Aubin of the *Montreal Gazette* as a duplicated newsletter in 1978, even before the organization's founding convention in 1979. The *Bulletin*'s Achilles' heal remains that it is awkward or impossible for most journalists to write critically about the media they know best – their own newsrooms. Even tenured journalism teachers may be unwilling to write too critically for fear of antagonizing the employers of future graduates. And over the years, both publications have paid little or nothing for articles – a further deterrent to people who *expect* to get paid for writing. Pseudonyms may sometimes be used to protect writers, but journalists are inherently suspicious of 'unnamed sources.' So it is refreshing to see, for instance, a *Globe and Mail* writer criticizing Thomson Newspapers.[42]

There are other periodicals dealing with Canadian media – *Canadian Broadcaster*, *RTNDA Newsletter*, and the *Press Review*, for instance – but these tend not to devote much space to issues, especially ethics.

It would be helpful if news managers made it clear that reading – and contributing to – all such publications is perfectly acceptable for their staff.

3 **Conducting media critiques.** It is curious how few Canadian media write about the media. A few bigger

dailies have genuine television critics – but does any have a newspaper critic?[43] Does any broadcast newsroom have a newspaper critic?[44] And given that there is only a handful of cities with genuine newspaper competition in Canada (Halifax, Toronto, Ottawa, Edmonton, Calgary, Winnipeg, and – in French – Montreal and Quebec City), there are few situations where one paper can keep an eye on another. (It could be said that the *Globe and Mail*, as a 'national' newspaper, provides competition in *every* community. If so, then how about having a staff newspaper critic?)

Even the few professional television critics are rarely tough and insightful, although TV is often regarded as one of the most potent influences on twentieth-century society.[45] Indeed, senior CBC producer Ron Haggart once branded most Canadian TV critics as ignorant, snobbish people who actually disliked TV.[46]

4 **Conducting surveys.** For our purposes, surveys come in two basic forms: those 'unscientific' questionnaires soliciting reader input into the paper, and more scientific studies of reader opinion for management purposes.

When the *Montreal Gazette* offered readers a chance to make judgments on ten controversial news scenarios, more than 400 wrote in, resulting in a double-page spread, 'You Were the Editor!'[47]

An earlier, similar *Toronto Star* poll titled 'You Be the Editor' said, by implication, 'Look, we have problems. It is not an easy life being a journalist, making these decisions. How far do we go? Put yourselves in our shoes and see how you get on.' Again, readers loved it and inundated the paper with responses. In both cases, the reader is given an opportunity to evaluate some of the ethical problems journalists regularly face. While this is not direct input into the running of the newspaper, it does involve the reader, making her feel she is being consulted.[48]

The *Winnipeg Free Press* has had astonishing results with its annual published surveys. In 1986, for instance, the paper tabulated 3,200 responses for 'Here's What Readers Say.'[49] The material included not only views on the state of the world (economics, schooling, lifestyles, etc.) but also on the paper itself. Two-thirds of the respondents that year were regular *Free Press* subscribers and had been for an average of sixteen

Several Canadian dailies have turned the tables on armchair critics and given readers an opportunity to judge news value. This *Toronto Star* page asked readers about naming people charged with crimes, naming rape victims, revealing the criminal record of a prominent citizen, reporting a judge's drinking problem, and sharing pictures of accident victims with competitors.

years. They called for more local, northern, business, world, and investigative news and more editorials and letters space (but NOT more crime reporting); they wanted less National Football League football and basketball and baseball coverage, but a bit more amateur sports coverage. These are valuable data, though skewed, of course, towards loyal older readers (average forty-seven years old, with 40 per cent of the households earning more than $40,000 and having two years of college).

The *Toronto Sun* has done a similar survey every year since 1973.[50] The Toronto tabloid also periodically runs a two-column-inch box inviting readers' views on a current issue, such as whether to publish the names of people charged with prostitution-related offenses. A selection of answers is published in the Sunday edition.

The other sort of survey is management-inspired, to privately solicit public opinion – typically to find out why they are reading less and watching more. The results of these surveys do NOT make it into the paper, but they may well influence newsroom policy on such issues as news/sports ratio, emphasis on local news, and which comic strips to run.

Both forms are useful. The informal polls can be particularly valuable in that they 'beckon' readers in, to share newspaper decision-making, and they can put the audience front and centre, with pictures and bylines of the readers, instead of the staff reporters, for a change.

5 **Applying peer pressure.** Peer pressure is rarely overt in newsrooms but is more likely to emerge as a casual comment over a beer in one of the few remaining press clubs ('Nice story, Ethel!').

Journalists seem not to be good organizers (several attempts to create reporters' groups in Ontario and Saskatchewan, for instance, have failed),[51] so there are few mechanisms for any formal censure of a journalist by other journalists. Occasionally, however, it does happen, such as when a BC radio station broke an embargo on a news release. Members of the legislative press gallery were so offended by this breaking-ranks that CFAX was expelled for a while from the gallery.[52] Occasionally, calls emerge for formal mechanisms for peer censure, and these will be explored later.

6 **Beckoning audiences.** The media can do much more to invite feedback. One method is to prominently publish the names and phone numbers of senior editors (beyond the formal listing required for protection under the libel laws). Increasingly, editors are answering their own phones, instead of being shielded by staff, to demonstrate their accessibility.

Here are a few other techniques tried in various places:

- 'Call the editors' night.' The *Calgary Sun* occasionally has editors staff telephones for an evening to respond to reader comments.[53] The danger here is that the practice can become just a token. Editors make themselves available for ninety minutes and then feel they can brush aside readers for the rest of the year.

- Action lines. Columns that go to bat for the reader, such as the one run for years by the *Toronto Star*, are immensely popular. As the paper intercedes for readers in their conflicts with city hall or big business, so they win friends and audience confidence: 'The paper *is* on our side.'

- Explaining the paper. The Middleton, New York, *Times Herald-Record* published a seven-part series, describing how the paper works, to coincide with American Newspaper Week in 1982.[54] The package was then collated into an eight-page tabloid supplement. Some of the headlines indicate the content: 'Who decides what's news?' 'Who runs this newspaper, anyway?' 'Readability vs. credibility: Good news is hard to find,' and 'Advertising, circulation write the bottom line.' Such packages are difficult to do without sounding like puff pieces. Staff writer Mike Levine commented that he was told to tell the truth, 'no holds barred,' and he acknowledged that the paper had previously 'done an absolutely terrible job' of explaining itself to its audience.[55] *Seattle Times* editors felt their editorial page was too intimidating so published a dummy of both it and the Op-Ed page (the page opposite the editorial page), with descriptive boxes all round, explaining what role each unit played (masthead, local column, guest column, letters, etc.).[56]

- Accuracy campaigns. Checking the accuracy of reporting by polling newsmakers after an event, discussing errors with staff, and recording errors in reporters' personnel files so they can be referred to during performance reviews all pay off. *Editor and Publisher*

writer Mark Fitzgerald notes that the concept of asking newsmakers their opinion of a story has been around for at least thirty years,[57] but he suggests it has recently been given a strong boost by newspaper ombudspersons. Fitzgerald quotes *Montreal Gazette* ombudsperson Clair Balfour as saying 70 per cent of those polled were pleased with the coverage, which is a good morale-booster for the reporters involved.

- Report to readers. The proprietors of some newspapers, such as *USA Today* and the *Wall Street Journal*, have published regular or sporadic open letters to their readers, reporting on the philosophy and health of their newspapers.

- Newspaper coupons. Some papers, such as the *Red Deer Advocate*, include a coupon in the paper asking readers to clip it and mail it in with their comments. The same paper also has a box at the top of page 2 each day titled 'Something wrong?' which invites comments and promises to act on them. A phone number and name are listed.

- Corrections policy. Does the newsroom have a clearly defined policy on willingly and quickly correcting errors? (See Chapter 9)

- Inviting the audience in. Many news media have occasional 'open houses.' But how many invite citizens – perhaps just one at a time – to attend editorial meetings? The Vancouver, Washington, *Columbian* has made a practice of it.[58]

- Phone policy. Do all newsroom staff answer phones politely and return calls promptly? Do they welcome story ideas (no matter how bizarre) and give out information gladly?

- Code of ethics. If a newsroom has one, is it actively promoted?

How such guidelines should be developed, and their enforceability and efficacy, are the subjects of the next chapter.

Finally, two other weapons in the fight for better newsroom/consumer relations need to be addressed. Both press councils and ombudspersons have to be primarily newsroom initiatives (they cannot be imposed by the community). But both represent a quantum leap in editorial determination to reach out to the readers. And each can involve a significant financial commitment.

Appeals to Press Councils

Press councils are a relatively recent phenomenon in Canada, and although they are now widespread (covering every province except Saskatchewan), they remain little known and often misunderstood, even by media people.

The basic premise of the press council was succinctly put by J. Allyn Taylor, then chairman of the Ontario Press Council, in his introduction to its 1988 annual report: 'The Council has a twofold role ... : to help improve the standards of journalism, and to preserve the right of the press to freedom of expression.'[59]

The first part of that mandate tends to involve adjudicating complaints from the public, and it is that which some journalists still resent. They see valuable newsroom time being taken up with explaining and defending past news judgments and the cross-examination of senior editors, sometimes by laypeople not entirely sympathetic with their 'I-don't want-it-good-I-want-it-Friday' philosophy.

Twenty years ago, such public accountability was unthinkable. Nobody, then, had the right to ask an editor *why* he wrote a particular headline, chose a gory picture, or slashed a letter-writer's purple prose (beyond everybody's fundamental right to march into a newsroom and thump on an editor's desk). Both the Davey and Kent commissions loudly espoused the press council concept, but many media people have deeply resented the idea.[60] Stu Keate, for instance, quite missed the point when he opposed early attempts to start a press council in BC. The *Vancouver Sun* publisher wrote to Victoria's mayor Peter Pollen, who was promoting the council concept: 'We have 245,000 critics – our readers – each day. If they feel injured, they may seek redress in person, or by letter to our editors. Failing satisfaction, they always have resort to the courts. It is not our intention to erode our editorial freedom by turning over direction of *The Sun* to a quasi-public body made up (if I understand your suggestion correctly) predominantly by our competitors.'[61]

As we have seen, the courts are rarely a useful tool. And those 245,000 critics may well feel that a two-inch letter on page 16 by no means redresses wrongs done in seventy-two-point type on page 1. (And nobody – not even the highly political mayor – wanted to 'turn over direction' of the newspaper to a press council, or wanted a council comprising 'competitors.' The Ontario council, for instance, comprises a chairperson, ten members of the general public, and ten members of the media sent by the participating newspapers. British Columbia has a chair plus four and four. If some of those members are competitors – in a loose sense – they are also co-defendants, more likely to support than to criticize each other.)

But if that is defensive, it is nothing to the paranoia demonstrated earlier by Brigadier R.S. Malone, president of F.P. Publications, which then owned the *Sun*, the *Globe and Mail*, and the *Winnipeg Free Press*. He told the Davey Commission:

I do not believe that any need for a press council has been demonstrated to date in this country or indeed exists. There is, of course, always the risk of the odd lapse but even in such rare instances I do not feel that the present situation warrants the greater risks which are inherent in any body which can exercise any control, pressure or threat over press freedom or the freedom of any editor or writer to express his views or report events without fear of being reported to a press council, or hauled before a board to answer every complaint that was lodged against him. If he has committed a crime the place for him to answer in is our proper courts of law.[62]

(No need, anywhere in Canada? Interestingly, the BC Press Council alone averaged nearly forty complaints a year in its first six years of operation, between 1983 and 1989.[63] And the larger Ontario Press Council averages about 150 complaints a year.[64] As for controlling or threatening press freedom, there seems to be no evidence of that occurring, anywhere, in democratic environments.)

But the fear seems to be endemic. Charles W. Bailey, former editor of the *Minneapolis Star and Tribune* and stalwart of the multi-media Minnesota News Council, was once asked why journalists seem to fear press councils: 'They think that if they accept the concept, pretty soon the council is going to tell the editor what to print as well as what not to print.' Obviously he does not share that view: 'I think the council idea is a very substantial plus for the newspaper, frankly, because it provides a kind of public monitoring, without legal jeopardy, where the people can go if they can't get satisfaction from the newspaper. It provides a public sounding board.'[65]

Does the press council inhibit news workers? Bailey, again: 'The generalized fears or inhibitions I think are absolutely groundless – without any foundation whatsoever. I have had no sense of that. Once in a while, someone will kid about an incident, saying "I wouldn't want to get before the News Council on *that*." What he really means is "We had better tighten up that story before we publish it." If there has been any effect at all, it hasn't been to inhibit us from working hard on difficult stories but to make us do it a little better.'[66]

The constitution of the BC Press Council lists eight objectives, starting with 'to preserve the established freedom of the press.' (This, despite Malone's fear of 'control, pressure or threat over press freedom.') Second, it lists 'to serve as a medium of understanding between the public and the press.' (That decidedly does not sound like 'turning over direction of *The Sun* ... to our competitors,' as Keate feared.)

The third objective is 'to encourage the highest ethical, professional and commercial standards of journalism.' And only in fourth place come complaints: 'To consider complaints from the public about the conduct of the press in the gathering and publication of news and opinion.'[67]

The other purposes include adjudicating complaints from the press about individual members of the public, reviewing access to information laws, lobbying governments, and publishing reports.[68]

One of the spin-off benefits from press councils adjudicating complaints against the media is that many of the complaints are rejected. A reader who had a complaint in the past, and was told by the editor that she was all wrong, would simply feel more resentful – finding the fox in charge of the chickens. But the reader whose complaint is thrown out by an objective, arm's-length press council is more likely to feel she has been given a fair hearing, and may even be persuaded that the newspaper was right.

There is no doubt that press councils can bog down in procedural wrangles, bureaucracy, and niceties; that they can be expensive to member papers; and that

complaints can take up valuable editors' time when they are forced to justify themselves to ill-informed and often bigoted lay critics. But surely the advantages outweigh the disadvantages. The Ontario council, for instance, operates on about $170,000, which covers paid help, an office, hearings, and the expenses of board members. As the council now has more than 100 member papers, including all of Ontario's forty-three dailies (total daily circulation, approximately 2.4 million), and operating costs are paid by an assessment on members based on circulation, the cost per paper is very modest. But it is crucial that the press councils remain lean and do not develop a self-perpetuating bureaucracy. The British Press Council groaned and eventually collapsed under the burden of a thirty-six-member council, with far too many participating papers to monitor – many of them provocative and sensational and hence constantly provoking many complaints – and an annual complaint list of well over 1,000.[69]

Similarly, the National News Council in the US died after eleven frustrating years, partly because it was so vast (covering the continent) and apparently needed upwards of $700,000 to operate, and partly because many papers cold-shouldered it, notably the *New York Times*.[70]

Another constant complaint about press councils is that they have no power – toothless watchdogs, with little bark, let alone bite.[71] Most press councils operate on an honour system, whereby each member paper publishes the results even if they are highly critical of the paper. That is all: no fines, no expulsion of members, no lifting of licences or cutting of newsprint quotas. And it is true that 'bad' papers will defy press councils, ignore admonitions, and give them the metaphorical finger. But the numbers are interesting. The 1988 Ontario annual report, for instance, notes that from its inception in 1972 to 1988, 276 complaints had actually been adjudicated, with 136 upheld and 134 dismissed. In other words, *half the complaints were thrown out*. In half the cases, the press came out the winners, with the member papers (all 113) publishing reports explaining how the complaints were evaluated and the reasons they were thrown out. *No* amount of self-justification by an editor could have the impact of these judgments.

What about the other half, the negative findings? There is an average of only eight or nine complaints upheld each year, across the whole province of Ontario, despite a circulation of 2.4 million daily newspaper readers, plus nearly one million weekly readers. In very crude numbers, at that rate, each member paper will suffer about seven complaints upheld against it every 100 years. Certainly a lot more complaints are *laid*, and time and money are expended on them until the plaintiff is satisfied or drops the matter before it ever gets to adjudication, but that is a small investment in goodwill.

It is evident from this that press councils are based on a spirit of volunteerism, and some critics thirst for a bigger stick with which to beat the media. Law professor Robert Martin, for instance, dismisses councils as powerless: 'If the unlimited proprietary rights of newspaper owners give rise to legitimate concerns, then press councils, whatever their other merits may be, simply do not address those concerns.'[72] But press councils are not designed to deal with the proprietary rights of press owners any more than a car is designed to float. There is plenty of cause for concern about the authoritarian and arrogant manner of some media barons, but nobody should expect press councils to solve that particular problem.

Why go to such lengths to justify a system that is already functioning effectively throughout Canada? Simply because one province still holds out against the concept. Saskatchewan has only four daily papers, two owned by Thomson and two by the Sifton family (Armadale Publishing), so it could be argued that the number of dailies simply could not sustain an independent council. However, the Alberta press council did, at one time, extend the hand of friendship to Saskatchewan dailies, if they wished to join, though this never happened. One senior Sifton manager once argued that his papers were so good there were not any complaints, and so a council would be a waste of effort.[73] But such swagger is – at best – poor PR. If, for instance, an editor makes a practice of privately answering letters to the editor that criticize his paper, instead of publishing them (as some do), then it may well look as if, indeed, there are no complaints.

Only in a few cases do broadcast listeners or viewers complain to a press council (only Quebec and Windsor councils include broadcasting). To fill this need, the Canadian Broadcast Standards Council was founded in 1989. This body – with a name that sounds vaguely like a division of some government consumer affairs branch – was actually created by the Canadian Association of Broadcasters at the insistence of the CRTC. The new council is very much a broadcast clone of the press councils, designed to adjudicate complaints against the commercial broadcasters.

All in all, press councils remain useful in Canada. This may simply be, in part, that the Canadian press does not indulge in the extremes of behaviour of a London *Sun* or *Sport*. Press councils are, perhaps, 'toothless,' but watchdogs should not have to bite people: their very existence should act as a deterrent. If nothing else, they act as a cheap form of insurance and thus deter governments from imposing much more oppressive press controls.[74]

Appeals to Ombudspersons

The Organization of News Ombudsmen remains a tiny and exclusive club. At last count only five newspapers in Canada and the CBC French service had members in this international group. Those papers are: the *Edmonton Journal*, the *Calgary Herald*, the *London Free Press*, the *Toronto Star*, and the *Montreal Gazette*. (For the record, that is four Southam papers and one independent.)[75]

In the entire United States there are only about thirty-two ombudspersons. In Britain, the concept had little acceptance until a deal was struck in early 1990, whereby twenty of the national dailies appointed ombudspersons in conjunction with revamping the press council.[76]

Why so exclusive? One immediate answer is cost. It looks like an extravagance to add a job to the payroll that commands a high salary and takes one of the most senior newspeople out of the newsroom, basically to criticize his or her colleagues. The innovative Louisville, Kentucky, *Courier-Journal* appointed the world's first newspaper ombudsperson in 1967, following the suggestion by A.H. Raskin in a June 1967 *New York Times Magazine*. The *Toronto Star* led Canada in 1972 (the same year it started the Ontario Press

Council), calling their ombudsperson 'Your man at *The Star.*'

To be effective, the ombudsperson – called reader representative in many papers – must be given the right to ask anybody working for his or her newspaper almost any question, and must be able to robustly criticize colleagues and superiors in print. Few publishers have the fortitude for that. Does it work? The Kent Commission concluded that 'the ombudsman kills two birds with one stone: he enhances the prestige of the paper, and endows it with a kind of moral conscience.'[77] For the appointee, it is a schizophrenic role. 'Newsmen are my friends and associates, but I don't really work with them,' commented Charles B. Seib, *Washington Post* ombudsperson, in an early interview: 'As ombudsman, I don't really work for the *Post*, although the *Post* pays my salary. I have to make myself constantly remember that I'm independent, that I'm the working representative of the reader.'[78]

An ombudsperson is unlikely to *harm* a newspaper. At worst he is a gadfly, asking embarrassing questions and printing embarrassing answers. At best he is a liaison, a bridge between paper and readers. The *Montreal Gazette*'s Clair Balfour told Canadian managing editors in 1988: 'Readers don't get an answer from newspapers. They do get an answer from city hall or the drugstore or the car dealer.'[79]

Ideally, the ombudsperson is a respected senior journalist, given a full-time post to act as the readers' advocate. He or she will be easily accessible to the public by telephone. He or she will have a job guarantee and will report directly to the chief executive officer, while being able to ask anybody anything – and write it. Ideally, the ombudsperson should be viewed as a conciliator rather than an adjudicator.

Are they expensive? Balfour told members of the Canadian Managing Editors' Conference at their 1 June 1988 meeting that there is a direct cost benefit: Problems can be solved before the paper loses valuable customers, advertisers, or circulation. Are they busy? Balfour said he gets an astonishing 4,000 complaints a year. (This compares with about forty complaints filed annually with the Quebec Press Council.) Balfour sees himself as heading off and resolving many complaints before they get to the 'serious' stage of being publicly

filed with the press council. Speaking in 1987 to members of the Canadian Daily Newspaper Publishers Association, Balfour listed the advantages of such reader representatives:

• Enhances credibility
• Neutral righter of wrongs
• Increases newsroom professionalism
• Saves management time by fielding complaints
• Saves money by defusing potential suits.[80]

Obviously only the most affluent media will establish their own audience advocates because of the very visible direct costs – perhaps $100,000 a year – but that cost may well be offset by the less visible benefits.

Many of the ideas outlined above involve value judgments being made by the participants, whether it be firing a reporter for plagiarism or responding to press council complaints about an infringement of privacy. Such judgments are difficult at best, and even more difficult without any formula by which to measure them. One suggestion frequently advanced to resolve this is the establishment of newsroom codes of ethics, the topic of the next chapter.

TOUGH CALLS

1 Some local citizens tell you – as radio news director – they want to start a 'news council' parallel to the existing press council to handle complaints about your station and others. How do you respond?

2 The newspaper's ombudsperson suggests your paper make a policy that all corrections be given equal prominence to the original error. Good idea?

3 The publisher disagrees with the editorial page position on a major issue and wants to write a column outlining his view. Is that legitimate, or is it an abuse of power? Does it make any difference if he wants it on page 1?

4 The publisher has a neat idea to make some money for the paper during the recession: charge ten dollars for publishing all letters to the editor. Good plan?

5 Media Watch – a group that monitors the media's coverage of feminist issues – wants you to provide space for a weekly Op-Ed column from them on media performance. Should you? What are the issues? Would it be any different if the request was from the Fraser Institute's media research office?

6 The station manager's spouse thinks it would be nice if all the senior TV newsroom personnel listed their office phone numbers with the credits at the end of the news show. The news director thinks everyone would be incessantly taking calls from screwballs. What's best?

7 A British barrister, studying the press council there, described it as a pet poodle, rather than a watchdog. Is that a fair tag for press councils in general? Should they therefore be abandoned?

Codes of Conduct

Why don't journalists have rules to live by, just as doctors and lawyers do?

In discussing – in the preceding chapter – the ways in which the news media can develop a closer rapport with news consumers, it has become increasingly evident that journalists need to be accountable to their audience. For this to work satisfactorily, some form of common yardstick may be useful, both to guide and to judge journalistic behaviour. A code of ethics is often suggested as a possible solution.[1]

Clifford Christians, one of the top US specialists in media ethics, sees a special connection between accountability and codes. Indeed, he suggests that because accountability is misunderstood, journalistic codes of ethics have bogged down: 'The reason, I believe, for our failure to move forward substantially regarding codes is a deficiency in understanding accountability.'[2]

Christians sees journalists as being accountable to three constituencies: to government, to themselves as professionals, and to the public.[3] He defines accountability as being called to judgment, with three possible results relating to these three categories: punishment (e.g., court penalties); censure by peers; or censure by the community. Christians then draws a vital distinction: 'Codes of ethics ... reasonably fit into the second category only – that of moral sanction among peers.'[4] On this basis, the role and application of journalistic codes become somewhat clearer. They cannot be imposed by government, they cannot conflict with constitutional freedoms, and they cannot be used by the public as a weapon with which to beat the media.[5] But they can be collegially created and enforced 'by those who share a recognizable community with them.'[6]

Given Christians's definition, obviously the creation of a code would not somehow resolve all complaints or, indeed, make the media better behaved. A code of ethics is no panacea but instead offers a regimen by which journalists can live better professional lives.

In terms of Christians's other two categories, in the view of this writer, the government, per se, should not be judging the media at all. The government is elected to govern, and the electorate, category three, will judge the behaviour of the press by its own mores – modified over time – and will instruct the legislature and the judiciary to enforce those standards with laws governing such areas as privacy and obscenity. It is precisely when governments start to legislate on their own behalf (such as with the uranium cartel cover-up discussed in Chapter 7) that press freedom is seriously threatened.

The Case Against Codes

There are clearly many serious difficulties with the concept of formalized codes, the most obvious of which relates to the nature of the business itself. One of the pleasures of being a journalist is the variety of work – no two days, no two assignments are the same – but it is therefore extremely difficult to develop an effective code that covers all eventualities. Very quickly, code writers will find themselves bogging down in picayune detail: 'If this ..., but what if that ...?'

To adapt a remark from another context, the Ten Commandments consist of 320 words, but the European Common Market directive on the export of duck eggs comprises 27,623 words.[7] 'Thou shalt not kill' cannot be equalled for economy of words and clarity of thought. The problems occur when one starts getting specific. Kill what? Are mosquitoes included? Does this include preventing conception? But the principle – the sacredness of life – is the overarching guide.

The strength of the Ten Commandments, then, is the principles they enunciate. They are guidelines, some of which may occasionally have to be interpreted according to the situation. (The person who refuses to kill a mosquito in malarial territory is obtusely following the letter of the law, rather than its spirit.)

The same approach must be taken to journalistic codes of ethics. They cannot be written in stone because there must be some room for flexibility, for wise and thoughtful debate, and for interpretation according to the situation. They should enunciate the spirit of good journalism.

In addition to the reservation offered above (that the job is so varied a code is difficult to apply), numerous other arguments are marshalled against journalistic codes. However, they are far easier to negotiate if we accept the view that codes are primarily tools for peer accountability. For instance, in the United States, it is sometimes argued that enforcing any code would be an infringement of the First Amendment. This immediately leads to furious waving of the freedom flag by journalists, and a breakdown in any debate. But when the framers of the Constitution wrote that 'Congress shall make no law ... abridging the freedom of speech or of the press,' they obviously had not intended to police the press. If, instead, we agree that codes are *internal* rules, only to be established and enforced within the industry, then the First Amendment argument collapses. No code of ethics would work if it were to be enforced by some external agency – a government-appointed, media-watch committee. The

motivation and enforcement has to come from within.

The Canadian Constitution is somewhat more circumspect. It guarantees the fundamental freedoms, 'subject only to such reasonable limits prescribed by law as can be demonstrably justified in a free and democratic society.'[8] This, then, is *almost* total freedom – total freedom, *except*. The principle of press freedom is vital and must not be debased, but it is not limitless. Nonetheless, media freedom remains entrenched, and nobody's freedom will be threatened if a newsroom develops its own code of ethics and mechanisms for enforcing that code.

Other critics imply that any code, even one developed democratically by an individual newsroom for itself, is the first step towards government control.[9] Two US journalism teachers, Jay Black and Ralph Barney, approvingly summarized other arguments against codes of ethics for journalism: 'They have few if any teeth; they are both unenforced and unforceable [*sic*]. They are incumbent upon members only, and the only sanction that can be applied against a member is expulsion from membership, sometimes a small penalty. The codes tend to be bland statements drawn up in response to public disenchantment with media operations.'[10]

However, these complaints are easy to refute. The issue of enforcement will be dealt with in detail later, but it is wide of the mark to say they are unenforceable. As cited in the previous chapter, many US publishers now report firing people because of ethical errors.[11] A survey in 1990, by this writer, of major Canadian news media yielded a number of incidents in which journalists were disciplined for unethical conduct.[12] But that is really beside the point. If codes are seen primarily as guidelines, then a heavy-handed enforcement of specific details is irrelevant.[13] While some rules are fairly universal, such as 'Thou Shalt Not Steal,' others, such as conflict of interest, are less well known and may need articulating.

Black and Barney say codes affect 'members only' and expulsion is the only punishment. But of course codes only affect the people they are meant to affect (medical ethics do not influence lawyers either). Is being fired so insignificant? And what of other punitive possibilities? There are many clear precedents in

Canada and the US where employees have been suspended for ethical misdemeanours, or switched to other assignments. Surely these are reasonable options?[14]

Finally, Black and Barney dismiss codes as 'bland,' being enacted only as a knee-jerk response to criticism. Bland may be an accurate if unflattering description, but must a code be full of fire and vitriol to be effective? And some codes may well be developed as a result of public criticism of the media, but does that limit or devalue them?

Such cavilling is unhelpful. It is reminiscent of John C. Merrill's blanket dismissal of codes as 'meaningless and illogical'[15] and his laboured demolition of the code of the Society of Professional Journalists (SPJ).[16] As Christians perceptively remarks, Merrill is faulting SPJ for being too all-encompassing.[17] It is far more difficult – even impossible – to write a meaningful code for a national organization such as the SPJ, representing thousands of journalists of every stripe, from coast to coast, than for those in one newsroom. As a result, the SPJ code is little more than a wish list.[18] The 'Statement of Principles' of the Canadian Daily Newspaper Publishers Association (CDNPA) suffered from the same limitation, but it aspired to be nothing more than just that: a statement of principles (see Appendix 1).

Survey Results

A survey of selected Canadian newsrooms, conducted by this writer in 1990 in conjunction with the current research, showed that codes of ethics were not widespread in the Canadian news industry but were evidently increasing fast.[19]

Questionnaires were sent to 156 separate newsrooms (plus press galleries, networks, industry associations, and journalism schools), with sixty responding (38 per cent). Of those, half (thirty-one) said they already had a code of some form, and another seven said they were working on one and would have it ready within a year. Four more respondents felt they ought to have a code but did not.

These figures certainly cannot be extrapolated across the whole industry, as only the larger newsrooms were polled, only the more ethically sensitized operations were likely to respond, and seventeen of the nineteen broadcast outlets who said they had a code were referring to the ready-made code from the Radio Television News Directors Association (see Appendix 2). In fact, only ten of the thirty-one newsrooms with codes actually had a code customized for their newsroom.

The survey found very few codes in daily newsrooms. In fact some respondents evidently forgot they had one. The Southam group, for instance, distributed a 'Newspaper Publishing Credo' to all Southam newsrooms in 1979, but several responding editors had evidently forgotten it by 1990. (It is only one page and is very general, but it does cover conflict of interest, fairness, access, accuracy, taste, freedom of the press, and advertisers' rights.)

Obviously, if a code exists, people have to know about it. More than half the newsrooms said they distribute copies of their code to staff, and half have them posted in the newsroom. In addition, a third of the newsrooms show their codes to job applicants before they are hired, so they know in advance the expectations. However, distributing a code does not necessarily make it stick. Many newsrooms go further, with memos and seminars. And when there are flagrant violations, there are repercussions.

Almost half of all the responding newsrooms reported having meetings or seminars on ethics within the last five years, and just as many had had memos on ethical issues circulated in the newsroom, covering topics ranging from freeloading (the most common topic) to privacy, handling suicides, identifying accident victims, and relations with police.

Managing editors and news directors were asked how ethical dilemmas were tackled, and more than half said they were discussed either on the spot or at regular meetings. (The other half split: two print editors said, surprisingly, that most issues were covered by union contract, and five – mostly print – said they were arbitrated by the senior editor.)

So the atmosphere seems to be largely democratic and consultative. However, a breach of ethics can be a firing offence, even in Canada. Fifteen of the sixty newsrooms reported that within the last five years somebody had been disciplined for an ethical lapse (and there may be more – several respondents did not answer that question; one or two respondents noted they had not worked in that newsroom that long; and other incidents may have been forgotten).

What sort of discipline? Three managing editors or news directors reported somebody was fired because of unethical behaviour; four reported news staff had been suspended; two reported staff had lost pay; six people were reprimanded; one person was assigned to a different beat; and one got a memo in his personnel file. Evidently ethics are being taken very seriously in Canadian newsrooms.

Disciplinary action for a breach of journalistic ethics may, of course, have nothing to do with the existence of a code. But the presence of a code will certainly reduce the number of people who, when challenged about an ethical infringement, can say, 'But I didn't know ...' And a code may also strengthen peer pressure. When colleagues drily remark in the bar, 'Are you sure you ought to march in the parade/run for mayor/write speeches for the government?' plans may be quietly changed.

But apparently Canadian newsroom codes are not very democratically developed. One-third of those responding (ten newsrooms) said their code had been developed by the managing editor or news director. Only three people said theirs had come from a newsroom committee, and two said they resulted from full newsroom meetings. (The other newsrooms said their codes were developed by 'other' methods.) To a complementary question about people's attitudes to the code, six news directors or managing editors said their codes were 'imposed' on the newsroom; thirteen said they were 'adopted' by news staff; and six said they were 'developed' by news staff. So the managers, at least, feel their codes have popular support, even though at least a third of them were developed top-down. It seems obvious that a code developed amongst peers and democratically adopted will have much more weight than one imposed by management.[20]

This relates to another perennial weakness of codes. Are they designed by management to tell staff how to behave, or are they developed collegially, to apply to everyone working for that medium? Eighty-one per cent of respondents said the code applied to everyone in the newsroom, including the managing editor or news director. However, very few said they apply right to the top: just three out of the thirty-one reported that

the publisher or station manager must answer to the code as well. Further research might usefully reveal whether other departments, such as advertising and circulation also have codes; there seems no reason to believe that only the newsroom needs such guidance.

It has been argued that publishers, station managers, and other top company executives march to a somewhat different drummer, that their central role is the prosperity of the operation and therefore they must be exempt from codes of ethics.[21] This seems to imply that senior management must, by definition, be unethical. However, if the code is seen – once again – as a set of guidelines, then it may well be applicable to even the company president. Her loyalty to the integrity and honesty of the operation should also be unquestioned. She, too, should eschew conflict of interest or abuse of power. Why should a publisher be exempt from guidelines on plagiarism or freebies? Her raison d'être may be different from the newsroom's, but the public may well perceive the misdemeanours of a publisher in just the same light as those of a copy clerk.[22]

Indeed, the UNESCO report on the international flow of news (entitled *Many Voices, One World*), though often confusing and even contradictory, makes a telling point when it suggests that proprietors may need codes of ethics *more* than their staff: 'It may also be noted in relation to codes that it is not journalists who need a high standard of ethics so much as their employers, who give orders that are often repugnant to the working reporter.'[23]

The Role of Codes

What good is a code? It is a touchstone. The act of making a code should be an important one for newspeople, focusing their attention on issues and on philosophy. Once in place, it gives journalists a starting point and a reason for discussion. But it must never be regarded as final and all-encompassing, because experiences, technologies, and situations all change and blend. The words on the wall matter far less than the daily deeds of the staff. The mere existence of a code will neither make the problems go away nor make journalists more ethical.

If a code also serves to assist the community in judging its media, so be it. Says John Quinn, a former president of the American Society of Newspaper Editors, 'The issue is credibility. A thoughtful ethics policy can be a major and needed step in promoting credibility.'[24]

So what should a code of ethics contain? Some, such as the Southam Newspaper Publishing Credo (see Appendix 3), are vastly generalized, outlining simply a communal philosophy, recognizing that situations are local and so must be solved locally. Others, like the CDNPA (now CDNA) Statement of Principles, outline broad positions on a few limited headings. (The British Code of Practice, developed by the dailies in 1989, is similar. See Appendix 4.) The more homogeneous the group – such as the Radio Television News Directors Association and the Periodical Writers Association of Canada – the more specific the code.

The most specific of all should be those designed for one newsroom only, such as that developed by the *Western Producer* newspaper in 1990. This commendable document (see Appendix 5) includes general principles – a devotion to 'reliable, relevant information' and freedom of the press – and then moves into the expected headings of Accuracy, Handling Errors, Fairness, Conflict, Plagiarism, and the need for a Multiplicity of Voices. Somewhat more unusual is its addition of the following: a determination to cite sources whenever possible, to maintain the integrity of photographs in the electronic darkroom, to separate editorial decisions from advertising influence, and to clearly label advertising and display it 'so as not to be confused with editorial content.' The code also announces the paper's policy on reporters identifying themselves, on their freelancing elsewhere, and on editing letters; and it bravely notes that though the paper is owned by the Saskatchewan Wheat Pool, the agency 'will be treated on the same basis as other major news sources.'

This code addresses precisely the ethical dilemmas likely to be encountered by the staff of this newspaper. The *Western Producer* is small and isolated,[25] and its staff will encounter problems unique to them, such as a commitment to cooperative principles, and whether reporters can join organizations of agrologists. A code with the broad sweep of, say, the CDNPA Statement of Principles would only lay the groundwork for them, without addressing their particular concerns. Yet a

narrower-based code (such as that written for CFPL-TV in London, Ontario, or even that prepared by the daily *Windsor Star*) would also omit some of their particular concerns and would contain many irrelevancies.

The temptation facing code writers, then, may be to narrow the focus of the document, basing it exclusively on the experiences of that newsroom. Yet here, too, there are dangers. If a code becomes too specific, it cannot address every situation, and participants may find themselves debating how many journalists can dance on the head of a pin, rather than the central issues of fidelity and integrity.

Let us examine, for a moment, a hypothetical case. The mythical *Daily Star-Reporter* has a code framed on the newsroom wall that clearly states: 'Thou Shalt Not Commit Plagiarism. Plagiarism Is A Firing Offence.' A staff editorial writer is found to have 'borrowed' the central two-thirds of an editorial on hunger in Africa from *The Plain Truth*, and the publisher wants to fire her and publish a grovelling apology as a gesture to the newsroom and the readers. However, the managing editor wants to transfer the writer to the sports department, publishing a brief apology. And the editorial page editor feels a reprimand is sufficient, maintaining it is all an internal matter.

What, then, are the issues? On the face of it, the issue is theft: stealing someone else's words, giving neither credit nor royalties. But plagiarism goes beyond that, to deliberately deceiving the audience: it is both theft and a lie. Yet anglophone editorials are traditionally anonymous. Does it matter who penned the words? Moreover, must justice be *seen* to be done outside the newsroom?

Does the writer's motivation matter? When challenged, the writer says rather weakly that she meant no harm, the original was phrased so well, she was encountering a serious family crisis at the time, and it will never happen again. Is the offence significantly different if it is committed by a habitually lazy writer trying to get to the golf course early rather than by a loyal staff member under stress?

Would the incident matter less if it occurred on the recipes page? If only two or three paragraphs were involved? Does the judgment differ if she admits she has done it once before? If she says it's the only time, but she is subsequently found to have done it before? Is it significant that, though the paragraphs are recognizable, they have been substantially rewritten? Is the same punishment appropriate for both the writer who has habitually passed off vast chunks of other people's writing as his own and the writer who once slipped in a couple of paragraphs from elsewhere?

Even with this incident, which seems at first blush to be a prima facie case deserving the punishment specified – firing – there are too many variables.

The *Western Producer* outlines its position simply and clearly: 'Plagiarism will not be tolerated. If any staff or outside writer is found to have deliberately copied someone else's work without attribution, the infraction will be publicly noted.'[26] In other words, the punishment meted out to the perpetrator is none of the public's business (and can be flexible, according to the circumstances), but the occurrence itself – the attempt to gull the audience – is very much the public's business. The readers deserve to be told, even if not a single reader spotted the incident.[27]

It therefore seems clear that codes – to be effective – must be both specific to the newsroom and yet not too narrow to exclude the myriad variables that occur there daily.[28] But it bears repeating that codes per se solve nothing. Their success hinges on the participants having the will to conduct themselves in an appropriate way. A code cannot be imposed on unwilling participants, but willing participants can develop (or participate in developing) a workable code because it will articulate the values to which they already subscribe.

What, then, of the argument of the respected John Merrill, particularly in *Existential Journalism*, that codes are unenforceable rhetoric? As Merrill remarks (as he proceeds to throw out the baby with the bathwater): 'A code of ethics hanging on the wall is meaningless; a code of ethics internalized within the journalist and guiding his actions is what is meaningful ... Theory without action is dead.'[29]

Ideally, every journalist would, indeed, develop a personal code of the highest integrity, and there are clearly some journalists who already live by such rules. But that nirvana is a long way off.[30] The situation is aggravated by reverse pressures, especially among fiercely competitive media, such as many tabloid news-

papers, to cut corners. It might be argued that newsroom codes are an interim measure, in effect until every individual journalist meets this rigorous standard. But whether journalism can ever attain such a sublime state – certainly beyond anything yet achieved by the other professions – remains to be seen. Journalism attracts all sorts of people for all sorts of reasons. Hence, when an editor says no code is necessary because it is "written in our hearts,"[31] that may mean that different things are written in different scripts, some more legible than others. Some journalists, inevitably, will be more idealistic than others; some will be more philosophical, others more pragmatic. Some will be driven by a need to serve the community, others by a search for glory, wealth, or even power. In such an imperfect world, some guidelines applicable to all would help, as they would serve as signposts on a foggy road.

Merrill's rugged individualism in fact presupposes that journalism can tolerate a virtual anarchy of values. The only alternative is that the individuals be remarkably like-thinking, homogeneous in their values and in their evaluating. Perhaps no profession – journalism, medicine, architecture, or law – should be so unanimous.

This issue – the unanimity required of the formalized profession – will be examined in the next and final chapter.

TOUGH CALLS

1 Your newsroom code specifies that victims of sexual assaults not be identified. The teacher of a remote one-room school in your circulation area has been charged with indecently assaulting students. Do you name the teacher and, hence, identify his students? Do you rewrite the code?

2 Activists in your newsroom have called for a code of ethics to be developed. The publisher replies that the paper's motto is its code: 'The policy of our paper is very simple – merely to tell the truth.' Will that suffice?

3 Your newsroom policy manual says there must be no exploitation of grief. You have a fine picture of a man weeping on a police car, after learning his entire family has been killed (see page 121). Do you run the picture? Where? How big? Does it make any difference if this is the *Tillsonburg Times* or the *Toronto Sun*?

4 The press gallery rules forbid conflict of interest, such as journalist-members working for the government on the side. One senior member is discovered to have written speeches for a minister. In the ensuing debate, several similar situations are uncovered, such as editing documents and preparing brochures. As president of the gallery executive, what do you think should be done?

18 Conclusion

Some critics of the news business have argued that codes of ethics are necessary before journalism can be viewed as a profession.[1]

It might be useful to conclude this study of journalism ethics in Canada by returning to two subjects touched on earlier: first, the question of professionalism, broached in Chapter 3, for this is a key issue of self-image, germane to ethics; and second, the question of freedom of the press, which is equally important to fully understanding the journalist's role in society.

Journalism as a Profession

Considerable ink has been expended on debating whether journalism is a profession.[2] Indeed, there seem to be a good number of people who feel that if journalism can be so designated, it will thus join the ranks of lawyers and doctors and so enjoy some dignity and respect not presently accorded its practitioners.[3] This is an unfortunate equation. Many journalists spend their careers observing professionals and seeing the reverence they are often accorded despite normal human frailty, and yet they themselves may be vilified for what they write about them – for perceived invasion of privacy, ghoulishness, sensationalism, superficiality, etc.

In a thoughtful essay on professionalism, Louis Hodges, a specialist in applied ethics, suggests that journalism is on the way to professionalism, but that it lacks three ingredients: a greater sense of service on the part of journalists (instead of a 'parent-child' relationship between journalists and audience); a sense of

nobility and achievement from that service; and a greater awareness of the need to contribute holistically to people's lives.[4] This is a tall order, not achieved overnight or by any single action. However, Hodges's concepts have, in fact, suffused the current study: the role of the journalist has been interpreted very much in terms of helping people to live richer lives and contributing to making a better world. The five Ws of ethics postulated in Chapter 1 are based on the journalist's relationship to her audience. The concept of the journalist taking responsibility for her actions shares Hodges's sense of service.

However, Louis Hodges takes the moral high ground. He quotes – presumably approvingly – a reference to the word 'profession' being defined as the antonym of the word 'commercial.'[5] And, inspired by a powerful Christian view, he sees journalism as one of 'the caring professions,' in which the worker becomes 'a true and humble servant,' performing 'sacrificial service.'[6] But why is it necessary to embrace this view before the journalist can behave ethically and professionally? For some, journalism may be – as Hodges maintains – a 'calling,' but for others there may be more prosaic motivations of fame and fortune, which nonetheless do not exclude ethical conduct.

Hodges proffers his view after examining more traditional definitions of the professions (notably Abraham Flexner's),[7] and finding that journalism falls far short of those. But the difficulty may lie with the appropriateness of the criteria themselves. Sometimes the simplest definition is the best, but Don Buckingham's definition, for instance, really is too general. Buckingham, associate director of law and public policy at the Westminster Institute for Ethics and Human Values, says: 'A profession is a group of individuals trained in a specific discipline, possessing a specialized knowledge and vocabulary which is made available to the general public.'[8] Journalism, surely, is much more than this.[9]

Perhaps more apposite in this context is Merrill's list of criteria for journalism to be judged a profession: rules of admission; an exclusive body of knowledge; a mechanism for expelling inadequate members; an elite inner circle; a code of ethics; and a roster of acceptable practitioners.[10] Merrill concludes baldly: 'Journalism is not a profession.' However, he warns darkly that journalism may be moving towards becoming a profession – and would be the worse for it. Merrill's fear – perhaps predictable given his strongly conservative position, expounded particularly in *The Imperative of Freedom: A Philosophy of Journalistic Autonomy* – is that individualism will be stamped out of journalists, 'making all journalists march to the same drummer.'[11] He calls for an alternative to professionalization: 'What is needed is a will to have more vigorous, vital and pluralistic journalism.'[12]

Undeniably, increased vigour, vitality, and pluralism would be advantageous to journalism. Merrill's concern has some basis, but he may be overcompensating. While there is not space here to fully debate Merrill's six criteria of a profession, it is clear that he is right in saying that journalism does not fully meet any of them. But are these the right criteria?

The argument is often made that medicine and law are professions, and therefore to gain professional status, journalism should match them. This presupposes that they constitute ideal role models for the journalist. But such regimes would only result in imposing a wholly unsuitable homogeneity on journalism.

Instead, and at the risk of indulging in semantics, it might help to limit this debate by using the adjective 'professional,' leaving aside the noun 'profession.' Thus it is not necessary to define 'profession'[13] in order to usefully ask, 'Do journalists deport themselves in a professional manner?'

What are the symptoms of this professionalism? Ethical sensitivity is certainly crucial. But after that the definitions are vague. Using the official US government definition, journalism is primarily intellectual and varied and requires judgment; it is difficult to standardize in terms of time; and it does require some specialized knowledge (interviewing, story-construction, literacy, logic, headline-writing, writing to videotape, etc.). It is Merrill's suggested criteria that do not fit and must be resisted. It is important that journalism *not* have narrowly defined membership and entry criteria. It is important that there *not* be an exclusive body of knowledge for entry or a roster of acceptable practitioners. Such limitations would bring a dangerous homogeneity to a skill that needs a vast range of expertises and experiences. Some of the best practitioners of journalism in Canada today have university degrees in philosophy, medicine, divinity, science, or law, rather than – or in addition to – a journalism degree. (And some may have no degrees at all.) If they were excluded in favour of a universal and exclusive 'journalism' degree, for instance, a most unfortunate mass production would ensue. Medicine, law, or accounting may not need this endless variety: Journalism thrives on it.

American academic Jeffrey Olen urges journalists to steer away from such mass-produced orthodoxy: 'And all sorts of eccentric journalism ought to be tolerated. Certainly, nothing along the lines of a bar association ought to decide which ones should not be tolerated. We do not, in short, need to be protected from "unprofessional" journalism. If anything, we need to be exposed to the widest variety of journalism.'[14]

Olen is concerned that promoters of organizations such as the Society of Professional Journalists (or, in the Canadian context, the Canadian Association of Journalists) will envisage their group as akin to the Law Society, and so be tempted to set rigid entry rules, with, for instance, a committee to sit in judgment on members and rescind their 'licence' to practise.[15] Journalism would be seriously diminished by this.[16]

Setting rules will not turn journalism from a craft to a profession. Perhaps British columnist Katharine Whitehorn has got it right when she reduces it to one element: 'Professions are only trades with more prestigious and established controlling bodies.'[17] Only the visible appearance of behaving in a professional way will bring communal respect. Indeed, there are already some newspeople who are clearly professionals of the highest calibre, such as the late Bruce Hutchison, although they lack many of the artificial yardsticks used by those wanting to formalize journalism as a profession.[18]

Nor are there any simple solutions. Tom Kent, who fathered the ill-fated Kent Commission, reviewed the professionalizing of Canadian journalism in a speech to members of the CIJ/CAJ: 'So what do we do? You will do all you can to raise standards by your own efforts, in your work, in the journalism schools, even in our weak press councils. But the main problem is with the media proprietors. It is to induce them to pay for more professionalism.'[19]

But it isn't even that simple. This is one problem that will not be solved by 'throwing money at it.' Journalists would be delighted if proprietors started paying them better, and this might at least induce the proprietors to respect them more, but it would not automatically make journalists better.

David Taras, looking at steady improvements in journalism, points to ethics as a major factor in this: 'The main tenets of a new professional awareness were that journalists had to develop ethical standards and guidelines, rigorous methods of reporting, and greater independence from publishers and owners ... The claim to professionalism was predicated on journalists taking responsibility for the fairness and accuracy of their work, having both education and training, and feeling some loyalty to the profession as a whole.'[20]

With this intellectual rigour, independence, and sense of fairness and accuracy, journalists will be seen as professionals. When the journalists' actions speak as loud as their words, then they will be seen as professional. When journalists are really good at their craft, they will recognize that the label is irrelevant, and they will then *be* professional.

Freedom of the Press

It may seem odd to leave a discussion of freedom of the press to the end of an examination of journalism ethics, when so many similar studies *start* with freedom, viewing it as the wellspring for all good journal-

ism. But by what right does the press have freedom, and how is it to be used?

Certainly the Canadian Constitution articulates freedom of speech and freedom of the press for all citizens.[21] This has been elaborated by the courts. Justice Brian Dickson, subsequently chief justice of the Supreme Court of Canada, wrote, 'We define freedom of the press as that degree of freedom from restraint which is essential to enable proprietors, editors and journalists to advance the public interest by publishing the facts and opinions without which a democratic electorate cannot make responsible judgments.'[22]

So democracy and freedom of the press are symbiotically entwined. But which comes first – freedom or the press?[23] The answer is freedom. Freedom of the press emerges from freedom of speech and thought, and is a benefit of being a Canadian citizen today. One does not have to be a good citizen to have freedom of the press: she who sets up a press in Canada today instantly has freedom, before printing a word. But if those first few words are, for instance, a call for the violent overthrow of government, then that freedom is forfeit. The freedom continues to be earned or lost depending on performance. And it brings with it clear responsibilities – the responsibilities of stewardship. As the Davey Commission pointed out years ago, the media – or the media moguls – do not 'own' freedom of the press: 'Too many publishers harbour the absurd notion that freedom of the press is something they own; their freedom of the press ... Of course, the exact opposite is the case. Press freedom is the right of the people.'[24]

The subsequent Kent Commission also felt freedom of the press was abused by proprietors: 'In a one-newspaper town it means nothing except the right of a proprietor to do what he will with his own ... [Because of concentration of ownership,] freedom of the press means, in itself, only that enormous influence without responsibility is conferred on a handful of people.'[25] Kent went on to endorse the CDNPA Statement of Principles, which states, in part, 'The Press claims no freedom that is not the right of every person ... [Its] over-riding responsibility is to the society which protects and provides its freedom.'[26]

So, what is the purpose of this much-vaunted freedom? Most people seem to agree that freedom of the media has a very specific purpose: to protect democracy. Indeed, the trenchant Walter Lippmann argued that the newspaper is 'the bible of democracy,' and that editors, handling the daily flood of news, carry out 'one of the truly sacred and priestly offices in a democracy.' Even the UNESCO Commission, not notable for its poetic vision, sees this sacerdotal role: 'It is this right of the public to know that is the essence of media freedom of which the professional journalist, writer and producer are only custodians.'[27]

Or, as Kent even more expansively and prosaically described it: 'The responsibility above all [is] to be the medium of record providing, by disinterested selection, investigation and interpretation, the information that is significant to the lives of Canadians in as comprehensive, balanced, fair, and understandable a way as is humanly possible.'[28]

This requires a very real sensitivity to journalistic ethics. Freedom of the press gives the people in the media enormous liberty, but it is liberty *to* not just liberty *from*. John Merrill summarizes this very usefully when he identifies two forms of press freedom: 'Positive freedom is the freedom to achieve some good, whereas negative freedom is the freedom from restraint.'[29] This partly explains why freedom is all-too-often invoked to shelter the press, rather than to shelter the community.[30]

John Hulteng puts it very neatly: 'To prevent further erosion, editors and reporters should refrain from excessive or unjustified appeals to public opinion. A knee-jerk invocation of press freedom every time some public official or special-interest representative criticizes the performance of the press will only harm the cause ... Cry "Wolf!" only when a genuine predator is on the prowl.'[31]

Freedom of the press is, therefore, freedom *from* restraint, within bounds, in order *to* inform, entertain, and enrich the audience, and it requires the exponents of it to take responsibility for what they do. It is this mandate that demands journalists be sensitized to ethics.

Red Light vs. Green Light Ethics
The concept of positive and negative freedom links well with another concept only recently thrown into the ethical mix: 'red light' vs. 'green light' ethics.

Apparently first suggested by Roy Peter Clark of the Poynter Institute for Media Studies in St. Petersburg, Florida,[32] the idea suggests that too much thinking about ethical issues has concentrated on what we may *not* do, whereas pro-active ethics suggests things that we *should* do. Clark urged journalists to 'think positive,' using their positive freedom for positive ethical decisions. This has been picked up and expanded recently by other journalism scholars, notably Jay Black and Ralph Barney in their essay on how ethics have changed in the decade since the *Washington Post*'s Pulitzer Prize debacle.[33]

Clark sees green light ethics as focussing on news staff as 'teams' (rather than individuals), driven by a sense of democratic duty, compassion, openness, mission, courage, ingenuity, and craftsmanship.[34] He cites dozens of cases of admirable American journalism and suggests that the best journalism is driven by the motives he lists. The best journalism, he implies, is not advocacy journalism (in the sense of promoting causes) but journalism that contributes to the community, even at its own expense – even if it means occasionally lying or aggravating a press council. He writes:

Green Light Ethics is, admittedly, a rhetorical device, a way of understanding ethics that empowers journalists rather than cripples them ... The Green Light shines from the very core of journalism. It is the reason why the best journalists get into the business in the first place. It is the beacon for those who want to report good stories, to reform democratic institutions, and to improve people's lives. Too many red lights turn journalists into cowards. The Green Light will make them brave.[35]

The Good News
Journalism in Canada is far from perfect. But it is far better than in many other countries of the world,[36] and it has improved immeasurably, even in the last twenty years. When journalists fret about the quality of the profession, they could do worse than re-read the Davey Commission's description of them in 1970:

How good are Canadian reporters? Good, but not as good as they could be. They lack, to begin with, the professional and technical competence of their counterparts in the United States and Britain. This is partly because their training is inferior and partly because neither the newspaper industry nor the members of the craft collectively are working to improve standards. In Britain, for instance, the industry-supported Press Council works constantly and effectively to establish standards of newspaper performance and to police the product. The Institute of Journalists plays a similar role within the profession. In Canada there are no press councils. Nor is there any other industry watchdog.[37]

This now seems hopelessly out of date, as the craft has developed so far in such a short time. A vastly higher proportion of Canadian journalists now have specialized journalism education; news people now *do* work collectively to improve standards (demonstrated particularly by the useful meetings and conferences of the Canadian Association of Journalists from coast to coast, and the CAJ publications); numerous press councils have been founded and are making real contributions to media understanding and accountability; and industry watchdogs, such as ombudspersons, Media Watch, and various media critics, have been established. All that has been achieved in little more than twenty years. As Peter Desbarats puts it: 'Whether it is regarded as a profession or a craft (or something in between), journalism has quite clearly become more professional in Canada in recent decades. Journalists nowadays are better educated, better paid, more aware of ethical issues, more conscientious in their work, and more accountable to society than at any time in our history.'[38]

Desbarats's five criteria are fascinating, as at least the last three bear on ethics. And it could be argued that if journalists' education includes formal journalism courses that deal with ethical concerns, these journalists may be better educated and more ethically sensitive.

Recurring throughout this study has been the theme of responsibility – on being aware that access to a trusting audience is a privilege. And while the emphasis has been on the newsrooms of the nation – broadcasting, newspapers, news agencies, and magazines – the same responsibility effects proprietors. The news media are not just – as Lord Thomson once remarked of his television franchises – 'a licence to print money,' cash cows to be milked dry. Media managers are accorded the right to operate and make a profit in return for providing, in the words of the Kent Commission, 'the information that is significant to the lives of Canadians in as comprehensive, balanced, fair, and understandable a way as is humanly possible.'[39]

The fear remains – indeed, the fear grows – that multinational conglomerates are less likely to be concerned about the welfare of their newspaper holdings (and their audiences) than are independents or small firms. There is increasing concern that Tom Kent was right when he warned a decade ago: 'The hard-headed business thing to do is to fill up the news hole as cheaply as possible, with wire-service copy and minimal local news gathered by junior reporters and stringers.'[40]

Media managers, therefore, also need to reassure the news consumers that they, too, recognize and respect ethical values. Every individual in a news operation – from makeup artist and advertising clerk to managing editor and network president – needs to remember that his or her relationship with the audience is symbiotic and sensitive. At a time when newspaper circulations are dipping, network television ratings are slipping, and radio audiences are fragmenting, all media employers and employees must recognize that credibility is crucial. Newsroom staff, as the front-line, must constantly remember that credibility is inextricably linked to ethics. It does not matter how fine the investigative journalism is, how colourful the pictures are, how effective the audio is, or how imaginative the documentary may be – without credibility, all is dust.

Appendixes

Appendix 1: Statement of Principles for Canadian Daily Newspapers, Canadian Daily Newspaper Publishers Association
(adopted April 1977; courtesy the Canadian Daily Newspaper Association)

I. Ethics

Newspapers have individual codes of ethics and this declaration of principles is intended to complement them in their healthy diversity. As individual believers in free speech they have a duty to maintain standards of conduct in conformance with their own goals.

II. Freedom of the Press

Freedom of the press is an exercise of the common right to freedom of speech. It is the right to inform, to discuss, to advocate, to dissent. The Press claims no freedom that is not the right of every person. Truth emerges from free discussion and free reporting and both are essential to foster and preserve a democratic society.

III. Responsibility

The newspaper has responsibilities to its readers, its shareholders, its employees and its advertisers. But the operation of a newspaper is in effect a public trust, no less binding because it is not formally conferred, and its overriding responsibility is to the society which protects and provides its freedom.

IV. Accuracy and Fairness

The newspaper keeps faith with its readers by presenting the news comprehensively, accurately and fairly, and by acknowledging mistakes promptly.

Fairness requires that in the reporting of news, the right of every person to a fair trial should be respected.

Fairness also requires that sources of information should be identified except when there is a clear and pressing reason to protect their anonymity. Except in rare circumstances, reporters should not conceal their own identity. Newspapers and their staffs should not induce people to commit illegal or improper acts. Sound practice makes a clear distinction for the reader between news reports and expressions of opinion.

V. Independence

The newspaper should hold itself free of any obligation save that of fidelity to the public good. It should pay the costs incurred in gathering and publishing news. Conflicts of interest, and the appearance of conflicts of interest, must be avoided. Outside interests that could affect, or appear to affect, the newspaper's freedom to report the news impartially should be avoided.

VI. Privacy

Every person has a right to privacy. There are inevitable conflicts between the right to privacy and the public good or the right to know about the conduct of public affairs. Each case should be judged in the light of common sense and humanity.

VII. Access

The newspaper is a forum for the free interchange of information and opinion. It should provide for the expression in its columns of disparate and conflicting views. It should give expression to the interests of minorities as well as majorities, and of the less powerful elements in society.

Appendix 2: Radio Television News Directors Association of Canada Code of Ethics

(revised 1986; courtesy the Radio Television News Directors Association Canada)

Recognizing the importance to a democracy of an informed public, the members of the RTNDA of Canada believe the broadcasting of factual, accurately-reported and timely news and public affairs is vital. To that end, RTNDA members pledge to observe the following Code of Ethics:

Article One:
The main purpose of broadcast journalism is to inform the public in an accurate, comprehensive and balanced manner about events of importance.

Article Two:
News and public affairs broadcasts will put events into perspective by presenting relevant background information. Factors such as race, creed, nationality or religion will be reported only when relevant. Comment and editorial opinion will be identified as such. Errors will be quickly acknowledged and publicly corrected.

Article Three:
Broadcast journalists will not sensationalize news items and will resist pressures, whether from inside or outside the broad-casting industry, to do so. They will in now way distort the news. Broadcast journalists will not edit taped interviews to distort the meaning, intent or actual words of the interviewee.

Article Four:
Broadcast journalists will always display respect for the dignity, privacy and well-being of everyone with whom they deal, and make every effort to ensure that the privacy of public persons is infringed only to the extent necessary to satisfy the public interest and accurately report the news.

Article Five:
Broadcast journalists will govern themselves on and off the job in such a way to avoid conflict of interest, real or apparent.

Article Six:
Broadcast journalists will seek to remove any impediments or bans on the use of electronic news gathering equipment at public proceedings, believing that such access is in the public interest. They acknowledge the importance of protection of confidential information and sources.

Article Seven:
News directors recognize that informed analysis, comment and editorial opinion on public events and issues is both a right and responsibility that should be delegated only to individuals whose experience and judgment qualify them for it.

Article Eight:
Broadcast journalists shall conduct themselves politely, keeping broadcast equipment as unobtrusive as possible. Broadcast journalists will try to prevent their presence from distorting the character or importance of events.

Article Nine:
In reporting matters that are or may be before the courts, broadcast journalists will ensure that their reporting does not interfere with the right of an individual to a fair trial.

Article Ten:
Reporting of criminal activities, such as hostage-takings, will be done in a fashion that does not knowingly endanger lives, hamper attempts by authorities to conclude the event, offer comfort and support or provide vital information to the perpetrator(s). RTNDA members will not contact either victim(s) or perpetrator(s)

of a criminal activity during the course of the event, with the purpose of conducting an interview for broadcast.

Article Eleven:

The RTNDA will seek to enforce this code through its members and encourage all broadcast journalists, whether RTNDA members or not, to observe its spirit. News directors will try whenever possible and within programming format constraints to publicize the existence of the Code of Ethics, and state that their news department adheres to the code. In any such announcement, it should be mentioned that copies of the code can be obtained by writing the RTNDA or the news director at the station.

Appendix 3: Southam Newspaper Publishing Credo
(dated 12 March 1979; courtesy Southam Newspapers)

There is no 'Southam' editorial policy. There are no rigid rules for producing a 'Southam' newspaper. Diversity and innovation are encouraged.

The responsibility for editorial content rests entirely with the divisional management. All editorial opinion is formed at the local level. In establishing its editorial position, each newspaper is encouraged to be positive in support of issues it believes to be for the common good and courageous in standing up against those it believes not in the best interest of the public. Comment should be fair and constructive.

Newspapers should reflect the lives and attitudes of the people within their community, including their concern for the well-being of our country as a whole. They should respect minority viewpoints and encourage active discussion in their pages of all aspects of society. Their news columns should present an accurate and balanced picture, uncoloured by the editorial opinions of the newspaper or the bias or prejudice of individual writers. They should bring to their public the widest possible range of news, information, comment and interpretation, subject only to general good taste and the laws governing obscenity, slander, libel and sedition.

The newspaper's columns should be open to per-

sons who disagree with it, although the right of access to news columns remains an editorial prerogative to be carefully guarded within the considerations of fair play and public interest.

Editorial employees participating in specific events should not report on those events.

Southam publishers shall maintain the highest possible standards of journalism by employing those individuals who best represent the ideals of a free and responsible press. Consideration of age, race, colour, creed, religion, sex, national origin or handicap, should not influence the hiring of staff. The ability and integrity of the individual should be the guiding factors in all cases.

Freedom of the press is a right of all Canadians, and one that publishers should preserve and defend. It is not a special privilege of the press, but a simple extension of the concept of freedom of speech. A corollary is the right of any purchaser to buy advertising space, subject only to consideration of truthfulness, decency, legality and the public interest.

The company charges its publishers with the responsibility to ensure that the trust and power inherent in publishing not be abused.

Appendix 4: The Code of Conduct of British Dailies
(printed 11 November 1989 in the Independent*)*

Declaration

We, the editors of all Britain's national newspapers, declare our determination to defend the democratic right of the people to a Press free from government interference.

In pursuing our campaigns for a freedom of information act and reform of libel and contempt law, we have also given due consideration to criticism of the Press in Parliament and by the public.

While supporting the Press Council, each individual national newspaper now accepts the need to improve its own methods of self-regulation, including procedures for dealing promptly and fairly with complaints.

Editors have agreed on a common Code of Practice and the establishment of systems of readers' representatives to take up complaints and breaches of the

Code. The representatives' authority will be set out in formal terms of reference. Representatives will safeguard standards of accuracy, fairness and the conduct of journalists. They will have the power to question journalists and editorial executives. They will have the right to require prompt publication of statements of correction and to have their findings published.

If a dispute cannot be settled in this way the right to appeal to the Press Council, of course, remains.

Code of Practice

Respect for Privacy
Intrusion into private lives should always have a public interest justification.

Opportunity for Reply
A fair opportunity for reply will be given when reasonably called for.

Prompt Corrections
Mistakes will be corrected promptly and with appropriate prominence.

Conduct of Journalists
Subject only to the existence of an overriding public interest, information for publication will be obtained by straight-forward means. Similarly, newspapers will not authorise payment to criminals or their families and associates to enable them to profit from crime.

Race, Colour
Irrelevant references to race, colour and religion will be avoided.

Appendix 5: Western Producer Editorial Code of Ethics
(dated 5 April 1990; courtesy The Western Producer*)*

Editor's note: Many newspapers have developed written statements to clearly define the ethical standards and principles they follow in obtaining, selecting and publishing news. Such codes of ethics acknowledge that professional journalists and responsible newspapers have a special obligation to help ensure the public

is well informed in democratic societies.

The following *Western Producer* code of editorial ethics was recently developed in consultation with editorial staff and approved by management as formal newspaper policy for the newspaper, including editorial supplements. It is published here so that readers can be aware of the standards this newspaper sets for itself, and so that readers can call it to account if those standards are not met.

I. General Principles
Western Producer journalists are individually and collectively committed to the highest ethical standards of professional journalism. Their role is to provide readers with reliable, relevant information. To ensure the greatest benefit to readers, editorial policies and procedures will be designed to support this goal.

II. Accuracy
Accurate, timely news reports and other informative articles are the foundation of the newspaper. Every effort will be made to provide readers with the latest news and to verify questionable information.

Complaints will be given full and prompt consideration. Significant errors will be promptly and prominently corrected.

Comments published within quotation marks must be exactly as written or spoken, except only for occasional minor grammatical editing that does not change the sense or tone of the quotation. Similarly photographs must not be electronically or otherwise altered to distort the actual scene.

III. Fairness
The newspaper will present balanced coverage of issues. Although it is rarely practical to include all sides of an issue in each individual article, representatives of all major viewpoints will be given an opportunity to comment during continuing coverage.

Every effort will be made to present news reports in neutral, factual fashion, enabling readers to make up their own minds on the issues.

IV. Attribution
As far as possible, all sources of information will be

disclosed to readers. Statements quoted in articles will be fully attributed to sources whenever possible. When there is no alternative to using anonymous sources to provide information needed by readers, the newspaper will make every reasonable effort to ensure the credibility of those sources.

Authorship of articles will be prominently identified, including whether the article was prepared by a staff writer or an outside source. Opinion and analysis will be clearly labelled as such, to distinguish it from news reports.

Plagiarism will not be tolerated. If any staff or outside writer is found to have deliberately copied someone else's work without attribution, the infraction will be publicly noted.

Advertising copy will be clearly labelled and displayed so as not to be confused with editorial content.

V. Conflict of Interest

Readers should be confident stories are printed in *The Western Producer* because journalists have judged them to be of value to readers, not because special interests are promoting the stories.

All actual or apparent conflicts of interest involving writers of articles or columns will be disclosed to readers. For example, a member of a political party who writes political analysis will be identified as a party member.

Whenever practical, journalists with potential conflict of interest in a topic should avoid writing about that topic and should not be assigned to do so.

Journalists cannot accept any substantive benefit from individuals or organizations they write about. *The Western Producer* will not accept free airline tickets or similar donations to assist news coverage. Scholarships and other programs not connected to news coverage, however, may be accepted with senior management approval.

Free lunches, drinks and similar favors should not be sought or routinely accepted. *Western Producer* staff are to pay their own way. This principle, however, should not be applied to the extreme extent of discourteous or disruptive refusal of normal hospitality, as in joining a farm family for lunch or coffee. Where such normal hospitality is accepted, there should be an attempt to reciprocate.

Business gifts should be discouraged, and no gifts may be accepted other than items of small intrinsic value like pens. If an employee receives a gift that cannot be returned for any reason, it must be turned over to the company so that it can be given to an appropriate charity or otherwise disposed of.

Western Producer news and business contacts must not be used by staff to solicit prizes for any function or contest.

Editorial staff will not become involved in outside employment that compromises journalistic performance. Articles for non-competitive news media are acceptable so long as *Western Producer* subscribers get reports designed for them an available to them first.

Nothing in this section should discourage journalists from participating in organizations of journalists, agrologists, or similar professional groups. So long as possible conflicts of interests are fully disclosed, *Western Producer* journalists should be free to develop their professionalism in both agriculture and journalism.

Ownership of *The Western Producer* by Saskatchewan Wheat Pool shall be noted in the newspaper masthead. In keeping with the owner's policy of encouraging and supporting independent, credible news coverage of agricultural issues for the benefit of Western Canadian farm families, Saskatchewan Wheat Pool will be treated on the same basis as other major news sources.

VI. News Sources

Western Producer reporters will clearly identify themselves as reporters and will indicate that statements may be published. Any exceptions, as in the case of special investigative projects, must be cleared in advance with senior management.

Guarantees of confidentiality to sources will be respected, within limits set by Canadian law.

VII. Opinion

The Western Producer will provide a forum for all legitimate expressions of Western Canadian rural opinion on current agricultural issues, within the constraints of available space and Canadian law.

While it is the Editor's policy to have the newspaper's primary opinion page (page 6) encourage and support co-operative principles and orderly marketing, additional topics and viewpoints will be welcome on other pages of commentary and analysis.

Selection and editing of reader letters for publication will be done with every effort to preserve the meaning and tone of the original letter.

The newspaper reserves the right to edit all articles on the basis of fairness, information value, taste, accuracy, grammar, clarity, style, and other editorial considerations.

VIII. Advertising Relations

Advertising and editorial operations will be independent. Although total advertising volume necessarily influences the total pages available for editorial copy, the existence or non-existence of individual advertising orders will not influence editorial decisions on writing, selection, or editing of specific news stories.

Purely advertising features will be clearly identified as such, and reporting staff will not be responsible for preparing material appearing in them. Editorial staff will be responsible for the content of general-interest supplements and features like the *Western Livestock Producer.*

IX. Professional Development.

Western Producer journalists will be encouraged to maintain high personal professional standards, seeking to improve their performance and knowledge by such methods as reading professional publications, participating in associations, attending seminars, and making use of other opportunities for professional self-development.

X. Freedom of the Press

The Western Producer supports the principle of a free press as one of the foundations of democracy and individual liberty.

Notes

Preface

1 J.C. Merrill, *The Imperative of Freedom: A Philosophy of Journalistic Autonomy* (New York: Hastings House 1974), 163.

2 I recognized at the outset that this study was going to be almost exclusively anglophone. It doesn't deal with the vast ethnic press in Canada because I'm not comfortable in Urdu, Chinese, or French, and because the value systems reflected in other-language media are significantly different. It would be a serious misreading of *le fait français* to suggest that Quebec values are identical to those of the rest of the country. The Napoleonic Code implies a vastly different approach to values. Radio Canada, for instance, operates under a totally different ethos from its anglophone counterpart. French journalists' attitudes to 'objectivity' and to anonymous editorials, for instance, are quite distinct from the anglophone approach. Francophone attitudes to violence and sensationalism in the media are vastly different. (There is no English-Canadian equivalent of *Allo Police* and *Photo Police!*) All this suggests that a totally separate book is needed for – and deserved by – the francophone media.

3 For photojournalism ethics, see L. Gross et al., eds., *Image Ethics: The Moral Rights of Subjects in Photojournalism, Film and Television* (Oxford: Oxford University Press 1988) and P.M. Lester, ed., *The Ethics of Photojournalism* (Durham, NC: National Press Photographers Association 1990).

4 Some people may argue that only a philosopher should write a book on ethics. Perhaps. But no philosophers have yet tackled Canadian journalism. There is an urgent need for a book – any book – on the subject in order to start the debate. The philosophers are welcome to follow my lead.

5 I recommend E. Lambeth, *Committed Journalism: An Ethic for the Profession* (Bloomington, IN: Indiana University Press 1986); D. Elliott, ed., *Responsible Journalism* (Beverly Hills, CA: Sage 1986); J.L. Hulteng, *The Messenger's Motives* (Englewood Cliffs, NJ: Prentice-Hall 1985); J. Hohenberg, *The Professional Journalist* (New York, NY: Rinehart & Winston 1983); C. Christians et al., *Media Ethics: Cases and Moral Reasoning* (White Plains, NY: Longman 1983); J.C. Merrill and S.J. Odell, *Philosophy and Journalism* (New York: Longman 1983); and particularly the recent book by E.D. Cohen, ed., *Philosophical Issues in Journalism* (New York: Oxford University Press 1992).

6 In an essay entitled 'Defining Press Responsibility,' in *Responsible Journalism*, ed. Deni Elliott (Beverly Hills, CA: Sage 1986), 13-31, Louis Hodges says: 'Society seems to promise the press freedom to function with the assumption that the press will serve society's needs for information and opinion.'

7 M. Norton, 'Ethics in Medicine and Law: Standards and Conflict,' in *Lawyer's Ethics*, ed. Allan Gerson (New Brunswick, NJ: Transaction Books 1980), 259.

Chapter 1: Values and Evaluation

1 J. Harvard, anchor, 'Media Ethics: An Inquiry into News Morality,' produced by CBC-TV Manitoba, 1983. This program was based on a one-day media ethics workshop conducted in Winnipeg by the Canadian Managing Editors' Conference.

2 These are outlined by J. Macquarrie in *Three Issues in Ethics* (Philadelphia: Westminster Press 1970), 105. This book is particularly useful since Macquarrie strives to write from a position of open humanism rather than theological dogma.

3 Ibid., 105.

4 Ibid., 74.

5 Ibid., 32-3.

6 Data supplied by Bryan Cantley, editorial director of the Canadian Daily Newspaper Association, in a private communication, October 1990.

7 Conrad Black is president and chairman of Argus Corporation. As a founder of Sterling Newspapers, he bought and later closed several British Columbia papers. It is fashionable to dismiss group-ownership in media as necessarily deleterious. However,

Mary Vipond, for one, suggests chains may sometimes be beneficial. See *Mass Media in Canada* (Toronto: Lorimer 1989), 86.

8 A. Bevins, 'The Crippling of the Scribes,' *British Journalism Review* 1, no. 2 (1990):13.

9 *UK Press Gazette*, 11 February 1991.

10 S. Keate, *Paper Boy: The Memoirs of Stuart Keate* (Toronto: Clarke Irwin 1980). Keate cites John F. Bassett, owner of the *Toronto Telegram* (p. 167) and R.S. Malone (p. 195) as glaring exceptions.

11 P. Rutherford, *The Making of the Canadian Media* (Toronto: McGraw-Hill Ryerson 1978), 51-2.

12 Ibid., 93.

13 Ibid., 52.

14 *Canadian Daily Newspaper Publishers Association (CDNPA) Research Newsletter*, June 1988, 1.

15 G. Henry, 'We Are Guilty, Says Editor,' *Guardian*, 24 September 1990, 24.

16 S. Klaidman and T.L. Beauchamp, *The Virtuous Journalist* (New York: Oxford University Press 1987), 113.

17 *CDNPA Research Newsletter*, October 1990, passim.

18 P. Desbarats, *Guide to Canadian News Media* (Toronto: Harcourt Brace Jovanovich 1990).

19 Larry Lamb, editorial director of the *Sun* and the *News of the World*, is quoted by S. Chibnall, *Law-and-Order News* (London: Tavistock 1977), 75.

20 This and subsequent quotations are extracted from responses to a survey of national dailies conducted by this writer in 1985. A more complete report and details of a more extensive survey conducted in 1990 are included in Chapter 17.

21 These five Ws were partly inspired by H. Eugene Goodwin of Pennsylvania State University, *Groping for Ethics in Journalism* (Ames, IA: Iowa State University Press 1983), during a discussion of questions that need asking at a conference on teaching journalism ethics at the University of Kentucky in 1988. The *H* was in part contributed by James Risdon, editor of the *Opasquia Times*, The Pas, Manitoba.

22 Kohlberg has a number of books and articles to his credit. He synthesizes much of this work in his essay, 'A Current Statement on Some Theoretical Issues,' in *Lawrence Kohlberg: Consensus and Controversy*, ed. S. and C. Modgil (Philadelphia: Falmer 1986), which is also usefully debated by others in the same book.

23 This simplification does not do justice to Kohlberg, as elements applicable to the current debate are emphasized. For a full explication, see Kohlberg, 'A Current Statement.'

24 Howe succeeded not only in cleaning up government patronage but in changing the law. For a full description of the celebrated case, see W.H. Kesterton, *A History of Journalism in Canada* (Toronto: McClelland & Stewart 1967), 21-2 and J.M. Beck, *Joseph Howe*, vol. 1 (Montreal and Kingston: McGill-Queen's University Press 1982), 129-46.

Chapter 2: The Nature of News

1 There are also a few, less helpful, definitions. For instance, Katharine Whitehorn cites (without a source): 'News is something that someone somewhere is trying to suppress. All the rest is advertising.' See K. Whitehorn, *Ethics and the Media* (Guildford: University of Surrey 1988), 13. There is also a grain of truth in the old maxim, 'News is what the city editor says it is.'

2 Steve Chibnall adds some criteria of news judgment which are uniquely his own and somewhat cynical, including 'simplification' (the tendency to oversimplify reality, eliminating shades of grey), 'titillation' (defined as 'the age-old recipe of the voyeur'), 'conventionalism' (where news fits into accepted formulae), and 'structured access' (in which journalists rely on official sources). See *Law-and-Order News* (London: Tavistock 1977), 23-41.

3 'Who's Bin Done,' *Sunday Times* magazine, 7 October 1990, 54-70.

4 *Seattle-Post Intelligencer*, 14 February 1971.

5 R.V. Ericson, P.M. Baranek, and J.B. Chan, *Visualizing Deviance: A Study of News Organization* (Toronto: University of Toronto Press 1987), 347.

6 Ibid., 348.

7 M-L. Galician and N.D. Vestre, 'Effects of "Good News" and "Bad News" on Newscast Image and Community Image,' *Journalism Quarterly* 64 (1987):399-405, 525, debate the issue and provide a good survey of the field.

8 But the news consumers are not credulous: A 1985/6 Gallup survey in the United States, titled 'The People and the Press,' found that readers rated the *Wall Street Journal*, CBS, *Time*, the *New York Times*, and other major media as highly believable – 73-87 per cent – but only 14 per cent believed the *National Enquirer*. Cited by Robert P. Clark, president of the American Society of Newspaper Editors, in 'The Slippery Subject of Credibility,' *Editor and Publisher*, 29 March 1986.

9 K. Nash, 'Cleopatra, Harlots and Glue,' in *The Quarrymen of History: Canadian Journalists Examine Their Profession*, ed. N. Russell (monograph no. 2, School of Journalism, University of Regina 1987), 12.

10 Ibid., 13.

11 Ibid., 17.

12 J. Black and R. Barney, 'Journalism Ethics Since Janet Cooke,' *Newspaper Research Journal*, Fall 1992/Winter 1993, 2-16.

13 D. Jones quoted in T. Griffin, 'Why Readers Mistrust Newspapers,' *Time*, 9 May 1983, 60. See also a survey titled 'For the People and the Press,' *Times-Mirror Centre* (AP), 15 November 1989.

14 R. Clark, 'Sore Points,' *Washington Journalism Review*, February 1985, 51.

15 *CDNPA Newsletter*, March 1990, 2.

16 Clark, 'The Slippery Subject of Credibility,' juxtaposes two important credibility surveys and finds that they contradict each other in important ways. But minuscule variations in questions produce significant differences, and different agencies interpret

their findings in different ways. So Gallup analyzed its survey results as being good news for newspaper editors, but the American Society of Newspaper Editors saw their survey as being bad news – though their statistics were often similar.

17 'Story on Canine Unit Has Schneider Upset,' Regina *Leader-Post*, 23 September 1983.

18 S.I. Hayakawa, *Language in Thought and Action* (New York: Harcourt, Brace 1949).

19 M. MacDonald, 'Haverstock Seizes Chance to Attack Provincial Gov't,' Regina *Leader-Post*, 5 June 1989, A4.

20 *Concise Oxford Dictionary of Current English*, 8th ed., ed. R.E. Allen (Oxford: Clarendon Press 1990), 627.

21 *Vancouver Sun*, 4 January 1980.

22 *Edmonton Sun*, 28 February 1986.

23 T. Phillips, 'The "Twisteroo" Ties Reporting the Usual to Noticing Irony,' *Journalism Educator*, Summer 1986, 35-7.

24 *Concise Oxford Dictionary of Current English*, 1102.

25 It is fashionable to label the news media as more sensational than they used to be, so it is instructive to note Paul Rutherford's description of outrageous behaviour amongst the news media at the turn of the century – just the beginning of what he calls a 'sixty-year "silly season" in news reports.' 'Obviously, the news of the mass daily was tinted a mild shade of yellow ... Sensationalism was rife in the daily press because it succeeded – it won attention.' See *Making of the Canadian Media*, 56-7.

26 Vancouver *Province*, 14 April 1983, 1.

27 *Calgary Herald*, 24 June 1984, B2.

28 Maggie Siggins, lecture at the University of Regina, 17 October 1985.

29 Anecdote courtesy of Frank Flegel, former news director of CKCK-TV, Regina, in personal communication.

30 Numbers represent additional newsstand sales, beyond the numbers predicted by the circulation department for that week.

31 C. Balfour, untitled column reprinted from *Montreal Gazette* in *Editor and Publisher*, 13 February 1988, 4-5. Balfour admitted that his numbers represent 'unexpected' extra sales and were all weekdays. Weekend circulation is always substantially higher, and ironically the largest seller of the year was a Saturday issue with a special section headlined 'Sex in the '80s: A Risky Business,' which dealt with sexual disease, practices, and attitudes. But sociologists might well label this a responsible public service, rather than sensationalism.

32 The Canadian Press *Stylebook*, ed. P. Buckley (Toronto: Canadian Press 1993), for instance, has several references to 'handling estimates.' See pp. 87, 132.

33 *New York Post*, 30 April 1986, 1.

34 S. Keate, *Paper Boy*, 178.

35 Great Britain, *Attitudes to the Press*, Social and Community Planning Research for the Royal Commission on the Press (London: HMSO 1977), 193.

36 For instance, a survey conducted for the 1970 Davey Commission showed that 'two out of three Canadians think their local daily is doing a good or excellent job in fulfilling its responsibilities to the public.' See Desbarats, *Guide to Canadian News Media*, 75.

37 C. Bailey, 'Wake Up – to Public Opinion,' *Editor and Publisher*, 7 July 1984, 16.

38 C. Black, 'The Press as a Scapegoat,' *Editor and Publisher*, 19 May 1984, 8.

39 J.P. O'Callaghan, 'Great Newspaper Debate: Publisher, Commissioner Tangle over Press Bill,' *Calgary Herald*, 6 October 1983, A5.

40 F. Bruning, 'Why People Distrust the Press,' *Maclean's*, 16 January 1984, 9.

41 As of 1 January 1994, there were 108 dailies in Canada, unchanged in several years, with a total weekly circulation of 35,716,000 or about 5,536,000 a day. Of some nine chains, three control about 60% of the total daily newpaper sales. Southam Newspapers (with 17 titles) has 27.5% of the total circulation; Thomson Newspapers (39 titles) has 20.5%; and Toronto Sun Publishing (10 titles) has 10.9%. Hollinger, with 12 titles, ranks sixth with a mere 3.7% of the total circulation, as its papers are all small. There remain some 13 independent daily titles, with 17% of the total circulation share. Data courtesy of Bryan Cantley, head of editorial services for the Canadian Daily Newspapers Association and the CDNA '1993 Circulation Data' leaflet, October 1993.

42 S. Keate, *Paper Boy*, 97.

43 Ibid., 195.

44 Ibid., 167.

45 Ibid., 219.

46 Fillmore is cited in Peter Desbarats, *Guide to Canadian News Media*, 100-1.

47 Desbarats concludes: 'There have been remarkably few attempts to interfere politically with the journalistic process ... [and] the evidence is that they were the exception rather than the rule.' See Desbarats, *Guide to Canadian News Media*, 49.

48 Ibid., 70.

49 Canada, *Report of the Royal Commission on Newspapers* [Kent Commission] (Ottawa: Queen's Printer 1981), 224.

Chapter 3: The Role of the Media

1 P. Desbarats, *Guide to Canadian News Media* (Toronto: Harcourt Brace Jovanovich 1990), 121.

2 P. Trueman, 'The Goldhawk Muzzle,' *Content*, March/April 1989, 11.

3 Ibid.

4 P. Rutherford, *The Making of the Canadian Media* (Toronto: McGraw-Hill Ryerson 1978), 57.

5 J.C. Merrill and S.J. Odell, *Philosophy and Journalism* (New York: Longman 1983), 174.

6 This and similar advertisements, which offered an engine attachment strongly condemned by the Consumers' Association of Canada, ran in a number of Canadian dailies in late 1987. For further discussion, see Chapter 4.

7 J. Hohenberg, *The News Media: A Journalist Looks at His Profession* (New York: Holt, Rinehart & Winston 1968), 22.

8 Cook was quoted by M. Polanyi, 'Holocaust Fact, Historians State,' *Globe and Mail*, 30 May 1985, 11.

9 Senator Hiram Johnson in 1917, cited in P. Knightley, *The First Casualty: From the Crimea to Vietnam*, rev. ed. (London: Quartet Books 1982), iii.

10 R. Harris, *Gotcha! The Media, the Government and the Falklands Crisis* (London: Faber 1983), 93. See also a useful discussion by John Pilger in 'Myth-Makers of the Gulf War,' *Guardian*, 7 January 1991, 23, who found some good examples from the Falklands War and the 1990-1 Gulf War.

11 Knightley, *The First Casualty*.

12 H. Dempsey, *The Wit and Wisdom of Bob Edwards* (Edmonton: Hurtig 1976), 74.

13 Telephone interview with Bruce Wark, 15 November 1993.

14 Wark's view is reinforced by Richard Starr in 'Where Was the Warning at Westray?' *Content*, December 1992, 10-13. Starr does point out that some journalists tried to put the safety angle on the news agenda, but notes that the lesson of history was largely ignored: between 1838 and 1952, 246 men had died from explosions in the Pictou coal mines.

15 Desbarats, *Guide to Canadian News Media*, 116-21. Desbarats was dean of the journalism school at the University of Western Ontario and a former reporter for the *Toronto Star* and Global TV.

16 Ibid., 121.

17 In the context of Canada's national broadcasting network, however, objectivity is not just an easy way out. The corporation has to serve all elements of society, and everyone is a self-appointed critic. The CBC is constantly under fire for not representing all views, including Parliament (as its funding agency), but is also roundly criticized for *not* being provocative enough. See L. Griffin, 'Strictly by the Book,' *Ryerson Review of Journalism*, Spring 1989, passim.

18 This is not a new idea. US president Thomas Jefferson, who had equivocal views on the press, suggested: 'Perhaps an editor might ... divide his paper into four chapters, heading the first, Truths; 2d, Probabilities; 3d, Possibilities; 4, Lies.' See *Writings* (New York: Library of America 1984), vol. 6, 55; vol. 11, 224.

19 W. Morgan, speech to the Canadian Communications Association, Victoria, BC, 1 June 1990.

20 Ibid.

21 M. Allen, speech to the annual conference of the Centre for Investigative Journalism, Toronto, 1985.

22 J.C. Merrill, 'Good Reporting Can Be a Solution to Ethics Problems,' *Journalism Educator*, Autumn 1987, 27-9.

23 J.C. Merrill, 'Is Ethical Journalism Simply Objective Reporting?' *Journalism Quarterly* 62, no. 2 (1985):391-3.

24 J.C. Merrill seems to show an evolving view in his works. The 1983 book says that 'objectivity in journalism is at best an elusive goal and probably an unrealistic one.' See *Philosophy and Journalism*, 174. But the 1987 article, by pitting objective reporting *against* 'morally inspired reporting' seems to call for objectivity. See 'Good Reporting Can Be a Solution,' 28.

25 Merrill and Odell, *Philosophy and Journalism*, 176.

26 Merrill, 'Is Ethical Journalism Simply Objective Reporting?' 391.

27 Merrill, 'Good Reporting Can Be a Solution,' 27.

28 Ibid., 28.

29 A. Medina, 'Fuddy Duddy Journalism,' eighth Minifie Lecture, University of Regina, Regina, 7 March 1988.

30 H. Hutchinson, 'Images, Self-Images and the Long String,' in *The Quarrymen of History*, ed. N. Russell, monograph no. 1, 64.

31 J. Miller, 'Rethinking Old Methods,' *Content*, September/October 1990, 25, was suggesting journalists need to rethink their own values, and he specifically criticizes 'scrumming' a politician, instead of digging into the government. But the two are not mutually exclusive. Reporters can still quote the officials – indeed, they *must* do so – but they can *also* do the digging and the tough questioning.

32 Desbarats, *Guide to Canadian News Media*, 123.

33 Ibid., 121.

34 Ibid., 123.

35 Hutchinson, 'Images, Self-Images and the Long String,' 68.

36 Desbarats, *Guide to Canadian News Media*, 122.

37 Ibid., 123.

38 Katharine Whitehorn recalls a delicious sign posted in the *London Daily Mirror* office: 'Never write down to your public. People who are less intelligent than you are can't read.' See K. Whitehorn, 'Ethics and the Media,' Leggett Lecture, University of Surrey, Guildford, UK, 9 November 1988, 8. But this reveals more about the newspaper management's attitude to the reporters than the reporters' attitude to the audience.

39 C. Lynch, 'How Celebrity Corrupts Journalists,' in *The Quarrymen of History*, ed. N. Russell, monograph no. 2, 47.

40 Desbarats, *Guide to Canadian News Media*, 122.

41 Canada, Special Senate Committee on Mass Media, *Report* [Davey Report], vol. 1 (Ottawa: Queen's Printer 1970), 84.

42 Hutchinson, 'Images, Self-Images and the Long String,' 64. The CTV network host and reporter was giving the sixth Minifie Lecture at the University of Regina.

43 How those decisions are made is beyond the scope of this study but is synthesized well by Peter Desbarats, *Guide to Canadian News Media*, 103-13. For further exploration, see also R.V. Ericson et al., *Visualizing Deviance: A Study of News Organization* (Toronto: University of Toronto Press 1987).

44 Paul Rutherford describes how the role of the press as unofficial opposition has grown in Canada in the last thirty years. See *The Making of the Canadian Media*, 107.

45 Lynch, 'How Celebrity Corrupts Journalists,' 47.
46 Rutherford, *The Making of the Canadian Media*, 35.
47 Ibid., 110.
48 Ibid., 111.
49 Desbarats, *Guide to Canadian News Media*, 17.
50 A. Siegel, *Politics and the Media in Canada* (Toronto: McGraw-Hill Ryerson 1983), 16-18; Fred Siebert et al., *Four Theories of the Press* (Urbana, IL: University of Illinois Press 1963).
51 Rutherford, *The Making of the Canadian Media*, 118. His fear of increased government control based on the social responsibility theory is well grounded. It was precisely this argument by the Kent Report that led to the creation of the proposed Daily Newspaper Act in 1983, which would have permitted considerable government interference in newspaper operation, including creation of a powerful Newspaper Advisory Council.
52 *Daily Mail*, 24 October 1990, 9.
53 Fotheringham was being interviewed about his career as sports writer and columnist by Vince Carling on *Media File*, CBC radio, 10 September 1986, and remarked, 'A sportswriter is really a columnist in disguise.'
54 D. Hodgson, 'House a Zoo as MPs Go Ape,' *Toronto Star*, 12 June 1986, 3.
55 Reported by M. Fitzgerald, *Editor and Publisher*, 15 December 1984, 11, 21.

Chapter 4: The Media and Money
1 One Colorado newspaper makes no bones about the connection, with the masthead motto, 'The *Aspen Flyer* is as independent as revenues permit.' Cited by Burton Benjamin during a conference on teaching journalism ethics, University of Kentucky, 26 October 1986.
2 The '*Yorkshire Ripper*' case was one fairly recent incident which brought out the worst in British media, with offers of up to £110,000 made to Rosemary Sutcliffe, the Ripper's wife. See UK Press Council, *Press Conduct in the Sutcliffe Case* (London 1983). Much closer to home was an incident in 1989, when the tabloid *London Mail* paid a reported $8,000 to Chantal Daigle to tell her story. The young Quebec woman had aborted a fetus despite her former fiancé's court battle to prevent her from having an abortion. Nora Ephron argues that television is far worse than print, paying huge sums for interviews ($100,000 to H.R. Haldeman, $15,000 to Gordon Liddy, and $600,000 to Richard Nixon for interviews with David Frost, all for Watergate stories; other sums to Marina Oswald, Sirhan Sirhan, and Lt. William Calley). She concludes cynically that the practice reminds us that 'there is no reason to confuse television news with journalism.' See N. Ephron, *Scribble, Scribble: Notes on the Media* (New York: Alfred A. Knopf 1978), passim.
   The syndicated US 'tabloid TV' shows are now carrying on this tradition. When William Kennedy Smith was charged with rape in Florida, a friend of the accuser was paid $40,000 by *A Current Affair* to talk about the case. The same show was reported to have paid a similar amount to Gennifer Flowers for describing her alleged affair with Bill Clinton, who was then running for the presidency.
3 It is ironic that chequebook journalism often seems to be related to hoaxes: a number of the incidents where news media have paid for news in the United States in the last twenty years have involved the search for chimeras – payment to people who falsely claimed they could reveal the whereabouts of Patty Hearst and others, for instance. See R.U. Brown, 'The Hoax Revived,' *Editor and Publisher*, 2 August 1975, 36.
4 C. Reed, 'Former Mafia Enforcer Paid for Interview,' Regina *Leader-Post*, 28 March 1984.
5 CBC, *Journalistic Policy* (Montreal: CBC Enterprises 1988), 41. The 1993 revision of this manual, retitled *Journalistic Standards and Practices*, leaves this statement virtually unchanged.
6 C. Reed, 'Victim's Mother Furious Drunk Paid to Tell Story,' Regina *Leader-Post*, 15 November 1984.
7 S. Alexander, 'Read All about It: Star Man Finds Gerda Munsinger,' in *The News: Inside the Canadian Media*, ed. B. Zwicker and D. McDonald (Ottawa: Deneau 1982), 164.
8 UK Press Council, *Declaration of Principles* (London 1966).
9 UK Press Council, *Press Conduct in the Sutcliffe Case*.
10 For further discussion see M.L. Stein, 'Checkbook Journalism,' *Editor and Publisher*, 14 April 1984, 12.
11 CBC, *Journalistic Policy*, 43.
12 M.K. Guzda, 'Exclusivity Dispute in Toronto,' *Editor and Publisher*, 14 September 1985, 15, 56.
13 Cited in A.C. Shepard, 'An AIDS Story,' *Washington Journalism Review*, January 1986, 10.
14 The PBS program *Frontline* documented some appalling chequebook journalism in connection with reporting sex changes attributed to Michael Jackson. See 'Tabloid Truth: The Michael Jackson Scandal,' 15 February 1994. The clear implication was that the worst excesses of British tabloid story-buying had recently been embraced by American 'tabloid television' shows such as *A Current Affair* and *Front Page*.
15 Dan Sheridan documents several US instances where journalists doing stories on cocaine use have had to pay informers to get into crack houses and to take pictures. See 'Crack Deal,' *Columbia Journalism Review*, May/June 1990, 14. Everette Dennis, speaking at a workshop on teaching journalism ethics, University of Kentucky, 26 October 1986, described journalism students at Columbia School of Journalism doing research on the homeless in New York and being asked for $5.00 per interview. Journalism students in Regina told this writer – their instructor – that while doing a documentary on prostitutes, they encountered one woman who demanded $50 for an hour's interview. Some media solicit news tips. Take for instance the frequently repeated slogan from CJME radio in Regina: 'We pay cash for news calls.'

16 The pioneer press critic Upton Sinclair seems to have coined the term, in his colourful critique of US journalism, *The Brass Check* (Pasadena, CA, 1920), 436. He says the brass cheque is in newsworkers' pay envelopes every week: 'The Brass Check is the price of your shame – you who take the fair body of truth and sell it in the market-place, who betray the virgin hopes of mankind into the loathsome brothel of Big Business.' Quoted in J.L. Hulteng, *The Messenger's Motives: Ethical Problems of the News Media*, 2nd ed. (Englewood Cliffs, NJ: Prentice-Hall 1985), 170.

17 A good advertising salesperson will keep her eyes open on behalf of the newsroom and will pass on story tips. That way she will earn the trust of the journalists and will be taken seriously if she comes up with story suggestions that coincide with clients' advertising plans.

18 A. Gardos, 'On the House,' *Ryerson Review of Journalism*, Spring 1989, 29.

19 Ibid., 28.

20 Ibid., 29.

21 Stettler, Alberta, *Independent*, 6 April 1988, B6.

22 Ituna, Saskatchewan, *News*, 3 May 1984.

23 Personal interview with reporter Darlene Rude.

24 Anonymous tip from staff member.

25 Anonymous tip from staff member.

26 Humboldt, Saskatchewan, *Journal*, 16 August 1989, C5.

27 Anonymous tip from staff person.

28 M. Hoyt, 'When the Walls Come Tumbling Down,' *Columbia Journalism Review*, March/April 1990, 35-8.

29 Ibid., 37.

30 Ibid.

31 These can also be scanned into a newspaper's computer system, but, increasingly, advertising agencies are sending their ads computer-to-computer via telephone modem, E-mail, or satellite.

32 These can be very helpful to fill a special section, such as a spring bridal supplement or special sections on gardening or back-to-school. There may be a dearth of real 'hard' news, so 'featurish' material from commercial concerns may be very welcome.

33 Only the very biggest newspapers can afford to retain skilled automotive writers, yet there are frequently dozens of car dealers in town, all clamouring for advertising on an 'automobile page,' and such a page is expected to contain editorial matter to catch readers. So the papers may be desperate for material to fill such pages. A similar situation will occur with 'travel sections' and sometimes even with 'family sections' (which used to be called women's pages and which attract substantial amounts of grocery and housekeeping advertising). Contrast sports pages, for which there are masses of bona fide news material.

34 This example is as it ran in the Lloydminster, Alberta, *Meridian Booster*. The two subsequent paragraphs mentioned the brand names four more times, and the headline, supplied by the company, read 'Corsica gets families' vote.' Equivalent advertising would have cost hundreds of dollars. Another example, titled 'Update dill pickle pleasures,' filled half the church page with two recipes promoting pickle experts, Bernardin of Canada. See Lloydminster, *Meridian Booster*, 18 August 1993, B11.

35 D. Dilks, ed., *News Canada*, August 1988, 6.

36 Ibid., 8.

37 'Publisher Hits Weekly Tobacco "News" Service,' *Editor and Publisher*, 15 December 1973, 15.

38 See S. Curtis, 'Ad Absurdum,' *Ryerson Review of Journalism*, Summer 1993, 36; Gardos, 'On the House'; D. Melman-Clement, 'Counterfeit Copy,' *Ryerson Review of Journalism*, Spring 1990, 56-60; and M. Strauss, 'Buying "News,"' *Content*, September/October 1990, 17-18.

39 K. Davey, 'Getting the Media We Deserve,' *Content*, July/August 1990, 14.

40 Melman-Clement, 'Counterfeit Copy,' 56. She describes a baby-faced Robert Fulford, who started at the Toronto *Globe and Mail* in 1956 by writing a sixteen-page jewelry supplement.

41 Ibid.

42 Strauss, 'Buying "News."' Strauss also questioned a piece in the *Lawyer's Weekly*, but that was subsequently challenged by the publisher, Michael Fitz-James, in *Content*, November/December 1990. Strauss, a *Globe and Mail* writer, asserts flatly that the sponsored column in her paper 'has confused at least some readers.' See 'Buying "News,"' 18.

43 Melman-Clement, 'Counterfeit Copy,' 58.

44 Ibid., 59.

45 Ibid.

46 Regina *Leader-Post*, 1986.

47 Regina *Leader-Post*, 2 November 1987. The same advertisement appeared in the Saskatoon *Star-Phoenix*, the Regina *Leader-Post*, the *Surdel Messenger*, Surrey, BC, and the New Westminster, British Columbia, *Columbian*, at least.

48 Personal communication from reporter Gerry Klein.

49 The four subheadings were: 'This rodeo's for you'; 'Raft your troubles away'; 'Galloping good time'; 'Meet you at the fair.'

50 *Editor and Publisher*, 23 October 1982, 14.

51 In particularly venal cases, there may be a reverse pressure on the newsroom. Katharine Whitehorn describes how *Daily Express* fashion writers were forbidden to mention any company by name if it did not advertise. See K. Whitehorn, 'Ethics and the Media,' 6.

52 Regina *Leader-Post*, 16 June 1987, C1.

53 *Western Living*, August 1991.

54 S. Keate, *Paper Boy: The Memoirs of Stuart Keate* (Toronto: Clarke Irwin 1980), 125.

55 A. Ross, 'Realtors Flex Muscle over "Offensive" Story,' *Content*, July/August 1990, 4-5.

56 Ibid., 4.

57 Ross notes that much of the cancelled advertising was moved to the opposition semi-weekly, *Kingston This Week*, part of the prosperous *Toronto Star* family. Less laudable is a 1989 incident

in which a new company was formed in Ontario to sell homes for a much-reduced commission. A Canadian Press report said that the federal Bureau of Competition was subsequently asked to investigate complaints about a dozen newspapers that refused to sell advertising space to the new firm when conventional brokers threatened to withdraw their ads. See C. Reed, 'Real Estate Firm Charges Flat Fee' (CP), Regina *Leader-Post*, 18 February 1989.

58 Veteran Canadian journalist Walter Stewart recalled that years ago *Today* magazine ran a cover story on cancer-causing products in the home. In revenge, he said, the cigarette companies, which were major advertisers, pulled their ads en masse. In a lecture to journalism students, University of Regina, Regina, 13 September 1987.

59 Publisher Ernie Neufeld at an ethics seminar sponsored by the Saskatchewan Weekly Newspapers Association, Regina, 15 September 1989.

60 Editor Dave Ramsay at an ethics seminar sponsored by the Saskatchewan Weekly Newspapers Association, Regina, 15 September 1989.

61 P. Desbarats, *Guide to Canadian News Media* (Toronto: Harcourt Brace Jovanovich 1990), 17.

62 C. Lynch, 'How Celebrity Corrupts Journalists,' 50. Journalistic payoffs are still widespread in some communities. Sang-Don Chun, a Korean journalist, described an incident in Seoul where a drunken police officer murdered several people. The city police telephoned all the local newsrooms and offered substantial bribes to each to suppress the story. The incident remained completely secret for several weeks, until one paper broke the silence and the others were forced to follow suit. (Private correspondence)

63 K. Whitehorn, 'Ethics and the Media,' 5.

64 D. Grotta, 'Travel Writer Sounds Off,' *Editor and Publisher*, 2 May 1987, 82.

65 I. Gillespie, 'The Flip Side of Freebies,' *Ryerson Review of Journalism*, Spring 1988, 21.

66 Ibid., 21.

67 Ibid.

68 Ibid.

69 Ibid., 20.

70 B. Rader, 'Food + Feed = Foolishness,' ASNE *Bulletin*, January 1973, 12-13.

71 L. Hobbs, 'Television,' *Vancouver Sun*, 21 January 1974.

72 Ibid.

73 K. Winner, 'Freebies and Junkets Are Fading,' in *Professional Standards Committee Report* (New York: Associated Press Managing Editors 1985), 10.

74 R.M. Evans, 'Freebies? Don't They Just Make You Sick?' *Guardian*, 5 May 1986.

75 See A. Prendergast, 'Mickey Mouse Journalism,' *Washington Journalism Review*, January/February 1987, 32 and A. Radolf,

'Junket Journalism,' *Editor and Publisher*, 18 October 1986, 16-17.

76 Cited in Gillespie, 'The Flip Side of Freebies,' 21.

77 Ibid.

78 A. Prendergast, 'Mickey Mouse Journalism,' 32.

79 *Globe and Mail*, 14 January 1978.

80 S. Overbury, 'Sports News: Real Stuff or Just a Game?' *Content*, January/February 1979, 3.

81 Ibid., passim; see also B. Zwicker, 'Media Must Pay Freight ...' *Content*, March/April 1978, 5. Media critic Barrie Zwicker cited the reaction of one sports editor when told press box seats for sports writers should be paid for: 'They can't be,' he said.

82 *Globe and Mail Style Book*, ed. E.C. Phelan (Toronto: *Globe and Mail* 1981), 20.

83 *Globe and Mail Style Book*, ed. J.A. McFarlane and W. Clements (Toronto: *Globe and Mail* 1990), 59.

84 That it still occurs was documented by Jacques Poitras in 1989, who concluded that the spotlight should now switch to amateur sport where much coverage is dependent on federal government subsidies. See J. Poitras, 'A Helping Hand,' *Content*, May/June 1989, passim.

85 T. Naumetz, 'Breaking Campaign Camp,' *Content*, January/February 1989, 15.

86 In many legislatures, the media still have not dealt with the issue of free press-gallery facilities. The several hundred people accredited to the Ottawa gallery, for instance, have free desk space, free parking, free stationery, free phones, use of the magnificent reading room and library of Parliament, and access to subsidized restaurants.

87 Keate, *Paper Boy*, 13.

88 Ibid., 10.

89 V. Sears, 'Politicians Are Losing Privacy,' *Toronto Star*, 27 September 1988, 26.

90 G. Turner, 'Companies' Cutesy Gimmicks Actually Bribes for Publicity,' *RTNDA Newsbreak*, December 1986.

91 Ibid.

92 A Brazilian journalist described his discomfort when, after being taken on a tour of a major new prophylactic factory, he was presented with a case of about 1,000 condoms. His editor decided they should be given to local agencies fighting AIDS. (Personal communication from Joao Fabio Caminoto, *Folha de Sao Paulo*.)

93 W.R. Garr, 'Listen Here, You Anti-Freebie Phonies!' reprinted from *Quill* magazine in *International Press Journal*, Fall 1974.

94 'Press Rejects Gifts Frills To Be Trimmed,' *Ottawa Journal*, 19 August 1975.

95 The 1988 national conference of the Canadian Community Newspapers Association wallowed in meals and receptions provided by more than thirty companies, including newsprint manufacturers, Canadian National Railways, Air Canada, and Canada Post (with whom the weeklies are forever fueding about poor delivery and sky-rocketing postal rates). The Saskatchewan

association's 1993 convention had fifteen sponsors, including Air Canada, SaskPower, and Canada Post. Many of these conferences have had substantial door-prizes and draws. Japan Airlines, for instance, gave a double return ticket to one lucky winner at the BC weekly publishers' conferences for years. Pure generosity? Perhaps, but one publisher, the late Herb Legg, Sr., wrote a florid seventeen-part series in his *Creston Review* about his pampered trip.

96 C.K. Johnson, 'Solving an Ethical Dilemma,' *Editor and Publisher*, 22 March 1986, passim. Johnson says her paper briefly tried returning all gifts, but found the postage was exorbitant.

97 'Press Council Questions Ethics Awards,' *Press Review*, Winter 1984-5.

98 C. Clark, 'Tainted Triumphs: The Great Awards Debate,' *Ryerson Review of Journalism*, Spring 1989, 33-4.

99 Ibid., 33.

Chapter 5: Conflict of Interest

1 Katherine McAdams's division of non-monetary conflicts into four categories does not seem particularly helpful. See 'Non-Monetary Conflicts of Interest for Newspaper Journalists,' *Journalism Quarterly* 63 (Winter 1987):700-5, 727. She identifies political ties, family ties, reporter-source antagonism, and reporter-source affinity, but the antagonism – in this writer's view – is rare or perverse (her example is an atheist being put on the religion beat), and even the affinity may provide more insight than conflict (her example is a lawyer being put on the court beat). Some of these factors also sometimes overlap.

2 This contrasts, happily, with the more Victorian view that employees were little more than the chattels of their Ebenezer Scrooge-like employers. BBC staff still tell tales of draconian control of their private lives within living memory. Katharine Whitehorn remarks that BBC director-general Lord Reith 'used to insist that announcers read the Nine O'Clock News in evening dress.' See 'Ethics and the Media,' Leggett Lecture, University of Surrey, Guildford, UK, 9 November 1988, 15. For more on this topic, see A. Briggs's, *History of Broadcasting in the United Kingdom*, vol. 2 (London: Oxford University Press 1970), passim.

3 The metaphor does not bear close scrutiny, as journalists do, of course, serve a number of masters, including the public, the proprietors, the editors, and their peers.

4 *Globe and Mail*, 4 December 1982.

5 Very few Canadian newsroom codes of ethics cover this practice. The *Code* of the Radio Television News Directors Association in Canada merely says: 'Broadcast journalists will govern themselves on and off the job in such a way as to avoid conflict of interest, real or apparent,' though some of the examples cited in the text may be seen as transgressing that. See RTNDA, *Code of Broadcast News Ethics* (Toronto: RTNDA 1986). However, the 'Code of Conduct' of the National Union of Journalists in Britain is quite specific on one aspect: 'A journalist shall not by way of statement, voice or appearance endorse by advertisement any commercial product or service save for the promotion of his/her own work or of the medium by which he/she is employed.' See National Union of Journalists (NUJ), 'Code of Conduct,' in *Rule Book* (London 1986).

6 *Vancouver Sun*, 21 March 1986. A similar incident occurred in the United States in 1980 when columnist George Will was accused of conflict because he covered the presidential candidates' debate for ABC-TV without revealing he had helped to coach President Reagan for the debate. See R. Burke, 'Jackson, Columnist Clash over Prejudice, Objectivity,' *USA Today*, 4 January 1988; McAdams, 'Non-Monetary Conflicts.'

7 S. Robertson, 'Hot Over Cold Water,' Saskatoon *Star-Phoenix*, 26 January 1986.

8 The first three examples come from R. MacGregor, 'What Will Become of the Other Charley Lynch?' *Toronto Star*, 16 October 1983.

9 J. Hunter, 'New Tapes Fuel Smith Controversy,' *Vancouver Sun*, 14 July 1990. The Sinclair-Smith incident was extremely complicated and deserves further discussion. In sum, a former radio reporter (then a cook) eavesdropped on Cabinet Minister Smith's radio-telephone calls. His audio-tapes suggested Smith was trying to interfere in a current court case and was having an affair with the radio reporter. When he gave the tapes to Broadcast News, the agency refused to use them, judging them to be an invasion of privacy (a debatable decision). They were subsequently offered to the New Democratic Party, which revealed them in the House, leading to Smith's resignation from cabinet and Sinclair's resignation from CKVU-TV. The privacy issue is irrelevant in this context, but the reporter clearly got too close to her source.

10 *Winnipeg Free Press*, 12 August 1986.

11 A. Fotheringham, *Birds of a Feather* (Toronto: Key Porter 1989), passim.

12 B. Yaffe, 'When Gallery Becomes a Hothouse,' *Vancouver Sun*, 18 July 1990, A9.

13 Interestingly, Yaffe does not recall any journalists questioning the advisability of her having dined with a politician, but the politician's party leader, Ed Broadbent, questioned whether the *politician* could be trusted after dining with a reporter.

14 Yaffe, 'When Gallery Becomes a Hothouse,' A9.

15 B. Kieran, 'The Too-Cosy Relationship of Margot Sinclair,' Vancouver *Province*, 15 July 1990, 5.

16 In fairness, it should be noted that Sinclair, in resigning, asserted firmly, 'My news reports have never been biased or compromised,' and her employers said she demonstrated 'nothing but the highest professional conduct' and at no time did she show any bias. See T. Arnold, 'TV Reporter Resigns, Threatens Lawsuit,' *Vancouver Sun*, 19 July 1990, A1.

17 Cited in C. Hoy, 'Reporters Forgetting Their Duty,' *Toronto Sun*,

25 March 1986, 18.

18 Cited in McAdams, 'Non-Monetary Conflicts,' 701. This proximity between sources and reporters takes on an even greater intimacy in the British context. For discussion, see M. Cockerell, P. Hennessy, and D. Walker, *Sources Close to the Prime Minister: Inside the Hidden World of the New Manipulators* (London: Macmillan 1984).

19 'Western Producer Editorial Code of Ethics,' *Western Producer*, 5 April 1990, 7.

20 'Conflict 2,' in *Editorial Department Policy Manual*, ed. C. Morgan (Windsor: *Windsor Star* 1989).

21 Ibid.

22 McAdams, 'Non-Monetary Conflicts,' 727.

23 *Vancouver Sun*, 19 July 1990.

24 Ibid.

25 For full reports of the debate, see *Vancouver Sun* and Vancouver *Province*, 12-19 July 1990, passim.

26 Cited in *CCNA Publisher*, December 1985 - January 1986, 12.

27 The *Huntsville Forester* pointed out that a number of other local weekly editor/publishers had also been politicians. One was a member of the Ontario legislature, one chaired the local district council, one was a school trustee, and another was both on council and the school board. See *CCNA Publisher*, December 1985 - January 1986, 12.

28 A. Barnes, 'Ethical Journalists Sometimes Have to Give Up a Little Freedom,' *St Petersburg Times* (Florida), 6 August 1989.

29 Ibid.

30 D. Brydges, editor-publisher of the Geraldton *Times Star*, in *CCNA Publisher*, March 1986, 4.

31 G. Rotering, 'Politics, Journalism Don't Mix,' *Nelson News*, 11 June 1979.

32 CBC, *Journalistic Standards and Practices* (Toronto: CBC Enterprises 1993), 29.

33 Ibid., 73. This and the preceding section have been considerably expanded in the 1993 edition of the policy manual, probably in part due to the fierce debate over the Dale Goldhawk case.

34 Ibid., 29.

35 Ibid., 94.

36 By-law 14, section 3a.

37 Such rules, written or implicit, are widespread in the Canadian news industry. For instance, when Larry Schneider, an agricultural reporter for CKTV in Regina, Saskatchewan, announced his plan to run for mayor, he was taken off the air. He subsequently dropped out of journalism when he became mayor and, later, MP.

38 By-Law 14, section 3cii.

39 L. McMahen, 'What's in a Name?' *Content*, July/August 1990, 15-17.

40 Ibid., 17.

41 The following description is heavily dependent on reports in *Content* magazine by Peter Trueman and Bronwyn Drainie and by Stephen Bindman's update in the CAJ *Bulletin*. See P.

Trueman, 'The Goldhawk Muzzle,' *Content*, March/April 1989, 11B; B. Drainie, 'Media Integrity,' *Content*, September/October 1989, 18-19; and S. Bindman, 'Conflict of Interest and the Goldhawk Case,' CAJ *Bulletin*, Spring 1991, 13.

42 Drainie, 'Media Integrity,' 19.

43 Peter Trueman maintains there is no evidence whatsoever of bias in Goldhawk's work. CBC could point only at the 'perception of bias' – but was reported to have received no complaints other than Lynch's.

44 This issue has also been touched on in Chapter 3 under the discussion of objectivity.

45 Duffy, then an Ottawa reporter for CBC-TV, was speaking to journalism students at the University of Regina, 22 October 1985.

46 T. Steve was speaking to a journalism class at the University of Regina in 1988.

47 Peterson was quoted by two journalism students in an unpublished research paper. See L. McIntosh and W. Cox, [No title], research paper, School of Journalism, University of Regina, 1986, 2. Peterson said Jackson was such a good writer, his daily was willing to 'take a little flak to gain his expertise.'

48 Religion can, on occasion, be equally contentious. An Associated Press reporter who expressed evangelical Christian views ran into difficulties with his company and was taken off the Montana state capitol beat. See M. Fitzgerald, 'A Sticky Question at AP,' *Editor and Publisher*, 13 October 1984, 9, 20.

49 Described by R. Tripp as 'a left-leaning alternative publication.' See 'Separating the Private from the Public,' *Content*, January/February 1991, 4.

50 Ibid., passim.

51 J. Lee, 'Journalists Faced Work-or-Walk Dilemma of Ethics,' *Vancouver Sun*, 2 June 1987, B3. To avoid any perception of conflict of interest, it should be noted that both Mason and Rotering were journalism graduates of Vancouver Community College, then directed by this writer.

52 Saskatoon *Star-Phoenix*, 1984.

53 C.P. Jorgensen, publisher of three small papers in Massachusetts, told staff in a 1984 memo: 'We are Republican newspapers. We do not intend to pay for paper and ink, or staff time and effort, to print news stories or opinion pieces which in any way might be construed to lend support, comfort or aid to political candidates who are opposed by Republican candidates in the November election.' Cited in M.K. Guzda, 'Write Pro-Republican Stories,' *Editor and Publisher*, 24 November 1984, 16. See also M.L. Stein, 'Political Involvement,' *Editor and Publisher*, 29 October 1988. By contrast, Charles Lynch described the way such politicization used to be rampant in Canada fifty years ago. See C. Lynch, 'How Celebrity Corrupts Journalists,' in *The Quarrymen of History*, ed. N. Russell, monograph no. 2, 50-1. George Bain noted that a company which owns a news operation may also stand to gain by political events, so this may influence its editorial stance. See G. Bain, 'The Debate over

Feathering Nests,' *Maclean's*, 20 January 1986, 46.

54 T. Pender, 'Reporters Barred from Covering Strike,' *Globe and Mail*, 15 February 1988.

55 Publisher Switzer announced that a non-union employee would be assigned to cover the nurses strike. But an out-of-scope management person would be just as suspect in this case as a union member.

56 'Conflict 1' in *Editorial Department Policy Manual*, ed. C. Morgan (Windsor: *Windsor Star* 1989).

57 McAdams, 'Non-Monetary Conflicts,' passim.

Chapter 6: Pack Journalism and Celebrity Journalism

1 Canada, *Report of the Royal Commission on Newspapers* ['Kent Commission'] (Ottawa: Queen's Printer 1981), 64. Though the definition is neat, it should not be taken as excluding editors and other news managers: the pack mentality can invade all levels of journalism, though it is most pronounced in press galleries.

2 P. Rutherford, *The Making of the Canadian Media* (Toronto: McGraw-Hill Ryerson 1978), 97. Probably the best known study of the pack in action is T. Crouse, *Boys on the Bus* (New York: Ballantine 1974). For the Canadian context, see Clive Cocking's equivalent study, *Following the Leaders: A Media Watcher's Diary of Campaign '79* (Toronto: Doubleday 1980).

3 The corridor scrum, where a gaggle of reporters besiege a source, contains two negative elements. Not only does the source control the questioning, only acknowledging the questions she wishes to answer and ending the event when she wishes, but because it is so visible, there is pressure on each reporter to come up with a story, especially if it is for radio or television, where live footage is all important. For a more complete description of the typical scrum, see D. Taras, *The Newsmakers* (Scarborough, ON: Nelson Canada 1990), 72.

4 Sawatsky was addressing journalism students at the University of Regina, November 1987, while holding the Max Bell Chair of Journalism.

5 A. Bevins, 'The Crippling of the Scribes,' *British Journalism Review* 1, no. 2 (1990):15.

6 Calamai, like Sawatsky, was speaking to journalism students at the University of Regina, February 1986, during his term as the Max Bell Visiting Professor.

7 R. Harris, *Gotcha! The Media, the Government and the Falklands Crisis* (London: Faber 1983), 144.

8 M. Fishman, *Manufacturing the News* (Austin, TX: University of Texas Press 1980), 78-83.

9 Sawatsky in his lecture to journalism students at the University of Regina, November 1987, while holding the Max Bell Chair of Journalism.

10 Ibid.

11 Ibid.

12 Because the Canadian Press news agency (CP), which serves virtually all dailies, covers Parliament gavel to gavel, the news media now tend to rely on CP for routine coverage, only staffing the more colourful and unpredictable question period.

13 P. Desbarats, *Guide to Canadian News Media* (Toronto: Harcourt Brace Jovanovich 1990), 131, echoes this, but also notes the Royal Commission on Newspapers' finding (p. 143) that another cycle develops during election campaigns, with TV newsrooms using newspapers to set the agenda, and newspapers using TV.

14 Sawatsky in his lecture to journalism students at the University of Regina, November 1987, while holding the Max Bell Chair of Journalism. Sawatsky's solution to pack journalism: specialize. He recommends young reporters carve a niche for themselves. He escaped the pack by inventing a hitherto-unknown energy beat for the *Vancouver Sun*.

15 Taras, *The Newsmakers*, 72.

16 Canada, *Report of the Royal Commission on Newspapers* ['Kent Commission'], 143.

17 P. Calamai, 'Discrepancies in News Quotes from the Colin Thatcher Trial,' in *Trials and Tribulations*, ed. N. Russell (monograph no. 1, School of Journalism, University of Regina 1987).

18 Ibid.

19 Calamai's examples of pack editing included the old *Winnipeg Tribune*, when it competed with the *Winnipeg Free Press*. On occasion, editors at both papers, seeing what the opposition led with in the first edition, remade the front pages, and so, in effect, traded headlines.

20 Calamai in his lecture to journalism students at the University of Regina, February 1986, during his term as the Max Bell Visiting Professor.

21 Ibid. Clark's tour was haunted by accidents and ineptitude. At every turn, Clark seemed to slip on stairs, lose his luggage, or ask ignorant questions. David Taras notes: 'Fotheringham's weapon is ridicule through cruel satire, and his flaying of Conservative Party leader Joe Clark in 1978 and 1979 was particularly venomous.' See *The Newsmakers*, 62. He adds later: 'Editors sought stories about Clark's bungling from their reporters, who were trying to outdo each other in finding gaffes and errors to report.' See *The Newsmakers*, 90. Walter Stewart maintains, however, it was not that simple. Speaking to journalism students during his term as Max Bell Professor at the University of Regina, 28 September 1987, Stewart suggested Doug Small, as pool reporter for Canadian Press on Joe Clark's Asian tour, found his CP superiors were getting nervous about his daily reports of Clark's ineptitude, so Small fed details to Fotheringham to reinforce his own copy.

22 The following description is based on this writer's own observation, accredited as one of the 229 media at the First Ministers' Conference. For further discussion of the event, see N. Russell, 'Staffing Levels as a Reflector of Quality,' *Canadian Journal of Communication* 16 (1991):118-28.

23 Even the Hatfield drug story could itself be seen as pack journal-

ism. The evidence of Hatfield having wild drug parties was extremely thin, largely based on the evidence of two unappetizing witnesses paraded on CBC-TV's *The Journal*. But the media seemed to have got tired of Hatfield's long reign in New Brunswick.

24 Another aspect of such events deserving further exploration is the pool coverage. To reduce the indignities of television cameras and lights, only two TV units were allowed into the auditorium at the Regina conference. The video captured by these discreet units was then fed to the huge press room and to all television stations wishing to use it. This meant that not only did all anglophone stations across the country get the same raw signal (ditto with the francophone), but that most accredited reporters watched the event on monitors in the press room, instead of going into the auditorium where they couldn't gossip or smoke. So they too saw only a limited view of events, usually close-ups of the speakers without the interchange and reactions of other key persons on stage. Clive Cocking remarks on similar phenomena on the election trail. See Cocking, *Following the Leaders*, 188. Calamai described such willingness to rely on second-hand observation as a symptom of pack journalism: 'There are plenty of people on the Hill now who will tape an event – then play back the tape to find out what happened.' See Calamai in his lecture to journalism students at the University of Regina, February 1986.

25 M.K. Guzda, 'Exclusivity Dispute in Toronto,' *Editor and Publisher*, 14 September 1985, 15, 56. Anthony Bevins notes that the British press behave in a very similar way: 'It is much easier to pander to what the editors want and all too often that is a pulverised version of the truth – the lowest common denominator of news. With their eyes firmly fixed on Press Association, they want what everyone else has got, regardless.' See 'The Crippling of the Scribes,' 15.

26 No account is taken here of the system of excluding competitors. Put simply, when a paper supplies CP with a story it has gathered, it is understood that the agency will deliver it to every paper *other* than those directly competing in the same community, i.e., a story from the *Toronto Sun* will be coded 'Toronto Out' so the computer will not forward it to the *Toronto Star* or the *Globe and Mail*.

27 P. Trueman, *Smoke and Mirrors: The Inside Story of Television News in Canada* (Toronto: McClelland & Stewart 1980), 153.

28 Primarily, the Natives sought resolution to long-standing land claims, but the incident was sparked by plans by the village of Oka to expand a golf course on ground that the Mohawk regarded as sacred.

29 See debate: R. Perigoe, 'Shades of Grey,' *Content*, May/June 1990, 18-19; A. Norris, 'Gazette Reporter Singled Out for Abuse,' *Content*, September/October 1990, 12-13; G. York, 'In Defence of the Truth,' *Content*, November/December 1990, 18-20; and R. Boswell, 'Oka: Crisis in Journalism,' *Content*, January/February

1991, 16-17.

30 J. Heinrich, 'Media Solidarity?' *Content*, September/October 1990, 14. For some thoughts on the 'Stockholm syndrome' in the journalistic context, see Wendy Mesley in L. Frum, *The Newsmakers: Behind the Camera with Canada's Top TV Journalists* (Toronto: Key Porter 1990), 189-90.

31 Much of the data on this incident were collected by two Regina journalism students, Sally Haney and Mitch Moneo.

32 Esther Fein, writing in the *New York Times* from Moscow, reported there were long segments each night on Soviet TV.

33 I. Ball, 'Rescue Not a Moment Too Soon For Bored US Viewers,' *Daily Telegraph*, 28 October 1988.

34 Ibid.

35 S. Haney and M. Money, 'It's Like Going Out and Freeing Bambi,' research paper, School of Journalism, University of Regina, Regina, SK, 1.

36 C. Laurence, 'Freed Whales are Reluctant to Head for the Open Sea,' *Daily Telegraph*, 28 October 1988.

37 Ibid.

38 Ibid.

39 J. Olen, *Ethics in Journalism* (Englewood Cliffs, NJ: Simon & Schuster 1988), 119.

40 Knowlton Nash, the first Minifie lecturer in 1981, has written two books of memoirs and was director of CBC-TV information programs for seven years, director of news for two years, CBC chief correspondent, and anchor of *The National* news for some years. Clark Davey, who gave the 1982 Minifie lecture, has been managing editor of the *Globe and Mail*, publisher of the *Vancouver Sun*, and publisher of the *Montreal Gazette*. William Stevenson (1983) has worked for several major dailies but is best known as the author of about a dozen books, including *A Man Called Intrepid: The Secret War* (New York: Harcourt Brace Jovanovich 1971). Charles Lynch (1984) was an Ottawa writer for Southam newspapers before becoming chief of Southam News and then a Southam columnist. He has written several books. Joe Schlesinger (1985) was CBC-TV Washington correspondent for more than a decade, before becoming a Parliament Hill commentator for CBC. Helen Hutchinson (1986) began in radio but ventured into CBC-TV in 1968 and joined CTV as a host in 1973. Allan Fotheringham (1987) wrote simultaneously for Southam News and *Maclean's* magazine for years, and gained a national TV audience as a panellist with *Front Page Challenge*. Ann Medina (1988) spent fifteen years with US television news before moving to Canada to join CBC in 1974. She earned a fine reputation as a national TV reporter until leaving in 1986 to try her hand at film. Peter Gzowski (1989) has a huge following for his CBC radio network morning show, *Morningside*. He also has produced several books and briefly hosted a TV program. Patrick Watson (1990), chairman of CBC, is perhaps most recently known as host of an epic TV series called 'Democracy.' Eric Malling (1991) was a program host with CBC-TV for some

years before joining CTV's *W5* in 1990. Pamela Wallin (1992) built a fine reputation with CTV but is now co-host of CBC's *Prime Time*. June Callwood (1993) has worked sporadically for the *Globe and Mail* for several decades as well as being a formidable social activist. Arthur Kent has worked primarily with NBC television news and is best known for his bold reporting from war zones.

41 For a more complete profile of Minifie, see N. Russell, 'James M. Minifie: A Sketch and Appreciation,' in *The Quarrymen of History: Canadian Journalists Examine Their Profession*, ed. N. Russell (monograph no. 2, School of Journalism, University of Regina 1987).

42 N. Ephron, *Scribble, Scribble: Notes on the Media* (New York: Alfred A. Knopf 1978), 156.

43 Knowlton Nash, 'Cleopatra, Harlots and Glue,' in *The Quarrymen of History*, monograph no. 2, 18. John Hulteng points at the emphasis on personalities that has developed through the trend towards 'Happy Talk' news. See J.L. Hulteng, *The Messenger's Motives: Ethical Problems of the News Media*, 2nd ed. (Englewood Cliffs, NJ: Prentice-Hall 1985), 120-2.

44 C. Lynch, 'How Celebrity Corrupts Journalists,' in *The Quarrymen of History*, monograph no. 2, 46.

45 Ibid.

46 Desbarats may simply be viewing the star anchorperson as passé. Discussing trends in TV elsewhere in his book, he refers to the golden age of network TV when anchors became the most highly paid journalists in history, and 'they not only reported news; they frequently made news, on- and off-camera.' Desbarats, *Guide to Canadian News Media*, 47. But the current chapter refers less to anchors and more to bona fide full-time journalists: those who report rather than merely voicing the news.

47 Desbarats, *Guide to Canadian News Media*, 85-6.

48 W. Stewart speaking to journalism students at the University of Regina, 28 September 1987.

49 J. Olen, *Ethics in Journalism* (Englewood Cliffs, NJ: Simon & Schuster 1988), 121.

50 Nash, 'Cleopatra, Harlots and Glue,' 18.

51 A. Medina, 'Fuddy Duddy Journalism,' eighth Minifie Lecture, University of Regina, Regina, SK, 7 March 1988, 9.

52 Olen, *Ethics in Journalism*, 120.

53 Ibid.

54 Taras notes how 'in the eye of the television lens, the party literally becomes the leader.' See *The Newsmakers*, 166, especially Chapter 6, 'The Television Election.'

Chapter 7: Manipulating the Media

1 Governments are nothing if not equipped to manipulate the media. It is very difficult to ascertain how many people are employed by the government to deal with the media, but in 1984 the government of British Columbia, as an austerity measure, said it would halve its public relations force, cutting 102 people.

2 H. Dempsey, *The Wit and Wisdom of Bob Edwards* (Edmonton: Hurtig 1976). CBC news anchor Knowlton Nash puts it more formally: 'It's why political parties alternately woo and castigate the media. They want to shape our reporting to their objective. And their objective is to win elections, not necessarily to be fair or honest or sometimes even accurate in what they say and do.' See K. Nash, 'Cleopatra, Harlots and Glue,' in *The Quarrymen of History: Canadian Journalists Examine Their Profession*, ed. N. Russell (monograph no. 2, School of Journalism, University of Regina, Regina 1987), 15. Of course, not all politicians are so self-serving. The late Tommy Douglas, leader of the New Democratic Party, would often deliver the same speech night after night on the campaign trail, though he knew reporters would find little new to report. But he felt his message to the electors was more important than developing thirty-second sound bites.

3 Saunders wrote this first for his newspaper, and later it was reprinted. See 'The Gag Order: "Censoring a Fact,"' *Content*, July/August 1982, A1-4.

4 Ibid., A2.

5 Ibid., A4.

6 A slightly similar situation occurred in Britain in 1966 after the Aberfan coal-tip disaster. The national government was embarrassed by the vivid reporting of the 144 deaths (including 116 children) when the dump collapsed onto a village. The secretary of state for Wales quickly announced a tribunal of inquiry with extensive powers and stated that 'any comment' on the incident might bring a contempt charge. The clear threat silenced the press. See W.C. Heine, *Journalism Ethics: A Case Book* (London, ON: University of Western Ontario 1975), 38.

7 The Freedom of Information legislation has in some ways made life more difficult for journalists, as civil servants can now decline to release information *unless* it is requested under an FOI search, which can be both slow and expensive. Attitudes to official secrecy in other countries are beyond the scope of this study, but D. Taylor, 'No Such Thing as a Secret Lunch,' *Guardian*, 8 February 1988, gives a fascinating insight into the Swedish view that 'secret papers and secret information are the exception.'

8 Occasionally, an irate government may try something more draconian. For instance, after the Doug Small incident (in which Small broadcast the contents of a leaked federal budget on Global-TV news), police charged Small with theft, presumably at the urging of government officials. However, the court peremptorily rejected the charge as politically inspired.

9 Once the writ of summons, announcing a libel action, is issued, the matter becomes sub judice until it is decided in court. Thereafter, further publication or comment may aggravate the action. Hence the writ effectively gags the recipient.

10 The classic British case involved the *Sunday Times* and the thalidomide scandal. Distillers Company (Biochemicals) Ltd. had manufactured a tranquillizer for use during pregnancy

which caused some 8000 babies worldwide to be born seriously deformed – many without arms or legs. The company was beseiged with more than 300 damage suits in the United Kingdom alone but only offered small out-of-court settlements to the plaintiffs. The *Sunday Times* researched the disaster, but the manufacturer won an injunction preventing publication. This was extended over four years before the newspaper ultimately got it reversed, and Distillers then substantially increased the settlements. See A.G. Pickerell, 'Thalidomide Injunction Lifted by Queen's Bench,' *Editor and Publisher*, 24 July 1976. The libel writ has also been frequently used as a gag in the United States. See, for instance, A. Radolf, 'The Libel Suit: A Political Weapon?' *Editor and Publisher*, 27 October 1984, 14-15.

11 Private communication, 6 March 1990.

12 G. Mungham, 'Grenada: News Blackout in the Caribbean' in *The Fog of War: The Media on the Battlefield*, eds. D. Mercer, G. Mungham, and K. Williams (London: Heinemann 1987), 291-310. In April 1989, aides of Alberta premier Don Getty called the province's news media at about 4:40 P.M., announcing a 5:00 P.M. news conference in Calgary. The timing of the conference, at which Getty announced he was running for by-election, having failed to get a seat in the recent general election, meant that there was virtually no chance to get a reaction from experts or even evaluation from press gallery old hands.

13 P. Desbarats, *Guide to Canadian News Media* (Toronto: Harcourt Brace Jovanovich 1990), 49, 166.

14 Licence statement, 29 March 1985.

15 T. Creery, 'More State Intrusion?' *Content*, January/February 1990, 15. Creery was a senior consultant to the Caplan-Sauvageau Task Force on Broadcasting Policy.

16 Ibid.

17 See, for instance, T. Crouse, *Boys On The Bus* (New York: Ballantine 1974) and W. Small, *To Kill A Messenger: Television News and the Real World* (New York: Hastings House 1970).

18 P. Trueman, *Smoke and Mirrors: The Inside Story of Television News in Canada* (Toronto: McClelland & Stewart 1980), 148.

19 C. Cocking, *Following the Leaders: A Media Watcher's Diary of Campaign '79* (Toronto: Doubleday 1980), 21, 58, 285, 288.

20 Cited in R. Laver, 'The Parties Concoct the "Line,"' *Maclean's*, 31 October 1988, 17-19.

21 Cited in W. Wallace, 'And Now the News,' *Maclean's*, 31 October 1988, 25.

22 Ibid., 25.

23 Ibid., 24-5.

24 Cited in T. Hargreaves, 'The Fight to Control Election News,' *Maclean's*, 3 September 1984, 42. The whole relationship between politicians and the media and the rise of television as a factor in political campaigning was very effectively outlined by Graham Fraser and Ross Howard, *Globe and Mail* reporters, in a five-part series titled 'Prime Time Politics,' 2-8 April 1988. The US experience is outside the purview of this study, but the Reagan admin-

istration appears to have tried every manipulative technique in the book, and this is well documented in a number of studies. See E. Clift, 'How the White House Keeps Reporters in Their Place,' *Washington Journalism Review*, June 1986, 9; M. Fitzgerald, 'Manipulating the Press,' *Editor and Publisher*, 12 May 1984, 9, 24; J.V. Lamar, 'The View from 30,000 Ft,' *Time*, 17 September 1984, 44; J. Snow, 'A Visitor in King Ronnie's Court,' *Mother Jones*, June/July 1987, 40-2; and M.L. Stein, 'Political Involvement,' *Editor and Publisher*, 29 October 1988.

25 Cited in L. Frum, ed., *The Newsmakers: Behind the Camera with Canada's Top TV Journalists* (Toronto: Key Porter 1990), 18.

26 CBC cameraman David Hall is cited in Frum, *The Newsmakers*, 193, as saying 'the parties go out of their way to make you like their guy, to make you part of the team, especially when you're the cameraman. And after a while you start trying to make the guy look good.'

27 One measure of the importance of TV news to politicians is that many federal and provincial cabinet ministers now have newspaper cutting services *and* TV monitoring services. For instance, Joe Ralko, a Saskatchewan press gallery veteran, reported that staff in that provincial legislature videotaped *every* television newscast and prepared summarized scripts for ministers by 8:30 A.M. each morning. See J. Ralko, private communication at the Regina legislature, 23 October 1987.

28 Estimate from M. Rose, 'A Fight Over Tory TV,' *Maclean's*, 11 January 1988, 19-20. This article is drawn on heavily for the subsequent material about the parliamentary news service.

29 Audio clips have been provided by many of the more advanced public relations offices for some years. M. Rose, 'A Fight Over Tory TV,' cites the Canadian Labour Congress as one source.

30 J. Kessel and J. Heinrich, 'Electronic News Releases,' *Content*, November/December 1988, 5.

31 An *Ottawa Citizen* reporter surveyed a dozen independent radio news directors across the country and found that 'few expressed any significant objections to using Tory-generated material.' See G. Weston, 'Tories Feed "News" to Radio Stations,' *Ottawa Citizen*, 26 October 1988, A1-2. A *Vancouver Sun* report on a similar British Columbian government operation found some stations using it, but it was viewed as highly politicized. See 'Broadcasts Branded as Propaganda,' *Vancouver Sun*, 12 March 1984.

32 Ibid.

33 M. Evans, CBC interview, *The Journal*, 2 December 1987.

34 Once again, accuracy is here confused with balance. The video and audio clips may be 'accurate' but they are far from a balanced, fair, and objective journalistic report.

35 See M. Evans, *The Journal*, 2 December 1987.

36 Kessel, 'Electronic News Releases.' The handout tape is far from an exclusively Canadian phenomenon. It is well developed, for instance, in the United Kingdom where the government's Central Office of Information is said to issue some 400 broad-

cast tapes a year, and the commercial firm of UNS Radio Services produces another 500 for private companies. Carl Gardner reported in 1986 that 'every day their (COI and UNS) sophisticated "news stories" are being played on the air by hard-up radio stations desperate for cheap editorial matter.' See C. Gardner, 'How They Buy the Bulletins,' *Guardian*, 17 February 1986.

37 Ralko, private communication.

38 For many editors, most press releases are rubbish – irrelevant to their publication, area, and audience. However, they know that some will provide story or picture ideas, a few will provide all the material for a story, and the occasional one will be ready to publish virtually verbatim. So none can be ignored, though the experienced editors learn to trust, or distrust, certain sources more than others.

39 CNW is a commercial operation delivering material by telex to newsrooms via equipment that is provided free of charge. The material delivered is therefore more immediate than materials delivered by mail.

40 Around 1989, the American news agency, United Press International, contracted with the United States Information Agency to distribute government material to thirty-three off-shore newsrooms. Some editors expressed dismay at the prospect. See 'Protests as UPI Starts Sending UPIA [*sic*] News,' *IPI Report*, November 1987, 7.

41 Both examples come from the 'Dossier Noir' cited in Chapter 6. See 'Dossier Noir: News Media-State Intrusions,' *Content*, April 1979, 38. For UK parallels see, for instance, S. Chibnall, *Law-and-Order News* (London: Tavistock 1977), passim.

42 J. Sawatsky, *Men in the Shadows: The RCMP Security Service* (Toronto: Doubleday 1980), 50-1.

43 'Spy Agency Used Reporter,' *Red Deer Advocate*, 24 September 1988, 4B.

44 Sawatsky, *Men in the Shadows*, 51.

45 See V. Malarek, 'Tinker, Tailor, Journalist, Spy,' *Globe and Mail*, 13 September 1986.

46 M.L. Stein, 'Political Involvement,' *Editor and Publisher*, 29 October 1988, passim.

47 J.E. Roper, 'Impersonating Journalists,' *Editor and Publisher*, 26 May 1984, passim.

48 C. Arvidson, 'FBI Intrigue Surrounds a Southam Correspondent,' reprinted from *Columbia Journalism Review* in *Edmonton Journal*, 17 September 1983.

49 Cited in A. Marro, 'When the Government Tells Lies,' *Columbia Journalism Review*, March/April 1985, 30.

50 Ibid.

51 George Bain suggests, for instance, that leaks occur because someone has a grudge against the minister, is mad at the government, hopes to enlist public support in an internal struggle, seeks the thrill of shaking governments, or is mischief-making. See 'One Thousand Wounds in the Body Politic,' *Report on Business*, November 1986, 25-9. For a more thorough analysis see B. Swain, *Reporters' Ethics* (Ames, IA: Iowa State University Press 1978).

52 'Records Show Minister Let Go For "Incompetence, Hysteria,"' Kingston *Whig-Standard*, 28 February 1985, 19.

53 J. Beltrame, 'Hatfield May Be Charged with Pot Possession Today,' *Edmonton Journal*, 26 October 1984.

54 'Drug Leak Questioned,' *Calgary Herald*, 24 October 1984.

55 For more Canadian examples, see Bain, 'One Thousand Wounds in the Body Politic.'

56 Ibid., 28.

57 P. Dempson, *Assignment Ottawa: Seventeen Years in the Press Gallery* (Don Mills, ON: General Publishing 1968), 101. Media historian Wilf Kesterton corroborates this scenario. See *A History of Journalism in Canada* (Toronto: McClelland & Stewart 1967).

58 The press officer can even select *who* will be invited; usually the more journalists, the better, but the source can be selective if that is seen as an advantage. For instance, in 1988, Premier Bill Vander Zalm of British Columbia invited just four reporters to a two-hour discussion of his controversial relationship with businessman Peter Toigo. Other journalists who found out about the session were livid. See K. Baldrey, 'Premier Angers Press Gallery,' *Vancouver Sun*, 28 April 1988.

59 Column by T. Nunn, Regina *Leader-Post*, 28 September 1984.

60 In British Columbia, visiting Ku Klux Klan organizers allowed a reporter and cameraperson from BCTV to film a cross-burning ceremony at a remote, secret location. Later the journalists asked themselves if the event would have happened at all if they had not been there, and if, in fact they had been 'used' to promote the white supremacist organization. Anecdote from Cameron Bell, then news director of BCTV, in private communication, September 1980. For a fascinating analysis of one such media campaign in the United States, see S.E. Rada, 'Manipulating the Media: A Case Study of a Chicano Strike in Texas,' *Journalism Quarterly* 54 (1977):109-13.

61 R. Maynard, 'Blitzing the Media,' *Report on Business*, June 1986, 71.

62 A. Collins, 'You're On!' *Canadian Business*, March 1987, 40-2.

63 The *Vancouver Sun* reported an incident that indicated that it is not just politicians and the captains of industry who are being coached to prepare for interviews. See 'The Instant Interview,' *Vancouver Sun*, 18 April 1987. The *Sun* described receiving a press kit for an interview with a book author, which included a complete synopsis (so the interviewee need not read the book) and six 'sample interview questions.'

64 For further discussion of such training techniques, see Der Hoi-Yin, 'Talking to the Media a Corporate Must,' *Vancouver Sun*, 5 July 1985 and D. Eisentadt, 'An Executive's Guide to Dealing with the Media,' *Financial Times*, 12 January 1985.

65 *UK Press Gazette*, 4 March 1991, 14.

Chapter 8: To Press or to Suppress?

1 Krickhahn then postponed the main event, reportedly unhappy with the media confusion. For a good summary of the situation, see S. Fine and A. Mitchell, 'Why a Suicide Plan Became a Spectacle,' *Globe and Mail*, 4 November 1993, A1, A5.

2 Advertising is outside the main thrust of this book. However, there have been many situations where the media have declined advertising on ethical grounds, and this sets the tone for the newsroom and the whole publication. See further examples in Chapter 13, note 19. Note, also, the apparent decision made recently by some British newspapers to reduce or eliminate advertising on their front pages.

3 The *New English Dictionary* defines a censor as 'one who exercises official or officious supervision over morals and conduct,' vol. 2, 218. The *Random House Dictionary of the English Language* refers to 'an official who examines books, plays, news reports ... for the purpose of suppressing parts deemed objectionable on moral, political, military or other grounds,' 238. *Webster's Third New International Dictionary* refers to 'a supervisor or inspector especially of conduct and morals ... An official empowered to examine written or printed matter ... in order to forbid publication ... if it contains anything objectionable,' 361. Thus the lietmotif is one of an 'official' who can forcibly suppress material.

4 The term 'auto-censorship' will be avoided here because of the pejorative overtones of censorship.

5 Media patriotism is explored effectively in D. Mercer, G. Mungham, and K. Williams, eds., *The Fog of War: The Media on the Battlefield* (London: Heinemann 1987), and is touched on by P. Knightley, *The First Casualty: From the Crimea to Vietnam*, rev. ed. (London: Quartet Books 1982). Note, for instance, Williams's finding that during the Vietnam War much of the audience demanded patriotic reporting. 'Many sectors of society were disquieted by material that appeared to favour the enemy and be derogatory to the U.S. armed forces.' See Mercer et al., *The Fog of War*, 219.

6 For example, in conjunction with a mock invasion of Winnipeg in 1942, which was designed to boost the sale of Victory Bonds, the *Winnipeg Tribune* published a four-page section resembling what the paper might look like if Germany had actually conquered the city. *Das Winnipeger Lugenblatt* was chillingly realistic. At the same time, there was, of course, wartime censorship. The United States media are much more frequently faced with the problem of withholding military information because they are so frequently in a war mode. For instance, in 1986, NBC News withheld its knowledge of plans to bomb Libya. See G. Garneau, 'Cooperating with the Military,' *Editor and Publisher*, 21 November 1987, 15, 32. The classic incident involved President Kennedy's request that newspapers withhold their advance information on the 1961 Bay of Pigs fiasco. Garneau concludes that the US media have 'responded favorably when valid national security questions are raised.' See Garneau,

'Cooperating with the Military.'

7 'News Media Blamed for Violence' (CP), *Vancouver Sun*, 3 June 1985, A8.

8 Trueman was speaking at the 1985 conference of the Centre for Investigative Journalism.

9 Some media have now developed guidelines for handling such incidents. For instance, Canadian Press/Broadcast News has instructed staff to tip off police if they learn of hostage or terrorist actions; they must not phone participants in hostage cases, report police counter-measures, or provide a platform for terrorist statements. See Canadian Press *Stylebook*, ed. P. Buckley (Toronto: Canadian Press 1993), 33-4.

10 J. Scanlon, 'Hostage Taking and Media Ethics,' *Carleton Journalism Review*, Spring 1980, 7.

11 'Police Praise Media,' *Calgary Herald*, 29 March 1978. Compare a similar incident on Long Island, New York; see 'Police Laud Newhouse Paper for Withholding Kidnap News,' *Editor and Publisher*, 30 November 1974.

12 Scanlon, 'Hostage Taking and Media Ethics,' passim. For further discussion of media and kidnappings, etc. in the US context, see N.D. Palmer, 'When Reporting Endangers a Life,' *Washington Journalism Review*, October 1986, 36-8.

13 It should be irrelevant to the debate on ethics that Small was subsequently charged with theft of the document, but exonerated by the courts.

14 Cited in C. Volkart, 'A Question of Ethics,' *Vancouver Sun*, 28 April 1989, A10.

15 Cited in P. Moreira, 'Auditor-Video,' Canadian Press, 2229ED, 24 October 1989.

16 Anyone who doubts that the copycat syndrome is a factor in news reporting should recall the D.B. Cooper incident. Cooper hijacked a Northwest Orient jet between Portland and Seattle in 1971. He demanded and got $200,000 and four parachutes, and then jumped from the plane. Despite huge publicity, neither he nor the money was seen again. But within one year, twenty-one other people tried the same thing (three died and eighteen were committed to jail or institutions). See L. Peter, *Why Things Go Wrong* (London: Allen & Unwin 1985), 52.

17 W. Grigg, 'Does Publicity in the Media Cause Waves of Food Tampering?' *Editor and Publisher*, 21 February 1987, 68, 70.

18 Ibid.

19 Cited in J. Jaben and D. Hill, 'The Suicide Syndrome,' *Washington Journalism Review*, July 1986, 10.

20 Ibid.

21 'TV News Has To Be Honest, Wallin Tells Awards Dinner,' Regina *Leader-Post*, 16 October 1985.

22 Interview with W. Chabun, 3 April 1990.

23 Ibid.

24 'Thief Turns Repeater,' *Vancouver Sun*, 13 December 1984.

25 P. Tivy, 'Pot Has Come a Long Way,' *Calgary Herald*, 22 February 1985.

26 In some situations, the same laissez-faire attitude may be overtly dangerous, such as in the case of the compact disc that appeared in western Canada in 1993 offering hints on how to make bombs, rob banks, and other crimes. The news media should not give such material any free publicity, and the community should press retailers to refuse to handle it. If the material is illegal, then the authorities can prosecute. But if it is not illegal, everyone loses if we insist that the police – or some other watchdog group – go through stores looking for the bothersome material. The next stop for such 'thought police' is the public library.

27 H. Winsor, 'A Power Elite Gets Its Way in Kitchener,' *Globe and Mail*, 7 February 1972.

28 The photographs showed members of a local motorcycle club, kneeling with their hands cuffed behind them, during a police raid which yielded one charge of possession of marijuana. The police were so livid that they cut the paper off from police news for several days. See R. MacDonald, 'In and Out of Court,' *CDNPA Newsletter*, July/August 1978, 1.

29 Canada, Special Senate Committee on Mass Media, *Report* [Davey Report], vol. 1 (Ottawa: Queen's Printer 1970), 87.

30 'Lemon,' CIJ *Bulletin*, Autumn 1987, 6.

31 For instance, during a strike at a Regina drugstore in 1986-7, the union gave television stations an advance list of where their picketers would be each day, providing that the media did not publicize the list. This way, the union got TV coverage of the picketers and the TV stations got the video they craved.

32 M. Kelly, 'Reporters Keep an AIDS Secret,' *Washington Journalism Review*, September 1989, 18. The 'Boy in the Bubble' story, described in Chapter 11, was similar. In the 'Baby Jane Doe' story, parents in Long Island decided to forego surgery for their baby, who was born with an incomplete spine, abnormally small head, and fluid on the brain. The baby was expected to die without the surgery, but to be in constant pain and remain paralyzed after the surgery. A right-to-life lawyer challenged the parents in court. The media never identified the family. See A. Radolf, 'A Well-kept Media Secret,' *Editor and Publisher*, 3 March 1984, 12, 18.

33 C. Lynch, *You Can't Print That!* (Edmonton: Hurtig 1983).

34 R. Sarti, 'Secret Stories of an Ace Reporter,' *Vancouver Sun*, 28 September 1983. Lynch mentions Roosevelt because the US media agreed not to show pictures of the US president in his wheelchair during the Second World War in case it would make him appear weak.

35 Ibid.

36 The quote, while representing widespread feelings, comes from Gordon Fisher, then managing editor of the *Vancouver Sun*, discussing the Doug Small budget leak story. See Volkart, 'A Question of Ethics.'

37 K. Fox, 'Asleep at the Wheel,' *Content*, September/October 1990, 20.

38 Ibid., 21.

39 Starting in 1993, a similar project has been introduced in Canada.

40 C. Jensen, 'Seven Deadly Sins of Journalism,' *Editor and Publisher*, 23 August 1986, 38, 48.

41 Ibid.

42 The *Edmonton Journal* won an 8-0 decision in 1984 against 'unreasonable search and seizure' by officials of the Restrictive Trade Practices Commission. The decision means that officials can no longer go on 'fishing expeditions' in newsrooms, but must first get formal search warrants based on reliable testimony. See 'Raid on Journal Unconstitutional: Supreme Court,' Regina *Leader-Post*, 18 September 1984.

43 The following examples come from 'Dossier Noir: News Media-State Intrusions,' *Content*, April 1979, 38-9: RCMP bugged the telephones of Agence de Presse Libre du Quebec in 1971 and burgled their offices in 1972; RCMP questioned reporters at the Trail, British Columbia, *Times* following publication of articles about RCMP; RCMP searched a reporter's home in Regina after the Regina *Leader-Post* ran his story on alleged police brutality (1976); RCMP used a search warrant to seize reporters' notebooks and contact lists at the *Vancouver Sun* and Vancouver *Province*, but their search warrants were thrown out by the courts (1977); Ontario Provincial Police with search warrants seized negatives from the *London Free Press*, regarding a scuffle on a picket line (1978); RCMP used search warrants to seize videotape from CBC and CTV (1978); police tried to seize film of a demonstration from CBC and Global, but both refused (1978); Ontario Provincial Police used warrants to try to obtain pictures of a demonstration from Global TV and the *London Free Press* (1978); Montreal police requested CBC to hand over videotapes of an interview with two exiled terrorists. For a last example, see 'Police Want Tapes of Terrorist Exiles, Radio-Canada Says,' *Calgary Herald*, 20 April 1978, A3

44 A *La Presse* reporter was called to testify at an inquest, although some seventy other witnesses were also summoned ('Reporters Made to Testify Too Often, Quebec Told,' *Montreal Gazette*, 24 December 1986); police seized videotape of a demonstration from a Montreal TV station ('Press Council Protests Seizure of TV Film,' *Montreal Gazette*, 7 April 1986); several Saskatoon newsrooms had to fight demands for material which was wanted as evidence in a private libel suit (J. Parker, 'Henderson's Lawyers Ask for Broadcasters' Tapes,' Saskatoon *Star-Phoenix*, 19 July 1988); police seized videotape of striking postal workers destroying a post office; police seized videotape of a demonstration from Quatre Saisons TV in Montreal ('Police Seize Videotape of Demonstration,' *Montreal Gazette*, 5 July 1987); RCMP searched the Canadian Press and Radio-Canada newsrooms in Montreal for material on the Canadian Security Intelligence Service ('Press Council Protests RCMP Raids,' *Montreal Gazette*, 6 August 1988).

45 See J. Wilson, 'The Long Finger of the Law,' *Guardian*, 17 September 1990, 25.

Chapter 9: Playing Fast and Loose with the Truth

1 Cited in R.U. Brown, 'The Hoax Revived,' *Editor and Publisher*, 2 August 1975, 36.

2 'No Dats, Cogs' (Reuter), Vancouver *Province*, 14 December 1970.

3 'April Fool,' photo caption, Vancouver *Province*, 3 April 1972.

4 'The Nymph Was a Myth' (Reuter), Vancouver *Province*, 11 May 1972.

5 'Collins' Comment Draws Wrist-slap,' Vancouver *Province*, 18 August 1972.

6 L. Winer, 'Gotcha!' *Columbia Journalism Review*, September/October 1986, 6.

7 At various times, Skaggs has announced forming a 'Fat Squad' to enforce diets on weight-watchers (1986); a gypsy group protesting the use of the word 'gypsy' in the gypsy moth; and a Cathouse for Dogs where clients could get 'a little tail for your dog.' See D. Gersh, 'Call Him Mr. Hoax,' *Editor and Publisher*, 14 June 1986, 48, 55 and Winer, 'Gotcha!' Another career hoaxer is Alan Abel, who got widespread publicity for his 'school for beggars' and once persuaded the *New York Times* to run his own obituary. A British equivalent is one 'Rocky' Ryan.

8 Gersh, 'Call Him Mr. Hoax,' 48.

9 Winer, 'Gotcha!' 6.

10 See C. MacDougall, *Hoaxes* (New York: Macmillan 1958).

11 'Women and Children Next,' *Vancouver Sun*, 17 October 1970.

12 J. Consoli, 'Canadian Papers Hoaxed,' *Editor and Publisher*, 27 March 1982, 13.

13 'Paper Fooled by Photo,' *Vancouver Sun*, July 1985.

14 D. Creswell, 'Dead Mouse in the Dog Biscuits Stuns Shopper,' *Edmonton Journal*, 10 September 1985.

15 Editor Steve Hume described the incident as a serious breach of ethics which was damaging to the paper's credibility and wondered aloud how it got into print. Ironically, the reporter was quoted as wondering how the story got on page 1.

16 Cooke, it will be recalled, wrote a Pulitzer Prize-winning story about an eight-year-old drug addict called Jimmy. But Jimmy didn't exist and could at best be described as a composite of several child addicts. Editors at the *Edmonton Journal*, the only Canadian paper ever to win a Pulitzer, were perhaps more sensitive than most to the mortification *Post* editors suffered when they returned their Pulitzer, and so may have been too quick to cut the reporter loose.

17 However, seriously abused media can resort to the court system. The London *Daily Mirror* successfully took a hoaxer to court after putting his fake story about drugs in prisons on its page 1. He was given a suspended jail term and fined the equivalent of $2,000 – but that was just what they had paid him. See *UK Press Gazette*, 29 April 1991.

18 The *New York Herald*'s story on 9 November 1874 had a thirteen-deck headline, beginning, AWFUL CALAMITY / The Wild Animals Broken Loose from Central Park / TERRIBLE SCENES OF MUTILATION / A Shocking Sabbath Carnival of Death.

19 This is not, of course, a peculiarly Canadian tradition. Many Western societies celebrate a 'feast of fools' during which time tricks are permissible. Certainly the British press has a long tradition of enjoying April 1st, and the London *Guardian* rarely lets the date go by without its own spoof.

20 Despite some cynics' questions, Dennis Bell's brilliant parrot stories may well have been entirely authentic. See W. Stewart, *Canadian Newspapers: The Inside Story* (Edmonton: Hurtig 1980). Certainly this writer has *seen* the memorial to an ancient parrot in the Carcross village cemetery.

21 *Upper Islander*, 30 September 1970.

22 *Upper Islander*, 10 March 1971.

23 On 1 April 1984, the Durand, Michigan, *Express* reported that Nissan would build a huge new plant in the depressed community. Among others, the unions were very disappointed to learn it was a hoax. See R. Sherefkin, 'Rood Joke,' *Washington Journalism Review*, June 1984, 11. In 1986, the Virginia, Nevada, *Territorial Enterprise* announced an open pit mine was to be built on main street. Citizens were very upset. See M.L. Stein, 'Hoax Sheet Has Town Up in Arms,' *Editor and Publisher*, 15 March 1986, 17, 34.

24 Is *anyone* sophisticated enough to spot all spoofs? This probably depends which side of bed you get out of. In 1993, the BC weekly *Gulf Islands Driftwood* announced the paper was launching a fax edition at $89 a month. *The Publisher*, journal of the Canadian Community Newspapers Association, earnestly reported the technological breakthrough (May 1993), though the *Driftwood*'s offer was dated 1 April.

25 A British parallel might be the TV programs *Crime Watch* or *Crime Stoppers*, both of which rely heavily on police input. The current affairs show *That's Life* is more journalistic, but also uses dramatizations. A January 1991 edition, for instance, featured sex abuse in private schools and included a re-enactment of the trial of a head teacher and two colleagues based on court transcripts.

26 Jennings apologized on air the next night, and the ABC team who made the segment was severely reprimanded. See R. Perigoe, 'Shades of Grey,' *Content*, May/June 1990, 19. For more, see W.G. Strothers, 'Troubles with Re-creating News,' NPPA *News Photographer*, November 1989, 25.

27 In the United Kingdom, 'Shoot To Kill' was a prime example of the genre. This four-hour ITV docudrama was effectively critiqued by Hugo Young, 'Shooting to Thrill,' *Guardian*, 15 October 1990.

28 Another program of the same ilk was called 'Inside the Summits,' broadcast by CBC on *The Journal*, 25 May 1988. It showed actors playing US president Reagan and Soviet premier Gorbachev meeting face-to-face in Reykjavik to discuss nuclear disarmament. The show was labelled 'dramatization,' but there wasn't much danger of audiences being misled. Reagan was more reminiscent of his character on the satirical show *Spitting*

Image than his real self.

29 Transcript from CAJ conference.

30 The policy manual specifies: 'Journalistic programs must not as a general principle mix actuality (visual and audio of actual events and of real people) with a dramatized portrayal of people or events. The audience must be able to judge the nature of the information received. The mixture of forms renders such a judgment difficult because it may lend the appearance of reality to hypothesis.' The code specifies that dramatization must be clearly identified, and 'any reconstruction or simulation must coincide as closely as possible with the event which it purports to portray.' See CBC, *Journalistic Standards and Practices* (Toronto: CBC Enterprises 1993), 77.

31 Transcript from CAJ conference.

32 Cited in J.H. Cuff, 'TV Re-creations Blur the Lines,' *Globe and Mail*, 11 November 1989, C3.

33 Ibid. See also Perigoe, 'Shades of Grey,' 18-19.

34 Cuff, 'TV Re-creations Blur the Lines,' C1.

35 Perigoe, 'Shades of Grey,' 18.

36 Ibid., 19.

37 Ericson cites further examples that his team observed in Toronto. One event, in which the RCMP lost some seized drugs, he describes as 'a blend of illusion and accounts of reality ... a reconstruction of what *may* have happened.' See *Visualizing Deviance: A Study of News Organization* (Toronto: University of Toronto Press 1987), 102, 274-8.

38 L. Lacey, 'CBC's Documentary Double-Speak,' *Globe and Mail*, 2 November 1993.

39 The television 're-ask' is faintly similar. With this technique, the reporter conducts an interview in which a source is filmed answering his questions. After the source departs, the camera operator re-positions the camera to film *the reporter* asking the same questions, perhaps more carefully phrased and smoothly delivered. The two can then be spliced together back at the studio.

40 CBS broadcast a 90-minute documentary titled 'The Uncounted Enemy: A Vietnam Deception' in 1982, alleging General William Westmoreland had deliberately misrepresented Viet Cong numbers to make it appear the US was winning the war. He sued for $120 million, but part way through the case he withdrew.

41 A. Medina, 'Fuddy Duddy Journalism,' eighth Minifie Lecture, University of Regina, Regina, SK, 7 March 1988, 7.

42 'M. Bell, "Marilyn's Story. I Felt I Was Swimming Forever,"' *Telegram*, 10 September 1954. The Marilyn Bell story has been recounted in several places, including W.H. Kesterton, *A History of Journalism in Canada* (Toronto: McClelland & Stewart 1967). The *Toronto Star* had signed up Bell for an exclusive interview after her swim, so the *Telegram* 'reconstructed' the saga. Val Sears, one of the *Telegram* team assigned to the story, concluded later in his autobiography, 'It was a magnificent phoney.' See V. Sears, *Hello Sweetheart ... Get Me Rewrite* (Toronto: Key Porter 1988), 119.

43 Some twenty years ago, United Press International ran a series of historical features, recreating great events in history as if they had just occurred and the reporter was right there – Columbus landing on America and the completion of the Great Wall of China, for instance. But audiences would have been absurdly naive to believe they were 'news' events, and each was preceded with an explanatory caveat.

44 Perigoe, 'Shades of Grey,' 19.

45 A sequel, in three parts, was aired nearly two years later, in 1979.

46 W. Rowland, *Making Connections* (Toronto: Norfolk Communications 1979).

47 See Z.N. Smith and P. Zekman, *The Mirage* (New York: Random House 1979), passim and N.D. Palmer, 'Going After the Truth – in Disguise,' *Washington Journalism Review*, November 1987, 22.

48 D. Crittenden, 'Agony Before Death,' *Toronto Sun*, 17 October 1982.

49 See Palmer, 'Going After the Truth,' 20-1.

50 See D. Davy, 'Burlington Man Mad as a Wet Hen,' *Hamilton Spectator*, 19 October 1989.

51 Sears, *Hello Sweetheart ... Get Me Rewrite*, 35.

52 NUJ *Rule Book*, 54.

53 CBC, *Journalistic Standards and Practices* (Toronto: CBC Enterprises 1993), 65.

54 Ibid.

55 L. Hodges, 'To Deceive or Not to Deceive,' *Quill*, December 1981, 9.

56 For further debate, see P. Braun, 'Deception in Journalism,' *Journal of Mass Media Ethics* 1 (1988):77-83 and N.D. Palmer, 'When Reporting Endangers a Life,' *Washington Journalism Review*, October 1986, 36-8.

57 Palmer, 'Going After the Truth,' 20.

58 The law forbids third-party taping ('bugging' a conversation in which one is not a participant) and insists that if broadcasters want to use taped material on air, they must have the interviewee's permission. In about eleven US states, it is illegal even to secretly tape conversations to which one is a party. See F. Talbott, 'Taping on the Sly,' *Quill*, June 1986, 47.

59 *Globe and Mail Style Book*, ed. J.A. McFarlane and W. Clements (Toronto: Globe and Mail 1990), 58-9.

60 T.L. Glasser, 'On the Morality of Secretly Taped Interviews,' *Nieman Reports*, Spring 1985, 17.

61 Talbott, 'Taping on the Sly,' 47.

62 Ibid.

63 See D. Shaw, 'The Canker at the Core of Journalism,' *Guardian*, 20 August 1984 and V. Clemence, 'Plagiarism ... the Cancer that Destroys the Very Soul of Journalism,' *Content*, January/February 1990, 18-19. Shaw's article was reprinted from the *Los Angeles Times*, where he was ombudsperson.

64 Clemence, 'Plagiarism,' 18.

65 C. Reed, 'Former Mafia Enforcer Paid for Interview,' (CP) Regina *Leader-Post*, 28 March 1984, 21.

66 D. Shaw, 'The Canker at the Core of Journalism.'

67 Ibid.

68 White cites a 1987 *Philadelphia Inquirer* guideline as a potential model: 'All material used in the construction of a story or column should be clearly attributed to the proper sources ... In addition to direct quotations, all paraphrased material, analyses, interpretations, or literary devices, such as distinctive descriptive phrases, should be attributed. Using another person's words, phrases or ideas without attribution is plagiarism, an offense which may be cause for dismissal.' See M.D. White, 'Plagiarism and the News Media,' *Journal of Mass Media Ethics* 4 (1989):278.

69 That plagiarism is treated seriously can be judged from other incidents: A *Chicago Tribune* writer had to resign in 1975 after part of one column was found to be plagiarized and part of another was false. In 1987, the *Pittsburg Press* fired a columnist whose column resembled one from the Rhode Island *Journal*. A *Newsweek* writer was fired after it was discovered that his article on the Calgary Olympics (Winter 1988) bore a close resemblance to a *Sports Illustrated* piece. A Saskatoon *Star-Phoenix* sports writer was fired in 1989 when parts of two columns were found to have appeared earlier in the *Globe and Mail*. See White, 'Plagiarism and the News Media,' passim, for details of these and others.

70 Shaw attributes more causes: 'Laziness, sloppy work habits, deadline pressure, writer's block, temporary – or chronic – emotional problems, basic dishonesty, a conscious or unconscious desire to be caught and punished.' See Shaw, 'The Canker at the Core of Journalism.'

71 D. McGillivray, 'Plagiarism: Phrase Filch or Mental Slip,' CIJ *Bulletin*, Spring 1989, 29.

72 Ibid.

73 Cited in Shaw, 'The Canker at the Core of Journalism.'

74 *Ethics and Policies*, staff manual of the *Ottawa Citizen*, 15.

75 Cited in P. Neely, 'Correcting Mistakes: More Papers Willing to Admit Errors,' APME *Credibility Report*, 1984, 9.

76 CBC, *Journalistic Standards and Practices*, 90.

77 The CBC carries very few corrections. This may reflect the high standards within all their newsrooms, but it may also indicate the ephemeral nature of broadcast news. The audience may be more likely to complain about a perceived error which leaps out from the newspaper page than about a few words quickly spoken and gone into the ether.

78 Canadian Press *Stylebook*, ed. P. Buckley (Toronto: Canadian Press 1993), 13. In this writer's experience working with Canadian Press, the agency lives up to this edict, conscientiously making corrections fully and quickly.

79 See D. Gersh, 'Corrections, Corrections, Corrections,' *Editor and Publisher*, 21 February 1987, 16, 57.

80 *New York Times*, 13 July 1987.

81 G. Garneau, 'New York Times Admits Error in Story that Tops Front Page,' *Editor and Publisher*, 18 July 1987, 12.

82 In one celebrated case, a citizen won a libel suit against a New Zealand newspaper, and when the original story was resurrected for a 'Twenty Years Ago' flashback story, he successfully sued again. (Source lost)

83 J. Vormittag, 'Handling Errors,' APME *1986 Report of the Newsroom Management Committee* (New York 1986), 32.

Chapter 10: The Media and Violence

1 K. Whitehorn, 'Ethics and the Media,' Leggett Lecture, University of Surrey, Guildford, UK, 9 November 1988, 2.

2 *Vancouver Sun*, 16 July 1990.

3 Papers were replete with 'the birth of a two-headed cow, the passage of a comet, the nasty habits of African cannibals or the exploits of a madman ... special attention to disasters and crime. Earthquakes, fires, shipwrecks, epidemics, train accidents and so on.' See P. Rutherford, *The Making of the Canadian Media* (Toronto: McGraw-Hill Ryerson 1978), 19.

4 Canadian Press, 'News Media Blamed for Violence,' *Vancouver Sun*, June 1985.

5 Only occasionally do the media indulge in purely gratuitous violence. One example is the *Toronto Sun* chain's 'Crime Flashback' series, which retells gruesome old murders in gory detail, often illustrated with drawings reminiscent of some Harlequin romance. The *Ottawa Sun*'s treatment of a Russian serial killer (15 November 1992) was similarly flamboyant. While other papers indulged in some gory reports of his trial, the *Sun* published a double-page spread with the scarlet headline two inches high: 'The Red Ripper.' Evidently this is giving the readers what they want in the Fleet Street tabloid tradition, as the *Sun*s prosper. And, as with the Sunshine Girls and Boys, if one doesn't like it, one doesn't have to buy it.

6 J. McLean, private communication, 1989.

7 R. Neil, 'To Screen or Not to Screen,' *Observer*, 6 December 1987, 75.

8 An informal survey of major Canadian dailies by this author in January 1994 turned up horrific news pictures that were never printed. Editors were asked if they ever withheld pictures because they were too gruesome, and they readily submitted shots of dead bodies, including some severed by railroad trains.

9 Cited in C. Van Doren, *Benjamin Franklin* (New York: Viking 1938), 100.

10 R. Neil, 'To Screen or Not to Screen,' 75.

11 A. Morrison, 'The Media Failing to Keep the Peace,' *Guardian*, 16 April 1983, 7.

12 See various examples in C. MacDougall, *News Pictures Fit to Print ... Or Are They?* (Stillwater, OK: Journalistic Services 1971).

13 Phone interview, 9 November 1993. Jarred said the decision to run the picture was made on deadline when he had nobody else to consult, but, as a result, 'We have a rule now: We won't run dead bodies again, because of the complaints.'

14 The risk is measurable on the Kohlberg scale: fear of public

recrimination may be outweighed by the social good achieved. But the journalists need not expect to be thanked for exposing a wrong in this way. When a Boston woman fled a tenement fire only to die when the fire-escape collapsed, many editors thought the brilliant and horrific photographs of her falling were justified because they might get conditions improved. Some 400 US dailies ran at least one picture – and were vilified from coast to coast for the decision. For further discussion see Chapter 11.

15 *Montreal Gazette* ombudsperson Bob Walker made the point while discussing the picture later, according to Catherine Buckie in the CIJ *Bulletin*.

16 Brassard and Burnside were among those editors quoted in a survey of how papers handled the story, which was done for *Moving Up*, the Southam in-house newsletter.

17 Webster was quoted in the *Montreal Gazette*'s ombudsperson's column, and cited in the *CDNPA Newsletter*.

18 Repetition of images is a real danger. When the *Challenger* exploded, the same stills or footage appeared on every front page and every telecast for days afterwards, so the audience was forced to relive the deaths of the crew time and time again. I, personally, was appalled at the end of the week to pick up my *Maclean's* magazine and find the same picture splashed across the front cover one more time. See 10 February 1986, cover.

19 The policy manual for the *Windsor Star* demands all stories mentioning suicides be cleared by a senior editor, and says that most should not be reported, unless they are very public or the rank or title of the person is significant. See *Editorial Department Policy Manual*, ed. C. Morgan (Windsor: *Windsor Star* 1989), law 10. CFPL-TV in London, Ontario, says similarly it 'does not cover suicides except in circumstances such as murder-suicide, public suicide, or when the person involved has a high public profile. Any exceptions require the approval of news management.' See *CFPL News Department Policy*, ed. J. MacDonald (London: CFPL-TV 1988), 26.

20 Bill Morgan, then director of CBC-TV news and current affairs, described the footage as going 'beyond violence to what I guess I'd call horror.' Quoted in an anonymous Canadian Press news story, 22 January 1987.

21 Ibid.

22 I am indebted to the CBC radio program *Media File* for some of the data on this story. They aired an item on the event, 3 February 1987.

23 Ibid.

24 Ibid.

25 *Weekly World News*, 21 January 1986.

26 Another very small example of this offensive use of verbal detail was faulted by the *New York Times* newsroom bulletin, *Winners & Sinners*, after it ran in the paper: 'A week after he went down with Pan American Flight 103, Michael Bernstein, or what they could collect of him, was still in Lockerbie, Scotland.' See *New York Times*, 30 December 1989. The line may be cute, but the

Reversibility Rule suggests that few people would want it written about themselves, for their children to read.

27 B. Basiia, 'Benoit Murder Case Like a Bizarre Soap Opera,' *Humber Log*, 8 February 1989, A5-7.

28 D. MacMillan, 'Playing Confucius,' *Content*, March/April 1986, 13.

29 *Saturday Night*, July/August 1993, 33, 34, 50, 55.

Chapter 11: Privacy

1 Cited in R. Lustig, 'Promises Are No Longer Enough,' *British Journalism Review* 1, no. 2 (Winter 1990):46.

2 Some roles, by definition, lose a degree of privacy. Royalty, for instance, attracts enormous public interest and is seen as virtually public property, from conception to the grave. Elected public officials, such as prime ministers, also must expect considerable public scrutiny by definition.

3 'The pictures don't show anything about slum life; the incident could have happened anywhere, and it did. It is extremely unlikely that anyone who saw them rushed out and had his fire escape strengthened. And the pictures were not news – at least, they were not national news. It is not news in Washington, or New York, or Los Angeles that a woman was killed in a Boston fire. The only newsworthy thing about the pictures is that they were taken. They deserve to be printed because they were great pictures, breathtaking pictures of something that happened.' See N. Ephron, *Scribble, Scribble: Notes on the Media* (New York: Alfred A. Knopf 1978), 62.

4 There were few complaints, but the *Toronto Star*'s ombudsperson recorded some.

5 It is not clear how the misleading cutline occurred. The Associated Press sent out a correction on the wire, but by then most papers had gone with the misleading original cutline. See 'Would You Run These Photos?' APME *Photo/Graphics Report* (New York 1986), 7.

6 J. Harvard, anchor, 'Media Ethics: An Inquiry into News Morality,' produced by CBC-TV Manitoba, 1983. This program was based on a one-day media ethics workshop conducted in Winnipeg by the Canadian Managing Editor's Conference.

7 John Harvard, then a journalist and subsequently an MP, was anchoring a CBC-TV program called *Media Ethics: An Inquiry Into News Mortality*. It was based on a 1993 media ethics workshop in Winnipeg sponsored by the Canadian Managing Editors Conference.

8 Ibid.

9 J.E. Brown, 'News Photographs and the Pornography of Grief,' *Journal of Mass Media Ethics* 2 (Spring/Summer 1987):77.

10 On shooting first and judging after, Brown says: 'An editor cannot decide whether to publish a picture if there is none to begin with.' See 'News Photographs and the Pornography of Grief,' 78. However, such value judgments are best made by experienced senior editors, not by line photographers or reporters in the field.

11 Carl Lindstrom in Brown, 'News Photographs and the Pornography of Grief,' 77.

12 Cited in Bruce Swain, *Reporters' Ethics* (Ames: Iowa University Press 1978), 66.

13 V. Sears, 'Politicians Are Losing Privacy,' *Toronto Star*, 27 September 1987, B1.

14 CBC, *Journalistic Standards and Practices* (Toronto: CBC Enterprises 1993), 44, 48.

15 Cited in J. Brady, *The Craft of Interviewing* (Cincinnati, OH: Writer's Digest 1976), 5.

16 N. Beloff, 'This Above All,' in *Questioning Media Ethics*, ed. B. Rubin (New York: Praeger 1978), 63. This may be a fairly recent development. The press had no such reservations a century ago, as cartoonists regularly described Prime Minister Sir John A. Macdonald's fondness for the bottle. Boozing was, perhaps, seen by some as an amusing peccadillo, where today alcoholism is viewed more seriously.

17 *New York Times* magazine, cited in 'A System for Chumps,' *Globe and Mail*, 7 May 1987, A7.

18 Blom-Cooper in Lustig, 'Promises Are No Longer Enough,' 46.

19 *New York Times*, quoted in *Globe and Mail*, 7 May 1987, A7.

20 V. Sears, *Hello Sweetheart ... Get Me Rewrite* (Toronto: Key Porter 1988), 203-4.

21 N. Lees, 'Fonyo Incident Sad for Everyone,' *Edmonton Journal*, 8 February 1985.

22 W. Stewart, *Canadian Newspapers: The Inside Story* (Edmonton: Hurtig 1980), 199.

23 Calamai, speaking during his term as Max Bell Professor of Journalism at the University of Regina, 25 October 1985.

24 In 1993, the Regina *Leader-Post* ran a list of people who owed the city substantial property taxes and, to its credit, included the name of a respected newspaper columnist.

25 Z. Olijnyk, 'Man Convicted of Sex Offences,' Regina *Leader-Post*, 28 September 1985, 3.

26 'PM-CRAFT-Priest,' Canadian Press wire story, 8 November 1989.

27 Harvard, 'Media Ethics.'

28 Cited in K. Whitehorn, 'Ethics and the Media,' 5.

29 As several of these are not specifically issues of privacy, they are discussed later, in the appropriate chapters.

30 L. Robin, 'Secrecy Surrounding Sauvé's Illness,' *Ottawa Citizen*, 1 February 1984, 5.

31 'Journalists Went Too Far in Search of Scoop,' *Vancouver Sun*, 13 July 1985.

32 One respected journalist, Harvey Schachter (a former president of the Centre for Investigative Journalism), characterized this incident as 'traditional scoop journalism ... But to the public it was an appalling scoop, a grossly impolite treatment of a minister's invitation to a photo opportunity that was not much different than if the reporter pilfered the budget.' See H. Schachter, 'Garbage Journalism,' CIJ *Bulletin*, Summer 1983, 7.

33 *Globe and Mail*, 6 May 1983.

34 Vancouver *Province*, 30 January 1986.

35 In a self-congratulatory story with the ten-page picture spread, the paper revealed something about the 'How?' of the piece, referring to their paparazzi as 'raiding' and 'skulking' to conduct their 'larky derring-do' and 'burglary.' See 'Who's Bin Done?' *Sunday Times* magazine, 7 October 1990, passim.

36 Private conversation between Steinke and this writer.

37 Details of this incident come from this writer's involvement in the case, as an 'expert witness' on journalism ethics at the grievance hearing.

38 Knowlton Nash, senior CBC-TV news anchor, recalls that President Lyndon Johnson once said he 'didn't want reporters writing about how many drinks he had or "when I go into a strange bedroom."' Until recently, says Nash, reporters tended to join such conspiracies to protect their sources. See K. Nash, *History on the Run: The Trenchcoat Memoirs of a Foreign Correspondent* (Toronto: McClelland & Stewart 1989), 253.

39 C. Rosner, 'Notes Show Manitoba Hardest Hit,' *Winnipeg Free Press*, 27 November 1984, 1.

Chapter 12: Naming Names and Revealing Sources

1 The Toronto nurse Susan Nelles was a powerful example of this. At the centre of a furious investigation into the sudden death of several babies in Toronto's Children's Hospital, she was ultimately exonerated of all complicity, but it took years for her to recover her reputation, after her name and face were exposed for months on the front pages of papers and every evening newscast.

2 For this reason, the *Toronto Star* newsroom employs a full-time clerk to keep track of individuals once they are named in the newspaper and appear in one of the seventy Metro Toronto courts. But that is a major investment of time and resources. See *The News: To Name or Not To Name* (Toronto: Ontario Press Council 1981), 13. The *Star* thus makes a point of publishing the final disposition of charges. The *Montreal Gazette* has a commendable policy to ensure even-handed treatment: if someone is reported on page 1 as being charged with an offence and he is acquitted, a report must also go on page 1.

3 Atlantic Press Council, *Annual Report* (Truro, NS: Atlantic Press Council 1993), 13.

4 In Mexico, persons charged may be pictured in the newspapers, holding the weapon they are accused of using or the item they are accused of stealing, even before the matter has gone to court. By contrast, the Swedish media generally choose not to name people facing the courts even after they have been convicted of major offences, unless they are very well known.

5 *Ottawa Citizen*, 12 March 1975.

6 Even the community weekly papers may be feeling the pressure to name names, rather than turn a blind eye. In a letter to the industry publication, *CCNA Publisher*, Fred A. Hatfield, editor of the Yarmouth, Nova Scotia, *Vanguard*, urged fellow editors to

stand and be counted: 'Perhaps if more diligent reporting practices were applied instead of the wishy-washy small town stuff that poses for journalism, communities across North America would not be faced with members of the clergy simply being shuffled out of communities after they abuse children, to set up shop in other small unsuspecting places.' See F.A. Hatfield, 'Publishing Names of Criminals Important Task for Newspapers,' *CCNA Publisher*, March 1992, 6.

7 R. Goodman, 'To Name or Not to Name the Accused?' *Toronto Star*, 11 January 1986, B2.

8 L. Hughes, 'That's the Role of the Courts,' *Edmonton Journal*, 17 February 1990.

9 The lawyer had been involved in an investigation of the police shooting of Native leader J.J. Harper. The implication of his arrest was that the police wanted to punish him. The city of Winnipeg ultimately paid him $120,000 in compensation. See 'Sex-assault Case Settled,' Regina *Leader-Post*, 16 October 1992, A6.

10 Rex V. Wright (1799): 'The general advantage to the country in having these proceedings made public more than counterbalances the inconveniences to the private persons whose conduct may be the subject of such proceedings.' This precedent and others are quoted approvingly in an insightful decision by Judge O'Brien of the Ontario High Court, 16 September 1983, in which he threw out an application to keep secret the names of thirty-two men charged with gross indecency in Orillia, Ontario.

11 When a prominent Calgary city employee was charged with sexual assault in 1991, the *Calgary Herald* chose to name him despite a court ban on revealing his identity. The man was given probation and ordered to do community work – a punishment that might have looked unduly soft if the entire event had been shrouded in secrecy.

12 The Canadian Bar Association voted in 1989 (by a narrow margin) in favour of the names of defendants in sex-trials only being published after conviction. See R. Walker, 'If Accused's Names Aren't Printed Secrecy May Endanger System,' reprinted from *Montreal Gazette* in *Press Review*, January 1990, 24. The media have to be particularly careful with such issues, as community values are continually evolving. For instance, drinking and driving used to be seen as almost funny and is now seen as irresponsible and deadly.

13 *Ethics and Policies*, staff manual of the *Ottawa Citizen*, 24-5.

14 K. Makin, 'The Long Arm of the Media,' *Ryerson Review of Journalism*, Spring 1989, 87.

15 'Deviance and control ... constitute the essence of all news judgments.' See R.V. Ericson et al., *Visualizing Deviance: A Study of News Organization* (Toronto: University of Toronto Press 1987), 4-5. 'There is an over-emphasis on murder, other forms of serious violence, and offences involving sexual aspects' (p. 45). There is evidence of 'deviance and crime being prime criteria of newsworthiness' (p. 151). But the research which Ericson et al. cite shows that crime only composes 4 per cent of print news in

Britain and 9 per cent in Chicago (p. 44). However, they are far from alone in this view. Contrast the view of the London *Sun* editor, quoted in Chapter 1, who felt crime was the readers' paramount interest. Or even that of the nineteenth century New York publisher, Charles A. Dana, who said: 'Whatever the Divine Providence permitted to occur I was not too proud to print.' Cited in J.L. Hulteng, *The Messenger's Motives: Ethical Problems of the News Media*, 2nd ed. (Englewood Cliffs, NJ: Prentice-Hall 1985), 150. Saying 'It's all *his* fault' does not free the journalist from making ethical decisions.

16 Hughes, 'That's the Role of the Courts.'

17 Clearly journalists are not 'ordinary citizens' in many contexts. They may, for instance, be seen as having considerably more power than most people, some may lose some privacy themselves when they become celebrities in their own right, and many forfeit basic rights, such as the right to be politically active. But they would be wise to ally themselves as closely as possible with the common citizen, rather than to view themselves as an elite.

18 E. Goodwin, *Groping for Ethics in Journalism* (Ames, IA: Iowa State University Press 1983), 250, 265.

19 The Americans have probably overdone the formalizing of these terms, but in some jurisdictions it may be useful. For instance, the US State Department has defined each phrase – 'off the record,' 'deep background,' etc. – very carefully in 'Guidelines for Talking with the Press.' Cited in C. Lewis, 'State Department Guidelines Spell Out Who May Say What,' ASNE *Bulletin*, April 1988, 5.

20 Canadian Press *Stylebook*, 27.

21 CBC, *Journalistic Standards and Practices* (Toronto: CBC Enterprises 1993), 51. Before this policy was fully formulated, the CBC had a salutary experience: A reporter alleged in a TV piece that a British Columbia cabinet minister had interfered with the justice system. When they were sued for libel, it became clear the inexperienced reporter could not produce reliable evidence – and his supervisors had never checked or insisted on corroboration. A similar incident hit the *Toronto Sun*, and both cost the newsrooms unusually huge libel damages – further reason for double-checking accuracy and ensuring sources *can* be revealed when necessary.

22 The way to avoid unnamed sources, says Steve Weinberg, executive director of Investigative Reporters and Editors Inc., is to follow the paper trail. Cited in D. Johnston, 'The Anonymous-Source Syndrome,' *Columbia Journalism Review*, November/December 1987, 54.

23 For a further good debate of these issues, see Johnston, 'The Anonymous-Source Syndrome'; J. Kettle, 'Protecting Sources,' *Content*, September 1978, 16; C. Lakshman, 'New Editor Bans Anonymous Sources,' *Content*, January/February 1990, 5-6; C. Law, 'The Shield Law Controversy,' *Carleton Journalism Review*, Winter 1977, 12-14; and J. Leslie, 'The Anonymous Source,'

Washington Journalism Review, September 1986, 33-5.

24 Sawatsky made the comment while speaking to journalism students at the University of Regina, during his term as the Max Bell Visiting Professor, 12 November 1987.

25 Lakshman, 'New Editor Bans Anonymous Sources,' 5-6.

26 Johnston, 'The Anonymous-Source Syndrome,' 54.

27 L.D. Boccardi, 'Name Names, Staff Letter Says,' *AP Log*, 13 February 1978, 1.

28 Canadian Press *Stylebook*, ed. R. Taylor (Toronto: Canadian Press 1989), 226.

29 *The Journal*, 4 January 1987.

30 The issues were fully debated by *Toronto Star* legal writer Harold Levy, who concluded that the information about prison conditions was sufficiently important to justify BCTV's action. See H. Levy, 'What Should We Do When the Cops Arrive?' *Content*, April 1987, 35-9.

31 N. Hall and G. Mason, 'Rogers will Stay – Premier,' *Vancouver Sun*, 9 May 1987, A1-2, B3.

32 Ibid., A2.

33 Many members of the BC press gallery, for instance, played weekly basketball games with members of the legislature. See D. Bramham, 'Reporters Reassess Ethics, Standards,' *Vancouver Sun*, 17 July 1990, B2.

Chapter 13: The Media and Sex

1 This view is strengthened occasionally by a brazen editor. See, for instance, the London *Sun* editor's statement, cited in Chapter 2, that sex is one of the quintet of public interests, along with crime, food, football, and money.

2 See, for instance, CBC's directive: 'Explicit scenes of nudity or eroticism must not normally be used. They are acceptable only if it is clear that they are essential to the information being conveyed in the program and that such information is itself important enough to warrant broadcast. Such scenes must never be emphasized or used primarily to shock or for sensation.' See CBC, *Journalistic Standards and Practices* (Toronto: CBC Enterprises 1993), 80.

3 It is worth remembering that two generations ago, men wore swimming-suits that covered their chests; and three generations ago, respectable women who went swimming changed in a mobile changing-hut that was then propelled directly into the sea, so that only their heads need be seen above water. Today Canadian authorities turn a blind eye to Wreck Beach, near Vancouver, where nude sun-bathing is the norm.

4 CBC, *Journalistic Standards and Practices*, 79.

5 J.C. Merrill has written at length on the topic, notably in *The Imperative of Freedom* (New York: Hastings House 1974) and *Existential Journalism* (New York: Hastings House 1977).

6 Merrill, *Existential Journalism*, 132.

7 See 'Ontario Press Council Objects to Toronto Sun "SUNshine Girls,"' *Editor and Publisher*, 7 December 1985, 17 for a brief

report of the case, or the 1985 annual report of the Ontario Press Council for more detail. Interestingly, the Press Council's 1978 booklet *Sexism and the Newspapers* is surprisingly dated, even though revised in 1981. This may indicate the major improvements that have occurred since it was developed.

8 The *Bulletin* of the Canadian Association of Journalists (formerly CIJ) and *Content* magazine have both paid attention to feminist issues in recent years, and feminism is frequently a key topic at CAJ conferences, spearheaded by the Women's Network activist group.

9 Some fairly recent, random examples from *Maclean's*: actress Tara Frederick (9 September 1991, 31); actress Kate Vernon (7 December 1992, 51); actress Kymberley Huffman (14 December 1992, 52); dancer Margaret Illmann (26 July 1993, 42).

10 J. Down, 'Sweet Sue's Got the Key to Skeleton,' *Calgary Sun*, 20 March 1987.

11 Canadian Press *Stylebook*, ed. P. Buckley (Toronto: Canadian Press 1993), 22-3.

12 Regina *Leader-Post*, 13 June 1984.

13 Canadian Press *Stylebook*, 22.

14 F. Denney, 'Banish All the Sexist Terms,' in *Sexism and the Newspapers* (Ottawa: Ontario Press Council 1978), 10-15.

15 Denney, 'Banish All the Sexist Terms,' 11-12.

16 For discussion of women in the newsroom, see P. Desbarats, *Guide to Canadian News Media* (Toronto: Harcourt Brace Jovanovich 1990) and L. Douris, 'Upwardly Immobile,' *Ryerson Review of Journalism*, Spring 1988, 40-3.

17 This is not to suggest, of course, that the audience is homogeneous – even an isolated Hutterite village has independent thinkers and a range of ages and attitudes. But the writer must be sensitive to the prevailing mood of the news consumers. It is impossible to please everyone. But the journalist must guard against aggravating large numbers *accidentally*.

18 J.B. Mays, 'Strong Poison,' *Globe and Mail*, 14 April 1990, C1.

19 Ibid.

20 The *Globe and Mail*, for instance, banned tobacco advertising in August 1986, well before the federal government restricted such advertisements, at a cost of about $100,000 a year. See D. Gersh, 'Toronto Globe and Mail Drops Tobacco Ads,' *Editor and Publisher*, 6 September 1986, 15. This followed the lead of some American newspapers that dropped tobacco ads in 1985. Some media also refuse advertising for 'happy-hours' (cheap drinks after work) and escort services (often fronts for prostitution). See M.K. Guzda, 'All the Ads Fit to Print,' *Editor and Publisher*, 26 January 1985, 7, 18.

21 D. Dutton, 'When Seduction Goes Too Far,' *Western Report*, 12 October 1987, 37.

22 The mass of detail and the deliberate chronology of the event matches the most salacious of British papers, the London *Sport*, which gleefully describes such incidents in articles surrounded by advertisements for sexual aids and obscene phone calls.

23 A. Boras, 'Step-Father Acquitted in Assault Case,' Regina *Leader-Post*, 18 September 1986, A3. (Allegations, of course, do not usually cause physical abnormality!)

24 Vancouver *Province*, 23 June 1983.

25 Vancouver *Province*, 4 October 1981.

Chapter 14: Hide the Paper: Here Come the Kids

1 CBC, *Journalistic Standards and Practices* (Toronto: CBC Enterprises 1993), 79-80. The Canadian Press, for instance, simply asserts that 'casual obscenity, blasphemy and vulgarity are not wanted in the news reports.' Editor Peter Buckley may well feel that, as the Canadian Press *Stylebook* is now used widely even by high school newspaper staffs, a list of banned words would itself cause offence. See Canadian Press *Stylebook*, ed. P. Buckley (Toronto: Canadian Press 1993), 18.

2 Cited in H.E. Goodwin, *Groping for Ethics in Journalism* (Ames, IA: Iowa State University Press 1983) 198.

3 For example, on 9 November 1993, the CBC *Prime Time News* showed a Newfoundland town councillor telling a reporter to 'Fuck off!'

4 CBC, 'A World of Words: The O.E.D.,' on *Ideas*, CBC radio, 12 and 19 October 1988.

5 T. Coleman, 'Gazumping Old Onions,' *Guardian*, 12 October 1972, 12.

6 H. Hebert, 'Lingua Frankly,' *Guardian*, 25 March 1974, 15.

7 J. Crosby, 'Villains of the Piece,' London *Observer*, 31 December 1972.

8 R.W. Burchfield, 'Four-Letter Words and the O.E.D.,' in *Times Literary Supplement*, 13 October 1972.

9 Details of this incident are taken from Goodwin, *Groping for Ethics in Journalism*, 200-1.

10 B. Evans, 'Foul Language Still Put To Test in Newsrooms,' *APME Writing and Editing Committee Report* (New York: APME 1984), 13-14.

11 Hutchinson was speaking to journalism students at the University of Regina, before giving the sixth Minifie Lecture, 24 February 1986.

12 Cited in Goodwin, *Groping for Ethics in Journalism*, 198.

13 *Globe and Mail*, 1 May 1986, A12.

14 Regina *Leader-Post*, 30 September 1989.

15 Ibid.

16 *New York Times*, 11 May 1987.

17 'Tone of the Times,' *Winners & Sinners*, 29 May 1987, 1.

18 Regina *Leader-Post*, 3 October 1988.

19 Personal communication from George Oake, then managing editor of the *Edmonton Journal*.

20 *New York Times*, 18 September 1988.

21 Cited in Goodwin, *Groping for Ethics in Journalism*, 206.

22 *Globe and Mail*, 13 January 1983.

23 See, for instance, *Toronto Star*, 21 September 1989, A3.

24 *Globe and Mail*, 22 April 1987.

25 *Globe and Mail Style Book*, ed. E.C. Phelan (Toronto: Globe and Mail 1981), 20.

26 *Globe and Mail Style Book*, ed. J.A. McFarlane and W. Clements (Toronto: Globe and Mail 1990), 'Obscene language.'

27 Ibid.

28 *Sunday Times*, 30 March 1986.

29 *Toronto Star*, 19 September 1989, A3.

30 *Guardian*, Spring 1988.

31 *Guardian*, 18 May 1987.

32 Canadian Press *Stylebook*, 289.

33 An example is 'Bloom County,' 21 March 1981.

34 *Toronto Star*, 20 September 1989, A12.

35 ASNE *Bulletin*, April 1986, 2514.

36 CBC, *Journalistic Standards and Practices*, 79-80.

37 *Napanee Beaver*, 8 September 1993, 1.

38 Saskatoon *Star-Phoenix*, 3 August 1993, B3.

39 Stuart Keate, long-time publisher of the *Vancouver Sun*, defended this paternalism very simply: 'It is a curious fact, not much thought about, that newspapers remain today one of the last bastions of media "respectability," while movies, literature and TV have all succumbed.' See S. Keate, *Paper Boy: The Memoirs of Stuart Keate* (Toronto: Clarke Irwin 1980), 147.

Chapter 15: Different Media: Different Problems

1 In this writer's experience working with Canadian Press many years ago in Halifax and Vancouver, there was rarely any opportunity to develop writing style or any rapport with individual papers. The overarching emphasis is on speed.

2 P. Desbarats, *Guide to Canadian News Media* (Toronto: Harcourt Brace Jovanovich 1990), 19.

3 P. Rutherford, *The Making of the Canadian Media* (Toronto: McGraw-Hill Ryerson), 57.

4 D. Taras, *The Newsmakers* (Scarborough, ON: Nelson Canada 1990), 52.

5 Hutchinson, quoted fully in Chapter 3, suggested, in the 1986 Minifie Lecture at the University of Regina, that journalists had a prime responsibility to put things in perspective – to put the beads of events on the string of time. See H. Hutchinson, 'Images, Self-Images and the Long String,' in *The Quarrymen of History: Canadian Journalists Examine Their Profession*, ed. N. Russell (monograph no. 1, School of Journalism, University of Regina 1987), 64.

6 Another factor of size, of course, is the press capacity, but even the most ethical proprietor is unlikely to give the newsroom much influence over that.

7 Only in the early 1990s has kenaf, as a wood substitute, been brought into production in the southern US. Its viability remains to be seen. Large areas of North America, outside the biggest urban concentrations, still have little or no newsprint recycling. Even the Toronto dailies only began serious use of recycled paper after Toronto City Council threatened in 1989-90

to ban newspaper boxes from city streets unless recycling was embraced. (This writer, who worked with a volunteer recycling group in British Columbia in the 1970s and early 1980s, was shocked to find nobody in the West was interested in buying the boxcar-loads of clean, sorted, and bundled paper. But the newsprint-hungry Japanese were prepared to buy it, despite the trans-Pacific shipping costs.)

8 The story, too, is abysmal, snidely reporting only the members of the royal family who missed the birthday party: 'Princess Margaret chose to stay with her friend Lord Glenconner in Scotland rather than be at her mother's side.' See London *Today*, 5 August 1988, 1.

9 It may be recalled that during the earlier discussion of violence and privacy, it was noted that the caption for a picture of the *Challenger* explosion made a vast difference to the reader's reaction to the picture.

10 J. Hohenberg, *The Professional Journalist: A Guide to the Practices and Principles of the News Media* (New York: Holt, Rinehart & Winston 1983), 19.

11 These photographic processes could be likened to the activities of the news writer and editor who cut, insert, move, substitute, and otherwise massage words. Their motives are – or should be – 'pure.' Like the photographers, they are aiming simply to communicate an image clearly and concisely.

12 See M. Evans, 'An Open Question: "Emphatically Accurate Photos,"' *News Photographer*, November 1989, 26-8; K. McGran, 'Now You See It, Now You Don't: The Ethics of Image Processing,' *Ryerson Review of Journalism*, Spring 1987, 4-5; S. Reaves, 'Ethics: Report Airs Editors' Debate on Principles,' *Electronic Times*, 9 October 1989, 1; and E. Rogers, 'Now You See It, Now You Don't,' *News Photographer*, August 1989, 16-19.

13 McGran cites a Toronto magazine executive who suggests it would be dishonest for the editor of a travel spread, which showed a sandy beach with luxury hotels, to excise an oil refinery visible in the background. See McGran, 'Now You See It, Now You Don't.'

14 Rogers, 'Now You See It, Now You Don't,' 18.

15 McGran, 'Now You See It, Now You Don't,' 5.

16 Ibid., 27.

17 Private communication.

18 For a useful treatment of the subject in a British context, see J. Tunstall and M. Dunford, *The ITC and the Future of Regional and National Television News* (London: Social Science Department, City University 1991).

19 CBC, *Journalistic Policy* (Montreal: CBC Enterprises 1988), 107.

20 C. Curtis, 'The Incredible Shrinking Newscast,' *Ryerson Review of Journalism*, Spring 1988, 6-7.

21 Ev Dennis confirms the deleterious effects of deregulation in the United States: 'Radio news is a disaster if we are to believe recent comments from the Radio and Television News Directors Association. Radio news, once nurtured and propped up by the Federal Communications Commission, fell victim to deregulation, which has caused many stations either to curtail their news operations drastically or to drop them altogether. The public, I believe, is badly served by this trend.' See E. Dennis, *Reshaping the Media* (Newbury Park, CA: Sage 1989), 63. He adds that the quality of local TV news has also deteriorated substantially in the United States.

22 Taras, *The Newsmakers*, 156.

23 The event was further muddied by an inflammatory commentary by Terence McKenna when this item was aired on the CBC-TV's *The Journal*, 4 December 1989.

24 CBC, *Journalistic Policy*, 34.

25 Ibid., 33. See also CBC, *Journalistic Standards and Practices*, 65.

26 CBC, *Journalistic Standards and Practices* (Toronto: CBC Enterprises 1993), 67.

27 James MacLean, private communication, 1989.

28 David Taras says the average television news story is roughly ninety seconds (150-250 words). He quotes one CBC producer as saying the ideal length for an interview clip is 12 seconds. See Taras, *The Newsmakers*, 102.

29 K. Nash, 'Cleopatra, Harlots and Glue,' in *The Quarrymen of History: Canadian Journalists Examine Their Profession*, ed. N. Russell (monograph no. 2, School of Journalism, University of Regina 1987), 20.

30 Zundel's trial occurred in 1985. For a full critique of media coverage, see N. Russell, ed., *Trials and Tribulations* (monograph no. 1, School of Journalism, University of Regina 1986).

31 Zundel appeared on *The National* eight times during the trial, wearing his colourful helmet. See Russell, 'Handling Hate,' 40.

32 Ibid.

33 Taras, *The Newsmakers*, 102-5.

34 Ibid., 107.

35 E. Malling, 'Recipes for Sacred Cow,' Minifie Lecture, University of Regina, Regina, 25 March 1991, 7.

36 Ibid. Malling's example is somewhat flawed. The fact that no one is killed when the Denver plane does a belly-landing is precisely what *does* make it news. It is just the sort of 'good news' the media are always being urged to report to offset the disasters.

37 Hutchinson, who gave the Minifie Lecture at the University of Regina in 1986, was quoted in Chapter 5.

38 Malling, 'Recipes for Sacred Cow,' 10.

39 Ibid., 23.

40 See, for instance, W. Small, *To Kill A Messenger: Television News and the Real World* (New York: Hastings House 1970), 70-3.

41 CBC, *Journalistic Standards and Practices* (Toronto: CBC Enterprises 1993), 62.

42 MPs used to express approbation in the Commons by slapping their desks; since TV was introduced, they have adopted the more dignified hand-clap. The TV cameras in the Ottawa Commons are not allowed to show long shots of the 'empty' House, and MPs 'load' the picture by clustering round whoever

is speaking, looking animated and approving. Few judges have permitted cameras in the courtroom, but the American experience seems to suggest that the presence of the camera tends to turn the court into a sort of Perry Mason performance. See also W. Small's description of TV's impact on political conventions in the United States in *To Kill A Messenger*, chapter 11.

43 McKenna was speaking at a conference of the Centre for Investigative Journalism in Ottawa, Spring 1989.

44 Some useful examples occurred years ago when the CBC showed its 'Connections' series on the Mafia in Canada: Some of those ambush interviews revealed much about the character of the people involved.

45 K. Nash, *History on the Run: The Trenchcoat Memoirs of a Foreign Correspondent* (Toronto: McClelland & Stewart 1989), 121.

46 *CFPL News Department Policy*, ed. R. MacDonald (London: ON: CFPL-TV 1988), 22.

47 John Owen was speaking to students at the School of Journalism, University of Regina, 18 January 1989.

48 K. Whitehorn, 'Ethics and the Media,' Leggett Lecture, University of Surrey, Surrey, UK, 9 November 1988, 9.

49 Malling, 'Time for a New Attitude,' 6.

50 J. Forsyth, 'I've Got You Taped,' *British Journalism Review* 1, no. 1 (1990):30.

51 CBC, *Journalistic Standards and Practices*, 75.

52 This writer recalls working for the BBC World Service at a time when society was more naive, and taking great pride in editing incoherent, stammering sources into mellifluous speakers. It was a feat of tape splicing, but it misrepresented the sources.

53 So-called 'open line' shows are outside this discussion, though the same guidelines may be appropriate.

54 Canada, 'CRTC Regulations,' paragraph 3. The CRTC has responsibility for licensing radio and television stations. However, as Peter Desbarats points out, the commission is largely toothless, in part because of its 'reluctance to employ the licence-renewal process rigorously as an instrument to improve program quality.' See Desbarats, *Guide to Canadian News Media*, 165.

55 Enright was speaking informally at a meeting of CBC radio producers to discuss ethics, at Niagara-on-the-Lake, 5 December 1989.

56 *Broadcasting Act*, section 3, 1.

Chapter 16: Righting Writing Wrongs

1 K. Whitehorn, 'Ethics and the Media,' Leggett Lecture, University of Surrey, Guildford, UK, 9 November 1988, 16.

2 J. Stott, 'Reader's Must Be First Concerned For Newspapers,' *Calgary Herald*, 13 May 1990. Many others have expressed the same concern. 'Journalists themselves don't like to be examined,' commented Allan Fotheringham. 'The universities have been bashed about, and the church and the medical profession and the legal profession (badly needed), but there has been surprisingly little X-raying of the press, which is usually on the lethal end of the stethoscope.' See *Birds of a Feather* (Toronto: Key Porter 1989), 8. The thoughtful *Chatelaine* editor Ivor Shapiro brought together several similar comments in 'No Comment,' *Saturday Night*, March 1989, 27-9.

3 Desbarats, *Guide to Canadian News Media* (Toronto: Harcourt Brace Jovanovich 1990), 156. Libel awards are not nearly as high in Canada, so far.

4 This is not just a 1990's thought: Wilf Kesterton tells of nineteenth-century readers smashing a Montreal press, wrecking a Kingston type room, and cutting off the ears of a St. John's editor and his shop foreman, because of dissatisfaction with editorial content. See *A History of Journalism in Canada* (Toronto: McClelland & Stewart 1967), 20-1.

5 J.L. Hulteng, *The Messenger's Motives: Ethical Problems of the News Media*, 2nd ed. (Englewood Cliffs, NJ: Prentice-Hall 1985), 112.

6 R. Adler, *A Day in the Life of the New York Times* (New York: Lippincott 1971), 79.

7 It is to be devoutly hoped that no self-respecting newsroom would countenance the old practice of faking letters in order to stir up controversy or fill space.

8 CBC, *Journalistic Standards and Practices* (Toronto: CBC Enterprises 1993), 89.

9 Cited in M. Campbell, 'Paper Writes Off Anti-Abortionist,' *Globe and Mail*, 19 April 1986.

10 M.L. Stein, 'Weeding and Rhetoric,' *Editor and Publisher*, 8 December 1984, 14.

11 The *Sun* tabloid newspapers continue the practice and presumably feel that readers are amused by the caustic one-liners. But it was one of the things readers complained about during a 'Talk to the Editors Night.' 'They cheapen you,' commented reader Esther Brody. Replied editor-in-chief Bob Poole: 'Sorry Esther, they're here to stay. And anyway, Editor Paul Stanway is so good with those quips.' See R. Poole, 'So Nice of You to Call Us,' *Calgary Sun*, 9 June 1988, 5.

12 For a more complete discussion of editors replying to letters, see Jim McClure, managing editor of the Lewiston, Pennsylvania, *Sentinel*, in 'Letters to the Editor,' *PNPA Press*, December 1984.

13 E. Franklin, 'Minding Your Manners,' *Washington Journalism Review*, December 1986, 33. For another clarion call for better responses to readers' letters, see David Lawrence, Jr., publisher of the *Detroit Free Press*, in 'Points On Credibility,' *Washington Journalism Review*, February 1985, 49-51.

14 S. K-Brooks, 'Unsigned Letter Runs as Lead Story,' *Editor and Publisher*, 2 July 1988, 14.

15 Sample solicitation: 'Moms, tell us how you juggle home and job,' *USA Today*, 31 October 1986, 1.

16 A. Radolf, 'A Place for Readers to Explode,' *Editor and Publisher*, 14 May 1988, 10.

17 Williams, in Canada, *Proceedings of the Special Senate Committee*

on Mass Media, vol. 1 (Ottawa: Queen's Printers 1969), 61.

18 *Vancouver Sun*, 22 October 1983, 5.

19 Franklin, 'Minding Your Manners,' 32.

20 C. O'Connor, 'Flaunting Its Feedback,' *Washington Journalism Review*, May 1985, 11.

21 On a somewhat smaller scale, CBLT-TV in Toronto has had an audience talk-back show called 'Soap Box,' where citizens are given time to air their views. See R.V. Ericson et al., *Visualizing Deviance: A Study of News Organization* (Toronto: University of Toronto Press 1987), 85.

22 Such shows need not be boring. Anne Robinson presented fragments of viewers' letters on the BBC's weekly *Points of View*, which were both engaging and outspoken. She showed clips from protested shows and gave every appearance of being on the viewers' side – a sort of audience advocate. Wednesdays, 8:50 P.M., for ten minutes.

23 W.B. Stewart, 'Canadian Social Systems and Canadian Broadcasting Audiences,' in *Communications in Canadian Society*, ed. B.J. Singer (Don Mills, ON: Addison-Wesley 1983), 31.

24 R. Rykken, 'Letters to Readers,' *presstime*, December 1989, 10, 12.

25 Stewart, 'Canadian Social Systems,' 30.

26 Ibid. This is going too far, but Franklin quotes one publisher (Arthur Wible, *Dallas Times-Herald*), as saying: 'We're all PR agents for our company.' See 'Canadian Social Systems,' 32.

27 The injunction (described in the discussion of media manipulation) remains a possible tool for irate citizens, but it is only for extreme situations where a libel is about to be committed. Hopefully, this weapon will be used rarely.

28 This writer filed a complaint with the Department of Consumer Affairs under misleading advertising legislation, but was told that he would not be allowed access to the results of their investigation and would not even be informed if there was a prosecution.

29 N. Russell, 'Handling Hate: Reporting of the Zundel and Keegstra Trials,' in *Trials and Tribulations*, ed. N. Russell (monograph no. 1, School of Journalism, University of Regina 1986), 46.

30 N. Barnett, 'Hartford's Car Wars,' *Columbia Journalism Review*, September 1985, 18-19.

31 For a further evaluation, see Arthur Siegel's skilfull dissection of the Kent Report in *Politics and the Media in Canada* (Toronto: McGraw-Hill Ryerson 1983), 146-50.

32 Vancouver *Province*, 18 August 1983.

33 *Vancouver Sun*, 5 November 1985.

34 Regina *Leader-Post*, 27 July 1977.

35 K. Makin, 'N.B. Station Denies Broadcast Abusive,' *Globe and Mail*, 5 May 1988 and *Vancouver Sun*, 1 June 1988.

36 Some of the early Canadian newspapers were started by political parties angry at the political stance of the existing papers. See P. Rutherford, *The Making of the Canadian Media* (Toronto: McGraw-Hill Ryerson), passim. In the 1960s, a newspaper war emerged in tiny Campbell River, British Columbia (population of about 12,000). Some citizens, mostly local retailers, were unhappy with a perceived 'sensationalist' stance of the two existing papers and so founded the *Mirror*, which flourished. The *Kamloops News* was started by a citizen to protest the Thomson-owned *Kamloops Sentinel* and eventually defeated the older paper.

37 On one occasion, the publisher of the *Vancouver Sun* bought space on a huge billboard near the *Sun* office to dispute the views expressed by a senior columnist.

38 Umbrella groups, such as the Canadian Daily Newspapers Association and the Radio Television News Directors Association, offer regular workshops across the country, to help reporters and editors do better work. In the United States, the Associated Press Managing Editors group has a lively Writing and Editing Committee, which publishes frequent newsletters for members.

39 The quality improvement concept might be characterized as a concerted attempt by management to improve the entire product. In a newspaper, this means firing up staff in all departments to care more about what they do and how they do it. Ways of measuring quality are sought in each department – such as counting the number of typographical errors – and a program is then instituted to set targets and monitor progress.

40 *Editor and Publisher*, 26 April 1986, 50.

41 Carleton University generously offered to help produce *Content* and subsequently provided space for the CIJ/CAJ office. The CIJ became increasingly mainstream (moving away from a purely investigative thrust). The resulting amalgamation of the *Bulletin* and *Content* was inevitable.

42 J. Partridge, 'Learning How to Compete,' *Content*, May/June 1990, 15.

43 There is nothing in Canada akin to Britain's 'Media Guardian' section in the *Guardian* every Monday, or *The Independent*'s Wednesday media page. Ron Verzuh makes the point that the 'alternative' press partly fill this gap, with sporadic articles in *This Magazine*, *Inner-City Voice* (Winnipeg), *Metropolis* (Toronto), and *Metro* (Ottawa). See R. Verzuh, 'Watchdogs on Society's Watchdog,' *Content*, July/August 1990, 25. Rick Salutin and Robert Fulford have both written regularly about media in the *Globe and Mail*, but almost exclusively from an Ontario perspective. *Frank* magazine writes wickedly about the media, but leans towards Parliament Hill gossip rather than constructive criticism.

44 The closest we have come in Canada in recent years has been CBC radio's *Media File*, an excellent little radio show condemned to the Saturday afternoon ghetto and then cancelled during the 1990-1 budget cuts. One of the few journalists in North America with a true media beat is David Shaw of the *Los Angeles Times*. Shapiro recalls that Shaw tried to get access to newspaper editorial board meetings, to describe the processes there, but was refused by the *New York Times* and the *Washington Post*. Shaw crisply labels this double-standard – covering other

corporate meetings but keeping your own secret – as 'hypocrisy.' See Shapiro, 'No Comment,' 28.

45 The classic critique of television in society is, of course, Neil Postman, *Amusing Ourselves to Death* (New York: Viking 1985).

46 R. Haggart, 'Problems of Printing Broadcasting,' *Content*, September/October 1988, 19.

47 *Montreal Gazette*, 27 March 1989

48 This has been much imitated, see C. Varcoe, 'You Be the Editor,' Regina *Leader-Post*, 16 January 1993.

49 *Winnipeg Free Press*, 22 February 1986.

50 Conducted just before Christmas, it comprises some 200 questions about reader news preferences, from world news to comic strips, and profiles the readers themselves in terms of income levels, jobs, education, and housing. This method is also becoming increasingly popular. See 'Record Reader Survey,' in *Kitchener-Waterloo Record*, 23 March 1992.

51 The clear exception to this, after a decade of struggle, is the Canadian Association of Journalists.

52 This is curious and unfortunate: The press gallery here chooses to censure a colleague on the grounds that he or she broke an embargo and hence failed to cooperate with an artificial deadline imposed by a news source and acquiesced to by the gallery pack. Yet, in 1990, when a reporter was caught advising the attorney general on how to handle the media, reading stories to him for his approval, and arranging late-night meetings with him, the gallery declined to act. See earlier discussion on conflict of interest.

53 This has been tried in several other newsrooms, such as the *Calgary Sun* and the Saskatoon *Star-Phoenix*.

54 M. Levine, ed., 'Inside the Times Herald-Record,' in the *Times Herald-Record*, Middletown, NY, 10-16 October 1982.

55 M. Levine, 'The Record Goes "On Record,"' in the *Times Herald-Record*, Tabloid reprint, 1982, 8.

56 *Seattle Times*, 29 June 1985, A15. The *Toronto Star* emulated this with a full-page analysis of its editorial and opinion editorial pages, titled 'Please Let Us Explain,' 26 December 1985. Such a full frontal approach to readers brings into question the view still held by some news managers that readers are 'probably not interested in newspapers.' See Shapiro, 'No Comment,' 28.

57 See M. Fitzgerald, '"Accuracy Checks" Grow in Popularity at Newspapers,' *Editor and Publisher*, 24 May 1986, 17.

58 Managing editor Denny Dible recalls a citizen sitting-in on the editorial meeting and challenging a decision to run a particular picture. Dible said 'her judgment was better than ours,' so they killed the picture. See M.L. Stein, 'Improving Credibility,' *Editor and Publisher*, 13 July 1985, 32.

59 J.A. Taylor, ed., *Annual Report* (Toronto: Ontario Press Council 1988), 1.

60 Canada, Special Senate Committee on Mass Media, *Report* [Davey Report], vol. 1 (Ottawa: Queen's Printer 1970), 87. See also Canada, *Report of the Royal Commission on Newspapers* ['Kent Commission'] (Ottawa: Queen's Printer 1981), 226.

61 S. Keate in his private letters to Pollen, who provided me with copies of his 1973 correspondence.

62 Canada, *Report* [Davey Report], 112.

63 British Columbia Press Council, *Annual Report* (Vancouver: BC Press Council 1989), 3.

64 Ontario Press Council, *Annual Report* (Toronto: Ontario Press Council 1987), 1.

65 C. Bailey, 'Wake Up – to Public Opinion,' *Editor and Publisher*, 7 July 1984, 18.

66 Ibid., 21.

67 British Columbia Press Council, 'Press Council Objectives,' in the pamphlet, *The British Columbia Press Council* (Vancouver: BC Press Council n.d.).

68 Ibid.

69 The reasons for the collapse of the British Press Council are not unanimously accepted. However, Geoffrey Robertson probably identified most of them, as author of a commission of inquiry into the council in 1986. He listed as its major shortcomings the following: delays in adjudication; procedural obstacles; lack of investigatory facilities; no monitoring of the press to see if they complied with rulings; lack of space given by papers to publish adjudications; and too many members on council, many of whom were ill-prepared for adjudication. See G. Robertson, 'The Watchdog That's a Poodle,' *UK Press Gazette*, 28 April 1986, 13. Ironically, one zealot, Bob Borzello, can take some of the responsibility for killing off the British Press Council. Borzello filed 220 complaints to the council regarding alleged racism or sexism between 1984 and 1990, thus helping to bring the whole mechanism to a halt. The new Press Complaints Commission will not allow third-party complaints, such as his. See M. Brown, 'Press Complaints Body Will Run Readers' Hotline,' *Independent*, 17 October 1990.

70 A. Radolf, 'National News Council Folds,' *Editor and Publisher*, 31 March 1984, 9, 28-9. For a discussion of the US experience, see D. Cassady, 'Press Councils – Why Journalists Won't Cooperate,' *Newspaper Research Journal*, Summer 1984, 19-25. For a history of the National News Council, see P. Brogan, *Spiked: The Short Life and Death of the National News Council* (New York: Priority Press 1985).

71 Typical in the Canadian context, for instance, is lawyer Robert Martin's article, 'Press Councils: Watchdogs with No Bite,' CAJ *Bulletin*, March 1986, 30.

72 Ibid., 30.

73 In a private telephone conversation with this writer.

74 The British Press Council was created by the British dailies after threats by the British government to legislate controls. When it ultimately folded in 1990, it was immediately replaced by the Press Complaints Commission, again to stave off threats of government intervention. Similar threats in the province of Manitoba provoked the press to start a council there. As Arthur Siegel neatly put it: 'The media as watchdog of government is

faced with the dilemma of government as watchdog of the media.' See Siegel, *Politics and the Media in Canada*, 234.

75 Bill Morgan, who heads the CBC's Office of Journalism Policy and Practices, is a sort of broadcast ombudsperson. He has described his relationship: 'The idea is that there will be someone who reports to the president and Board of Directors ... who has no affiliation with the programming line.' See his speech to the Canadian Communications Association, 2 June 1990.

76 See Brennan, 'Slow Progress for Watchdogs,' *UK Press Gazette*, 28 April 1986, iv-v.

77 Canada, *Report* [Kent Commission], 151.

78 I.W. Hill, 'Seib Is His Name: News Is His Game,' *Editor and Publisher*, 18 January 1975, 44.

79 Balfour speaking at a CMEC annual conference in St. Catharine's, ON, June 1988.

80 C. Balfour, 'Ombudsmen Do More than "Bird-Dog" Writers,' speech to the Canadian Daily Newspaper Publishers Association, reprinted in *Press Review*, Fall 1987, 24.

Chapter 17: Codes of Conduct

1 The literature on codes of journalism ethics is scarce, though there has been an increase since the inception of the *Journal of Mass Media Ethics* in the US in 1985. For a world overview, see the UNESCO survey by Clement Jones, *Mass Media Codes of Ethics and Councils* (Paris: UNESCO 1980), now seriously dated. Of special interest are Clifford Christians, 'Enforcing Media Codes,' *Journal of Mass Media Ethics* 1 (1985):14-21 and K. Schneider and M. Gunther, 'Those Newsroom Ethics Codes,' *Columbia Journalism Review*, July/August 1985, 55-7. See also the analysis of two surveys, D. Anderson, 'How Managing Editors View and Deal with Ethical Issues,' *Journalism Quarterly* 64, no. 2 (1987):341-5 and D. Pritchard and M.P. Morgan, 'Impact of Ethics Codes on Judgments by Journalists,' *Journalism Quarterly* 66, no. 4 (1989):934-41. Many codes are cited throughout the discussion. For a broadside attack on codes, see J.C. Merrill and S.J. Odell, *Philosophy and Journalism* (New York: Longman 1983), Chapter 6 and J. Black and R.D. Barney, 'The Case Against Mass Media Codes of Ethics,' *Journal of Mass Media Ethics* 1 (1985-6):25-36.

2 Christians, 'Enforcing Media Codes,' 15.

3 Ibid., 16.

4 Ibid., 17.

5 These distinctions are vital. But Christians misses one point. He concludes that codes are a peer tool only, and insists that people commit an error in logic if they believe that the existence of press councils will deter governments from interfering with media. But surely it does not matter if the belief is erroneous, so long as government believes it too? Similarly, he notes that it is an error of logic to argue that the existence of codes will improve media credibility. But, likewise, surely it does not matter, so long as the public shares the same belief?

6 Ibid., 16.

7 The original aphorism, source unknown, was developed to show the idiocy of bureaucracy run wild, contrasting the brilliant brevity of the Lord's Prayer and the Gettysburg Address with the outrageous prolixity of the ECM duck egg rules. I have substituted the Ten Commandments because they more closely parallel a code of ethics, but purists will note that the length of the Ten Commandments is debatable, as there are two versions (Deuteronomy 5 and Exodus 20) and they include some asides. My '320 words' refers to the entire statement contained in Exodus 13:2-17 inclusive. In the Anglican liturgy, for instance, this is very much abbreviated.

8 Canada, 'Canadian Charter of Rights and Freedoms,' *Constitution Act* (Ottawa: Supply & Services 1982), part 1, clauses 1 and 2.

9 Eugene Goodwin summarizes some of the anti-code arguments in *Groping for Ethics in Journalism* (Ames, IA: Iowa State University Press 1983), 5-7. Clifford Christians quotes some examples, dismissing them as 'logically fallacious.' See 'Enforcing Media Codes,' *Journal of Mass Media Ethics* 1 (1985):18.

10 Cited in Black and Barney, 'The Case Against Mass Media Codes of Ethics,' 27.

11 See, for instance, Prof. Douglas Anderson's 1985 survey in which nearly a quarter of the ninety-six responding US managing editors said they had fired someone for unethical conduct. See 'How Managing Editors View and Deal with Ethical Issues,' *Journalism Quarterly* 64 (1987):341-5.

12 The survey is fully reported below. However, to the question: 'Has anybody been disciplined in your newsroom in the last five years for an ethical error?' one-quarter of the respondents (of sixty newsrooms) said yes.

13 A negative enforcement may also be in effect in some environments. There seems little doubt that some of the most unethical material appearing in British tabloids, such as chequebook journalism, results from – or is at least facilitated by – peer and management pressure to beat the competition – to get the story at any cost.

14 Of the few who described incidents in the survey of Canadian newsrooms for this research, six said reprimands were issued, two said offenders were suspended from duty, and two reported firings.

15 J.C. Merrill and S.J. Odell, *Philosophy and Journalism* (New York: Longman 1983).

16 Ibid., 137-45; J.C. Merrill, *Existential Journalism* (New York: Hastings House 1977), 129-32.

17 'The codes of national associations cannot be as practical, itemized, and comprehensive. John Merrill ... legitimately scourges them.' See Christians, 'Enforcing Media Codes,' 19. Merrill does not beat about the bush, calling the SPJ code 'fuzzy and generalized ... high-sounding rhetoric.' See Merrill, *Existential*

Journalism, 132. But his thesis – that the ideal journalist is an existentialist (one who does not give in to pressures, does not conform, and is committed to independence, freedom, and truth) – will not suit every newsworker.

18 This was confirmed in 1987, when the SPJ agonized over its right to censure member-journalists for unethical activity and eventually voted to drop that power from its constitution. For a full discussion, see M. Fitzgerald, 'Self-Censure Clause Dropped,' *Editor and Publisher*, 21 November 1987, 9, 43. For a parallel incident, see the defeat of similar powers by the American Society of Newspaper Editors. See J.L. Hulteng, *The Messenger's Motives: Ethical Problems of the News Media*, 2nd ed. (Englewood Cliffs, NJ: Prentice-Hall 1985), 206.

19 The survey design was strongly influenced by Douglas Anderson. However, Anderson addressed only daily managing editors, and also requested recipients to respond to a series of ethical scenarios. The present writer felt this both limited the scope and deterred the respondents. The purpose here, then, was threefold: to establish whether codes were widespread in larger Canadian newsrooms, to obtain copies of codes, and to ascertain how ethical dilemmas were currently resolved.

20 Donald M. Gillmor, Silha Professor of Media Ethics and Law at the University of Minnesota, puts it well: 'I would argue that individuals working in concert, the employees of an editorial department or a newsroom, those persons who gather and present the news, should develop their own ethical boundaries through experience, discourse and dialogue as a substitute for the ethics of hierarchy. Authority figures, whether they be editors or publishers, should never be the only source of ethical direction. This is not to say that a chief editor could not coordinate such an ethical process or be involved in it. Readers and other members of the public could be consulted periodically, but they cannot be responsible or accountable for day-to-day ethical decisions.' See D.M. Gillmor, 'Broken Promises: Where Law and Ethics Met,' *Social Responsibility: Business, Journalism, Law, Medicine* 19 (1993):38-9.

21 Schneider and Gunther report: 'Publishers argue that they must get involved in their communities to protect their investment in their newspapers.' They conclude that 'publishers are unlikely to submit themselves to codes barring outside business, civic, or political interests.' See 'Those Newsroom Ethics Codes,' 57.

22 The 1978 *Toronto Sun* conflict incident, described in Chapter 4, illustrates this. To recap, the *Sun* had been editorializing against free passes being used by Air Canada staff; airline staff then spotted the newspaper publisher's wife travelling to Europe on a free first-class ticket worth $1,500. An airline employee was quoted as describing this as 'hypocritical.' See 'Air Canada Staff Feels *Sun* Hypocritical about Passes,' *Globe and Mail*, 14 January 1978. At the time, the *Toronto Sun* evidently lacked a policy on the issue, and the editor-in-chief was quoted as criticizing the acceptance of free passes. A company-wide policy should eliminate such

internal contradictions.

23 UNESCO, *Many Voices, One World*, report of the International Commission for the Study of Communication Problems (Paris: UNESCO 1980), 242.

24 J.C. Quinn and E.C. Patterson, 'Why Your Paper Should/Should Not Have a Written Code of Ethics,' ASNE *Bulletin*, October 1984, 13.

25 The *Western Producer* is published in Saskatoon, SK. It is a substantial, tabloid-sized weekly, circulating throughout the Canadian prairies, and read avidly by a loyal farming audience. Although tied to the grain producers cooperative, its newsroom (consisting of some nine writers and editors and led by its uncompromising editor, Garry Fairbairn) maintains a laudable distance from its parent company.

26 'Western Producer Editorial Code of Ethics,' *Western Producer*, 5 April 1990, 7.

27 The nature of punishments is beyond the scope of this study. However, it is clear that the public deserves to be informed and deserves an apology. It is also vitally important to flag the offending article in the morgue to prevent the embarrassment of it turning up again in the paper, perhaps in a year-end review or a 'Ten Years Ago' column.

28 'One newsroom' in this case includes the network of newsrooms of the CBC, a series of homogeneous newsrooms with some central control and one journalistic policy guiding all of them.

29 Merrill, *Existential Journalism*, 66.

30 It is difficult to accept Merrill's assumption that this total individualism is, indeed, the paradise he proclaims. It could equally be seen as an awful anarchy, with every journalist having unique values – one believing, for instance, that privacy of the individual is paramount, while another maintains the welfare of the community is over-riding. Who arbitrates? Which values should prevail?

31 Two editors were quoted in Chapter 1 as believing codes are 'written in our hearts.'

Chapter 18: Conclusion

1 For instance, John Merrill lists a code of ethics as a prerequisite of a profession. See J.C. Merrill and S.J. Odell, *Philosophy and Journalism* (New York: Longman 1983), 119. See also D. Taras, *The Newsmakers* (Scarborough, ON: Nelson Canada 1990), 53 and P. Desbarats, *Guide to Canadian News Media* (Toronto: Harcourt Brace Jovanovich), 80.

2 See, for instance, J. Olen, *Ethics in Journalism* (Englewood Cliffs, NJ: Simon & Schuster 1988), 29-31; K. Whitehorn, 'Ethics and the Media,' Leggett Lecture, University of Surrey, Guildford, UK, 9 November 1988, 4; Merrill and Odell, *Philosophy and Journalism*, 119-121; H.E. Goodwin, *Groping for Ethics in Journalism* (Ames, IA: Iowa State University Press 1983), 50-5. For a Canadian perspective, see Desbarats, *Guide to Canadian News Media*, 80; Taras, *The Newsmakers*, 53; T. Kent, 'We Told

You So ,' *Content*, July/August 1990, 12-13; Canada, Special Senate Committee on Mass Media, *Report* [Davey Report], vol. 3 (Ottawa: Queen's Printer 1970), 192.

3 See, for instance, Roy Copperud's columns in *Editor and Publisher*, especially 'Professionally Speaking,' 19 March 1988, where he spurns the description of journalism as a 'trade' and hopes a journalist 'surely matches the competence of a teacher.' Is it a trade, a calling, a skill, or a craft? Some practitioners may feel uncomfortable with a label such as trade, equating their skill with electricians and carpenters. But that discomfort only reflects their own insecurity. However, it's not an open-and-shut issue even for the 'established' professions. For instance, Don Buckingham, examining professionalism amongst lawyers, asks, 'Is law a business or a profession?' See D. Buckingham, 'Professionalism or Profit: Re-Examining Legal Ethics,' *Westminster Affairs* 6, no. 1 (1993):3.

4 L. Hodges, 'The Journalist and Professionalism,' *Journal of Mass Media Ethics* 1 (1986):36.

5 Ibid., 34.

6 Ibid., 36.

7 Flexner wrote, 'Is Social Work a Profession?' in *School and Society*, 26 June 1915. Cited in Hodges, 'The Journalist and Professionalism,' passim.

8 Buckingham, 'Professionalism or Profit,' 3.

9 To be fair, Buckingham adds that a profession is 'usually limited in number and is entrusted, by the public, to obtain knowledge and dispense it according to standards of ethical conduct which are more onerous than those of society generally.' He also adds that 'self-governance' is an attribute of many professions. Most of this simply doesn't fit journalism. Must the definition change – or journalism? See 'Professionalism or Profit.'

10 Merrill and Odell, *Philosophy and Journalism*, 191-20.

11 Ibid., 121.

12 Ibid.

13 The *Concise Oxford Dictionary*, 8th edition, offers, as its primary definition, 'A vocation or calling, esp. one that involves some branch of advanced learning or science (e.g. the medical profession).' Inevitably, this inspires parallels with medicine and law. Gene Goodwin introduces an 'official' definition, citing the US National Labor Relations Act, which states (to paraphrase) that a professional employee is one who is engaged in work predominantly intellectual and varied in character, involving discretion and judgment, difficult to standardize in terms of time and requiring specialized advanced intellectual study as opposed to a general academic education or apprenticeship. This comes a lot closer to the nature of journalism. But the NLRB has ruled that for *its* purposes, journalism is *not* a profession. See Goodwin, *Groping for Ethics in Journalism*, 50.

14 Olen, *Ethics in Journalism*, 30.

15 Perhaps the Canadian Association of Journalists is immune to such pettiness. However, members spent years debating chang-ing the name of the group from the Centre for Investigative Journalism, as if it seriously mattered, and this was followed by a concerted push to drive membership 'over the "magic 1,000" level.' See L. McMahen, 'What's in a Name?' *Content*, July/August 1990, 17. Where's the magic? Why does it matter? The North American journalists' union, the Newspaper Guild, has consistently opposed journalism being described as a profession, not on philosophical grounds, but because it might weaken collective bargaining or members might not get paid overtime. See Goodwin, *Groping for Ethics in Journalism*, 51. And the British equivalent, the National Union of Journalists, has raised a lot of hackles by its political activism. In 1991, during the Gulf War, the national executive voted to condemn military intervention in the Gulf, and, in 1986, they sent a telegram to Libya condemning the US bombing of Tripoli. See 'NUJ Exec Backs Peace Movement,' *UK Press Gazette*, 11 February 1991. How can union members report credibly when 'they' have recorded such opinions? (Contrast Ann Medina's assertion, 'It isn't our job to stir up protest against what we feel is wrong.' A. Medina, 'Fuddy Duddy Journalism,' eighth Minifie Lecture, University of Regina, 7 March 1988, 11.

16 To focus debate, it might be helpful to construct a hypothetical 'Act Respecting the Profession of Journalism,' akin to laws setting up medical and legal associations. This act might: (a) empower senior journalists to form a society to which all journalists must belong in order to practise; (b) prescribe qualifications for applicants; (c) prescribe training and examinations for applicants; (d) conduct disciplinary proceedings with regard to the conduct of members; and (e) fine or strike members from the roll, as deemed necessary. Many admirable journalists now practising might be ineligible to work, if such a law were passed.

17 Whitehorn, 'Ethics and the Media,' 4.

18 Hutchison became a reporter for the *Victoria Times* in 1918 and continued writing a trenchant editorial-page column once a week for the *Vancouver Sun*, into his 90s. His sixteenth and final book appeared in 1991.

19 Kent, 'We Told You So,' 13.

20 Taras, *The Newsmakers*, 53.

21 'Everyone has ... freedom of ... expression, including freedom of the press and other media of communication.' Canada, 'Canadian Charter of Rights and Freedoms,' *Constitution Act* (Ottawa: Supply & Services 1982), sec. 2.

22 Cited in V. Sears, 'Politicians Are Losing Privacy,' *Toronto Star*, 27 September 1987, B1.

23 Chronologically, the printing press was invented before freedom of the press was enunciated. William Caxton brought the first press to Britain in 1476. Richard III's parliament of 1484 passed an act controlling foreign imports but expressly excluding publications, writers, and printers. For a full discussion, see F. Siebert, *Freedom of the Press in England* (Urbana: University of Illinois Press 1965) and Nick Russell, 'Press Freedom: Born on a Vellum

Scroll,' unpublished paper.

24 Canada, *Report* [Davey Report].

25 Canada, *Report of the Royal Commission on Newspapers* ['Kent Commission'] (Ottawa: Queen's Printer 1981), 217.

26 CDNPA, *Statement of Principles*, Appendix 1, ss. 2, 3.

27 UNESCO, *Many Voices, One World*, report of the International Commission for the Study of Communication Problems (Paris: UNESCO 1980), 233.

28 Canada, *Report of the Royal Commission on Newspapers* ['Kent Commission'], 234.

29 Merrill and Odell, *Philosophy and Journalism*, 157.

30 See for instance, a little filler in the *Press Review*, 'It seems freedom of the press does not extend itself to university engineering students. Bowing to pressure, the engineering society at the University of Waterloo has agreed to stop publishing a controversial tabloid which the school's vice-president labelled sexist, racist and obscene.' *Press Review*, June 1983.

31 J.L. Hulteng, *Playing It Straight: A Practical Discussion of the Ethical Principles of the American Society of Newspaper Editors* (Chester, CT: Globe Pequot Press 1981), 17. The press doth protest too much. Stu Keate, for instance, bemoaned the Davey Commission survey finding that 51% of respondents said newspapers should be subject to some form of control. But if one asks, 'Should the media be free to publish whatever they want, or should there be some sort of control?' most lay-people will quickly answer, 'Control,' as the implied alternative is unbridled yellow journalism. It is surprising that it was only 51%. Kent reported that a 1978 study in Canada showed 'a small number of persons' thought the press should have complete freedom; half the respondents thought the media should have limited freedom; and 20% favoured media rules to be drawn up by an external agency. In other words, more than 70% favoured press controls. See Canada, *Report of the Royal Commission on Newspapers* [Kent Commission], 34.

Media people sometimes substitute the word 'censorship' for 'control,' suggesting that any form of control is an outrage. See N. Fillmore, quoted by Desbarats, *Guide to Canadian News Media*, 100. Ed Lambeth cites an example of a student reporter, so anxious to protect press freedom, that when a computer scientist asked to check a story for accuracy after being interviewed, he refused, and hence ran a story containing a horrendous error. See E. Lambeth, *Committed Journalism: An Ethic for the Profession* (Bloomington, IN: Indiana University Press 1986, 35. There is also Patrick O'Callaghan's furious attack on proposals to limit chain newspaper ownership as the ultimate threat to democracy. See 'Great Newspaper Debate: Publisher, Commissioner Tangle over Press Bill,' *Calgary Herald*, 6 October 1983, A5, though most people would agree that the trend itself is a threat to democracy.

32 At a journalism ethics workshop given at the Poynter Institute for Media Studies in St. Petersburg, FL, in 1991. Details taken from Clark's unpublished paper: 'Red Light/Green Light: A New Paradigm for Journalism Ethics.'

33 Black and Barney, 'Journalism Ethics Since Janet Cooke,' *Newspaper Research Journal*, Fall 1992/Winter 1993, 2-16.

34 Clark, 'Red Light/Green Light.'

35 Ibid., 29.

36 Such a claim is, of course, difficult to document. However, the International Press Institute issues an annual review of press freedom around the world, and Canada regularly rates very high. John Merrill, in rating world newspapers, consistently gives Canada very high marks. See Merrill, *Global Journalism* (New York: Longman 1983), passim.

37 Canada, *Report* [Davey Report], vol. 3, 192.

38 Desbarats, *Guide to Canadian News Media*, 80. The applause, however, is far from universal. Conrad Black, the Canadian newspaper tycoon, apparently takes great pleasure in belittling journalists – his employees – as 'effete lazy undisciplined dilettantes,' see B. Zwicker and D. McDonald, eds., *The News: Inside the Canadian Media* (Ottawa: Deneau 1982), 244, and as 'ignorant, lazy, opinionated, intellectually dishonest and inadequately supervised,' see C. Black, 'A Black View of the Press,' *Carleton Journalism Review* 2, no. 4 (1979/80):11. Perhaps, now that he owns more than 200 newspapers, his view has changed, but his 1993 autobiography gave no hint of it.

39 Canada, *Report of the Royal Commission on Newspapers* ['Kent Commission'], 234.

40 O'Callaghan and Kent debate, see 'Great Newspaper Debate,' and 'We Told You So,' respectively.

Bibliography

Adler, R. *A Day in the Life of the New York Times*. New York: Lippincott 1971

Alexander, S. 'Read All About It: Star Man Finds Gerda Munsinger.' In *The News: Inside the Canadian Media*, ed. B. Zwicker and D. McDonald. Ottawa: Deneau 1982

Anderson, D. (1987). 'How Managing Editors View and Deal with Ethical Issues.' *Journalism Quarterly* 64 (1987):341-5

Arvidson, C. 'FBI Intrigue Surrounds a Southam Correspondent.' Reprinted from *Columbia Journalism Review* in *Edmonton Journal*, 17 September 1983

Atlantic Press Council. *Annual Report, 1993*. Truro, NS: APC 1993

Bain, G. 'The Debate over Feathering Nests.' *Maclean's*, 20 January 1986, 46

Balfour, C. 'One Thousand Wounds in the Body Politic.' *Report on Business Magazine*, November 1986, 25-9

Barnett, N. 'Hartford's Car Wars.' *Columbia Journalism Review*, September 1985, 18-19

Bastian, G. *Editing the Day's News*. London: Library Press 1923

Beck, J.M. *Joseph Howe*. Montreal and Kingston: McGill-Queen's University Press 1982

Bell, D. 'Parrot Reformed but Hates Everyone.' In *CP Stories of the Year, 1972*. Toronto: Canadian Press 1972, 18-20

Beloff, N. 'This Above All.' In *Questioning Media Ethics*, ed. B. Rubin. New York: Praeger 1978

Bevins, A. 'The Crippling of the Scribes.' *British Journalism Review* 1 (1990):13-17

Bindman, S. 'Conflict of Interest and the Goldhawk Case.' *CAJ Bulletin*, Spring 1991, 13

Black, C. 'A Black View of the Press.' *Carleton Journalism Review* 2 (1979/80):10-12

Black, E. *Politics and the News*. Toronto: Butterworths 1982

Black, J. and R.D. Barney. 'The Case Against Mass Media Codes of Ethics.' *Journal of Mass Media Ethics* 1 (1985/6):25-36

Boswell, R. 'Oka: Crisis in Journalism.' *Content*, January/February 1991, 16-17

Boynton, P.R. and D. Boynton. *Sweepers in the Corridors of Power: Canadian Broadcast Journalism*. Toronto: Butterworths 1986

Braun, P. 'Deception in Journalism.' *Journal of Mass Media Ethics* 3 (1988):77-83

Briggs, A. *History of Broadcasting in the United Kingdom*. London: Oxford University Press 1970

British Columbia Press Council. *Annual Report*. Vancouver: BC Press Council 1989

Brogan, P. *Spiked: The Short Life and Death of the National News Council*. New York: Priority Press 1985

Brown, J.E. 'News Photographs and the Pornography of Grief.' *Journal of Mass Media Ethics* 2 (1987):75-81

Bruning, F. 'Why People Distrust the Press.' *Maclean's*, 16 January 1984, 9

Buckie, C. 'Dead Girl's Brother Speaks Out.' *CIJ Bulletin*, Spring 1990, 4

Buckingham, D. 'Professionalism or Profit: Re-Examining Legal Ethics.' *Westminster Affairs* 6 (1993):1-3

Calamai, P. 'Discrepancies in News Quotes from the Colin Thatcher Trial.' In *Trials and Tribulations*, ed. N. Russell. Monograph no. 1, School of Journalism, University of Regina, Regina, SK, 1986

Cameron, J. *Cameron in The Guardian, 1974-1984*. London: Grafton 1987

Canada. Special Senate Committee on Mass Media. *Report* [Davey Report]. 3 vols. Ottawa: Queen's Printer 1970

—. *Report of the Royal Commission on Newspapers* [Kent Commission]. Ottawa: Queen's Printer 1981

Canada. *Broadcasting Act*. Ottawa: Supply and Services 1991

Canadian Broadcast Standards Council. *Code of Ethics*. Ottawa: CBSC 1988

Canadian Broadcasting Corporation. *Journalistic Policy.* Montreal: CBC Enterprises 1988

—. *Journalistic Standards and Practices.* Toronto: CBC Enterprises 1993

Canadian Press. Canadian Press *Stylebook*, ed. P. Buckley. Toronto: Canadian Press 1993

Canadian Radio-Television and Telecommunications Commission. *Guidelines for Open Line Programs.* Ottawa: CRTC 1988

Cantley, B. 'Photo of Victim Provoked Strong Reader Reaction.' *CDNPA Newsletter*, December 1989, 1

Cassady, D. 'Press Councils – Why Journalists Won't Cooperate.' *Newspaper Research Journal*, Summer 1984, 19-25

CFPL-TV. *CFPL News Department Policy*, ed. J. MacDonald. London, ON: CFPL-TV 1988

Chibnall, S. *Law-and-Order News.* London: Tavistock 1977

Christians, C. 'Enforcing Media Codes.' *Journal of Mass Media Ethics* 1 (1985):14-21

Christians, C., K.B. Rotzoll, and M. Fackler. *Media Ethics: Cases and Moral Reasoning.* White Plains, NY: Longman 1983

Clark, C. 'Tainted Triumphs: The Great Awards Debate.' *Ryerson Review of Journalism*, Spring 1989, 31-6

Clark, R. 'Sore Points.' *Washington Journalism Review*, February 1985, 51

Clemence, V. 'Plagiarism ... the Cancer that Destroys the Very Soul of Journalism.' *Content*, January/February 1990, 18-19

Clift, E. 'How the White House Keeps Reporters in Their Place.' *Washington Journalism Review*, June 1986, 9

Cocking, C. *Following the Leaders: A Media Watcher's Diary of Campaign '79.* Toronto: Doubleday 1980

Cohen, E.D., ed. *Philosophical Issues in Journalism.* New York: Oxford University Press 1992

Creery, T. 'More State Intrusion?' *Content*, January/February 1990, 14-15

Crouse, T. *The Boys on the Bus.* New York: Ballantine 1974

Curtis, C. 'The Incredible Shrinking Newscast.' *Ryerson Review of Journalism*, Spring 1988, 6-7

Curtis, S. 'Ad Absurdum.' *Ryerson Review of Journalism*, Summer 1993, 36

Davey, K. 'Getting the Media We Deserve.' *Content*, July/August 1990, 13-14

Dempsey, H. *The Wit and Wisdom of Bob Edwards.* Edmonton: Hurtig 1976

Dempson, P. *Assignment Ottawa: Seventeen Years in the Press Gallery.* Don Mills, ON: General Publishing 1968

Dennis, E. *Reshaping the Media.* Newbury Park, CA: Sage 1989

Dennis, E. and J.C. Merrill. *Media Debates: Issues in Mass Communication.* White Plains, NY: Longman 1991

Desbarats, Peter. *Guide to Canadian News Media.* Toronto: Harcourt Brace Jovanovich 1990

Douris, L. 'Upwardly Immobile.' *Ryerson Review of Journalism*, Spring 1988, 40-3

Drainie, B. 'Media Integrity.' *Content*, September/October 1989, 18-19

Dutton, D. 'When Seduction Goes Too Far.' *Western Report*, 12 October 1987, 37

Elliott, D., ed. *Responsible Journalism.* Beverley Hills: Sage 1986

Ephron, N. *Scribble, Scribble: Notes on the Media.* New York: Alfred A. Knopf 1978

Ericson, R.V., P.M. Baranek, and J.B. Chan. *Negotiating Control: A Study of News Sources.* Toronto: University of Toronto Press 1989

—. *Visualizing Deviance: A Study of News Organization.* Toronto: University of Toronto Press 1987

Evans, W. 'Foul Language Still Put to Test in Newsrooms.' In *Report of Writing and Editing Committee.* New York: Associated Press Managing Editors 1984

Fetherling, D. *The Rise of the Canadian Newspaper.* Toronto: Oxford University Press 1990

Fishman, M. *Manufacturing the News.* Austin, TX: University of Texas Press 1980

Forsyth, J. 'I've Got You Taped.' *British Journalism Review* 1 (1990):30-4

Fox, K. 'Asleep at the Wheel.' *Content*, September/October 1990, 20-1

Franklin, E. 'Minding Your Manners.' *Washington Journalism Review*, December 1986, 30-4

Frum, L., ed. *The Newsmakers: Behind the Camera with Canada's Top TV Journalists.* Toronto: Key Porter 1990

Galician, M-L. and N.D. Vestre. 'Effects of "Good News" and "Bad News" on Newscast Image and Community Image.' *Journalism Quarterly* 64 (1987):399-405, 525

Gans, H. *Deciding What's News: A Study of CBS Evening News, NBC Nightly News, Newsweek, and Time.* New York: Vintage 1980

Gardos, A. 'On the House.' *Ryerson Review of Journalism*, Spring 1989, 26-9

Gerald, J.E. 'Press Councils: Help or Hindrance?' *Nieman Reports*, Summer 1983, 18-21

Gillespie, I. 'The Flip Side of Freebies.' *Ryerson Review of Journalism*, Spring 1988, 20-1

Gillmor, D.M. 'Broken Promises: Where Law and Ethics Met.' *Social Responsibility: Business, Journalism, Law, Medicine*, ed. L.W. Hodges 19 (1993):24-39

Glasser, T.L. 'On the Morality of Secretly Taped Interviews.' *Nieman Reports*, Spring 1985, 17-20

Globe and Mail Style Book, ed. E.C. Phelan. Toronto: Globe and Mail 1981

—, ed. J.A. McFarlane and W. Clements. Toronto: Globe and Mail 1990

Goodwin, H.E. *Groping for Ethics in Journalism*. Ames, IA: Iowa State University Press 1983

Griffin, L. 'Strictly by the Book.' *Ryerson Review of Journalism*, Spring 1989, 42-6

Griffith, T. 'Why Readers Mistrust Newspapers.' *Time*, 9 May 1983, 60.

Gross, L., J.S. Katz, and J. Ruby, eds. *Image Ethics: The Moral Rights of Subjects in Photographs, Film and Television*. Oxford: Oxford University Press 1988

Haggart, R. 'Problems of Printing Broadcasting.' *Content*, September/October 1988, 19-24

Hargreaves, T. 'The Fight to Control Election News.' *Maclean's*, 3 September 1984, 42

Harris, R. *Gotcha! The Media, the Government and the Falklands Crisis*. London: Faber 1983

Hatfield, F.A. 'Publishing Names of Criminals Important Task for Newspapers.' *CCNA Publisher*, March 1992, 6

Hausman, C. *Crisis of Conscience: Perspectives on Journalism Ethics*. New York: Harper Collins 1992

Hayakawa, S.I. *Language in Thought and Action*. New York: Harcourt, Brace 1949

Hayes, D. *Power and Influence: The Globe and Mail and the News Revolution*. Toronto: Key Porter 1992

Heine, W.C. *Journalism Ethics: A Case Book*. London, ON: University of Western Ontario

Heinrich, J. 'Media Solidarity?' *Content*, September/October 1990, 14

Henderson, M. 'A Tale of Three Newspapers.' *Content*, July/August 1990, 10

Hodges, L. 'To Deceive or Not to Deceive.' *Quill*, December 1981, 9

—. 'The Journalist and Professionalism.' *Journal of Mass Media Ethics* 1 (1986):32-6

Hohenberg, J. *The News Media: A Journalist Looks At His Profession*. New York: Holt, Rinehart & Winston 1968

—. *The Professional Journalist: A Guide to the Practices and Principles of the News Media*. New York: Holt, Rinehart & Winston 1983

Hoyt, M. 'When The Walls Come Tumbling Down.' *Columbia Journalism Review*, March/April 1990, 35-8

Hulteng, J.L. *Playing It Straight: A Practical Discussion of the Ethical Principles of the American Society of Newspaper Editors*. Chester, CT: Globe Pequot Press 1981

—. *The Messenger's Motives: Ethical Problems of the News Media*. 2nd ed. Englewood Cliffs, NJ: Prentice-Hall 1985

Hutchinson, H. 'Images, Self-Images and the Long String.' In *The Quarrymen of History: Canadian Journalists Examine Their Profession*, ed. N. Russell. Monograph no. 1, School of Journalism, University of Regina, Regina, SK, 1987

Jaben, J. and D. Hill. 'The Suicide Syndrome.' *Washington Journalism Review*, July 1986, 10-11

Jarzab, T. 'Freebies: A Continuing Journalism Problem.' *Carleton Journalism Review*, Winter 1980, 6-10.

Jefferson, T. *Writings*. New York: Library of America 1984

Johnston, D. 'The Anonymous-Source Syndrome.' *Columbia Journalism Review*, November/December 1987, 54-5

Jones, C. *Mass Media Codes of Ethics and Councils*. Paris: UNESCO 1980

Keate, S. *Paper Boy: The Memoirs of Stuart Keate*. Toronto: Clarke Irwin 1980

Kelly, M. 'Reporters Keep an AIDS Secret.' *Washington Journalism Review*, September 1989, 18

Kent, T. 'We Told You So ...' *Content*, July/August 1990, 12-13

Kessel, J. and J. Heinrich. 'Electronic News Releases.' *Content*, November/December 1988, 5

Kesterton, W.H. *A History of Journalism in Canada*. Toronto: McClelland & Stewart 1967

Kettle, J. 'Protecting Sources.' *Content*, September 1978, 16

Kilgour, D. 'No Small Affair.' *Ryerson Review of Journalism*, Spring 1990, 8-9

King, L. 'Press Gallery Airs Money / Ethics Issue.' *Content*, May/June 1990, 3-4

Klaidman, S. and T.L. Beauchamp. *The Virtuous Journalist*. New York: Oxford University Press 1987

Knightley, P. *The First Casualty: From the Crimea to Vietnam*. Rev. ed. London: Quartet Books 1982

Kohlberg, L. 'A Current Statement on Some Theoretical Issues.' In *Lawrence Kohlberg: Consensus and Controversy*, ed. Sohan and Celia Modgil. Philadelphia: Falmer 1986

Lakshman, C. 'New Editor Bans Anonymous Sources.' *Content*, January/February 1990, 5-6

Lamar, J.V. 'The View from 30,000 Ft.' *Time*, 17 September 1984, 44

Lambeth, E. *Committed Journalism: An Ethic for the Profession*. Bloomington, IN: Indiana University Press 1986

Laver, R. 'The Parties Concoct the "Line" In Order To Get the "Sound Bite."' *Maclean's*, 31 October 1988, 18-19

Law, C. 'The Shield Law Controversy.' *Carleton Journalism Review*, Winter 1977, 12-14

Leslie, J. 'The Anonymous Source.' *Washington Journalism Review*, September 1986, 33-5

Levy, H. 'What Should We Do When the Cops Arrive?' *Content*, April 1979, 35-9

Lewis, C. 'State Department Guidelines Spell Out Who May Say What.' ASNE *Bulletin*, April 1988, 5

Lorimer, R. and J. McNulty. *Mass Communications in Canada*. Toronto: McClelland & Stewart 1987

Lorimer, R. and D. Wilson. *Communication Canada: Issues in Broadcasting and New Technologies*. Toronto: Kagan and Woo 1988

Lustig, R. 'Promises Are No Longer Enough.' *British Journalism*

Review 1 (1990):44-8

Lynch, C. *You Can't Print That!* Edmonton: Hurtig 1983

—. 'How Celebrity Corrupts Journalists, and Other Tall Tales.' In *The Quarrymen of History*, ed. N. Russell. Monograph no. 2, School of Journalism, University of Regina, Regina, SK, 1987

McAdams, K.C. 'Non-Monetary Conflicts of Interest for Newspaper Journalists.' *Journalism Quarterly* 63 (Winter 1987):700-27

MacDougall, C. *Hoaxes.* New York: Macmillan 1958

—. *News Pictures Fit to Print ... Or Are They?* Stillwater, OK: Journalistic Services 1971

McGillivray, D. 'Plagiarism: Phrase Filch or Mental Slip.' CIJ *Bulletin*, Spring 1989, 29-30

McGran, K. 'Now You See It, Now You Don't: The Ethics of Image Processing.' *Ryerson Review of Journalism*, Spring 1987, 4-5

McMahen, L. 'What's in a Name?' *Content*, July/August 1990, 15-17

MacMillan, D. 'Playing Confucius.' *Content*, March/April 1986, 13-14

Macquarrie, J. *Three Issues in Ethics.* Philadelphia: Westminster Press 1970

Makin, K. 'The Long Arm of the Media: A Critical Cause and Effect.' *Ryerson Review of Journalism*, Spring 1989, 87-8

Marro, A. 'When the Government Tells Lies.' *Columbia Journalism Review*, March/April 1985, 29-41

Martin, R. 'Press Councils: Watchdogs with No Bite.' CAJ *Bulletin*, March 1986, 30

Maynard, R. 'Blitzing the Media.' *Report on Business*, June 1986, 70-4

Melman-Clement, D. 'Counterfeit Copy.' *Ryerson Review of Journalism*, Spring 1990, 56-60

Mercer, D., G. Mungham, and K. Williams, eds. *The Fog of War: The Media on the Battlefield.* London: Heinemann 1987

Merrill, J.C. *Existential Journalism.* New York: Hastings House 1977

—. *The Imperative of Freedom: A Philosophy of Journalistic Autonomy.* New York: Hastings House 1974

—. 'Good Reporting Can Be a Solution to Ethics Problem.' *Journalism Educator*, Autumn 1987, 27-9

—. 'Is Ethical Journalism Simply Objective Reporting?' *Journalism Quarterly* 62 (1985):391-3

Merrill, J.C. and S.J. Odell. *Philosophy and Journalism.* New York: Longman 1983

Miller, J. 'Rethinking Old Methods.' *Content*, September/October 1990, 23-5

Miller, M. and K. Swift. *The Handbook of Nonsexist Writing.* New York: Harper & Row 1988

Nash, K. *History on the Run: The Trenchcoat Memoirs of a Foreign Correspondent.* Toronto: McClelland & Stewart 1989

—. 'Cleopatra, Harlots and Glue.' In *The Quarrymen of History: Canadian Journalists Examine Their Profession*, ed. N. Russell. Monograph no. 2, School of Journalism, University of Regina, Regina, SK, 1987

National Union of Journalists. 'Code of Conduct.' In *Members'*

Handbook. London 1986

Naumetz, T. 'Breaking Campaign Camp.' *Content*, January/February 1989, 15-16

Neely, P. 'Correcting Mistakes: More Papers Willing to Admit Errors.' APME *Credibility Report*, 1984, 9-10

Negrine, R. *Politics and the Mass Media in Britain.* London: Routledge 1989

Newman, J. *The Journalist in Plato's Cave.* Cranbury, NJ: Associated University Presses 1989

Norris, A. 'Gazette Reporter Singled Out for Abuse.' *Content*, September/October 1990, 12-13

Norton, M. 'Ethics in Medicine and Law: Standards and Conflicts.' In *Lawyers' Ethics*, ed. A. Gerson. New Brunswick, NJ: Transaction Books 1980

O'Connor, C. 'Flaunting Its Feedback.' *Washington Journalism Review*, May 1985, 11

Olen, J. *Ethics in Journalism.* Englewood Cliffs, NJ: Simon & Schuster 1988

O'Neill, T. 'Have Laptop Will Travel.' *Content*, July/August 1990, 11

Ontario Press Council. *Annual Report.* Toronto: Ontario Press Council 1988

—. *The New To Name or Not to Name.* Ottawa: Ontario Press Council 1981

—. *Press Ethics and Freebies.* Ottawa: Ontario Press Council 1978

—. *Sexism and the Newspapers.* Ottawa: Ontario Press Council 1978

Osler, A.M. *News: The Evolution of Journalism in Canada.* Toronto: Copp Clark Pitman 1993

Ottawa Citizen. Ethics and Policies, staff manual. *Ottawa Citizen*, n.d.

Overbury, S. 'Sports News: Real Stuff or Just a Game?' *Content*, February 1979, 3

Palmer, N.D. 'Going After the Truth – in Disguise.' *Washington Journalism Review*, November 1987, 20-2

—. 'When Reporting Endangers a Life.' *Washington Journalism Review*, October 1986, 36-8

Partridge, J. 'Learning How to Compete.' *Content*, May/June 1990, 5

Patterson, P. and L. Wilkins. *Media Ethics: Issues and Cases.* Dubuque, IA: W.C. Brown 1991

Perigoe, R. 'The Media and Minorities.' *Content*, September/October 1990, 10-12

—. 'Shades of Grey.' *Content*, May/June 1990, 18-19

Poitras, J. 'A Helping Hand.' *Content*, May/June 1989, 29-30

Postman, N. *Amusing Ourselves to Death.* New York: Viking 1985

Prendergast, A. 'Mickey Mouse Journalism.' *Washington Journalism Review*, January/February 1987, 32-5

Priestland, G. *The Dilemmas of Journalism.* Guildford, UK: Lutterworth 1979

Pritchard, D. and M.P. Morgan. 'Impact of Ethics Codes on Judgments by Journalists: A Natural Experiment.' *Journalism Quarterly* 66 (1989):934-41

Quinn, J.C. and E.C. Patterson. 'Why Your Paper Should/Should Not Have a Written Code of Ethics.' ASNE *Bulletin*, October 1984, 12-13

Rada, S.E. 'Manipulating the Media: A Case Study of a Chicano Strike in Texas.' *Journalism Quarterly* 54 (1977):109-13

Rader, B. 'Food + Feed = Foolishness.' ASNE *Bulletin*, January 1973, 12-13

Radio-Television News Directors Association of Canada. *Code of Broadcast News Ethics*. Toronto: RTNDA 1986

Ramsey, D. and D.E. Shaps. *Journalism Ethics: Why Change?* Los Angeles: Foundation for American Communications 1986

Reaves, S. 'Ethics: Report Airs Editors' Debate on Principles.' *Electronic Times*, 9 October 1989, 1

Rivers, W.L. and C. Mathews. *Ethics for the Media*. Englewood Cliffs, NJ: Prentice Hall 1988

Rose, M. 'A Fight Over Tory TV.' *Maclean's*, 11 January 1988, 18-19

Rose, T. *Freeing the Whales: How the Media Created the World's Greatest Non-Event*. New York: Birch Lane Press 1990

Roshier, R. 'The Selection of Crime News by the Press.' In *The Manufacture of News*, ed. S. Cohen and J. Young, 40-51. Beverly Hills, CA: Sage 1982

Ross, A. 'Realtors Flex Muscle Over "Offensive" Story.' *Content*, July/August 1990, 4-5

Rowland, W. *Making Connections*. Toronto: Norfolk Communications 1979

Russell, N. 'Handling Hate: Reporting of the Zundel and Keegstra Trials.' In *Trials and Tribulations*, ed. N. Russell, Monograph no. 1, School of Journalism, University of Regina, Regina, SK, 1986

—. 'James M. Minifie: A Sketch and an Appreciation.' In *The Quarrymen of History: Canadian Journalists Examine Their Profession*, ed. N. Russell. Monograph no. 2, School of Journalism, University of Regina, Regina, SK, 1987

—. 'Staffing Levels as a Reflector of Quality.' *Canadian Journal of Communication* 16 (1991):118-28

Russell, N., ed. *The Quarrymen of History: Canadian Journalists Examine Their Profession*. Monograph no. 2, School of Journalism, University of Regina, Regina, SK, 1987

—. *Trials and Tribulations: An Examination of News Coverage Given at Three Prominent Canadian Trials*. Monograph no. 1, School of Journalism, University of Regina, Regina, SK, 1986

Rutherford, P. *The Making of the Canadian Media*. Toronto: McGraw-Hill Ryerson 1978

Saunders, J. 'The Gag Order: "Censoring a Fact."' *Content*, July/August 1982, A1-4

Sawatsky, J. *Men in the Shadows: The RCMP Security Service*. Toronto: Doubleday 1980

Scanlon, J. 'Hostage Taking and Media Ethics.' *Carleton Journalism Review*, Spring 1980, 7-8

Schachter, H. 'Garbage Journalism.' CIJ *Bulletin*, Summer 1983, 7-8

Schneider, K. and M. Gunther. 'Those Newsroom Ethics Codes.' *Columbia Journalism Review*, July/August 1985, 55-7

Sears, V. *Hello Sweetheart ... Get Me Rewrite*. Toronto: Key Porter 1988

Shepard, A.C. 'An AIDS Story.' *Washington Journalism Review*, January 1986, 10

Sherefkin, R. 'Rood Joke.' *Washington Journalism Review*, June 1984, 13

Sheridan, D. 'Crack Deal.' *Columbia Journalism Review*, May/June 1990, 14

Siegel, A. *Politics and the Media in Canada*. Toronto: McGraw-Hill Ryerson 1983

Singer, B. *Communications in Canadian Society*. Don Mills, ON: Addison-Wesley 1983

Small, W. *To Kill A Messenger: Television News and the Real World*. New York: Hastings House 1970

Smith, Z.N. and P. Zekman. *The Mirage*. New York: Random House 1979

Snow, J. 'A Visitor in King Ronnie's Court.' *Mother Jones*, June/July 1987, 40-2

Sotiron, M., ed. *An Annotated Bibliography of Works on Daily Newspapers in Canada, 1914-1983*. Montreal: Sotiron 1987

Southam Inc., 'Newspaper Publishing Credo.' Distributed to Southam newsrooms 30 November 1972, revised 12 March 1979

Starr, R. 'When Was the Warning at Westray?' *Content*, December 1992, 10-13.

Stewart, S. *From Coast to Coast: A Personal History of Radio in Canada*. Montreal: CBC Enterprises 1985

Stewart, W. *Canadian Newspapers: The Inside Story*. Edmonton: Hurtig 1980

Stewart, W.B. 'Canadian Social Systems and Canadian Broadcasting Audiences.' In *Communications in Canadian Society*, ed. B.J. Singer. Don Mills, ON: Addison-Wesley 1983

Strauss, M. 'Buying "News."' *Content*, September/October 1990, 17-18

Strothers, W.G. 'Troubles with Re-creating News.' NPPA *News Photographer*, November 1989, 25

Talbott, F. 'Taping on the Sly.' *Quill*, June 1986, 43-8

Taras, D. *The Newsmakers*. Scarborough, ON: Nelson Canada 1990

Tripp, R. 'Separating the Private from the Public.' *Content*, January/February 1991, 4-5

Troyer, W. *The Sound and the Fury: An Anecdotal History of Canadian Broadcasting*. Toronto: Personal Library 1980

Trueman, P. *Smoke and Mirrors: The Inside Story of Television News in Canada*. Toronto: McClelland & Stewart 1980

—. 'The Goldhawk Muzzle.' *Content*, March/April 1989, 11

Tunstall, J. 'News Organization Goals and Specialist News Gathering Journalists.' In *Sociology of Mass Communication*, ed. D. McQuail. London: Penguin 1972

Tunstall, J. and M. Dunford. *The ITC and the Future of Regional and National Television News*. London: City University 1991

UK Press Council. *Declaration of Principles.* London: UK Press Council 1966
—. *Press Conduct in the Sutcliffe Case.* London: UK Press Council 1983
UNESCO. *Many Voices, One World* ['The MacBride Report']. Report of the International Commission for the Study of Communication Problems. Paris: UNESCO 1980

Van Doren, C. *Benjamin Franklin.* New York: Viking 1938
Verzuh, R. 'Watchdogs on Society's Watchdog.' *Content,* July/August 1990, 25
Vipond, M. *Mass Media in Canada.* Toronto: Lorimer 1989
Vormittag, J. 'Handling Errors.' *1986 Report of the Newsroom Management Committee.* New York: Associated Press Managing Editors 1986

Wallace, W. 'And Now the News.' *Maclean's,* 31 October 1988, 24-5
Western Producer. 'Western Producer Editorial Code of Ethics.' *Western Producer,* 5 April 1990, 7
White, M.D. 'Plagiarism and the News Media.' *Journal of Mass Media Ethics* 4 (1989):265-80
Whitehorn, K. *Ethics and the Media.* Guildford: University of Surrey 1988
Windsor Star. Editorial Department Policy Manual. Edited by C. Morgan. Windsor, ON: *Windsor Star* 1989
Winer, L. 'Gotcha!' *Columbia Journalism Review,* September/October 1986, 4, 6
Winner, K. 'Freebies and Junkets are Fading.' *Professional Standards Committee Report.* New York: Associated Press Managing Editors 1985

York, G. 'In Defence of the Truth.' *Content,* November/December 1990, 18-20

Zwicker, B. 'Media Must Pay Freight ...' *Content,* March 1978, 5
Zwicker, B. and D. McDonald, eds. *The News: Inside the Canadian Media.* Ottawa: Deneau 1982

Illustration Credits

Index

Printed and bound in Canada by D.W. Friesen & Sons Ltd.

Copy-editor: Carolyn Bateman

Proofreader: Joanne Richardson

Book design: George Vaitkunas

Typefaces: Minion, Meta, Trixie and Univers